The KILLERS Among Us

AN EXAMINATION OF SERIAL MURDER AND ITS INVESTIGATION
SECOND EDITION

STEVEN A. EGGER, PH.D.
University of Illinois at Springfield

Prentice Hall

Upper Saddle River, New Jersey 07458

Library of Congress Cataloging-in-Publication Data

Egger, Steven A.
    The killers among us : an examination of serial murder and its investigation / Steven A.
Egger.—2nd ed.
        p.   cm
    Includes bibliographical references and index.
    ISBN 0-13-017915-9
      1. Serial murders.   2. Serial murderers.   3. Serial murder investigation.   I. Title.

    HV6515.E34 2002
    364.15'23—dc21

                                                                          2001036404

Publisher: Jeff Johnson
Executive Acquisitions Editor: Kim Davies
Assistant Editor: Sarah Holle
Managing Editor: Mary Carnis
Production Management: Stratford Publishing Services
Production Editor: Judy Ashkenaz, Stratford Publishing Services
Interior Design: Stratford Publishing Services
Production Liaison: Adele M. Kupchik
Director of Manufacturing and Production: Bruce Johnson
Manufacturing Buyer: Cathleen Petersen
Senior Design Coordinator: Miguel Ortiz
Formatting: Stratford Publishing Services
Marketing Manager: Ramona Sherman
Printer/Binder: R. R. Donnelley & Sons, Inc.
Copy Editors: Alice Vigliani and Judith Bellamy
Proofreader: Marsha Kunin
Cover Designer: Miguel Ortiz
Cover Illustration: Kevin Belford, SIS/Images.Com
Cover Printer: Phoenix Color Printers

Pearson Education LTD.
Pearson Education Australia PTY, Limited
Pearson Education Singapore, Pte. Ltd
Pearson Education North Asia Ltd.
Pearson Education Canada, Ltd.
Pearson Educación de Mexico, S.A. de C.V.
Pearson Education – Japan
Pearson Education Malaysia, Pte. Ltd

10 9 8 7 6 5 4 3 2
ISBN 0-13-017915-9

To my mother, for her love, creativity, and support.

The fundamental act of humanity is to refuse to kill.

—Elliott Leyton, in *Compulsive Killers:
the Story of Modern Multiple Murder*, 1986, p. 33

Contents

Preface

The first edition of this book, published in 1998, was my second attempt to provide an overview of the phenomenon of serial murder and to discuss its investigation. This was essentially an update of my first book on serial murder, *Serial Murder: An Elusive Phenomenon,* published in 1990 by Praeger Publishers. This second edition of *The Killers Among Us* provides an expanded overview and exploration of the phenomenon of serial murder and its investigation using the same basic format as the first edition. Minor editorial revisions have been made throughout the book.

Part I has been updated and expanded, with the addition of minor myths to the major myths of serial murder discussed in Chapter 1 and the inclusion of additional theories of the etiology of serial murder in Chapter 2. A discussion of a number of serial killers in the United States and internationally has been added to Chapter 3. My essay, "Serial Killing of the Lambs in Our Dreams: Concept of the 'Less-Dead,' " now stands alone as an introduction to Chapter 4 on victims, which has been completely rewritten by Kim Egger to include the results of a preliminary analysis of her database of 1,246 serial killers identified worldwide between 1990 and 1999. Chapter 5, which discusses mass media treatment of serial murder, has been completely rewritten and expanded.

Part II now includes seven case studies of serial killers rather than four. The study of Jeffrey Dahmer, which appeared alone in Part IV of the first edition, is now included with the other case studies. Two additional case studies are new to this edition. The case study of Joseph Miller, written by Don Larson, describes Miller's killings in the Chicago and Peoria, Illinois, areas. The case study of Jerry Marcus, written by Linda Kreuger, describes Marcus's killings in three southern states. Marcus is unique among the seven case studies in that he is African American and also because most of his victims were women he knew. Chapter 13 presents a cross-case analysis of these seven case studies.

Only minor changes have been made in Part III since the status of serial murder investigation has remained essentially unchanged.

As in the first edition, Part IV briefly discusses the future of the phenomenon and of its investigation.

This book is intended for a variety of audiences. Students attempting to understand the phenomenon of serial murder and its investigation will find the book useful. It is designed as a text for a separate course on serial murder or as a supplement to a variety of college and university courses, including Criminology,

Criminal Justice, Victimology, Deviant Behavior, Penology, Criminal Investigation, and Abnormal Behavior. Crime writers should find this book useful as a research tool. It is my hope that criminal investigators will also find this book useful in dealing with serial murder investigations or in becoming prepared to respond to such an investigation.

Acknowledgments

I would like to acknowledge the assistance of the following people, without whom this book would not have been possible:

- Professor José Sanmartin, director of the Queen Sofia Center for the Study of Violence, Valencia, Spain, for inviting me to speak and share my research with others at the International Workshop on Violence and Psychopathy in November 1999.

- Richard Griffiths of CNN Special Reports, Producer of *Murder by Number*, a two-hour television program on serial murder, and Cable News Network, Inc., for providing me with the original transcripts and research material used in producing *Murder by Number*, first broadcast in January 1993.

- Professor David Canter, University of Liverpool, for inviting me to England to present at the second International Conference on Investigative Psychology in April 1993; at the third conference in September 1994; at a special conference in May 1995 to share my ideas and concepts with police officials from around the world; and, in September 1998, at the fifth International Conference, entitled New Directions in Offender Profiling.

- Leo Meyer, deputy director of the Illinois Department of Corrections (retired), for his interest in my research and for taking me on tours of both death row facilities in Illinois, where in front of one cell I had a brief conversation with the late John Wayne Gacy.

- Captain Bobbie Prince of the Texas Rangers (retired) and the late Sheriff Jim Boutwell of Williamson County, Texas, for their patience and support of my interviews with serial killer Henry Lee Lucas.

- Jim Sewell, director of the Florida Law Enforcement Executive Institute, Florida Department of Law Enforcement, for valuing my research, inviting me to speak at the Institute in Tallahassee, and introducing me to Paul Decker.

- Paul Decker, deputy warden of Starke Prison in Florida, for providing me with the opportunity to interview serial killer Ottis Toole.

- Michael Reynolds, author of *Dead Ends,* the true account of serial killer Aileen Wuornos, for his continued support and willingness to discuss some tough issues with me at any time.

- To my colleagues who have researched the difficult phenomenon of serial murder: Eric Hickey, Candice Skrapec, Ron Holmes, Philip Jenkins, Richard

Krause, Jack Olsen, Roy Hazelwood, Robert Ressler, D. Kim Rossmo, Jack Levin, James Fox, Stephen Giannangelo, and others who continue to observe and study this phenomenon.

- To the Canadian anthropologist and writer Elliott Leyton, considered by many of us who have studied this horrific crime to be the "father" of serial murder research, for his willingness to share his analysis of the serial murder phenomenon and his encouragement of my research.

- And to all homicide investigators everywhere, but especially to Sergeant Frank Salerno (retired) of the Los Angeles County Sheriff's Office, who has investigated many serial murder cases, including the "Night Stalker" and "Hillside Strangler" cases; to Lieutenant Ray Biondi (retired), who investigated the Sacramento "Vampire Killer" and the Gerald Gallego serial murder cases; and to Robert Keppell (retired) of the Washington State Attorney General's Office, who worked on the Ted Bundy case and on the Green River Task Force, and who recently developed the Homicide Investigative Tracking System for his state.

- To the researchers, law enforcement officers, and students who attended the First International Conference on Serial and Mass Murder at the University of Windsor, Ontario, in April 1993. For the first time, many us who study and write about serial murder were together at the same time and place, agreeing or agreeing to disagree on a number of issues.

- To Thomas Guillen of Seattle University in Seattle, Washington, and Tory Creti of the University of North Texas in Denton, Texas, for their review of the manuscript.

- To all the students at the University of Illinois at Springfield who took my serial murder course and who were frustrated with so many questions and so few answers. By asking all those questions, we learned from each other.

- To Bob Ladendorf, for his interest and the continued support he has provided to me through his personal clipping service.

- To the National Crime Faculty at Bramshill Police College in England, who were gracious hosts to my wife, Kim, and me in May 1996.

- And finally, to Kim, my best friend, colleague, and partner, for her sociological research and steadfast support for my research and writing. Without her and her research support, all this would have never been published.

About the Author

Steven A. Egger is professor of Criminal Justice at the University of Illinois at Springfield. He was formerly interim dean of the School of Health and Human Services at the University of Illinois. He was project director of the Homicide Assessment and Lead Tracking System (HALT) for the state of New York. HALT, which was the first statewide computerized system to track and identify serial murderers, has become the model for the development of a number of other statewide systems.

Dr. Egger has been conducting research on serial murder since 1983. He holds B.S. and M.S. degrees from the School of Criminal Justice, Michigan State University. He has a Ph.D. in Criminal Justice from Sam Houston State University, where he completed the first dissertation on serial murder in the world. He has worked as a police officer, homicide investigator, police consultant, and law enforcement academy director. His other research interests include the epistemology of criminal investigation, police interagency networking, and the future predator.

He is the author of *Serial Murder: An Elusive Phenomenon* (Praeger, 1990), editor of a series of monographs entitled Criminology and Crime Control Policy for Praeger, and series editor of a series entitled Issues in Criminal Justice Controversy, under contract to Allyn and Bacon. He has lectured on serial murder in England, Canada, the Netherlands, and Spain.

Dr. Egger and his wife, Kim, are currently working on an encyclopedia of serial murder, which will include entries on over seven hundred serial killers.

Kim A. Egger studied at Purdue University and has a B.S. in Psychology from the University of Illinois at Springfield. She is currently pursuing a master's degree in Law and Psychology. She has co-authored, with Steven Egger, a chapter on the victims of serial murder in a monograph on victimology. For the past ten years she has been developing a database on serial killers, which currently holds information on 1,246 serial murderers. She has lectured at Purdue University, the University of Illinois at Springfield, and Brazosport College, Texas.

Don Larsen is a detective with the Springfield, Illinois, Police Department. He holds a B.S. in Criminal Justice from the University of Illinois at Springfield.

Linda Kreuger was formerly a part-time patrol officer with the Sangamon County Sheriff's Office. She is currently employed in Rehabilitation Administration for the state of Illinois. She holds a master's degree in Rehabilitation from Southern Illinois University.

Both Don and Linda were previously enrolled in Steven Egger's course on serial murder at the University of Illinois at Springfield.

Future Prey

There is a crime
We know not where,
For many crimes
Are there and here
And here and there.
Few care.
Victims no longer feel.
For many others,
The crimes are not real.
Many of the crimes
Are past tense
And seem to have
No sense of sense.
For those victims yet to be found
Many have perished without a sound.
The cycle of horror goes round and round.
Such visions of violence and death
Are only nightmares of our young.
Later acted out in real.
Life snuffed in the deal.
All for power, lust and greed.
Chartering our lives as prey
For the future predator deed
Is there, and here and everywhere.

—STEVEN A. EGGER

PART I

THE SERIAL MURDER PHENOMENON

Chapter 1 introduces the reader to the crime of serial murder, briefly summarizes the book, and identifies the six major myths and some of the less well known myths about serial killers. Chapter 2 discusses and reviews the various theories that attempt to explain why the serial killer kills. Chapter 3 provides examples of known serial killers as well as unsolved serial murder investigations in the United States and across the globe. Chapter 4, a discussion of serial murder victims written in collaboration with Kim Egger, introduces and explains the concept of the "less-dead" victims of serial killers. Chapter 5 discusses how the mass media report on serial killers and how the media generate a number of myths and inaccuracies regarding serial murder.

CHAPTER 1

Serial Murder

I agree that the serial murder problem out there is a tragic and horrendous problem,
which plagues society and all that is human and decent. But I am not now, nor have I
ever been, a serial nor even a uni-murderer.

—Kenneth Bianchi, convicted serial killer, in a letter to CNN refusing an interview
(CNN, 1993)

Introduction

This book is about serial murder—the crime that Kenneth Bianchi claims he has
not committed. It is an attempt to tell the reader all that we know, or think we
know, about serial murder. The phenomenon of serial murder is elusive. At the
beginning of the undergraduate course on serial murder that I teach at a state university in central Illinois, I tell my students that by the time they complete the
course they will know less about serial murder than their neighbors, friends, and
acquaintances do. The students become less uncomfortable with this fact as they
begin to understand the extent of false information and mythology that serial murder generates in the mass media. Most people learn about serial murder from television, newspapers, and film. This media information frequently takes the form of
hype and, unfortunately, contains a number of myths, inaccuracies, and outright
falsehoods.

Serial murder is not a new crime in America. In the late 1880s, Herman Webster
Mudgett, alias Henry Howard Holmes, considered by some to be "America's first
serial killer," killed twenty-seven women in his "Murder Castle" in Chicago, Illinois (Wilson & Seaman, 1992, p. 8). Mudgett was hanged in 1896. But this is not a
book about the history of serial murder. Rather, it is primarily a book about the serial murders that have been committed over the past twenty years, since the phenomenon was first identified as a unique type of homicide.

As a society, we have very little tolerance for homicide. When we can see some
logic or rational reason for the killing, however, our tolerance for such an act is
somewhat greater. If we lose a family member, loved one, or friend as a result of a

3

homicidal act, knowing the motive for such an act may reduce our anger or temper our grief. Most homicides occur because of an interpersonal conflict between a killer and a victim who have a prior relationship. It is much harder to find the rationale for an act of murder when the killer and the victim appear to have been strangers.

The reasoning behind the murder of a stranger defies our understanding, and such murders tend to increase our level of fear because of the apparent randomness with which victims are chosen. We are a violent society, prone to killing our friends, loved ones, and even acquaintances. But to kill a stranger, unless it is during the commission of another crime, is a definite threat to our society, an act that places us all at risk. A killer who intentionally chooses a stranger as his victim threatens our very social order.

Unfortunately, the mass media provide information that promotes the bottom line: What will sell newspapers? What will cause viewers to turn the television dial to a specific channel? What will attract moviegoers? The profit motive drives all of these industry questions. Editors and producers add hype and myth to the topic at hand when the information is not appealing or sexy enough to lure the reader or viewer. This has certainly been true of talk-television programs, made-for-TV movies that are "based on the actual facts," and movies in theatrical release. In the past, television producers and newspaper journalists were the culprits behind the myths surrounding the crime of serial murder. With the 1991 film *Silence of the Lambs,* however, Hollywood became the mythmaker. Ever since Hannibal Lecter (brilliantly portrayed by Anthony Hopkins) first stared out from movie screens that year, most people discussing serial murder think of this horrific, yet entertaining, killer as the typical serial murderer. The sequel to this very profitable movie, *Hannibal,* which opened in 2001, continues to perpetrate a number of serial-killer myths.

Defining Serial Murder

Serial murder was originally described, in early 1980, as "lust murder" (Hazelwood & Douglas, 1980). The term "serial murder" was first used sometime in 1982 or 1983. The criminal investigative pioneer Pierce Brooks, who first conceptualized the Violent Criminal Apprehension Program (VICAP) now being run by the Federal Bureau of Investigation (FBI), may have been the first to use the term "serial." Others, however, such as retired FBI agents, claim to have used the term first. No one knows for sure who coined the term, but it has been with us ever since.

Numerous efforts have been made to define the phenomenon of serial murder. The national media began to define serial murder in early 1984, when *Newsweek* magazine differentiated between "serial" and "mass" murder by describing only the former as an act in which the killer explodes in one homicidal rampage (Starr et al., 1984). Darrach and Norris noted in *Life* magazine that "unlike traditional mass murderers, who suddenly crack under pressure and kill everybody in sight, serial murderers kill and kill and kill, often for years on end" (1984, p. 58). Nevertheless, until about 1989 the news media continued to refer to serial murder as "mass murder," even though the two are decidedly different.

Mass murder is a single horrific incident in which a killer annihilates a number of victims. Mass murderers are people like Richard Speck, who killed seven nurses in Chicago, Illinois, on July 13, 1966, or James Oliver Huberty, who walked into a McDonald's restaurant in San Ysidro, California, and killed twenty patrons before turning a gun on himself.

Despite disagreements regarding the definition of serial murder, serial murder is very different from mass murder. For the law enforcement community, "serial murder" usually refers to sexual attacks and the resulting death of young women, men, or children, committed by a male killer who tends to follow a distinct physical or psychological pattern. Although many researchers define serial killers as those who kill a minimum of three or four victims, a more reasonable approach would be to consider two similar homicides as an example of serial murder until proved otherwise. When law enforcement apprehends a serial killer, that murderer may be just beginning a "harvest" of victims. In other cases, a killer may be killed by a resisting victim or may die of natural causes before adding to his victim count.

Over the past few years, I have worked to develop a serial murder definition that will be useful to law enforcement officers investigating multiple homicides. The definition I have developed has seven major components that may serve as flags to alert investigators to the possibility that a serial murderer is operating in their jurisdiction:

A serial murder is defined as occurring when:

- One or more individuals (in many cases, males) commit a second murder and/or subsequent murders.
- There is generally no prior relationship between victim and attacker (if there is a relationship, it will be one that places the victim in a subjugated relationship to the killer).
- Subsequent murders occur at different times and have no apparent connection to the initial murder.
- Subsequent murders are usually committed in a different geographical location.
- The motive is not for material gain; it is for the murderer's desire to have power or dominance over his victims.
- Victims may have a symbolic value for the murderer and/or they may be perceived to lack prestige, to be unable to defend themselves or alert others to their plight, or to be powerless given their situation in time, place, or status within their immediate surroundings.
- Victims typically include vagrants, the homeless, prostitutes, migrant workers, homosexuals, missing children, single women (out by themselves), elderly women, college students, and hospital patients.

I will use the preceding definition throughout this book. This, however, is not the only definition in use. The FBI uses a briefer definition of a serial killer as "someone who has murdered three or more victims, with a cooling off period in between each of the homicides" (CNN, 1993). Brooks et al. (1988) define serial murder as follows:

> [a] series of two or more murders, committed as separate events, usually, but not always, by one offender acting alone. The crimes may occur over a time ranging from hours to years. Quite often the motive is psychological, and the offender's behavior and the physical evidence observed at the scene will reflect sadistic, sexual overtones. (p. vii)

Besides drawing a distinction between serial and mass murder in definitions, it is also necessary to differentiate the serial murderer from other killers. Other definitions developed provide this distinction to a greater or lesser degree. Some have argued that the apparent lack of rational behavior and the presence of compulsive premeditation distinguish the serial murderer from other killers (Norris, 1989). Others argue that the stranger-to-stranger relationship between killer and victim, who are likely to be of similar socioeconomic status, provides this distinction (Holmes & DeBurger, 1988).

Why Do They Kill and Kill Again?

I felt a kind of madness and ungovernability in perverted sexual acts. I couldn't control my actions, because from childhood I was unable to realize myself as a real man and a complete human being.

—Andrei Chikatilo, Russian serial killer, convicted of fifty-two homicides, November 21, 1990

Much of the early research on serial murder focused on the sexual component of this crime to explain the killer's motivation. Psychologists have referred to this sexual component in a number of ways: Those "who suffer from a deviation or perversion of the sexual impulse" (de River, 1949, p. 99) "kill because of an underlying basis of sexual conflicts" (Revitch & Schlesinger, 1981, p. 281). "They [serial killers] usually have few normal social and sexual relationships. In fact, they often have had no experience of normal sexual intercourse" (Lunde, 1976, p. 53). Some criminologists focus on the sexual component by stating: "The serial killer, motivated by sex and sadism . . . favors immediate gratification, regardless of the consequences" (Levin & Fox, 1985, p. 225).

Other researchers disagree, arguing that the sexual component either is overstated or is simply an instrument of the killer, not the motivating factor behind the act. For these researchers, the focus of study is on the power relationships or the issue of control. The motivation is then enhancing the killer's sense of control and domination over his victims. The motivational dynamics of serial murder seem to be consistent with research on the nature of rape, which is considered to be a power and dominance crime (Egger, 1985b). This similarity becomes even more evident when one considers that it may take only a small increase in the fury of the rapist or the struggle of the victim to change a violent rape into a murder.

Elliott Leyton (1986) identifies relative and absolute deprivation as the provocation for the serial killer's frustration. Viewing these killers from a cultural perspective, Leyton rejects the arguments of excitement or victim conquest and views these murderers as reacting to their own denied ambitions.

Wilson and Seaman (1983) view the serial killer's violent acts as a result of what the philosopher Jean-Paul Sartre has called "magical thinking"—that is, thinking that cannot possibly accomplish its objective. In the case of the serial murderer, however, such thinking is apparently nothing more than a lack of self-control and an unwillingness to delay gratification. These characteristics of the serial killer, though possibly valid, still do not tell us the killer's motivation.

Norris (1989) describes a "serial killer syndrome" made up of twenty-two patterns of episodic aggressive behavior as factors of predisposition for the killer. Norris, however, offers no empirical documentation or references for the development of this syndrome. To many, this "syndrome" is seriously lacking as an explanation of the serial killer's motivation.

The terms "psychopath" and "sociopath," frequently used by psychologists and psychiatrists to describe the apparently motiveless serial murderer, are both obsolete. The *Diagnostic and Statistical Manual of Mental Disorders,* when first published in 1952 by the American Psychiatric Association, referred to "sociopathic personality" (code 52). The fourth revision of this manual (*DSM-IV*; American Psychiatric Association, 1994) refers to such behavior as "antisocial personality disorder" (code 301.7). In lay terms, persons suffering from antisocial personality disorder are not considered mentally ill or grossly out of touch with reality. Nevertheless, they are unable to experience love or empathy as a result of family rejection and frustration of their basic needs. They lack a sense of moral guilt and are unable to control their drive for immediate gratification. They will rape and murder as easily as they will lie and cheat.

Many social science researchers have found trauma, abuse, and neglect in the childhood of serial killers (Ellis & Gullo, 1971; Hazelwood & Douglas, 1980; Reinhardt, 1962). The social and psychological deprivation consistently identified in the childhood of serial killers would certainly indicate a strong correlation between such a childhood and serial killing. However, such a childhood can also be identified in many people who do not go on to become serial killers. Correlation does not equal causation. Indeed, if such a correlation were revealed to be the central causal factor of the serial murderer, the United States would have thousands and thousands of serial killers, given the current disturbing statistics on child abuse and neglect in this country. A terrible childhood may contribute to the serial killer's makeup, but it is apparently only one factor in the etiology of serial killing.

Hickey (1985) has noted that there is a strong and common belief that pornography, drugs, alcohol, or insanity is the direct cause of serial murders. Although these factors may contribute to serial murder, there is no empirical or direct evidence that they are the direct causes of the serial killer's behavior.

It may simply be (as I have begun to believe) that the search to gain control over his or her own life by using violence and sex to control and dominate others is the central causal factor in the development of the serial killer. Explanations of the serial killer's behavior are discussed in Chapter 2.

Who Are These Serial Killers?

These are the most infamous and best known serial murderers:

- Ted Bundy, who was convicted of three homicides in 1979 and 1980 in Florida and who is believed to have killed at least twenty-eight women between 1974 and 1978
- The "Hillside Stranglers" Kenneth Bianchi and Angelo Buono, who killed at least nine women in the Los Angeles, California, area in 1977 and 1978, after which Bianchi killed two women on his own in Bellingham, Washington, and was then caught
- John Wayne Gacy, who killed thirty-three young men in the Chicago area between 1972 and 1978
- Arthur Shawcross, who killed eleven women in 1988 and 1989 in and around Rochester, New York, shortly after he was paroled from prison, where he had been serving a sentence for killing an eight-year-old girl in 1972 (Shawcross was also suspected at the time of killing a ten-year-old boy)
- Wayne Williams, who was found guilty in 1982 of the killing of two young men, following the "Atlanta Child Murders" investigation in Atlanta, Georgia
- Richard Ramirez, the "Night Stalker," who was found guilty in 1989 of thirteen murders, five attempted murders, eleven sexual assaults, and fourteen burglaries in California
- Henry Lee Lucas, convicted of eleven murders in Texas, West Virginia, and Michigan and still suspected by law enforcement agencies in twenty-seven states of having killed another 162 people
- Aileen Wuornos, who killed seven men in central Florida in 1990 before she was arrested

Solo Predators

A number of serial killers operate as loners, stalking, luring, and killing their victims with no assistance from others and with no witnesses to their horrific deeds. Ted Bundy and John Wayne Gacy are two well-known solo serial killers. A brief life history of these notorious serial killers may tell us something about serial murderers who kill alone.

Ted Bundy

Theodore Robert Bundy was born out of wedlock on November 24, 1946. In 1951 his mother married John C. Bundy, who adopted Ted and had his last name changed to Bundy. Although Ted suspected he was illegitimate, he was never told this by his parents. Many suspect that learning the circumstances of his birth had a decided effect on Bundy's behavior, but there is no direct evidence of this.

Bundy's heroes were politicians, and he was an active volunteer in political campaigns. His goals in life were to become a lawyer and to work in politics. After receiving a bachelor's degree in psychology, he attended law school. During the early 1970s he committed a number of larcenies and burglaries in the Seattle area, but he was never caught (Michaud & Aynesworth, 1983).

Bundy is believed by law enforcement authorities to have committed over twenty-five murders of young women and girls in five states between 1974 and 1978. He was eventually convicted of three homicides in Florida and was executed in 1989.

John Wayne Gacy

John Wayne Gacy was born on May 17, 1942, in Chicago. As a boy, Gacy talked about wanting to be a policeman. He was closer to his mother than to his father, who drank a lot and, when drunk, would call him a sissy and a mama's boy.

Gacy attended two vocational high schools but dropped out of the second school in his sophomore year. He was married in Chicago and then lived in Springfield, Illinois, and Waterloo, Iowa, where he was convicted of sodomy for forcing homosexual relationships with young boys. While Gacy was serving his sentence in an Iowa prison, his wife divorced him.

Gacy was paroled to Chicago in 1970, and his killing of boys and young men began in January 1972. In December 1978, Gacy became a suspect in the disappearance of a fifteen-year-old boy in Des Plaines, Illinois, a northern suburb of Chicago. Gacy was arrested, confessed to the killings, and was subsequently convicted of killing thirty-three young men and boys. He was executed in May 1994.

Team Killers

> We went out as friends. We had our arguments, as far as arguments we worked 'em out. Me and Ottis never been in a fist fight. Friendship is further than anythin' else.
>
> —Henry Lee Lucas, October 1984

In a number of cases, murders are committed by two or more offenders working together. Such group serial murder is certainly not a rare occurrence. Jenkins (1989) identified twelve cases out of fifty-two serial murder cases (23 percent) in which ten or more victims were killed by such a team of killers. For example, Henry Lee Lucas was assisted in most of his killings by Ottis Toole, his homosexual partner; Kenneth Bianchi assisted Angelo Buono, his cousin, in their killing spree in Los Angeles County, California; Douglas Clark involved his girlfriend, Carol Bundy, in a number of bizarre and sadistic murders of prostitutes; Roy Norris and Lawrence Bittaker cruised the beaches of southern California in their "Murder Mac," a customized van in which they killed a number of their victims. Jenkins (1989) found that a common factor of these team killings was the killers' attempt to control victims through "absolute sexual domination" (p. 11).

Some serial killers may prefer to operate in pairs in order to make the abduction or murder of the victim an easier task. Hickey (1997) who surveyed 399 serial killers, found 110 offenders who appeared to have at least one partner in committing their homicides.

England's "Moor Murders," a gruesome series of three child murders committed by Ian Brady and Myra Hindley, provide evidence that group serial murder is not unique to the United States. Brady was a stock clerk and Hindley was a typist. Shortly after they met, they became lovers, and Brady began teaching Hindley about his favorite interests: Nazism and the philosophy of the Marquis de Sade. Brady and Hindley abducted their victims and forced them to pose for pornographic pictures before they were killed; in one case, they recorded the screams of a ten-year-old girl before they strangled her.

Henry Lee Lucas and Ottis Toole

Possibly the most prolific team of serial killers was Henry Lee Lucas and Ottis Toole. In 1960, Lucas was convicted of killing his mother and sentenced to twenty to forty years' imprisonment in Michigan. He was paroled in 1970, rearrested in 1971 for attempted kidnapping, and sentenced to four to five years. Paroled again in 1975, Lucas married a woman whom he abandoned in 1977.

In 1976, Lucas teamed up with Ottis Elwood Toole, a homosexual living in Jacksonville, Florida. Until 1983, Lucas traveled across the country with Toole and Toole's niece and nephew. They are believed to have killed a number of people during this time. In 1983, Toole returned to Florida, where he was arrested for arson in Jacksonville, found guilty, and sentenced to twenty years in prison.

In 1983, Lucas was arrested in Texas. Shortly after his arrest, he began confessing to the killing of scores of people across the country. Law enforcement agencies began to take some of his confessions seriously when his statements were matched with the facts, evidence, and location of unsolved murders. Lucas was convicted of a total of ten charges of homicide in Texas and West Virginia. He received the death penalty for one of these convictions in Texas, and spent time on death row until his sentence was commuted to life. Toole was incarcerated in Florida at a maximum-security prison, where he later died. Even today, Lucas and, in many cases, Toole are considered suspects in over a hundred homicides.

The Hillside Stranglers

Another killing team—dubbed by the media the "Hillside Strangler" before they were identified—was the serial killer pair of Kenneth Bianchi and his cousin Angelo Buono.

Bianchi, who had always wanted to be a police officer, applied for police work after his move to California but was not hired. He lived with his half cousin Angelo Buono in Glendale, a suburb of Los Angeles, where Buono ran an auto upholstery business out of his home.

Between October 1977 and February 1978, Bianchi and Buono abducted, tortured, and strangled ten young girls in the Los Angeles County area. They abducted most of their victims by posing as police officers. Bianchi then left California and traveled to Bellingham, Washington, where in January 1979 he sexually assaulted and strangled two young girls in an unoccupied house in Bellingham and then left the girls' bodies in the trunk of their car on a little-used city street. He quickly became a suspect and, under hypnosis, claimed to have a multiple personality and confessed to both the Bellingham killings and the "strangler" killings in Los Angeles, in which he implicated Angelo Buono as an accomplice.

Bianchi was found to be faking his multiple personality. He pled guilty to the killings in both Washington and Los Angeles. In return for being spared a death sentence, he testified against Buono, who was found guilty in nine of the ten murders and was sentenced to life imprisonment. Bianchi was returned to Washington for incarceration.

They Are All Around Us

To understand serial murder, it is important to address a number of issues. First, serial murder is generally referred to as a stranger-to-stranger crime. What does this mean? In addition to the well-known cases of solo and team killers briefly noted in this chapter, we need to look more broadly at this phenomenon. Who are the serial killers? What do they look like? How many are there? These and other general topics are discussed in Chapter 3.

Serial Murder Victims

When they were being killed, there wasn't anything going on in my mind except that they were going to be mine. . . . That was the only way they could be mine.

—Edmund Kemper, March 1974

Research on serial murder has focused on finding similarities among murderers. The victims of serial killers have largely been ignored. Serial killers seem to prey on people who are vulnerable or easy to lure and dominate, but little else is known about the victims of serial murderers except that they are almost always strangers to the murderer. They appear to be selected because they happened to cross the path of the serial murderer or because their physical appearance held some symbolic significance for the killer. Vulnerable victims may simply happen to be in the area where the killer is hunting, or their appearance may trigger the selection, or the opportunity and the victim's availability in a specific location may contribute to their fatal selection.

The high-risk lifestyles of some victims (such as some homosexuals, cult members, released mental patients, skid-row alcoholics, and prostitutes) certainly contribute to their victimization. These killers seem to pick victims whom they can dominate. The serial killer does not care about his victims or have any feelings of remorse. The issue of victims is covered more fully in Chapter 4; as an introduction to that chapter, I have provided a separate essay on his concept of the "less-dead."

Investigation of Serial Murder

Serial killers frequently are not captured until they have killed a number of victims. The problem lies with law enforcement; it is not that these killers have any special skills that allow them to elude the police. "Linkage blindness," the crux of this law enforcement problem, is a term I coined in 1984 to refer to a communication problem among law enforcement agencies in the United States. The problem also exists in other countries. Briefly stated, "linkage blindness" is a major weakness in law enforcement's ability to respond to and identify the serial killer.

"Linkage blindness" occurs because:

- Police do not exchange investigative information on unsolved murders with police agencies in different jurisdictions.
- Police do not exchange investigative information on unsolved murders in different command areas within the same jurisdiction.
- Police do not share or coordinate investigative information on unsolved murders very well between individual officers.
- Very little networking of information and sources relating to unsolved murders occurs between the police.

I have documented this problem of linkage blindness in a number of serial murder cases (1990). Although it is not the only problem associated with the investigation of serial murder, linkage blindness is the major problem in the police response to serial murder. Other investigative problems relate to and originate from this important problem. The problems of investigating serial murder are presented in Chapter 13 with reference to the "linkage blindness" that occurred in the John Wayne Gacy, Henry Lee Lucas, Kenneth Bianchi, and Ted Bundy cases, presented as case studies in Chapters 6 through 9, respectively. In addition, three new chapters have been added to this edition. Chapters 10, 11, and 12 present three case studies, on serial killers Jerry Marcus, Joseph Miller, and Jeffrey Dahmer, in which problems of linkage blindness can be found. These seven case studies are followed in Chapter 13 by a brief comparative and cross-case analysis of these seven serial killers.

Chapter 14 refers to the major problems of investigating a serial murder. In attempting to determine the best response to serial murder by law enforcement, I have been documenting different responses for a number of years. Chapter 15 documents fourteen police responses to serial murder. These responses are primarily from the United States, but in some instances examples of police responses in England are used, primarily because information on criminal investigations is shared between these two countries more readily than most. Canada is also cited in these responses because it shares a long border with the United States and is an English-speaking country.

Throughout this book, I will attempt to disabuse the reader of a number of myths about serial murder that unfortunately are promulgated with abandon by mass media journalists and entertainment industry writers. Any attempt at objectivity or factual reporting on a serial killer is colored with the sensationalism of journalists and fiction writers competing for the public's interest in these killers, who are shown as randomly killing strangers on our city streets, in our parks, or on university campuses. Reliable factual reporting of these crimes is marred by the hype and horror seen in newspaper columns and in the thirty-second sound bites of prime-time television programs.

The Myths of Serial Murder

The Silence of the Lambs, released in 1991, was a popular movie that has probably done more than any other single film, book, or television program to promote the mythology of serial murder. Other movies about serial killers, thriller novels, the recent increase in true-crime accounts of serial killers, and the frenzied media treatment of such recent events as Ted Bundy's execution in Florida, or of the crimes of Richard Ramirez, the "Night Stalker" and self-professed Satanic worshiper from California; Arthur Shawcross, who killed at least ten prostitutes in the Rochester, New York, area from 1988 to 1990; and Jeffrey Dahmer, whose grisly acts need no introduction, have promoted a number of myths regarding serial murder. Media reporting of unsolved serial murder cases, such as the "Green River Killer," the San Diego killings in the early 1990s, and the "Gainesville Slayer" (finally identified as Danny Rolling), have added to these myths. The fact that serial murder is a growing media industry is addressed in Chapter 5.

Six major myths about serial killers are ingrained in the public's understanding of serial murder:

1. All serial killers had terrible childhoods, were beaten by their parents, and were sexually abused.
2. Serial killers are "mutants from hell," who do not resemble the average person in appearance and mannerisms.
3. Serial killers prey on anyone who crosses their path and spend no time at all selecting their victims.
4. Serial killers have an uncanny ability to elude the police for long periods of time.
5. The serial killer fits the profile of a sex-starved man-beast, driven to kill because of a horrible childhood and the way society has treated him. He has had an unusual relationship with his mother. He travels alone across large geographic areas of the country and has an in-depth knowledge of police criminal investigative procedures, which allows him to elude local, state, and federal law enforcement. He is an insane and cowardly maniac who preys on the weak and helpless.
6. The Federal Bureau of Investigation investigates all serial murderers because most of them cross state lines.

A number of lesser myths also deserve mention, as they create additional confusion for the public and members of our criminal justice systems about the phenomenon of serial murder. These myths, selected from the list offered by researchers Fox and Levin (1999, pp. 81–92), are as follows:

1. There is an epidemic of serial murder in the United States.
2. Serial killers are inspired by pornography.
3. Serial killers can be identified in advance.
4. All serial killers are sexual sadists.
5. Serial killers select victims who somehow resemble their mothers.
6. Serial killers really want to get caught.

Like all myths, these include a little of the truth. But myths are not really helpful in dealing with the serial killer. In fact, myths make understanding these killers and catching them all the more difficult. My goal in writing this book is to clarify issues related to serial murder and to provide a better understanding of how serial murder is investigated. Clarifying some of these issues and analyzing the investigation process should give readers a better idea of where we go from here.

The last part of the book deals with the future. Chapter 16 addresses the future of the phenomenon of serial murder. Finally, Chapter 17 deals with the future of serial murder investigation.

CHAPTER 2

Why Do They Kill and Kill and Kill?

I am beyond good and evil. I will be avenged. Lucifer dwells in all of us.

—Richard Ramirez, the "Night Stalker," on being sentenced to death for thirteen murders, November 7, 1989

Of all the carnivores, only two lack built-in inhibitions against killing members of their own species—rats and man.

—Konrad Lorenz

You know I am a nurse of society. I am cleaning up all the rubbish. At work, I swept streets. Now I'm cleaning up a different kind of rubbish.

—Russian serial killer Ilshat Kusikov, who killed and ate his victims.

Serial Killers on the Couch: Explanations

The killing of a stranger cannot be seen as motivated by previous interpersonal friction in the killer–victim relationship but, rather, must be viewed as the outcome of some other interpersonal motive. Although the ability to identify and capture serial killers is the critical short-term objective of law enforcement, it is becoming increasingly important to understand why these killers behave as they do. As these murderers are identified, apprehended, and studied, descriptions of them have developed. Older references in the literature tend to reflect a Freudian orientation to the phenomenon of serial murder.

Some researchers classify theories that explain behavior into very broad categories. For example, researchers examining serial murder might classify theories of the behavior and motivation of the killer as falling within three general areas: sociological, psychological, and cultural. Others would add a fourth category, biological. The problem with placing the behavior of serial killers into specific categories of identified behaviors is that behaviors found in serial killers do not necessarily fall neatly within any tidy theory.

Was John Wayne Gacy like Ted Bundy? How is Andrew Cunanan, who killed five men from Minnesota to Florida, different from Arthur Shawcross, who killed eleven women in the Rochester, New York, area? Was Herbert Richard Baumeister, who was considered to be a family man but who may have killed sixteen young gay men in the Indianapolis area and who committed suicide in Canada, any different from Robert Yates, reportedly also a devoted family man, who killed at least eleven prostitutes in the Pacific Northwest? Answers to these questions are not readily apparent. Gacy and Bundy have been executed; Cunanan and Baumeister committed suicide. That leaves us with Shawcross and Yates, whose only similarity may have been in their choice of victims.

Some researchers study serial killers from within their own academic frame of reference. A sociologist, for example, will concentrate on those behaviors or characteristics that tell us something about serial killers in the aggregate. Sociologists attempt to use data and empirical evidence from a large group of subjects (in this case, serial killers) to explain what these subjects are "like."

Psychologists and psychiatrists, by contrast, are in the business of studying individuals, and much of their research is reported in the form of clinical case studies. Data from clinical studies of larger populations of subjects are frequently reported in journals and research reports. Psychiatrists, unlike psychologists, hold a medical degree, and their research frequently combines biological and social science information about their subjects.

Cultural explanations of serial murder behavior are provided by anthropologists, sociologists, social psychologists, and a number of other social science researchers who look to broader issues—historical development, media influence, trends, marginalization of certain members of society, and the like.

Biological explanations of serial murder generally deal with genetic factors, such as the XYY chromosome; neurological factors (brain abnormality or dysfunction); and biochemical factors (chemical imbalances in the brain).

All of these disciplines have contributed to our understanding of serial murder. However, many theories and explanations of serial murder behavior combine more than one of these disciplines. These are theories that do not fit neatly within a single discipline or theoretical framework.

For instance, consider the case of the Russian serial killer Ilshat Kusikov. St. Petersburg police charged Kusikov with the murders of three men in November 1995; they fear he also killed many more victims, including women and children. On the day Kusikov was arrested, police found two human legs, severed below the knee, and two forearms cut from the elbow in his apartment. When he was arrested, Kusikov begged the police to take his jars of dried human ears and buckets of human bones—so they wouldn't go to waste, he said.

Little is known of Kusikov's childhood except that his father strangled his mother when he was eleven years old. Records from Tadjikistan, where he grew up, show that he had an intense interest in surgery. He is reported to have had an incestuous relationship with his brother following the death of his mother. Also at this time, he developed an obsession with human physiology and was able to have orgasms while watching surgical operations on television. In the early 1970s, Kusikov worked as a welder before he was diagnosed as schizophrenic and began receiving a disability pension from the government.

When Kusikov's killings began, his wife, who had been an outpatient at the same mental hospital where her husband was treated, walked out on their two-year marriage after he attacked her with a knife. By this time, Kusikov was drinking excessively, eating dogs, and leaving the rotting corpses of cats in his apartment. He also was drinking his own urine and becoming sexually aroused by the smell of human excrement.

In his confession to Dr. Valery Ivanov, a Russian psychiatrist and expert on serial killers, Kusikov stated that he always committed the murders on the day he received his disability pension check. He would invite one of his "friends" to his apartment to drink vodka. When he and his companion were very drunk, Kusikov would make homosexual advances to his friend. If these advances were refused, Kusikov would become very angry and would strike his "friend" in the back of the head with a knife handle before slitting the victim's throat. He would then strip himself and his victim and would dismember the victim with a meat cleaver. Finally, Kusikov would cook his victim's heart, liver, and other body parts (Wroe, 1999).

Sources of Serial Murder Theories and Explanations

Research on serial murder behavior is based on five basic sources of information, each of which is historical; that is, we observe, view, and analyze these sources after the fact. We attempt to determine the motivation or explanation of the killings on the basis of what the killer has accomplished. We do not try to determine a theoretical basis for the killing until after the killer is in custody. (Analysis of behavior prior to the capture of the killer, which is used to catch the killer, is referred to as psychological profiling, investigative profiling, or simply profiling. This investigative approach is covered later in this book, in Part III.) Once this information is available, we can begin to look at the killer's background in a variety of ways in order to determine why this person has repeatedly killed. Information that is analyzed includes the following:

1. Specific homicide scenes
2. An identified pattern in a series of murders
3. The serial killer's confessions
4. Characteristics of the victims of serial murder
5. Published research on serial murder

The scene of a killing tells us something about the killer or killers. Where the killing took place, how the victim was killed, how the victim's body was left to be found, whether the victim was hidden from view or displayed for all to see, and what methods were used to subdue or torture the victim—these are all characteristics or descriptions of the kill site that allow researchers to deduce explanations about the killer's motivation.

A pattern or series of murders known to have been committed by an identified serial killer may give us insight into the serial killer's mind. In this case, the researcher has a larger view of the killer's acts from which to begin to understand the motivation for such killings. The similarities and possibly also the differences between these murders provide a clearer picture of these crimes.

The confessions of the serial killer usually provide most of the information used in developing an explanation for his killings. The killer states first to police, and frequently later to the news media, book writers, and researchers, what he has done. In nearly all instances the killer is asked why. The killer may not know or understand why he has committed these horrific acts, or he may well understand (at least in his own mind) why he has killed. The acts themselves and how they were accomplished are important for the police to know in order to charge the killer with his crimes.

The "why" is not required for criminal prosecution, but it is something everyone in interested in knowing. We are all curious. How much of the killer's confessions regarding his motives is fact and how much is fiction? The killer may be honestly telling why he thinks he killed, or he may be telling the police and others what he thinks they want to hear, based on his perception of what serial killers do, his audience's perception of the serial killer, or both. This is definitely a problem for researchers who attempt to determine the killer's motive from his confession.

Information about the victims of serial killers may give researchers a clue to motive. What type of person has the killer selected for his victims? Are they simply those who happen to cross his path and provide the opportunity for a "kill" or an abduction? Or do these victims have some symbolic significance for the killer? Were they selected, abducted, or killed in similar locations? Information about victims might answer some of these questions and thus lead to a theory about the killer's motivation.

Published research on serial murder forms the basis of a number of theories and explanations of serial murderers' behavior. This research provides the basis of scientific knowledge, as scientists either attempt to replicate earlier experiments or try to experiment with different variables to prove or disprove a hypothesis. This research builds toward the development of theories that can be tested against facts. However, human behavior cannot be subjected to laboratory conditions or manipulated to reveal changes or differences. Social scientists attempt to collect and quantify behavioral data that can be tested against a hypothesis or used to develop a theory, which in turn can be tested against further observations of behavior. To quantify behavioral information, the behaviors must be classified into variables and frequencies of variables. This is not an exact science.

Although there has been some published research on serial murder since the mid-1980s, much of the research on this crime has not been empirically based, and the data that have been collected have been limited in scope. The lack of empirical research causes a problem in studying serial murder. Information about these murders and murderers is not readily available because it is not collected systematically by government agencies. Within the *Uniform Crime Reports* collected by the federal government from federal, state, and local police jurisdictions, serial murder falls within the much larger category of homicide. In the absence of any official reporting mechanism, researchers have had to build their own databases from a variety of sources.

In addition to research published in journals and monographs, a great deal of information has been published in newspaper accounts, electronic media, true-crime books, and government publications. All of this may or may not be reliable or valid. Even research published in journals or monographs may be of questionable reliability or validity. In fact, all of the data should be considered suspect, but it is all we have and all we are likely to have for a while.

One way to approach information about serial murderers' behavior is to consider oneself an observer of the serial killer's actions. Because we cannot observe the actual killings, we must limit ourselves to what is observable before and after the apprehension of the killer.

Prior to the killer's apprehension, we can observe:

- The victims
- The crime scenes
- The areas surrounding the crime scenes
- The scenes of the abductions
- The areas surrounding the abductions

After apprehension, we can observe:

- The background of the killer
- The physical characteristics of the killer
- What the killer says about the killing

We can then aggregate these observations of the killings and the killer with observations of other killings and can attempt to make observations across cases.

Common Characteristics of Serial Killers

Many researchers of serial murder derive their theories about serial killers from the common behavioral characteristics that seem to be found in single case studies, small groups of case studies, or information about a number of killers. These common characteristics are observed in a variety of places that fall within the five major sources of information described earlier.

Single case studies provided a great deal of our information about serial killers in the early research into this phenomenon. Individual case studies are still conducted today, but more and more of our information on serial murder behavior comes from the combination of small groups of case studies. In addition to serious research using a case study approach, much of the true-crime literature relies almost entirely on case studies, whether of a single case or of a number of cases. It is up to serious researchers and students of this material to discriminate between

The Misbegotten Son (1993), a study of the serial killer Arthur Shawcross by Jack Olsen, who is well known for his painstaking research in writing crime books, and the more recent books written about Jeffrey Dahmer, many of which reached bookstores within weeks or months of the national reporting of this case from Milwaukee, Wisconsin.

Information on serial killers can also be found in so-called encyclopedias of serial killers, mass murderers, spree killers, and the like (Lane & Gregg, 1992; Newton, 1990). In addition, a number of books that claim to give the reader all of the information available on general categories of murder list and briefly describe these murders and murderers (Linedecker, 1990). Few if any of these books provide us with completely reliable or valid information about serial killers. For the most part, as with true-crime books, the authors and editors of these books have been under pressure to publish quickly in order to respond to the public's continuing fascination with serial murder (see Chapter 5 for a more detailed discussion of serial murder as a media growth industry).

Empirical Works

Holmes and DeBurger (1988) and Eric Hickey (1997) have provided us with a great deal of information about the behavioral characteristics of serial killers, based on databases of serial killers that they themselves have collected and on my own work (Egger, 1990a), which synthesized some of their research and other research much more limited in scope.

The challenges faced by these researchers are great, given the problems of collecting this information, as noted earlier. Data and descriptive information on the serial murderers or their victims are almost always missing. Reaching back more than ten or fifteen years to collect information on earlier killers only adds to the researcher's problems.

Holmes and DeBurger (1988) examine the behavioral backgrounds of serial killers and, from these, develop a typology or classification of serial murder (see Chapter 3). Their data set consists of 110 serial murderers, and they provide examples from this group. Analysis of these serial murderers (apparently all males) reveals three common central core characteristics in their behavioral backgrounds (adapted from Holmes and DeBurger, 1988, pp. 49–50, 63):

1. "The basic sources of the repetitive homicide pattern are psychogenic." The serial killer's psyche includes the norms, values, beliefs, perceptions, and propensities that result in the killing. Sociogenic factors provide context for these propensities but are not considered the immediate cause of the killing.

2. "Motives that impel and justify the repeated acts of homicide have an intrinsic locus; they are structured and rooted within the mind of the murderer." The killing is the expression of the killer's desire to kill; in most cases the motive is not material gain, political power, or other external rewards.

3. "The serial killer's homicidal behavior is expressive of the interlocking motives and propensities that predominate in his mind and personality. His behavior is therefore oriented toward psychological gain." Given the killer's psychological drive to kill, the more murders committed, the greater the buildup of psychological gain.

Holmes and DeBurger (1988) argue that although serial murder is psychogenic, social and cultural elements in American society tend to enhance the probability of serial killings. They cite the emphasis on violence and thrills in our entertainment industry, the common view of violence as a normal way of dealing with problems, the anonymity and depersonalization of urban society, and the mobility of Americans as factors that all serve the homicidal propensities of the serial killer. Meloy (1989) refers to this as a psychosocial approach to serial murder, in which psychogenic factors are central to the mind of the murderer but are greatly influenced by the sociocultural context.

Hickey's (1997) research is based on his collection of data on 399 serial murderers (62 females and 337 males) who killed between 1800 and 1995. Although this is indeed a large database of serial killers, the information Hickey presents is not specific to the behavioral characteristics of the serial killer, because Hickey's focus is on the victims, and much of his data is historical, in some case going back 195 years.

Although Hickey (1997) does give us a close look at female serial killers, his data set numbers only 62. Historical research tends to provide more general information on female serial killers than on men because of the women's notoriety in newspapers, crime books, and historical documents. The data on male serial killers are not presented in total, nor does Hickey discuss many behavioral characteristics of this sample. Rather, he identifies subsets of the data when discussing specific types of male killers or highlighting various important characteristics.

Hickey's analysis of female serial killers deals primarily with the emergence of these killers as a distinct type and with their selection of victims. In discussing their motives and methods, Hickey does shed some light on their behavioral characteristics. From limited biographical data on each killer, he did find that a number of them had histories of child abuse, extreme poverty, and unstable relationships. In a taxonomy of motives developed from his data, Hickey states that their motives "appear to center on financial security, revenge, enjoyment, and sexual stimulation" (1997, pp. 223–224). Of the 62 female killers described, he listed the motive as "money sometimes" in 47 percent of cases. Because Holmes and DeBurger, among others, believe the primary motive of the serial killer is psychological, this could be seen as a drive to achieve creature comforts. However, the second most common motive among these female killers is listed as "money only," in 27 percent of cases. A number of researchers would exclude these cases because the motive is material. However, a number of these killers may be "black widows," who kill their husbands or relatives for insurance compensation. Hickey notes that some of these killers' motivation for money may simply represent their attempt to meet an unfulfilled need; for others, psychological needs and economic needs are one and the same.

Hickey (1997) found that very few of the female killers had a criminal history. Their primary method of killing was the use of poison, and almost half used poison exclusively.

Hickey's empirical data on male serial killers' behavioral characteristics are first described for all of the males in his database and then for various subgroups of killers. For all males, he found that these killers were not highly educated and generally did not hold professional or skilled jobs. Further, they did not commonly use firearms as their sole means of killing. He found mutilation in over half of the cases and strangulation or suffocation in one-third. Hickey notes that the act of killing must be viewed as a process, given that a number of these serial killers have tortured, beaten, and mutilated their victims prior to death.

Hickey also addresses the issue of motivation for all males. Although sexual motivation was listed most frequently by these offenders, only 9 percent gave it as their sole reason for killing; 46 percent listed it as their motivation "sometimes." "Enjoyment" was listed frequently, and "money only" was listed by only 7 percent of these killers. Rarely were these motives listed as the sole reason. Hickey notes that many of the stated motives of the killers in his study "may actually have been methods by which they achieved ultimate power and control over other human beings" (Hickey, 1997, p. 155).

Although Hickey no longer provides percentages of the total database, he argues that solo killers who kill women can be referred to as "lust killers" because of the sexual nature of their criminal assaults. He further argues that the primary motive of this group is control. In comparison to all other male serial killers, they were more prone to rape their victims or carry out bizarre sexual acts on the victims, to have a history of sex-related crimes, and to have spent time in prison or mental institutions. Hickey found that one-third of this subgroup had experienced previous social or psychological problems and that two-thirds of these 198 male serial killers had experienced prior incarceration in prison or a mental institution. In 62 of the male offenders, Hickey found some form of childhood trauma, ranging from rejection and an unstable home to poverty and a prostitute mother.

A Multidisciplinary Theory

Mitchell (1999), in a critical examination of the current literature on serial murder, advocates a multidisciplinary model, incorporating the disciplines of sociology, psychiatry, biology, and psychology, which he refers to as an "integrated model." Mitchell's theory integrates pathological foundations with developmental consequences and includes a cycle for maintenance—that is, for continuing to kill. Mitchell's theory involves four major factors:

- *Foundation of pathology:* Biological predisposition (genetics) interacts with familial factors (such as physical abuse) and sociocultural factors (such as a violence-prone society). Either environmental trauma or biology alone is not seen as sufficient to cause the development of a serial murderer. It is their interaction that is important.

- *Developmental consequences:* Biology and the environment combine to produce individuals' personality characteristics, cognitive style, and mental health. However, diathesis stress (genetics, environment, and stressors) is a cause of personality difficulties, distorted cognitive style, and psychiatric morbidity (the probability of mental illness). These arise from interaction between their pathological antecedents and also through interaction among themselves (for example, there are likely to be significant and magnifying interactions between fantastic withdrawal and paraphilic development—occurring by sexual arousal through deviant or bizarre images or activities).

- *Initial homicidal episode:* The effect of stressors (e.g., a significant event like rejection or maternal death) may cause an initial homicidal episode. Such an episode may differ from subsequent murders in its level of planning and instrumentality; it may be unplanned, as with Dahmer's first victim (see Chapter 12) or when the intention is to silence a rape victim. However, if the murder is associated with relief (from stress), sexual gratification, relief from positive psychotic symptoms (in the case of a visionary killer), and success in evading capture ("I got away with it"), then the operant processes will contribute to a cycle of maintenance. Otherwise, the potential serial murderer may kill only once.

- *Maintenance cycle:* The positive effect (or relief from negative effect) is followed by a period that is not easily treated in which there may be relief from the "compulsion" to kill. Reliving the crime through "trophies" from the crime scene and mental imagery with masturbation reinforces the association between killing and positive experiences. Eventually, the offender's cognitive state will be challenged by an aversive experience (stressor), leading to cognitive decline. A negative inward response will be followed by a restorative attempt—the negative outward response, or homicidal response. The relief provided by the homicidal episode is sufficient to restart the cycle. In some cases, there need be no stressors to precipitate a further homicidal episode—merely a desire for further gratification in the absence of cognitive decline (adapted from Mitchell, 1999, pp. 26, 27).

Such an integrated theory may indeed provide us with an explanation of how biological predisposition toward committing aggressive acts combines with various events that act as triggers to cause such an individual actually to commit a homicidal act.

Case Studies

A number of researchers and authors have used combined case studies in their analysis. Others have used case studies or interviews as an empirical basis for their analysis. Still others have based their analysis on a very small number of case studies, and in some instances analysis and conclusions have been based on single case studies. Holmes and DeBurger (1985), in an earlier work, utilize information from five case studies from which they make certain generalizations regarding mobility and types of killers. In their later work (1988), they provide a case study of Ted Bundy, including the results of an interview with Bundy. However, the Bundy case study is used primarily to examine how a well-known serial killer corresponds to empirical research presented earlier in their book; this case study is not used as the basis of these authors' conclusions regarding serial murderers.

Hickey (1997) used brief case studies to provide examples of his subgroups and to highlight various characteristics of each subgroup. Ressler et al. (1986), in their analysis and interviews of thirty-six sexually oriented murders, concluded "that the motivation for murder is a complex developmental process that is based on needs for sexual dominance at the destructive expense of the victim" (p. 284). They also note that "[t]he victim and offense must be seen as having symbolic meaning to the offender reflecting violent sadistic fantasies" (p. 285).

The Case Study

Apsche (1993) used the case study of Gary Heidnik to reach certain conclusions regarding serial murder. Between November 1986 and March 1987, Heidnik kidnapped six women in Philadelphia and held them as sex slaves in the cellar of his home in order to have them produce his offspring. One of these women died while hanging from the cellar rafters and was dismembered by Heidnik. A second victim was electrocuted by Heidnik, who then disposed of her body in New Jersey. Heidnik was found guilty on two counts of first-degree murder, five counts of rape, six counts of kidnapping, four counts of aggravated assault, and one count of deviate sexual intercourse.

Apsche analyzed Heidnik's background and behavior through interviews with him and other information collected regarding his criminal trial. In his analysis of Heidnik, Apsche was attempting to develop a new diagnostic category for the serial killer.

Apsche argues that the characteristics found in Heidnik were very similar to those of other serial killers. He found an insatiable obsession, an almost instinctual drive, that pushes these killers to fill their empty lives with an overactive fantasy life leading to ritual murder. Apsche argues that serial killers are manipulative; they attempt to control the world around them. Apsche found serial killers to have a strong feeling of inadequacy and found that these individuals, as children, never felt the intimacy of bonding with their parents. Although Apsche's research relies a great deal on the work of others (Norris, 1989; Ressler et al., 1988), he also argues that many serial killers attempt suicide and that all attempt to get help. He argues that these killers "appear to want to stop what is about to happen yet they always regain control of themselves to prevent their discovery" (Apsche, 1993, p. 18). Heidnik, as one example, attempted suicide a total of thirteen different times.

Apsche calls for much more research into the mind of the serial killer. He notes that his efforts to understand the serial killer are only a first step.

Abrahamsen (1985), who interviewed David Berkowitz (the "Son of Sam"), described him as "a human being inexorably driven to destroy himself and others" (p. xii). Abrahamsen found Berkowitz to be totally indifferent to the fate of his victims and to have an urge to kill (and, when the time was ripe, to confess). Berkowitz, as his own detective, became, in a sense, the victim as well as the victimizer through his confessions (p. 215). Such a description could apply equally well to other well-known serial killers like Danny Rolling, John Wayne Gacy, or Dennis Nilsen.

Other Studies

Other researchers have analyzed serial killers from a combination of sources and found similar behavioral characteristics in these killers. J. Paul de River categorized what we now refer to as serial killers as "lust killers" who suffer from "a deviation or perversion of the sexual impulse" (1958, p. 99). They are "cold, calculating and egotistically sadistic" (p. 120). Guttmacher (1960) states that many of these sadistic killers vent their hostile impulses through cruelty to animals; their real hatred, however, is not against animals but against their fellow humans.

In discussing these compulsive homicides, Revitch and Schlesinger (1981) argue that the majority of these crimes have an underlying basis in sexual conflicts and that most sex murders belong to this group. Serial murderers, according to Lunde (1976) are sadistic murderers who are apt to repeat their crimes. He describes the sadistic murderer as one who kills, mutilates, or abuses his victims to achieve sexual pleasure and who may choose victims with specific occupations or characteristics. Lunde (1976) states: "They usually have few normal social and sexual relationships. In fact, they often have had no experience of normal sexual intercourse" (p. 53). The sadistic murderer is one of the most common types of killers of strangers and, of all types of murderers, is the most likely to repeat his crime, according to Lunde. Brittain (1970) describes the sadistic murderer as one "excited by cruelty, whether in books or in films, in fact or fantasy" (p. 202). Levin and Fox (1985) state: "[T]he serial killer, motivated by sex and sadism, is hardly deterrable. His sociopathic disposition favors immediate gratification, regardless of the consequences" (p. 225).

There is no consensus among behavioral scientists, even when they look at the same data, for the reasons that so many Americans kill one another (Rose, 1979). Banay (1956) notes that the reasons given for the act of homicide by an individual are misleading because the true cause is masked by other "logically" understandable explanations. Banay concludes that there is simply no logic in murder (p. 193).

Dr. Emanuel Tanay, a forensic psychiatrist, notes that the serial killer does not give any visible signs of derangement, even under the most expert examination. Tanay interviewed Theodore Bundy and found no overt psychopathology in examining him. Dr. Helen Morrison, who reportedly spent a number of hours with John Wayne Gacy, believes the serial killer is a new personality type (Berger, 1984).

Psychopaths or Sociopaths?

Serial murderers are frequently described as psychopaths by social scientists and in the mass media. Psychopaths have a personality disorder involving a range of affective, behavioral, and interpersonal characteristics. Primary personality characteristics of psychopaths include a lack of empathy, guilt, or remorse toward those who suffer from the results of their actions, and a callous disregard for the feelings, rights, and welfare of others (Cleckley, 1964). Psychopaths are typically egocentric, selfish, glib, deceitful, callous, impulsive, manipulative, sensation-seeking, and irresponsible; they act as if they had no conscience. They resist any social convention or norms and ignore social and interpersonal obligations. Because of this, they frequently come into contact with the criminal justice system (Hare, Forth, & Strachman, 1992).

The worst murderers in the world are frequently described as psychopaths. They are not the most numerous, but they are the ones who commit the motiveless crimes that shock and puzzle society today. The word "psychopath" is the one that psychologists and psychiatrists use to describe the behavior of the motiveless serial murderer. They have also used the term "sociopath," which is more commonly used by sociologists to emphasize the social interaction of the behavior.

Cleckley (1964) identifies a number of marks or attributes of psychopaths, whose behavior is not readily understood in terms of mental deficiency, neurosis, or psychosis. These primary attributes include unreliability, insincerity, pathological lying, and egocentricity; poor judgment and impulsivity; lack of remorse, guilt, or shame; an inability to experience empathy or concern for others, or to maintain affectionate attachments; an impersonal and poorly integrated sex life; and an unstable lifestyle, with no long-term plans. Beyond such general attributes, the psychiatric and psychological literature does not allow us to develop a set of the common characteristics of serial murderers. This is a result of the individual case approach used by psychologists and psychiatrists to study and classify such criminals. Dr. John Liebert, a psychiatrist at the University of Washington, has stated: "We have some basic clinical knowledge of serial murderers that allows us to rule people out. What we don't have is how to rule them in" (Berger, 1984, p. 1).

Levin and Fox (1985) found the terms "sociopath" and "psychopath" used interchangeably to describe serial murderers who repeated acts of brutality and sadism because they lacked conscience or a sense of guilt. For Levin and Fox (1985), these terms

> [a]pply to those individuals who are not mentally ill, not grossly out of touch with reality, but who are incapable of experiencing normal amounts of love and empathy. Though psychologists don't know for sure, they speculate that some people become sociopaths because of rejection; the sociopath lacks a sense of responsibility, guilt, or morality and is unable to have lasting and meaningful relationships. He has trouble postponing impulsive behavior, is immature, and is unaffected by the rewards and punishments which might ordinarily inhibit immoral action.

This type of individual is often implicated in behaviors ranging from cheating and lying, on the one hand, to rape and murder, on the other. (pp. 71–72)

Dr. Joel Fort, a psychiatrist who testified at the trial of the serial murderer Edmund Kemper in Santa Cruz, California, defined the sociopath as having

[a] morality that is not operating by any recognized or accepted moral code, but operating entirely according to expediency to what one feels like doing at the moment or that which will give the individual the most gratification or pleasure. It includes an absence of conscience. (Godwin, 1978, p. 300)

For example, Luke Karamazov, a convicted serial killer, is described by Hilberry (1987) as "on the whole . . . well satisfied with his own composure, his lack of feeling [for his victims]" (p. 88). Hilberry quotes Karamazov as stating: "I had a certain detachment, if you can visualize. There has to be some part of me left out" (p. 88).

The *Diagnostic and Statistical Manual of Mental Disorders (DSM)*, first published in 1952 by the American Psychiatric Association, referred to a "Sociopathic Personality" (code 52), as previously noted in Chapter 1. The terms "psychopath" and "sociopath" were replaced in the third edition of the *DSM (DSM-III, 1980)* with the term "antisocial personality disorder." The fourth and revised edition of this manual, commonly known as *DSM-IV*, refers to such behavior as "antisocial personality disorder" (1994, code 301.7).

The case of Kenneth Bianchi illustrates the utility of such a diagnosis using *DSM-III-R*. Bianchi was diagnosed with "antisocial personality disorder 301.70," a diagnosis that requires that at least three of twelve criteria be met prior to the age of fifteen years. Bianchi's history indicated that he (1) persistently lied from an early age, (2) had school grades that were consistently below his estimated intellectual ability, and (3) chronically violated rules at home and at school. This diagnosis further requires at least four of nine manifestations of the disorder after the age of eighteen. In Bianchi's case, he displayed (1) an inability to maintain consistent work behavior, (2) failure to accept social norms with respect to lawful behavior, (3) an inability to maintain an enduring attachment to a sexual partner, and (4) a failure to honor financial obligations. *DSM-III-R* adds two additional requirements: (1) a pattern of continuous antisocial behavior in which the rights of others are violated; and (2) that the behavior noted cannot be attributed to severe mental retardation, schizophrenia, or manic episode (American Psychiatric Association, 1989).

In the classroom, I ask my students to measure their own general behavior against these characteristics, excluding the last two requirements of the diagnosis. It is obvious from their reactions that quite a few (if they are being honest with themselves) have or have had similar behaviors during these periods in their life. The point is that *DSM-IV* does not provide us with a set of characteristics or criteria from which to predict homicidal or serial homicidal behavior. Once the serial killer is identified, we can retrospectively, with hindsight, find the character trait or flaw. As Hickey (1997) and others have noted, offenders do not always come from the same background or mold. Each evolves from very different events in their lives and in the situations they encounter, and they respond to these events and situations in very different ways. J. Reid Meloy, a noted psychiatrist, has argued that the criteria for this diagnosis are "too descriptive, inclusive, criminally based, and socioeconomically skewed to be of much clinical or research use" (1988, p. 6).

Hare (1993) and others have argued that the antisocial personality disorder criteria in *DSM-III-R* are primarily measurements of antisocial and criminal behavior and do not measure the affective and interpersonal characteristics of the personality disorder, commonly referred to as psychopathy.

Professor David Canter of the University of Surrey provides a different and perhaps more practical perspective on the use of the terms "psychopath" and "sociopath":

> They [serial killers] may be labeled psychopath or sociopath; both are curious terms that imply a medical, pathogenic origin yet in fact describe someone for whom no obvious organic or psychotic diagnosis can be made. The seemingly informed technical term is therefore more an admission of ignorance than an effective description. (Canter, 1994, p. 263)

Thus the utility of the terms "psychopath," "sociopath," and "antisocial personality disorder" is that they provide us with a set of typical characteristics or a typical lack of certain characteristics. The terms allow us to assign a group of attributes to certain individuals. The terms and their descriptors may allow us to see who does not fall within these categories, but may not let us identify those who specifically fit the labels. These terms advise us that such individuals lack a conscience and have no sense of empathy for their victims, but the terms do not allow us to predict such behavior. The terms may have a socioeconomic bias that causes those using the criteria to overlabel certain types of people. Finally, as David Canter has noted, these terms may simply be an admission that we in fact do not know why these individuals act as they do.

Giannangelo (1997) argues for a new and separate classification in the *Diagnostic and Statistical Manual of Mental Disorders* for the behavior of a serial killer. He argues that such a classification, which he labels as "homicidal pattern disorder," should be listed under "Impulse-Control Disorders Not Elsewhere Classified" (*Electronic DSM-IV*, 1994, p. 269).

Giannangelo describes this homicidal pattern disorder as having the following characteristics:

A. Deliberate and purposeful murder or attempts at murder of strangers on more than one occasion.
B. Tension or affective arousal at some time before the act.
C. Pleasure, gratification, or relief in commission or reflection of the acts.

D. Displays personality traits consistent with diagnosis of at least one Cluster B Personality Disorder (Antisocial, Borderline, Histrionic, Narcissistic).

E. Understands the illegality of actions and continues to avoid apprehension.

F. Murders are not motivated by monetary gain, to conceal criminal activity, to express anger or vengeance, in response to a delusion or hallucination, or as a result of impaired judgment (e.g., in dementia, Mental Retardation, Substance Intoxication). (Giannangelo, 1997)

In short, the terms "psychopath," "sociopath," and "antisocial personality disorder" allow us to define our label and to characterize those who seem to fit the label, but not to explain their behavior. They allow us to put many serial killers into a group or category—to classify the serial killer. The problem, however, remains for those who are asking why. The group, category, or classification goes no further toward an answer. It remains an enigma—indeed, an elusive phenomenon.

Inadequate Socialization

Theories regarding inadequate socialization or childhood trauma are frequently cited in the homicide literature with reference to the serial murderer. Storr (1972) states that human cruelty (describing the acts of torture, mutilation, and dismemberment committed by serial murderers) is "a phenomenon which can only be understood if we take into account the fact that many people suffer from persistent feelings of powerlessness and helplessness which date from a very early period in childhood" (p. 76).

The intense rage of the serial killer may mirror the horrors suffered in childhood. An intense hatred bred in childhood can now be directed at his victims. Reinhardt's (1962) case studies of "multicides" (mass and serial murders) found a prevalence of histories of neglect and early years spent in extreme social and psychological deprivation:

They gave preponderant evidence of never having experienced normal communication with a dependable, understanding part of the social world about them. They had no workable system of social or personal frames of reference. (p. viii)

Willie (1975), who concurs with Reinhardt, found that the most common feature in the family backgrounds of these murderers was the violent punishment inflicted on the child, and that there "appears to be no other factor which is as specific in the family backgrounds of homicidal offenders" (p. 168).

FBI agents Hazelwood and Douglas (1980) state:

Seldom does the lust murderer come from an environment of love and understanding. It is more likely that he was an abused and neglected child who experienced a great deal of conflict in his early life and was unable to develop and use adequate coping devices (i.e., defense mechanisms). (p. 4)

Ellis and Gullo (1971), in their extensive reading of the case histories of murderers, found the following:

Whenever sufficient material is given on the murderer's background, it is consistently found that (1) his upbringing, particularly in relation to being treated kindly by his parents and his being emotionally close to them and to his other family members, left much to be desired; and (2) from an early age, he acted peculiarly, especially in his interpersonal relations with others, and began to get into some kind of school, social or vocational difficulties. (p. 158)

Serial murderers are frequently found to have unusual or unnatural relationships with their mothers. Lunde (1976) notes: "Normally there is an intense relationship with the mother. Her death is often one of those fantasized during adolescence. Later on, she may become one of the victims" (p. 53). "Many serial murderers have had intense, smothering relationships with their mothers—relationships filled with both abuse and sexual attraction" (Starr et al., 1984, p. 105).

Bjerre (1981), in his classic study of murder, states:

Time after time during my studies among murderers I was struck by the fact that just the most brutal criminals—men who, however different their psychological natures may have been in the beginning, and who had a stereotyped incapacity to conceive their fellow creatures as anything but dead matter or as the means to the satisfaction of their animal lusts; in other words men who for a long time had been cut off from any sort of association with humanity—were nevertheless frequently attached to their mothers by bonds which seemed even stronger than those which one ordinarily finds between mother and son. (p. 81)

Sex As a Motive

The killer's sexual orientation is not a consistent correlate in known serial murderers. As West (1987) notes, "there is no reason to suppose that the likelihood of becoming homicidal is associated with a particular sexual orientation" (p. 194). For example, DeSalvo, Bundy, and Kemper preferred females as sexual partners and as prey, whereas Gacy, Nilsen, and Corll preferred males in these roles.

Elsewhere, I have argued that sex is only an instrument used by the killer to obtain power and domination over his victim (Egger, 1990a). Although the sexual component is frequently present in a serial murder, it is not the central motivating factor for the killer but merely an instrument used to dominate, control, and destroy the victim.

Dr. Helen Morrison, who has reportedly interviewed a number of serial murderers, argues against a sexual theme in serial murder. She states: "The incidence of sadomasochistic sex is very high. The incidence of mass murders is not, at least in the sheer number of perpetrators" (McCarthy, 1984, p. 1). Storr (1972) also discounts the sexual nature of sadomasochism or cruelty. He argues that "sado-masochism is less 'sexual' than is generally supposed, and is really a 'pseudo-sexual' activity or preoccupation, much more concerned with power relations than with pleasure" (Storr, 1972, pp. 74–75). The emphasis on power relations or control was, for Levin and Fox (1985), an important characteristic of serial murderers. They state:

> Domination unmitigated by guilt is a crucial element in serial crimes with a sexual theme. Not only does sadistic sex—consensual or forcible—express the power of one person over another, but in serial homicides, murder enhances the killer's sense of control over his victims. (p. 72)

Nature and Nurture?

Dr. Park Elliot Dietz believes that serial killers are produced by a combination of genes and the wrong parents. When asked to imagine what it would take to create another Ted Bundy, John Wayne Gacy, or Edmund Kemper, Dr. Dietz states:

> Start with an abusive, criminal father and a hysterical, alcoholic mother; torture the boy as erotically as possible; have the naked mother spank him and sleep with him until age 12; bind and whip him regularly; have the mother sexually arouse him and punish him for his erections; let the mother appear promiscuous while condemning prostitutes; leave detective magazines around the house for him to find; and encourage him to watch R-rated slasher films and violence against glamorous women. (Simon, 1996, p. 311)

Simon (1996) argues, however, that becoming a serial killer is, to some extent, an exercise of choice. As a practicing psychiatrist he has been impressed with some of his patients who have overcome great personal difficulties. One patient with a severe manic depressive illness, who was married and ran a successful business, told him, "Doc, it's not the cards you're dealt, it's how you play them" (p. 311).

Variations on Power and Control

Levin and Fox (1985) contend that the serial murderer is trying to achieve a feeling of superiority over the victim and to triumph or conquer by destruction. Further, "As the serial killer becomes more and more secure with his crime, however, he may also become increasingly more sadistic and inhumane" (p. 67), and "[T]he pleasure and exhilaration that the serial killer derives from repeated murder stem from absolute control over other human beings" (p. 68). The psychological need to control and the wish to command the fate of those around them is, for Fox and Levin (1985), often evident in serial murderers. However, Ressler et al. (1986), in their study of thirty-six sexually oriented murderers, found every indication that the killers' motivation was a complex developmental process based on needs for sexual dominance which in turn were based on violent sadistic fantasies.

Sewell (1985) analyzed the case of Ted Bundy from the literature dealing with Bundy and from Sewell's own involvement as an investigator of the Chi Omega sorority house murders committed by Bundy at Florida State University. The purpose of Sewell's analysis was to apply Megargee's "algebra of aggression" (Megargee, 1982) to Bundy's behavior. Megargee's multidisciplinary approach to criminal behavior contends that "an individual automatically weighs alternatives and chooses a response to a situation which maximizes his/her benefit and minimizes potential pain and distress" (Sewell, 1985, p. 15).

Sewell (1985) argues that the behavioral characteristics of Ted Bundy provide a clear application of Megargee's algebra of aggression:

> Bundy's overall violent response exemplified an instigation to aggression which was grounded in his rage against women and magnified by his need for excitement, attention, and ego gratification. His habit strength drew on his repeated successful acts of violence . . . to obtain control of the victims and the unsuccessful attempts by a number of states to charge him with these crimes. A number of situational factors added to his predisposition towards violence as an acceptable response. (p. 47)

Sewell concludes that "it would appear that Bundy chose a violent response as an acceptable reaction to many situations" (p. 24).

Similarities to Rape

As I have noted elsewhere (Egger, 1985), the motivational dynamics of serial murder seem to be consistent with the findings of research on the nature of rape. Power would appear to be a vital component of both crimes. Although this is only conjecture, with no empirical foundation, the similarity of these acts becomes evident when one realizes that "it may take only a small increase in the desperation of the assailant or the resisting victim to convert a violent rape into a murder" (West, 1987, p. 180).

David Canter (1994) has also noted this similarity in his research. Canter states:

> [M]en I have spoken to who have admitted a series of rapes have often also admitted that they would have killed subsequent victims if they had not been caught. Rape has the same roots as murder. The difference between rape and murder lies in the form and degree of control the offender exerts over his victims. (p. 257)

The implication of Canter's statement is that the motivations of these two violent acts may be similar. However, the motivational dynamics of both violent acts are complex, and their similarities may explain only a certain level of action—in this case, the form and degree of control—and not necessarily the inner thoughts and drives of the violent actor.

FBI Agent Roy Hazelwood (now retired) readily agreed, in discussions, that there was a similarity between serial rape and serial murder—that both are repetitive, among other things. He agrees with my view that there is a power component to each crime and that further study is needed to determine if the motivational factors are similar in these crimes.

It is certainly true that rape is part of the criminal histories of many serial murderers. In some cases, these rapes are found to have been committed months or even years before any act of murder is committed. In other cases, the killer may vary his crimes, raping some of his victims and killing others. The crimes of James Edward Wood (Figure 2.1) illustrate a varied serial pattern of rape and murder, as well as a number of robberies.

FIGURE 2.1 James Edward Wood's Trail of Crime

1961:	Auto theft, Idaho Falls, Idaho.
November 23, 1967:	Stabs two women in Bossier City, Louisiana, and rapes one of them.
1967–1971:	In prison in Angola, Louisiana.
1971–1975:	Robbery suspect in Missouri, Arkansas, Texas, and Louisiana.
December 24, 1976:	Kills woman, Shreveport, Louisiana.
July 1977:	Armed robbery, Baton Rouge, Louisiana.
1979:	Suspect in two murders, Louisiana; convicted of rape, Ruston, Louisiana.
1979–1986:	In prison, Angola, Louisiana.
March 1987:	Robbery suspect, Oklahoma.
October 24, 1992:	Rapes Alton, Illinois, woman.
October 25, 1992:	Rapes and shoots Jamie Masengill, Bridgeton, Missouri.
October 27, 1992:	Robs restaurant, suburban Denver.
November 28, 1992:	Rapes fifteen-year-old girl, Pocatello, Idaho.
March 13, 1993:	Robs sandwich shop, Pocatello.
March 27, 1993:	Robs Tyhee County Store, Pocatello.
June 9, 1993:	Rapes fourteen-year-old girl, Pocatello.
June 19, 1993:	Rapes prostitute near Salt Lake City after robbing a restaurant.
June 23, 1993:	Robs restaurant, Idaho Falls.
June 27, 1993:	Robs Poppa Paul's Café, Pocatello.
June 29, 1993:	Kidnaps eleven-year-old Jeralee Underwood, Pocatello.

| June 30, 1993: | Murders Jeralee Underwood, Idaho Falls. |
| July 6, 1993: | Caught by police and confesses. |

Source: Data taken from *St. Louis Post Dispatch,* February 27, 1994, p. 4.

Other experts concur that rapists can escalate into killers. The criminal psychologist Ronald Weiner, who specializes in treating sexual predators, finds some rapists who "during the course of attacking a woman will wind up killing her. And like it! So their liking for rape escalates into murder" (Mariani & Stover, 1999, p. 1).

Biological Predisposition

There is currently a developing body of literature suggesting that certain biological characteristics may cause an individual to commit violent acts or may contribute to violent actions. These biological characteristics may be certain abnormalities in the brain, either genetic traits present from birth or abnormalities caused by trauma or brain damage.

For example, Adrian Raine, a professor of psychology at the University of Southern California, Los Angeles, recently completed a series of psychological studies of Danish men, schoolboys in York, England, and murderers on California's death row that all point specifically to mild brain dysfunction in early life as playing a crucial role in determining whether a young boy turns into a violent man. Raine's research results strongly imply that birth complications can lead to mild brain damage that may go unnoticed throughout childhood, yet may predispose a boy to violent behavior in adulthood. Raine suggests that birth complications may have produced the prefrontal dysfunction that goes on to lead to low levels of arousal, which in turn results in a tendency to commit violent crime. Raine states: "We suspect that under-aroused people seek out arousal to increase their levels back to normal. One way to do this as a kid is to join a gang, burgle a house or beat somebody up" (Connor, 1994, p. 19).

Dr. Jonathon Pincus, a noted neurologist, believes that a combination of factors, including brain damage and psychiatric impairment, produces illogical thinking and paranoia in the serial killer. The other factor that he believes is always present in these killers is physical and/or sexual abuse. Brain damage alone will not cause a person to be violent, but when brain damage, abuse, and psychiatric impairment are all present, "those factors interact, and produce a very violent person" (CNN, 1993).

The serial murderers seen by Pincus have been a bit less obviously nueurologically impaired than those who are not serial murderers and less psychiatrically impaired than those who are not able to function in society at all. All had been abused sexually and physically. Pincus suggests that "a number of them [serial murderers] have had episodic disorders of mood that have made them unable to control their impulses at a particular time" (CNN, 1993). The fact that serial murderers have a mood disorder may explain, according to Pincus, why these murderers don't kill all the time but only kill when their mood swings dictate such behavior.

Dr. Richard Restak, a neurologist and neuropsychiatrist, disagrees with Pincus. He argues that serial murderers have not been found to have episodic dyscontrol. In fact, these killers are often stalkers, who follow their victims. Restak argues that society has difficulty understanding and putting a person like a serial killer into a framework.

> Circular arguments start from the idea anybody will have to be crazy in order to do this, and this person did it, and therefore they must be disturbed. . . . It's easy to say they must be insane, or they must be suffering from some mental disorder. But it's also a way of eliminating, or I should say refusing to look at the outer limits of human freedom, and even human evil if you will. (CNN, 1993)

Dr. Restak thinks that psychiatry and, to a lesser extent, neurology are being asked to explain, in a court of law, behavior that the public has difficulty understanding. Rather than explain behavior from a Freudian perspective, which juries, judges, and the public have all rejected, the idea of brain damage is being proposed and discussed. Restak argues that "behavior doesn't necessarily imply brain damage at all" (CNN 1993).

Restak sums up the current state of psychiatric and neurological knowledge of the serial killer by stating:

> I think we're at the beginning, we're going to study different brain functions with pet scans, and new computer-assisted electroencephalograms, and things like that, but I don't think we're going to turn up some type of magic bullet, or magic key that's going to explain this. . . . [W]e've learned more about the brain in the last ten years than we did in the previous two hundred. So you could say that about any particular behavior that you want to look at, serial killers as well as anything else . . . but I don't think we are going to predict or prevent, because not every person that fits a certain profile goes on to become a serial killer. The current state about knowledge of the brain of serial killers is at a very elemental level. (CNN, 1993)

Restak (1992) further states: "However much one might wish otherwise, neurology will never entirely solve the mystery of why some people kill others, much less explain why some murderers derive pleasure from their actions" (pp. 20, 21).

Dr. Richard Kraus, a rural psychiatrist from New York, has taken a somewhat different approach to studying the biology of the serial killer. Kraus studied Arthur Shawcross, a serial killer who was convicted of killing eleven women in the Rochester, New York, area between 1988 and 1989. Kraus's examination of Shawcross revealed some unusual results. Kraus (1995) states:

In this case, there was no predisposing family history of alcoholism, violence, criminality, or psychiatric disorder and no evidence of parental abuse, neglect, abandonment, or cruelty. However, at age seven years, this "bright, well-dressed, neat" child (as he was then described) was beginning to exhibit solitary aggressive conduct disordered behaviors which set him apart from his family, alienated him from his peers, and probably contributed to his becoming a loner. In the years that followed, his life style became that of repeated aggressive and anti-social behaviors, with convictions for burglary, arson, manslaughter, and finally, the serial homicides of 11 women. (p. 2)

In examining Shawcross's medical history, Kraus found a number of serious accidents. When he was nine, Shawcross suffered leg paralysis and was hospitalized for one week. At age sixteen he suffered a skull fracture and a cerebral concussion. When he was twenty, he was accidentally struck in the head with a sledgehammer and, that same year, was involved in an auto accident. In each of these instances he suffered a cerebral concussion. The following year, Shawcross fell from a ladder. His prison records show numerous complaints of passing out, headaches, and similar problems. Shawcross also received a 10 percent medical disability for numbness in his left hand, related to a military injury suffered when he was in Vietnam (Kraus, 1995).

Shawcross stated that his homicides were due to an "uncontrollable rage . . . it wasn't everyone, just certain ones [who] were more aggressive . . . the first one, she bit me . . . some tried to rob me . . . some belittled me . . . some didn't care . . . one threatened to tell my wife [about his infidelities]" (Kraus, 1995, p. 11).

Kraus found that Shawcross was not too impaired to understand the nature and consequences of his acts or to know that what he did was wrong. But Shawcross did have a "hair-trigger" temper and would lose control when provoked or under stress (Kraus, 1995, p. 12).

A battery of psychological tests on Shawcross revealed a primary diagnosis of antisocial personality disorder. Laboratory examinations revealed that Shawcross had a 47, XYY karyotype chromosome. Kraus found a great deal of controversy in the research literature on this XYY chromosome condition and whether or not it was suggestive of abnormality in some men. Further lab tests also revealed that Shawcross had ten times the normal level of krytopyrroles, which, according to Kraus's research, "correlated with marked irritability, rages, terrible problems with stress control, diminished ability to control stress, inability to control anger once provoked, mood swings, poor memory, a preference for night time, violence and antisocial behavior" (Olsen, 1993, p. 506).

In summary, Kraus (1995) found that:

These clinical findings revealed a matrix . . . of genetic, biochemical, neurological, and psychiatric impairments, which at least partially explain the ". . . actual inner workings . . ." of this serial killer. . . . Such a matrix of findings in one individual can reasonably be expected to result in behavioral disturbance. While biological

influences do not control behavior or predetermine outcomes, this case demonstrates that criminal tendencies do have biological origins. (p. 27)

Dr. Paul Britton (1999), a British forensic psychologist, argues that serial killers

would seem to be born without the capacity to develop a normal range of emotion. They seem unable to recognize that other people have feelings as important
as their own. They are impervious to remorse or guilt. They neither give love nor
receive it. Often the adults they become have an intense need for excitement. They
may also feel "society" has let them down or failed to give them the acclaim they
merit. These are the budding serial killers, psychopaths and sociopaths." (Features, p. 1)

Anthropological Viewpoint

Wilson and Putnam (1961) state: "If man is deprived of meanings beyond his
everyday routine, he becomes disgusted and bitter, and eventually violent. A society that provides no outlet for man's idealist passions is asking to be torn apart by
violence" (p. 233). Wilson and Seaman (1983) carry this line of thinking one step
further by attempting to examine the thoughts of those who commit murder. In
addition to extending and developing the argument for unmotivated resentment
as a prerequisite for such violence, these authors also attach an explanation for
what they label "motiveless viciousness" (p. ix). "Such violence, as frequently
committed by the serial killer, is the result of Sartre's magical thinking, that is,
thinking that cannot possibly accomplish its objective" (Wilson & Seaman, 1983,
p. xii). However, such an etiological argument seems specious given the fact that
such thinking is apparently nothing more than a lack of self-control and an unwillingness to delay gratification. Explanations of this nature are, indeed, almost trite;
they are frequently found in the more mainstream true-crime literature.

Elliott Leyton (1986) argues that multiple murders are a "kind of sub-political
and conservative protest which nets the killer a substantial social profit of revenge,
celebrity, identity and sexual relief" and which "is viewed by them as a mission or
crusade" (p. 26). For Leyton, these killings are "a kind of rebellion against the
social order" (p. 26), "a protest against their [the killers'] perceived exclusion from
society" (p. 27).

Leyton (1986) concludes by rejecting arguments of sexual excitement or of conquest over the victim. He argues that motivation is, rather, a solution to problems
resulting from denied ambition. Multiple murderers act "to relieve a burning
grudge engendered by their failed ambition" (p. 298).

Leyton, an anthropologist, expands upon a frequently cited explanation for
homicide when he identifies deprivation, both relative and absolute, as the provocation for the multiple murderers' frustration. From a cultural perspective, the
multiple murderer (Leyton includes both mass and serial murderers) is, then,

a profoundly conservative figure who comes to feel excluded from the class he so devoutly wishes to join. In an extended campaign of vengeance, he murders people unknown to him, but who represent to him (in their behavior, their appearance, or their location) the class that has rejected him. (p. 23)

Are They Simply Evil?

Is it sufficient to identify serial killers as evil persons? Such individuals are certainly not good persons! Are they followers of Satan? Vampires? Demons with superhuman powers? Do serial killers represent the dark side of humanity?

Philip Jenkins (1995) provides an interesting commentary on evil and serial murder:

When the 20th century began, it was obvious to all educated people that this would be a great age of science and enlightenment. As this black age slouches towards its conclusions, it is clear that science has failed either to understand or to subdue the beast within humanity and the highest form of enlightenment might be to admit this fact. At the very least, let us agree on the failure of language to offer an acceptable terminology for the beast, the darkness, for whatever metaphor we choose to employ for that intuitively obvious reality. If not "evil," what? (p. 19)

To conceive of the concept of "good," we must logically acknowledge the concept of "evil." One cannot exist without the other. Such philosophical discussions go beyond the scope of this text. They are, however, worth noting for the reader.

Problems with Explanations

There are, indeed, a number of different theories claiming to explain the behavior of the serial killer. Norris (1989) in *Serial Killers,* presents a list of behavior patterns, which he offers as the epistemology of the "serial killer syndrome" (p. 212). These twenty-two patterns are symptoms of episodic aggressive behavior, which for Norris provides a profile of predisposition. Norris contends that these patterns or profiles are the "combined symptomatology of hundreds of serial killers" (p. 242). It would seem that the reader must accept such a statement as fact on the basis of Norris's assertion of having interviewed "more than a dozen serial killers" (p. 210) and that the remaining data for such a synthesized symptomatology stem from interviews of secondary data sources. Such acceptance is indeed difficult, given the total lack of empirical documentation, footnotes, or references in Norris's work.

Few, if any, of the theories of serial murder described here have been tested empirically against a large number of serial killers. Frequently, psychologists and other researchers who have interviewed serial killers have approached their interviews using a structured format or protocol intended to verify an already developed theory of the behavior. Frequently, when those interviewed have provided information inconsistent with already established theories, the information obtained is dismissed as unimportant or irrelevant.

We are still locked into a single-factor approach or the belief that a common profile of "the serial killer" exists and that all serial killers have certain common characteristics. The mass media tend to drive this approach by constantly asking for a "profile" of the serial killer. But it is quite possible that when we fail to consider those characteristics of serial killers that do not distinguish these killers from other nonkillers with similar characteristics, we are missing an important, even critical, ingredient in the behavior of serial murder. It may be the presence of these nondistinguishing characteristics of serial killers *in combination with* other factors, that drives the desire of these killers to kill and kill again. More research in this area is undoubtedly necessary.

CHAPTER 3

They Are All Around Us

It has been widely stated by psychiatrists and lay writers that in our culture every killer must be psychopathic. That implies a rosy view of our society. It leaves out the terrible aspects of normality (however defined) in a violent age. We flatter ourselves if we believe that our social conditions are so far above reproach that only mentally ill adults and children can commit violence.

—Fredric Wertham, *A Sign for Cain*, 1966, p. 17

Violence is good for those who have nothing to lose.

—Jean-Paul Sartre, *Le Diable et le Bon Dieu*

We Are Strangers to One Another

In modern society, we are creating strangers of each other. As we become strangers, we begin to see others more as objects and less as human beings. Our connections with others become tenuous and fleeting. Interpersonal relationships are short-lived. A sense of alienation grows within us, often tempered only by a strong desire to maintain our social status, advance our careers, or ensure a relatively comfortable existence.

As we walk past a homeless man huddled over a grate in the sidewalk we don't see him as a man. He is not a human being, one of us, but only one of "them"—one who is different, probably dangerous, and certainly not worthy of society's attention. Were our eyes to see this man as a human being, they would tear with emotion. But as we walk on, our eyes remain dry, furtively focusing on those around us in anticipation of an attack.

The vestiges of our humanity have been driven inward, protected within our inner selves. This is not only a result of our alienation but also comes from our ever-present fear of the stranger. In anticipation of falling prey to the stranger, or perhaps from the memories of prior victimization, we remain a part of society yet hold ourselves apart from most of its members. Only those close family members and the few we call friends continue to have meaning for us as human beings. Essentially, each of us is alone: one among the many.

We place great value on individual success. We focus on what we need to do to survive, maintain our lives, and continue. The others with whom we must interact demand only minimal, impersonal involvement. As we negotiate with others for mutual profit, we may try to convince ourselves that we have control over our own lives. As we move about increasingly among strangers, however, we have little control over these strangers. And to the extent that we are seen as prey by some of these strangers, we are reminded that predators are all around us. It is a realization that can make us feel truly isolated and very much alone.

Who Are They?

Who are these serial killers? To answer that question, we should first look briefly at some of the better known serial killers in our society.

Jeffrey L. Dahmer's deadpan stare is known to most people who ever watch TV or glance at a copy of *Time, Newsweek,* or *People.* In July 1991 Dahmer was charged by Milwaukee police with the death of sixteen young men in that city; he was also charged with the death of one young man in Ohio. He confessed to killing and dismembering his victims and, at his trial, pled guilty but insane. The judge decided Dahmer was sane and sentenced him to fifteen consecutive life sentences in Wisconsin, a state that prohibits the death penalty. Dahmer was killed in prison in 1994.

Arthur Shawcross pled innocent to the murders of ten women. His lawyers argued that he was legally insane, but he was found guilty of second-degree murder and was sentenced to a minimum of 250 years in prison in New York. He also pled guilty to killing an eleventh victim (Olsen, 1993).

Richard Ramirez, dubbed the "Night Stalker" by the press, claimed to worship Satan. He was convicted of thirteen murders and thirty felonies by a California jury and is currently incarcerated in San Quentin Prison in California (Linedecker, 1991).

Theodore Robert Bundy, discussed at length in Chapter 9, is well known.

Shortly after his arrest on suspicion of killing an eighty-four-year-old woman, Henry Lee Lucas, discussed in Chapter 7, confessed to having killed sixty people.

Wayne Williams pled innocent to the killing of two black youths in Atlanta, Georgia, but an Atlanta jury found him guilty of two counts of murder and he was sentenced to two consecutive life terms in Georgia (Isaacson, 1982). At the time, police believed that Williams was responsible for killing twenty-four young people in what were referred to as the "Atlanta Child Killings." By linking Williams to these other murders, prosecutors effectively closed the files on twenty-nine young people who had been murdered or were missing.

Police in DesPlaines, Illinois, found the bodies of most of the young men killed by John Wayne Gacy Jr. in a crawl space under Gacy's house. Gacy is discussed in detail in Chapter 6.

Donald Harvey's co-workers called him the "Angel of Death." It seemed that whenever he was working as a nurse, someone died in the hospital. Harvey was charged with killing hospital patients in Ohio and Kentucky and was convicted of thirty-seven murders, seven aggravated murders, and one felonious assault. He pled guilty to avoid the death penalty. He claims to have killed eighty-seven people (CNN, 1993) and is believed by others to have killed an additional twenty-three victims (Hickey, 1997, p. 178).

"Hillside Stranglers" Angelo Buono and Kenneth Bianchi were accused of killing ten young women in the Los Angeles, California, area. Bianchi was convicted of two killings in Bellingham, Washington, after his claim of having a multiple personality was found to be a hoax. Bianchi is discussed in Chapter 8.

Patrick Wayne Kearney pled guilty to killing thirty-two young men between 1975 and 1978, in what were referred to as the "trash bag murders" in the Los Angeles area. These victims were dismembered and dumped in trash bags. Kearney received two concurrent life sentences (see Godwin, 1978; Newton, 1988).

Over a thirteen-month period in 1976 and 1977, the "Son of Sam" shot thirteen young men and women in eight different incidents in New York City. Six of these victims died. David Berkowitz, a twenty-four-year-old postal worker, was charged with these crimes. Claiming that a dog told him to kill, he pled guilty to the murders of five women and one man and was sentenced to twenty-five years to life (see Abrahamsen, 1985).

Juan Corona was convicted in January 1973 of the slayings of twenty-five migrant farm workers in California. The prosecution argued that these were homosexual murders, but a motive for these killings was never firmly established. Corona was sentenced to twenty-five consecutive life terms. An appeals court ordered a new trial, and he was again convicted of all of these murders (see Kidder, 1974; Lane & Gregg, 1992).

Albert DeSalvo claimed to be the "Boston Strangler," but police lacked evidence to bring him to trial for the murders of thirteen female victims, killed between mid-1962 and early 1964. DeSalvo was tried and convicted for unrelated assaults and was sentenced to life imprisonment. He was stabbed to death in his cell in 1973 (see Frank, 1967; Lane & Gregg, 1992; Rae, 1967).

Westley Allan Dodd was the first person in over thirty years to be executed by hanging in the United States. Dodd was convicted in 1993 of the kidnapping, rape, and murder of three small boys. Prior to these murders, he claimed, he molested young boys virtually nonstop for fifteen years (CNN, 1993). Dodd is quoted as saying that if he were ever freed, "I will kill and rape again and enjoy every minute of it" (CNN, 1993).

Lawrence Bittaker and Roy L. Norris began committing a series of rapes, torture, and murder of teenage girls during the summer of 1979 in California. They had met in prison the previous year. They dumped their last victim, naked and mutilated, on the lawn of a suburban house so they could see the reaction of the press. They were found guilty of five murders and twenty-one other felonies, including rape, torture, and kidnapping. Norris received forty-five years to life in prison, and Bittaker received the death penalty (see Markman & Dominick, 1989).

Known by the media as the "Sunset Slayer," Douglas D. Clark, together with his partner, Carol Bundy, abducted and murdered six young prostitutes and runaways from Hollywood's Sunset Boulevard during the summer of 1980. Clark was found guilty of all six murders and sentenced to death. Bundy, who testified for the prosecution, received two sentences of twenty-seven years to life and twenty-five years to life, to run consecutively. Clark continues to deny all involvement in the murders (see MacNamara, 1990). Clark still claims that Bundy (no relation to Ted Bundy) did all the killings and was attempting to duplicate Ted Bundy's crimes (Michael Reynolds, personal communication, February 5, 1991).

Jerome Brudos, at seventeen years of age, forced a young girl at knifepoint to pose in the nude. As a result, he spent nine months in a mental hospital. Nine years later, between 1968 and 1969, he began killing young women in his garage under a special mirror he had installed to feed his fantasies. He was convicted of three murders and is serving three consecutive life sentences at the Oregon State Prison (see Rule, 1980).

On August 21, 1992, Benjamin Thomas Atkins confessed to killing eleven women in the Detroit, Michigan, area. During his lengthy confession, he "explained to police in detail how he raped and strangled the 11 women in Highland Park and Detroit from the fall of 1991 to the spring of 1992" (*Detroit Free Press*, May 23, 1993). The bodies of his victims, all black women suspected of drug use and prostitution, were found nude or partially clothed in abandoned buildings. Atkins was found guilty on eleven counts of murder and one count of rape and was sentenced to life without parole (*Detroit Free Press*, May 23, 1993).

Richard Angelo, referred to as the "Angel of Death" by the media, worked as a supervising nurse in the intensive care and coronary care units of Good Samaritan Hospital in Long Island, New York. He had conducted experiments on field mice with the drugs Pavulon and Anectine, and in 1987 he began using these drugs on patients to put them into cardiac arrest. In some cases, Angelo would revive these patients; in other cases, the patients would die. When a surviving patient complained, an investigation was initiated and thirty-three bodies were exhumed. Angelo was convicted of second-degree murder and manslaughter for injecting four patients with a deadly drug and was sentenced to fifty years' to life imprisonment. He is suspected of having killed as many as twenty-five patients (see Linedecker & Burt, 1990).

Florida law enforcement officials believe Christine Falling murdered six young children. She was found guilty of murdering three children who were under her care as she worked as their babysitter. When she is released, she says, she wants to babysit for young children again. She told CNN, "I just love kids to death" (CNN, 1993).

Gerald Gallego and his wife, Charlene, went on a killing spree, abducting young women in search of the perfect sex slave and then murdering them. Charlene lured the women to the car Gerald was driving and often held a gun on the women while Gerald raped them. This team of killers murdered at least ten young women between 1978 and 1980 (see Biondi & Hecox, 1988).

John Joseph Joubert IV says that he had a fantasy of cannibalism from the time he was six or seven years old. He was convicted of killing three young boys near Omaha, Nebraska, in 1983, and he is believed to have killed others. He is on death row at the Nebraska State Prison (see Pettit, 1990).

As part of a plea bargain to avoid the death penalty, Robert Berdella confessed to killing six men in Kansas City, Missouri, in the late 1980s. All of his victims were killed by injections of an animal tranquilizer after he had tortured them and used them as his sex slaves for a number of days. Berdella then dismembered the bodies. One of his victims escaped, and police subsequently found skulls and a number of pictures of the victims in his apartment. Berdella died in prison of a heart attack in October 1992, following a lengthy series of interviews with British television journalists (see Clark & Morley, 1993).

There are four serial killers who play bridge together on California's death row. They have been convicted of killing a total of forty-nine people. One of these card players is William Bonin, known as the "Freeway Killer," who killed fourteen young men and boys between August 1979 and June 1980. Another player, Randy Kraft, was convicted in 1989 of killing twenty-four young men. Authorities believe he may have killed as many as sixty-three people. The third card player is Lawrence Sigmund Bittaker, who, with Roy Norris, committed five murders. The fourth is Douglas Clark (the "Sunset Strip Killer"), who was convicted of killing six prostitutes and runaways during the summer of 1980 (see MacNamara, 1990).

Kenneth Allen McDuff was on death row for the murders of three teenagers in Fort Worth, Texas, in 1966. His sentence was commuted to life in 1972, and in 1990 he was paroled. Less than two years later he was suspected of killing at least six women in Texas. The body of one of McDuff's victims was discovered just three days after his release from prison. After he was profiled on the television program *America's Most Wanted* in May 1992, a viewer spotted him in Kansas City, Missouri, where he was arrested. He was convicted in 1993 of killing a pregnant convenience store clerk in Temple, Texas, and he is still a suspect in the disappearance of several women in the Temple, Texas, area. He was sentenced to death and was executed in November 1998 (see Fair, 1994).

Roy and Faye Copeland, a farm couple from rural northern Missouri, celebrated their fiftieth wedding anniversary in separate jail cells shortly after they were arrested for killing five transient farm workers with a .22 caliber rifle and burying them on the farm (see Miller, 1993). Roy recently died of natural causes in a Missouri prison.

In 1964, when Edmund Kemper was fifteen years old, he killed his grandparents and was committed to a California state hospital for the criminally insane. In 1969 he was released as "cured." Then, in an eleven-month period, he murdered six young female hitchhikers and also murdered his mother. After murdering his mother, he drove to Pueblo, Colorado, where he called the local police and confessed to the murders (see Cheney, 1976; Leyton, 1986).

After his arrest, David Martin Long told police: "I've got something inside my head that clicks sometimes. It just goes off" (Sare, 1986, p. 1). Four of these lethal "clicks" resulted in the violent deaths of five women whom Long killed with an ax.

Wayne Nance killed at least four people in Montana between 1974 and 1986 and is suspected by police of killing others. Nance was referred to as "Montana's baby-faced serial sex murderer." Unlike most of the killers described here, Nance was acquainted with his victims. One of them was the mother of one of his high school classmates (see Coston, 1992).

Charles Ng, along with Leonard Lake, tortured and killed at least eleven women in Ng and Lake's survivalist bunker near Wilseyville, California, between 1981 and 1983. They are believed to have killed at least fourteen additional women during this time. Lake committed suicide shortly after his arrest for theft in June 1985. Ng, who was with Lake at the time, escaped and fled to Canada. The car that Ng and Lake were driving led police to the killers' hideaway, a torture-murder bunker in Calaveras County. Ng was arrested in Canada in 1985 and, in September 1991, was finally extradited to California, where he was arraigned on eleven counts of murder. Police found Lake's diary in the bunker. He wrote, "God meant women for cooking, cleaning house and sex and when they are not in use they should be locked up" (Associated Press, September 29, 1991; see also Harrington & Burger, 1993). In 1999 Ng was found guilty of eleven counts of murder for the killing of three women, six men, and two infants.

In 1997 Andrew Cunanan went on a killing spree that left five men dead in Minnesota, Illinois, New Jersey, and Florida. The media called him "a gay thrill-killer who committed random murders." Following the death of his fifth victim, the internationally famous clothes designer Gianni Versace, police finally tracked Cunanan to a houseboat in Miami. Before police could apprehend him, he committed suicide.

Once a month, between April and December 1995, Robert Silveria killed someone riding the rails. He killed in Oregon, Kansas, and Florida. In addition to the eight killings in 1995, he is suspected of killing dozens more. Nicknamed "Sidetrack," Silveria was a heroin addict who belonged to the Freight Train Riders of America (FTRA), an organization formed by Vietnam veterans who wear lightning-bolt tattoos, are considered welfare outlaws, and have links to far-right militia and racist groups such as the Aryan Nations. Past and present members of this group are suspected by police of having committed some three hundred murders nationwide. Silveria would wait until his victims were asleep and then beat them to death with a blunt object or a baseball bat. He would then assume the identity of his victim in order to collect more public welfare. When he was arrested in Oregon, he had twenty-eight food stamp accounts around the country and was picking up $119 per month from each one (Kershaw, 1999).

The South Side of Chicago spawned at least four serial killers between 1992 and 1999. In June 1995 Hubert Geralds Jr. was charged with the murder of six women, some of whom had children. Most of his victims were drug users, and some had turned to prostitution to finance their drug habits. Geralds's murders were particularly difficult for the police to solve because there was little indication of foul play. Geralds's method of killing his victims was to smother them by covering their noses while pressing his thumb on the victim's throat, leaving no marks associated with strangling.

Derrick Flewellen is accused of strangling two women during the same time period that Geralds was killing. Ralph Harris, a third suspected serial killer, was charged with killing five men, all believed to have been robbery victims.

In May 1996 Gregory Clepper was charged with killing eight women who apparently objected when he refused to pay them for sex. His victims, according to police, had all been drug addicts and prostitutes. All had been sexually assaulted, strangled, and left in trash containers on the South Side.

Recently, another serial murder was identified as occurring on the South Side of Chicago. Andre Crawford was arrested by Chicago police in January 2000 and charged with killing ten women and raping eleven other women between 1993 and June 1999. Crawford confessed these crimes on videotape to the police. A DNA sample from Crawford linked him to seven murder victims and to one woman who survived a brutal assault. Most of Crawford's victims were strangled or received blunt trauma injuries. Many victims had arrest records for drugs and prostitution.

Dana Gray lived to shop, and, when the money ran out, other people paid for her spending sprees with their lives. Her first victim was sixty-eight-year-old June Roberts; Gray strapped her to a chair, strangled her with a telephone cord, and then smashed her in the face with a wine bottle. Her second victim was fifty-eight-year-old Dorinda Hawkins, an antique store clerk, whom Gray strangled and left for dead. Hawkins survived the attack. Gray's third victim was Dora Beebe, eighty-seven, whom Gray hit with an iron and then strangled. Within minutes of each murder or attack, Gray was indulging her "shopaholic" tendencies, running up bills of thousands of dollars with the money and credit cards of her victims. Gray was sentenced to life without parole for the two murders and one attempted murder; police believe she is also responsible for three more murders. Gray's only explanation for her crimes was, "I had this overwhelming need to shop" (Grant, 1999, p. 26).

In November 1998 Wayne Adam Ford, a truck driver, walked into the Humboldt County sheriff's station in Eureka, California, holding the severed breast of a woman. He proceeded to confess to four murders of women hitchhikers and prostitutes. He was convicted of these four murders.

And the list goes on, and on, and on, and on. Currently, my files contain information on hundreds of these serial killers. And the list keeps growing.

Appearances Can Be Deceiving

In February 1999, heavily armed Russian police stormed an apartment in Nizhniy Tagil, a small town in the Ural Mountains, after receiving reports that its owner was a serial killer who had murdered dozens of women. This report came from a neighbor who had often seen the suspect transporting body parts in large bags at night. After being held at gunpoint, the man confessed to being a mannequin trader. Needless to say, he was released and not charged.

Although this incident may seem humorous and even ludicrous, in fact the police did respond appropriately when they took the report seriously. To do otherwise, particularly when serial killers are known to have been operating across the former Soviet Union, would have been poor police procedure at best.

What Do They Look Like?

Unlike the serial killer Hannibal Lecter in the film *Silence of the Lambs*, serial murderers do not look like killers, nor does their appearance reflect an ultimate evil. Unfortunately, serial killers simply do not stand out on our city streets, in suburban neighborhoods, or on our highways, as anything other than the average person. Once a Ted Bundy, Henry Lee Lucas, or John Wayne Gacy is identified, some are quick to comment on the killer's appearance: "He has an evil eye." "He sure looks like a serial killer." "I wouldn't want to meet him in a dark alley late at night." Without a criminal identity, however, in most instances the serial killer looks just like anyone else.

Even though a number of people retrospectively reinterpret the background and appearance of a serial killer after he or she has been caught, many others marvel at the fact that these killers look like the "boy next door," just your "average Joe," or "just like any other normal person." Jeffrey Dahmer certainly doesn't look like a killer, and neither do many of the other serial killers briefly described in this chapter. The normal outward appearance of the serial killer seems to dumbfound many people and remains a fascination for many more.

They May Be Your Neighbors

Robert Hansen was considered a family man and a respected community member in Anchorage, Alaska, where he owned a bakery and was a member of the local chamber of commerce. Yet in early 1984 he entered a plea-bargaining agreement in which he admitted killing seventeen women and raping thirty more women in the Anchorage area. Hansen tortured his victims in his home while his family was away and then killed them with a high-powered rifle after releasing them in rural areas outside Anchorage, where he also buried his victims.

Like Hansen, Robert Yates Jr. was considered an upstanding community member and a good neighbor in Spokane, Washington. Yates killed prostitutes in the Pacific Northwest; at least eleven Spokane women lost their lives to his brutal assaults, which began in 1996. Not until two years later, however, at the end of 1998, did Spokane authorities admit that they were dealing with a serial killer. Before he was identified as a serial killer, Yates, a father of five, appeared to all, including his wife and father, to be simply living the American dream. Yates was finally arrested in April 2000 because of the hard work and persistence of Spokane detectives. One of his victims was buried in his backyard. After his arrest, Yates pled guilty to two 1975 killings in Walla Walla, Washington, and to the killing of Stacy Hawn in 1988. The first case, the killing of a college couple, had remained unsolved for a quarter century. The case of Stacy Hawn had also gone unsolved. No one suspected the involvement of Robert Yates Jr., and his admission to these killings came as a shock to the victims' relatives, who had never suspected that the man they had been reading about for many months had been their children's killer. Authorities suspect that the modus operandi of these crimes may have established the future pattern of killings of Spokane prostitutes (*Seattle Times*, October 18, 2000). In October 2000 Yates was taken to Tacoma, where he was found guilty of killing two additional women.

Some Are Very Quiet and Hard to Spot

When Joel Rifkin confessed to having murdered seventeen prostitutes in the New York City area, a high school classmate described him as "quiet, shy, not the kind of guy who would do something like this." When David Berkowitz was convicted of six "Son of Sam" murders committed in 1976 and 1977 in New York City, a former friend from his army days stated, "He was quiet and reserved and kept pretty much to himself." Berkowitz's boss said, "That's the way he was here, nice—a quiet, shy fellow." Juan Corona was convicted of twenty-five murders of itinerant farm workers in California in 1971. Following Corona's conviction, a friend described him as a very quiet person: "That's the kind of man he is—kept to himself and never said much, for the most part." When Jeffrey Dahmer confessed to having killed and dismembered seventeen people in Milwaukee and Ohio in 1991, a friend of one of Dahmer's victims said, "He [Dahmer] didn't have much to say about anything, just 'Hi, nice to meet you.' He seemed quiet." And when Westley Allan Dodd was arrested and eventually executed in 1993 for the kidnapping, rape, and murder of three small boys, one of his neighbors stated, "Wes seemed so harmless, such an all-around, basic good citizen" (CNN, 1993).

Some Take Years to Catch

Unabomber

In July 1994 the FBI announced that for the past eight months they had been posting messages on the Internet, seeking assistance in their efforts to locate a suspect who, since 1978, had detonated seventeen bombs around the United States, killing three persons and injuring twenty-three. The most recent bombings had occurred in June 1993, when a medical geneticist in Tiburon, California, and a Yale University computer science professor were severely injured by mail bombs.

This was the first known use of the Internet, often described as an "information superhighway," in a major criminal investigation. In mid-December, the FBI began posting a request for tips in the so-called Unabomber case on the Internet's World Wide Web via a server at the NASA/Ames Research Center in Moffett Field, California.

In September 1995, the *New York Times* and the *Washington Post* (after extensive soul-searching and a number of meetings with officials of the U.S. Justice Department), published the Unabomer's thirty-five-thousand-word Manifesto. And in

January 1996, David Kaczynski found papers written by his brother, Ted, that were very similar in nature to the Unabomber's Manifesto.

On April 3, 1996, after a nearly two-month stakeout and a search of a home in Lombard, Illinois, federal law enforcement agents arrested Ted Kaczynski as a suspect in the Unabomber case. During this arrest, agents found explosive chemicals and bomb-making material in Kaczynski's remote mountain cabin in Stemple Pass, Montana, where he had lived for the previous twenty-five years. In 1998 Kaczynski was sentenced to life in prison without parole in a plea agreement.

A Number of Serial Killers Have Not Been Caught

A number of still-unsolved homicides are believed to be the work of serial killers. Unsolved murders that appear to be serial can be found in most states of the United States. The following cases are only a few examples.

California

When the bodies of four women were found in the East San Gabriel Valley and nearby Chino, California, in the fall of 1993, authorities said the killings did not appear to be linked. The victims were all black and in their thirties, they had been strangled, and their bodies had been thrown into business parks or along the roadside. But investigators said that these similarities were happenstance and that the murders were not the work of a serial killer. They said that the bodies of eight slain women had been found dumped in Los Angeles in November alone. The San Gabriel Valley murders, officials reasoned, were just part of an abnormally high monthly tally of dumped bodies.

But after the body of a fifth woman was found in the San Gabriel Valley on December 30, 1993, the Los Angeles County sheriff's department and the Pomona police department indicated that three of the deaths were considered to be linked and that two other victims also might be connected ("Police seek," *Los Angeles Times*, January 7, 1994, Part B, p. 3).

On May 30, 1993, Los Angeles police began seeking public help in finding a Jeep driver who, they said, had killed three black men and wounded a fourth in a series of shootings since January of that year. The attacks occurred within a three-block radius in the Harbor City area near San Pedro. The suspect was described as a white man, age twenty-five to thirty-five, with red hair, driving a Jeep that was possibly red in color. The killings occurred on January 31, February 14, and April 15, 1993. The last attack, in May, resulted in the wounding of a thirty-eight-year-old man. No one has ever been charged with these shootings ("Police seek killer," *Sacramento Bee*, May 30, 1993, p. B3.).

Texas

Over the past twenty-nine years, more than thirty women and girls have been murdered and dumped in the bayous along the fifty-mile stretch of Highway I-45 between Houston and Galveston. In addition, six more girls disappeared from this area and were never found. Despite the work of a task force set up by the Houston

FBI office and the surrounding police agencies whose jurisdictions were involved, not a single case has been solved. Don Clark, special agent of the FBI's Houston office, stated: "Clearly there is more than one deranged individual out there. We think we are dealing with two, or possibly three serial killers. But we don't even know if they are local or transient" (Miller, 1999, p. 10). The only thread that apparently links all these crimes is the very busy I-45, which joins a national freeway network north of Houston. Anyone committing a crime in the Houston area could be more than twelve hundred miles away within twenty-four hours without breaking the speed limit.

For example, four unsolved murders were probably committed by the same killer within this group of unsolved homicides outside of League, Texas, in the I-45 corrridor. The skeletal remains of Heidi Villareal Fye, age twenty-five, a waitress reported missing on October 10, 1983, were found on April 4, 1984. The body of Laura Lynn Miller, sixteen, reported missing September 14, 1984, was found on February 2, 1986. The remains of "Jane Doe" and another unidentified victim, "Janet Doe," were found on February 2, 1986, and September 8, 1991, respectively. Local police believe these four women were victims of an "organized serial sexual offender" but have not been able to link the murders to any suspects ("FBI tests fail to link suspect," *Houston Chronicle*, May 12, 1994, p. 20). Efforts to identify Jane Doe and Janet Doe have been unsuccessful.

New York

A number of unsolved killings of prostitutes and alleged drug addicts in Rochester, New York, since 1989 raised fears that another serial killer was at work—just two years after Arthur Shawcross, as discussed earlier, was convicted in a series of slayings in that area. Since September 1992 the bodies of four women with a history of prostitution and drug abuse have been found within a few miles of one another near the Lake Ontario State Parkway in northwestern Monroe County. The bodies of another ten women with similar histories have been found elsewhere in the Rochester area since 1989. Police are searching for two other missing women.

Following the 1990 conviction of Shawcross, who killed primarily prostitutes, police and sheriffs set up a program to pursue all missing persons cases aggressively. "Now we chase every lead," said Captain Lynde Johnston. "We immediately get dental records and other things to help with identifications. We treat them all like potential homicides" ("Search for a serial," *Newsday*, July 4, 1993, p. 45). Police still have no suspects in these murders.

Although they avoid the term "serial killer," investigators have nevertheless repeatedly drawn parallels to the investigation of Arthur Shawcross, who was sentenced to life in prison for killing eleven women, many of them prostitutes and drug addicts, in the Rochester area between 1988 and 1989. Nor was the "Pennsylvania Train Station Sniper" (also referred to as the ".25 caliber killer") ever caught by New York City police, who sent out the following teletype on July 9, 1985.

Att—BALLISTICS UNITS—HOMICIDE UNITS—DETECTIVE UNITS—CRIME ANALYSIS UNITS

PENN STATION TASK FORCE, comprised of members of the Long Island Rail Road police Dept., AMTRAK Police Dept., and New York City Police Dept. is attempting to identify the person responsible for seven (7) "Sniper Shootings: (including one homicide) which have occurred in and around the Penn Station Rail Road Station at 7th Ave. and 32nd Street, Manhattan, New York.

The first shooting occurred on 4/28/83 at 2225 Hrs. The victim was a F/W age 50 and lived in a women's shelter for the homeless at 257 W. 30th Street, Manhattan. The victim was shot from the second story ledge of the shelter and through a partially open window.

The second shooting occurred on 4/28/83 at 0030 Hrs. The victim was a security officer for the hotel (no distinctive clothing worn) and was in a basement corridor. The victim was a M/W age 25. Location was approx. two blocks away from the women's shelter.

The third shooting occurred on 6/29/83 at 222 Hrs. The victim was a M/W, artist, 29 Yrs. of age. he was shot from a second story ledge and through a partially open window. The location is adjacent to the women's shelter (Loc. of 1st victim).

The fourth shooting occurred on 7/31/83 at 0335 Hrs. The victim was a F/W 55 Yrs. of age who resided in the same building and room as victim number one. She was also shot in the same manner as victim Nbr. one.

The fifth shooting occurred on 12/4/83 at 1730 Hrs. The victim was a railroad worker at the Penn Station. He was a M/W 38 Yrs. of age. He was shot while walking on the platform, lover level of the station. Victim was not wearing any distinctive clothing. The location of the Sta. is three blocks from the women's shelter.

The sixth victim was shot on 12/20/83 at 2110 Hrs. The victim was a M/W 61 Yrs. of age. He was a RR worker and was shot in the same Loc. as the fifth victim.

The Seventh and "last" victim was a M/W 29 Yrs. of age. He was a RR worker and was shot and killed on 2/21/84 in the same Loc. as victims five and six except that he was approx. 60 feet further west on the platform.

All areas of the train station, hotel and women's shelter are accessible through a sub terrain network of tunnels which run beneath the RR station.

All shooting have been ballistically matched to the same 25 caliber weapon. The ammo used in the shootings were either "Aguila" or R&P 25 caliber rounds. In each shooting all injuries were either to the chest, neck or head areas of the victims.

Anyone with similar shooting, please contact the task force.

Source: New York State Police teletype, July 9, 1985.

Louisiana

The body of a thirty-year-old woman, clad in nothing but pink socks, was discovered by two crawfisherman shortly after dawn Sunday, February 21, 1993, in a ditch alongside a two-lane blacktop road in a rural stretch of St. Charles Parish near New Orleans, Louisiana. The woman, whose body had been there for several days, had been strangled. The next morning, another strangled, naked female body was discovered seven hundred feet down the road. The St. Charles Parish sheriff's office determined that the second body had been there less than twelve hours. Both victims were known prostitutes. After these murders were linked to a murder in September, sheriff's investigators discovered that New Orleans had ten similar cases.

"We haven't linked all these murders to one suspect," Sergeant Sam Fradella of the New Orleans police said of the unsolved Louisiana cases. "The murders are similar; the victims are similar. But we can't call this a serial killing. We're handling each one as an independent murder" ("Search for a serial," *Newsday,* July 4, 1993, p. 45). However, as of April 1996 the bodies of twenty-six women have been found along roadways and in swamps within a sixty- to seventy-five-mile radius in the greater New Orleans area.

Indiana, Kansas, Missouri, Texas

What are now referred to as the "I-70 Robbery-Murders"began on April 8, 1992, with the slaying of a shoe store clerk in Indianapolis. Three days later, the owner and a clerk at a Wichita, Kansas, bridal shop were slain. The killings continued on April 27, 1992, with the slaying of a ceramics store clerk in Terre Haute, Indiana. Eight days later, a Western footwear shop clerk in St. Charles, Missouri, was killed. Another murder occurred May 7, 1992, in Raytown, Missouri, outside Kansas City, where a curio shop clerk was killed. Five of the six victims in the Midwest were women; the sixth was a man with long hair tied in a ponytail. All were shot in the head. None of the stores involved had security alarms, and all were robbed of the little money available. Ballistics tests revealed that the same .22 caliber weapon had been used in all of these homicides. Authorities then began examining three killings in the Dallas–Fort Worth, Texas, area, that appear to be similar in nature (Detective Plummer, St. Charles, Missouri, police, personal communication).

Washington and Oregon

Since 1982, King County, Washington, authorities have sought the so-called Green River killer, blamed for the deaths of up to forty-nine women in Washington and Oregon. In 1986 the following teletype was sent out to all U.S. law enforcement agencies:

ALL POLICE DEPARTMENTS
(CITY, COUNTY, STATE, NATIONWIDE)
MSG H22KING COUNTY POLICE OCTOBER 17, 1986

THE KING COUNTY POLICE DEPARTMENT–GREEN RIVER TASK
FORCE, SEATTLE, WASHINGTON, HAS BEEN INVESTIGATING A SERIES
OF FEMALE HOMICIDES WHICH OCCURRED FROM APPROXIMATELY
JULY 1982 THROUGH MARCH 1984. IT IS THE OPINION OF THE FBI'S
BEHAVIORAL SCIENCE UNIT, AS WELL AS OTHERS FAMILIAR WITH
SERIAL MURDERS, THAT THIS KILLER WILL NOT STOP UNTIL HE IS
CAUGHT, OR MOVES FROM THE AREA. SINCE THERE HAVE BEEN NO
MURDERS IN KING COUNTY ATTRIBUTED TO THIS KILLER SINCE
APPROXIMATELY MARCH 1984, IT IS HIGHLY PROBABLE HE HAS
MOVED AND IS KILLING ELSEWHERE. IT HAS ALSO BEEN DOCU-
MENTED THAT SERIAL MURDERERS HAVE CHANGED THEIR MODUS
OPERANDI TO AVOID DETECTION.

RECEIVING AGENCIES ARE REQUESTED TO ADVISE THE KING
COUNTY POLICE DEPT–GREEN RIVER TASK FORCE OF ANY SERIAL
MURDERERS AND THEIR MODUS OPERANDI WHO HAVE OPERATED
IN THEIR JURISDICTION SINCE MARCH 1984. IT SHOULD BE EMPHA-
SIZED THAT INFORMATION IS BEING SOLICITED ON SERIAL HOMI-
CIDES IN YOUR AREA, NOT JUST THOSE WHOSE MODUS OPERANDI IS
SIMILAR TO THAT OF THE SERIAL MURDERER WHO OPERATED IN
KING COUNTY. IN EVALUATING WHETHER A "SERIAL MURDERER"
HAS OPERATED IN YOUR AREA, IT MAY BE USEFUL TO NOTE THAT A
"SERIAL MURDERER" GENERALLY REFERS TO A NUMBER OF MUR-
DERS BY A SINGLE PERSON OVER A PERIOD OF MONTHS—OR, OCCA-
SIONALLY YEARS. EACH KILLING IS USUALLY A DISCRETE EPISODE,
BUT THERE IS USUALLY A COMMON MOTIVE, METHOD, AND/OR
TYPE OF VICTIM.

A REPLY IS REQUESTED REGARDLESS OF WHETHER THE RESPONSE
IS POSITIVE OR NEGATIVE. ALL REPLIES SHOULD BE DIRECTED TO
THE ATTENTION OF ANTHONY M. CARUSO, OR FRANK ATCHELY,
GREEN RIVER TASK FORCE, (206) 433-2013.

Washington

A list of twenty-nine unsolved killings and twelve cases of disappearance of
women in King, Snohomish, and Pierce counties in the state of Washington since
1985 was given to the press in 1993. Officials say that the Green River killer
stopped murdering young women in the Seattle area in 1984. Many of these forty-
one cases involved prostitutes or young, street-wise teenagers. This was the first
public acknowledgment that a killer or killers were killing in the Seattle area since

the Green River Task Force was disbanded in 1990 (UPI, January 22, 1993). These killings remain unsolved.

Florida

It would appear that one or more serial murderers may have been at work in Florida. In January 1993, the Marion County sheriff's office spokesman reported that eighteen women had been killed and dumped in remote areas in Florida between late 1991 and January 1993. All of the victims were believed to be prostitutes, and no arrests have been made. In describing these murders, the spokesman indicated that nine victims were found in Brevard County, four in Volusia County, three in Lake County, and one each in Marion and Pasco Counties. He also reported that four of the victims had been found in the state of Indiana and three in Tennessee. This spokesman, nevertheless, downplayed the possibility that these murder represented the work of a serial killer ("Officials compare similar," *St. Petersburg Times*, January 8, 1993, p. 6B).

Massachusetts

In the New Bedford, Massachusetts, area, the district attorney's office and the police spent years investigating the killings in the late 1980s of eleven women, all of whom had connections to drug use and prostitution in the Weld Square area. All of them also had small children. Most were strangled to death and abandoned along the major highways that ring New Bedford. Although a man was charged in one of those killings, the case was dismissed for lack of evidence. The killings did not continue and remain unsolved (see Smith & Guillen, 1991, for an excellent analysis of a serial murder investigation and its problems).

Connecticut

In Connecticut, investigators created a task force in 1980 to seek the killer responsible for strangling two Waterbury prostitutes in 1988 and 1989. The task force was disbanded a few months later without a conviction.

Pennsylvania, Kentucky, Tennessee, Mississippi, and Arkansas

Between October 1983 and April 1985, eight female victims, some of them redhaired prostitutes, were found strangled and left along highways in five states bordering the Ohio and Mississippi Rivers. The case remains open, and no viable suspects were ever identified ("Red-haired victims," April 25, 1984).

Michigan

Michigan police never identified the "Oakland County Child Killer." The victims were two young boys and two young girls, killed in 1976 and 1977. A task force was formed to catch the killer but was finally disbanded when all leads had been exhausted (see McIntyre, 1988).

California and New York

During the period from October 1966 through October 1969, California was the scene of a series of baffling murders committed by an unknown person who signed himself variously "r-h," "Z," "the Zodiac," "a friend," "A Citizen," and "Red Phantom." The "Zodiac Killer," who killed six people and wounded two others, and who wrote to the San Francisco police, taunting them, was never identified (see Graysmith, 1976).

Twenty-one years later, between March and June 1990, a serial killer calling himself the "Zodiac Killer" shot and seriously wounded four people in the Brooklyn and Queens boroughs of New York City. The fourth victim died three and a half weeks after he was shot in the back. Newspapers received letters signed "The Zodiac" in which the writer provided details about the killings that, according to police, only the killer could know. The writer claimed that he intended to kill one person for each of the twelve signs of the Zodiac, the chart used by astrologers to predict the future. A task force of fifty detectives, formed in June 1990, did not make a arrest in this case (*Newsday,* June 20–July 8, 1990). The killer eventually shot nine victims, three of whom died. Heriberto Seda was arrested June 18, 1996, in his Brooklyn apartment, where he allegedly shot his sister and then held police at bay for three hours. He was convicted of three counts of murder and sentenced to eighty-three years' imprisonment (Newton, 2000). Prior to his conviction, Seda told the arresting detectives that he was envious of Ted Bundy and "wanted to be as good as [Bundy] was in getting victims"(Donohue, 1996, p. 32).

Kansas

Between October 1989 and March 1990, four Native Americans were found murdered in Lawrence, Kansas. Leaders of the Arapaho and Cheyenne tribes, suspecting that these deaths were the work of a serial killer, asked the FBI to investigate. Local authorities, however, claimed that the homicides were unrelated ("Plains mystery," August 16, 1990).

Maryland

In Suitland, Maryland, a suburban community adjacent to the District of Columbia, five young black women were killed within a two-month period in December and January 1987. Their bodies were found in a wooded park in Suitland. All had been sexually assaulted and stabbed to death. No one was ever charged with these murders ("'Classic' serial killer suspected," *Schenectady Gazette,* February 12, 1987, p. 2).

Female Serial Killers

"So, I would have to say that to the families. I mean, that guy's gonna . . . 'You stupid bitch, you killed my husband.' Or whatever, you know, or my brother or somethin'. And I'd just have to say to 'em, listen, what they were gonna do to me. I would be probably turning around if I had survived it and say, 'You stupid bastards. You almost killed me,

you almost raped me, you almost beat the shit out of me.' . . . So I can't really say they were sweet."

—Aileen Wuornos, female serial killer, videotaped confession, January 16, 1990

Relatively little has been written about female serial killers. In 1990, I wrote the following about gender and serial killers:

> One characteristic of the serial murderer not addressed in the literature is that there are very few instances in which a serial murderer is a female. Instances of female mass murderers can be found but relatively few serial murderers have been identified. This sexual differentiation may lead researchers to study maleness and its socialization as an etiological consideration. However, the lack of this obvious distinction has apparently precluded such study. (Egger, 1990a, p. 22)

Given Hickey's (1997) research and recent reports of female serial killers (Aileen Wuornos, Christine Falling, and Dorothea Montalvo Puente), it appears that this gender distinction may be less pronounced than I have previously indicated. Women certainly are capable of killing serially, but they do not do so as often as men.

Hickey's (1997) analysis of sixty-two female serial killers revealed that most used either some poison (45 percent) or poison only (35 percent) in at least some instances to kill their victims. Hickey refers to female serial killers as the "quiet killers" (p. 106). Many of the serial killers in Hickey's data set could be described as either "black widows," who killed their husbands, or nurses who victimized their patients. Hickey (1997) correctly notes that these serial killers seem to be almost invisible to the news media and frequently are able to kill over long periods of time before they are noticed by law enforcement.

Most of the known female serial killers appear to have been motivated primarily by financial gain, although the psychopathology is undoubtedly much more complicated. Like their male counterparts, most of them came from broken homes, were sexually abused by parents or relatives, or experienced other emotionally traumatic experiences in their youth.

In a number of cases, female serial killers have had a prior relationship with their victims. In other words, some of their victims were not strangers. Also, a number of these female killers murdered in part for their own material gain. In some cases, material gain was their sole motive. The presence of a relationship prior to killing their victim (unless the victim had been placed in a subjugated role in relation to the killer) and a motive of material gain do not fit my definition of a serial murderer, provided in Chapter 1. For instance, the female killers Marybeth Tinning, Velma Barfield, and Dorothea Puente, to be discussed, could all be considered killers who murdered for material gain, whether for insurance money, to cover other crimes, or for the social security checks of the victims. Certainly in these three cases the killers knew their victims and forced them into a subjugated role.

In the case of female serial killers, the reader will have to make a judgment as to whether some of the killers described briefly in this section should be considered serial killers. It may be that some female serial killers are exceptions to my definition of serial murder, or perhaps that female serial killers demand a separate serial murder definition. In fairness to others who would expand the definition to include the motive of material gain and the existence of a prior relationship (see Hickey, 1997), and in keeping with my desire to continue to study serial murder with an open mind, killers who do not strictly meet my definition are included.

Aileen Wuornos had to agree to go with her victims for the purpose of having sex with them in order to kill them. Wuornos, who was incorrectly labeled this country's first woman serial killer by the FBI, killed seven middle-aged men in north central Florida between November 1989 and the summer of 1990. The following is part of her confession to Florida police:

I just . . . I have to say it, that I killed 'em because they got violent with me and I decided to defend myself. I wasn't gonna let 'em beat the shit outa me or kill me, either. And I'm sure if they found out I had a weapon on me, which was very easy to find, 'cause I always had it in plain view where I could grab it quick, and if after the fightin' they found it, they would've shot me. So I just shot them. I really can't believe I'm in here tellin' you guys this. But I'm glad because I feel very guilty. Uh . . . I don't think I should live. I think I should die. I'm not gonna commit suicide. I'm gonna get right with the Lord and live a normal life until I'm to die or I die a normal death, but I don't think I'm . . . I should live. I think I should die because I killed all those people. Well, I think it was like self defense, myself, but no one can judge that but God. . . . And then when I shot him the first time, he just backed away. And I thought . . . I thought to myself, well, hell, should I, you know, try to help this guy or should I just kill him. So I didn't know what to do, so I figured, well, if I help this guy and he lives, he's gonna tell on me and I'm gonna get for attempted murder, all this jazz. And I thought, well, the best thing to do is just keep shootin' him. The stupid bastard woulda killed me so I kept shootin'. You know. In other words, I shot him and I said to myself, Damn, you know, if I didn't . . . shoot him, he woulda shot me because he woulda beat the shit outta me, maybe I woulda been unconscious. He woulda found my gun goin' through my stuff, and shot me . . . this dirty bastard deserves to die anyway because of what he was tryin' to do to me. (Transcript of Aileen Wuornos's confession, January 16, 1991, p. 7)

Wuornos was sent to Florida's death row on January 31, 1992, for the shooting death of one of her victims.

After the fifth infant died while under the care of baby-sitter Christine Falling, the State of Florida's Health Rehabilitative Services formed a task force to investigate these deaths. Dr. Bob Wray was asked by this task force to interview Falling to determine any psychological reason for these killings. Falling confessed to Dr. Wray that she had killed these infants.

STATEMENT OF DR. BOB WRAY TO
CNN CORRESPONDENT RICHARD ROTH

Well, she really couldn't say why she did it. The first child and I believe the third and the last child she alleged that she heard voices telling her to kill them. Two of the infants she didn't say that she heard any voices at all. On two of the people she alleged that she had some kind of weird sensation, as though she was taken over. And she killed them literally being in another personality. The other one or two times, which of course overlapped, she just said she had sort of automatic movements. For example, the first child, she said she just automatically moved her hands from the waist to the neck and as she was looking the child in the face she saw this poor child change from red to purple and she kept choking this child until it didn't twitch anymore. And the others are probably somewhat the same, although that's the only one I remember that she went into that kind of grim detail in describing. One of 'em, I think the fourth child, was actually her step niece. She was in the car with the child's mother. The child's mother, her step sister, went into a store, she strangled the child right there in the car. And when the mother came out and they drove down the street and the mother noticed the child was not moving and discovered she was dead. (CNN, 1993)

In some cases it is difficult to label a person as a serial killer because he or she has not been convicted of a number of murders. Many consider Genene Jones a serial killer, although she was convicted of only one killing. When she was found guilty of the murder of fourteen-month-old Chelsea McClellan at a pediatrics clinic in Kerrville, Texas, Jones received the maximum sentence, ninety-nine years. As the child's nurse, she had injected the child with the drug Anectine. Genene was further sentenced to sixty years in prison for "injury to a child" for injecting a child with heparin. Jones is still suspected by Texas authorities of being responsible for at least thirteen other deaths of infants under her care at Bexar County Hospital between February 1981 and January 1982 (Brown & Edwards, 1992; Elkind,1990; Moore & Reed, 1988; Scott, 1992).

Marybeth Tinning is another woman who is widely considered to be a serial killer, although she was convicted of only one murder. Tinning had nine children, and she is suspected of killing most of them. When her adopted child was brought into the hospital emergency room in 1981 (after a number of her children had died of sudden infant death syndrome), doctors were suspicious and performed an autopsy. The child was found to have died of pneumonia, and no evidence was found to prove otherwise. When Tinning's last child was born in 1985, she too died. Tinning was charged with her death, was found guilty of depraved indifference to human life, and received a prison sentence of twenty years to life. During the trial, Tinning admitted to killing two of her other children by smothering them. She was never charged with these other deaths (see Egginton, 1989).

Margie Velma Bullard Burke Barfield was tried for only one of her murders, when she poured rat poison into her fiancé's beer in 1978. However, she also confessed to having poisoned her mother, in 1964, and an elderly man and woman whom she had cared for as a nurse and housekeeper, in 1977. She is suspected by many people of having committed many more murders. Barfield was convicted in 1978 of first-degree murder of her fiancé and became the first woman to be put to death since 1962 when she was executed by lethal injection on November 2, 1984, by the State of North Carolina (see Newton, 1990; Scott, 1992).

In early November 1988, a volunteer social worker who had placed a client in Dorothea Montalvo Puente's boarding house in downtown Sacramento, California, near the state capitol, began to look for her client. The client's social security checks had been cashed regularly, but the social worker had not seen her client since August of that year. Sacramento police found seven bodies buried in Puente's yard, and Puente was arrested after fleeing to Los Angeles. The results of the police investigation led to Puente's being charged with nine deaths. At her trial, prosecutors maintained that she was killing her tenants so she could cash their social security checks.

On August 26, 1993, Puente was convicted of killing three of her tenants during the 1980s. At her trial the jury deadlocked on six other murder counts. When the jury also became deadlocked during the penalty phase, the judge declared a mistrial. Under California law, because she was convicted of serial killing, Puente was sentenced to life in prison without the possibility of parole. Unlike many other serial killers, Puente still maintains her innocence. She admitted to cashing the checks of some of her tenants but claimed, "I have not killed anyone." One explanation Puente gave for the seven bodies in her yard was that all the victims had died of natural causes. The media and her defense attorneys made much of Puente's grandmotherly appearance and the fact that she had given much to her boarders and to the Mexican American community in Sacramento. These arguments may be the reason that jurors deadlocked on whether or not she should receive the death penalty (see Blackburn, 1990; Norton, 1994; Wood, 1994).

Categories and Types of Serial Killers

An examination of the spatial dimensions of serial murder reveals a multitude of geographic and chronological patterns, which provide us with little similarity among either victims or offenders. The frequency of these events ranges from a matter of hours to months or even years. The only source, in most cases, is the memory of the murderer himself through his confessions and the patterns of killings identified by police or the news media. Nevertheless, some limited typologies and/or categories of serial murder were found in the literature.

Serial murderers are generally considered to be mobile, moving from city to city and state to state. Robert Keppel, the chief criminal investigator for the Washington State Attorney General's Office, who investigated the Theodore Bundy case and was also involved in investigating the Green River Killings in the Seattle area, characterizes serial murderers as tending to be highly mobile, ready to move quickly to another town after committing several killings that might lead to their detection (Lindsey, 1984). Theodore Bundy is reported to have left victims across the country, from Seattle, Washington, to Pensacola, Florida. Killings by Henry Lee Lucas are suspected by law enforcement agencies in twenty-seven states. Levin and Fox (1985) found that serial murderers have become more geographically mobile, as society has in general.

Many serial murderers travel continually. Whereas the average person might put 10,000 to 20,000 miles a year on his car, some serial murderers have traveled 100,000 to 200,000 miles a year by automobile (Sonnenschein, 1985). However, not all serial murderers are so mobile; some commit their killings within a relatively small geographic area. For instance, John Wayne Gacy committed his killings in and around the suburbs of Chicago. Robert Hansen committed his killings within the Anchorage, Alaska, area, even though he buried his victims in rural areas outside Anchorage.

Ressler et al. (1984) found that a number of serial murderers have been fascinated with law enforcement. They found several who had posed as law enforcement officers in order to lure their victims, some who held positions as security guards, and some who actually worked as auxiliary police. Some serial murderers are so fascinated by detective work that they school themselves in police procedures and investigative techniques. For example, Theodore Bundy worked for the King County Crime Commission in Washington; Wayne Williams often photographed crime scenes; John Wayne Gacy had a police radio in his home; and Edmund Kemper frequented a bar near police headquarters and questioned off-duty officers about the murders he had committed. Robert Keppel states, "A lot of them [serial murderers] seem to know something about police routine and are kind of police buffs (Lindsey, 1984, p. 7).

When one refers to the serial murderer, it is frequently understood that such an individual is mobile, as discussed. Cecil Wingo, chief investigator for the Harris County, Texas, medical examiner (retired), describes serial murderers in geographic terms. He has coined the terms "megastat" and "megamobile." The megastat commits killings over time in a single, static urban environment. The megamobile killer is mobile, moving over great stretches of geography as he commits his killings (Egger, 1984a, p. 352). Holmes and DeBurger (1985) use the terms "geographically stable" and "geographically transient." They define the former as one who typically lives in a particular area and kills his victims within the general region of his residence and the latter as one who travels continually throughout his killing career (pp. 6, 7). Holmes and DeBurger further differentiate between these two types, stating that for the "geographically stable" serial murderer, "[v]ery frequently, the motive is sexual in nature and the predator may slaughter a selected group of victims" (p. 6). This assertion is, however, based on only three cases (John Wayne Gacy, Albert Fish, and Wayne Williams). Hickey's (1985) geographic typology of serial murder is a more fully developed attempt. He identifies three different types: the "traveling or mobile," the "local," and the "place-specific." Hickey states:

> Mobile murderers are those individuals, almost exclusively male, who move from city to city and across state lines, killing victims at random, or seeking out a specific type of victim. These killers tend to appear friendly and helpful to their victims and usually take considerable precaution against being caught, i.e. Edmund Kemper. (p. 9)

> [T]he local serial murderer stays in close proximity to his city or community. Again, almost exclusively male, these killers usually have a specific type of victim, i.e. prostitutes in the Green River Killings or the young males in the Atlanta Child Murders. (p. 10)

> [T]he place-specific serial murderer, or the killer who repeatedly murders in the same place. This type of killer usually operates in nursing homes, hospitals or in private homes. Either male or female these murderers kill for reasons of financial security, "mercy" killing, hatred of a particular group of people such as infants, handicapped or the elderly as well as motives of violence and sex. . . . i.e. Ed Gein; John Gacy; . . . i.e. Herman Webster Mudgett. (p. 10)

Hickey's (1985) typology is based on a historical literature review in which he reports to have identified "117 men and women in the United States who can be identified as serial murderers. An additional 47 serial murderer cases were collected from foreign countries" (p. 3). Hickey, however, provides no specific references for these cases, nor are his selection criteria identified.

Legal classifications of murder (first-degree, second-degree, etc.) and classifications based on assailant–victim relationships tend to ignore many of the dynamic aspects of the event in the study of serial murder. The classification of murder according to its motive appears to have provided a somewhat more productive method of examining serial murder in the literature. Jesse (1924, p. 13), in her classic study of motive, provides six "natural" groups of motives:

1. Gain
2. Revenge
3. Elimination
4. Jealousy
5. Lust of killing
6. Conviction

Jesse (1924) divides her fifth group into two categories: lust-murders in which the satisfaction of lust is the actual killing, without any sexual connection with the victim, and lust-murders committed at the same time or directly after the sexual act as part of the sexual gratification.

Megargee (1982) classifies aggressive acts as having either instrumental or extrinsic motivation (that is, the aggressive or violent behavior serves as a means to some end) or angry or intrinsic motivation, in which the injury to the victim is an end in itself. It is his first category that concerns us here, as the motive of sexual gratification is frequently identified in cases of serial murder.

Guttmacher (1960) refers to purely sadistic homicides as lust-murders. Karpman (1954) describes the perpetrators of lust-murders as nearly always psychotic and as sexually impotent. J. Paul de River (1958) defines lust-murder as occurring when death has been caused by torture brought about to relieve sexual tension. The lust-murderer gains sexual gratification only through physical injury or torture of the victim (p. 99). Lust-murder is further described by de River (1958) as being accompanied by acts of perversion such as vampirism, cannibalism, and necrophilia (p. 40). Nettler (1982) refers to this as intentional lust-murder or sadistic murder.

Hazelwood and Douglas (1980), early pioneers with the FBI who examined serial murder, describe two types of lust-murderers. The "organized nonsocial" is seen as a totally egocentric, amoral individual who can be superficially charming and manipulative of others. His crimes are committed with method and "expertise." The "disorganized asocial" type is described as a "loner" with feelings of rejection who has great difficulty in interpersonal relationships. His killings are less cunning and are done on impulse. These killers generally select female victims, although male victims are not unknown.

Nettler (1982) provides a further description of the lust-murderer:

[F]or such men, the act of killing a woman is itself sexually stimulating. . . . Many have intercourse, in varied fashion, with the corpse before and after mutilating it. . . . The distinctive significance of sadistic killers is that they commit "butcher murders" without being psychotic. By legal standards, they are in touch with reality. They do not kill under the direction of a delusion. (p. 131)

Revitch and Schlesinger (1978) refer to lust-murders as compulsive homicides that are stimulated by a combination of social pressures, resulting in a weakening of authority and controls. However, lust-murder does not necessarily mean serial murder, which often appears to be random and motiveless.

How Many Are There in the United States?

What is the prevalence of serial murder? How many serial murderers are there? How many people do they kill? Is serial murder on the increase? The literature provides no definitive answers to any of these questions. Is serial murder a contemporary phenomenon, or is it a recently discovered problem with a long history? The research provides us with a somewhat clearer answer to this question.

Serial murder, as indicated earlier, is generally a stranger-to-stranger crime. Thus, one must look to this category of homicide to attempt to determine the number of serial murders, since no evidence is found in the literature of monitoring or tabulating this phenomenon. In the past, homicides have typically been separated into three categories: About one-third have been between intimates—family members or lovers; one-third have been between acquaintances; and one-third have been between strangers. In the 1960s the rate in the last category began to rise dramatically, while the other two have remained relatively stable (Meredith, 1984). Frank E. Zimring, director of the University of Chicago's Center for Studies in Criminal Justice, says that this classification needs to be examined much more carefully. He states, "That's as specific as police agencies get with that category [between strangers], and it's not enough. We need to know who these strangers are and why the rate is going up" (Meredith, 1984, p. 44).

Morris and Bloom-Cooper (1964), analyzing victim–killer relationships in homicides in England between 1957 and 1962, find that it was "abundantly clear that homicide 'out of the blue,' in which the victim is struck down without reacting in any way, is exceptionally rare" (p. 325). This has certainly changed, at least in the United States. Kiger (in Egger, 1990a) found a dramatic increase in the number of homicides in which the victim and offender were strangers or their relationship was unknown. Godwin (1978) found a dramatic increase in stranger-to-stranger killings, and he argued that these types of slayings were becoming more and more prevalent, quadrupling in the 1970s (p. 7). Gilbert's (1983) analysis of homicides in San Diego found that between 1970 and 1980, nearly 50 percent of all homicide victims did not know their killers. During this period, there was a 60 percent increase in all reported violent crimes, and the criminal homicide rate increased from 7.8 to 10.2 per 100,000 population (FBI, 1983).

The Centers for Disease Control (1982) analyzed all homicides reported to the Federal Bureau of Investigation between 1976 and 1979. Results of this analysis revealed that during this period 13 percent of the homicides were committed by strangers, and in 29 percent of the offenses the offenders were unidentified. In analyzing the same data for circumstances of the homicides, 20 percent were found to be indeterminable. In most instances, serial murders would be found within these categories since they are frequently stranger-to-stranger killings or murders in which the circumstances may not yet be determined.

In 1999, 15,533 criminal homicides (that is, persons who were murdered) were reported nationally to the FBI, for a rate of 5.7 per 100,000 population. This represents an 8 percent decrease from the previous year, a 28 percent decline from 1995, and a 34 percent decline from 1990. If we look back from 1999 over a thirty-three-year period, the rate of murders has now decreased to the same rate as in 1966 (U.S. Department of Justice, 1999). In 1965 the total was 9,850 and in 1993 it was 24,526, or a 149 percent increase. The rate per 100,000 for the same period rose from 5.1 to 9.5, or an 86 percent increase (FBI, 1994). So when population increases are taken into account, the murder rate still shows a dramatic increase during that time. The 1993 rate was 9 percent higher than in 1989 and 20 percent higher than in 1984. If we look at five- and ten-year periods, we still see a dramatic increase until the mid-1990s, when murder rates began to decline dramatically.

Even though the murder rate is down significantly, this does not tell us whether serial murder has in fact decreased with the overall trend. If we knew the total number of serial murders or the rate of serial murder at a point in time, we could extrapolate from that point, assuming an increase consistent with the total murder increase. Unfortunately, we simply do not have good data. Serial murders are not counted in official crime statistics, and even if they were, given the nature of the crime, we would still be missing an unknown percentage. In other words, a number of these murders would not be counted because they were never identified as such or linked to other murders by law enforcement authorities. So we are in a quandary.

Estimating the number of serial murders in a given period of time is problematic. The best evidence available for determining the prevalence of serial murder comes from two major sources: identified trends within the overall murder count over time and totals based on newspaper reporting of serial murder.

Homicide trends in stranger-to-stranger murders, or where the relationship between the killer and victim is unknown, do provide some evidence that suggests an increase in serial murder. This does not give us a magic number, but it does indicate the magnitude of the problem. As noted earlier, the relationships between victim and offender in homicide cases have changed dramatically since the 1960s. In the past, the vast majority of murders were committed by individuals who had formed some type of relationship or acquaintance with their victims. This is no longer the case. In 1965 only 5 percent of murders were committed in unknown circumstances. In 1992 this figure had increased to 28 percent. In 1992, murders by strangers and unknown persons represented 53 percent of all murders in the United States that were reported to the FBI (U.S. Department of Justice, 1994). In 1999 the figure for murders by strangers or where the relationship was unknown was 51.3 percent of the total, very close to the 1992 figure. Whereas in 1965 nearly one out of three (31 percent) murder victims was killed by a person or persons within his or her family, in 1999 the figure had fallen to only 13.8 percent, supporting the trend away from murders within a family (FBI, 1999). The FBI and others generally attribute this increase in murders by strangers or in unknown circumstances to the nation's drug trade. Although this may account for some of these murders, it is also reasonable to consider at least part of this increase to be the result of serial murder.

The *Vital Statistics of the National Center for Health Statistics* documents cause and nature of death in the United States, but their statistics are not collected to reveal motive or relationship between victim and offender, nor do police agencies collect or maintain information of this type. Darrach and Norris (1984) found that at least 120 serial killers had been captured or singled out by the police in the last twenty years; however, the authors did not indicate how this number was derived and did not provide any documentation for this claim.

It would appear that the mass media are currently the only other source (in addition to examining overall trends in murders reported to the FBI) from which to quantify serial murders in this country. Serial murders come to the attention of the print media when a serial murderer is apprehended and his killings are revealed or when a series of murders occurs within a relatively small geographical area and their multiplicity becomes evident over time. Press attention and column space thus provide a means of accumulating a more aggregate picture of this phenomenon. Fox and Levin (1983) utilize this data source in examining multiple murders. They state, "Because of the newspaper publicity associated with extreme acts of aggression, we believe that our selection procedure uncovered most of the acts of multiple murder committed during the time period under investigation" (p. 3). The information collected from this data source (forty-two mass murderers between 1974 and 1979) was also apparently used by Levin and Fox (1985) in their book on mass murder. Dominick (1978) found that newspapers devote a great deal of column space to a few sensational crimes, especially the more spectacular homicides. Without extensive survey research to provide an inventory of serial murders from each law enforcement jurisdiction, newspaper research is the only currently available source of this information. The problem with this approach is that many unsolved murders may be the work of serial killers. Without a serial murderer's confession, numerous unsolved murders will remain separate, distinct homicides that will receive little if any attention in major newspapers.

A great deal of cross-checking and backtracking is necessary to research serial murderers through newspaper content analysis. Two strategies can be utilized initially: a search for an identified serial murderer or a search for identified serial murders. The former, used by Egger (1984a) in a preliminary search of the *New York Times Index* from January 1978 to June 1983, revealed a total of fifty-four serial murderers, each of whom who had reportedly killed four or more persons and had been identified by the paper during this time period.

Any attempt to determine the number of serial murder victims is fraught with the same problems as determining the number of serial murderers. In addition, known victims of homicide probably will not be identified as possible serial murder victims unless their demise has occurred within a relatively small geographic area, as in the Green River Murders in the Pacific Northwest, or their assailant has been apprehended and confessed to the murders, as in the cases of Lucas, Gacy, Bianchi, and others. Also, the victims of serial murder sometimes are not found, or, if they are found, it may be next to impossible to determine their identity. Alfred Regnery, former administrator of the Office of Juvenile Justice and Delinquency Prevention, U.S. Department of Justice, contending that many missing children are the victims of serial murderers, stated, "Because the bodies of the victims are not always found, we have no idea what the real number is" ("Serial murder victims," *Houston Post,* November 11, 1983, p. 1). Robert O. Heck, a U.S. Justice Department official, has stated that each year more than four thousand bodies are found abandoned on lonely hillsides, in city Dumpsters, or beside rural roads and are never identified (Lindsey, 1984). However, Heck's statistics are only an estimate, with no empirical basis; there is no mechanism for collecting such information. In discussing the number of serial killers, Levin and Fox (1985) state, "Indeed, one can only speculate that many of the more than five thousand unsolved homicides in the nation each year are the work of a few very effective killers" (p. 186).

Whether or not the incidence of serial murder is increasing is a question frequently addressed in the contemporary literature, with a great deal of focus on the increase in stranger-to-stranger or motiveless homicides. Those who contend that there is such an increase base their argument largely on the increase in the number of apparently motiveless killings in the 1960s and 1970s (Nelson, 1984). Law enforcement officials assert that history offers nothing to compare with the spate of such murders that has occurred in the United States since the beginning of the 1970s. These officials concede that more murders than are generally recognized could have occurred in the past. They may have gone unnoticed because detectives in widely scattered jurisdictions did not connect the crimes. However, officials still maintain that the incidence of murders with no apparent motive is definitely increasing.

Ressler et al. (1984), in a paper presenting the results of a two-year study on serial or series murder, state:

> The beginning of such stranger, motiveless murders was first noticed by the media in the mid-sixties when the "Son of Sam" killer, David Berkowitz, stalked victims in New York and gunned them down with a .44 pistol without apparent motive. Since that time there has been a considerable upswing in these types of murders and in the past decade the rate has climbed to an almost epidemic proportion. (p. 1)

To illustrate the scope of this problem, Ressler et al. (1985) cite a newspaper indexing report on the occurrence of mass murders and serial murders from 1982 through July 1984. They conclude that the figures from this report "dramatically illustrate the increase in mass murders as well as the category of serial murders" (p. 3). Although the information presented from this newspaper indexing report by Ressler et al. does tend to show an increase in serial murders, with ten in 1982, twenty-seven in 1983, and twelve in the first seven months of 1984, there are severe limitations to these data. First, the total number of murders in the first seven months of 1984 may reflect a decrease if seasonal variation in serial murders is discounted. This total of twelve murders in seven months reflects an average of only 1.7 per month, compared to 2.25 per month for the previous twelve months and 0.83 for 1982. If the incidence of murders is linear, then the total number of serial murders for 1984 would be fewer than twenty-two. Although linearity of serial murder occurrences is not assumed, the limited time frame of thirty-one months is not sufficient, given the data presented, to permit the conclusion that serial murder is increasing or to imply a definite trend in this phenomenon. True, the data reflect an increase within the thirty-one-month period, based upon twelve-month increments or a portion thereof. This does not, however, represent a trend. Even more problematic is the fact that the data presented by Ressler et al. represent only those data reported as occurrences of serial murder and subsequently reported in the newspapers indexed in the report.

The U.S. Justice Department has hesitated to refer to serial murder as an epidemic, but the volume of cases of serial murder has certainly brought more attention to the phenomenon. Roger Depue, former FBI director of the National Center for the Analysis of Violent Crime, stated: "It isn't just a matter of being more aware of [serial murders]. The actual number seems to be increasing" (Starr, 1984, p.100).

Others who argue that serial murder is increasing attribute the increase to violence on television or the growth of sadistic pornography. Pierce Brooks, a recognized homicide expert, argues that the increased mobility of Americans is partly to blame for the rise in serial homicides. Brooks states: "We are becoming more of a society of strangers" (Berger, 1984, p. 1).

Zahn (1980) also notes that there has been a definite increase in stranger murders and in cases where the offenders remain unknown (p. 124). Zahn further states that "with careful monitoring of these types of homicides that are occurring differing allocations to solve the problems associated with these types might occur" (p. 128). The problem, however, is that there is no such monitoring on a national scale. The *Uniform Crime Reports* and preliminary content analysis of newspaper accounts reveal that the occurrence of serial murder is a persistent and possibly increasing phenomenon in our society. It is possible, however, that serial murder is stable in rate and that any "increase" is the result of rising awareness and media reporting procedures. Newspaper stories of serial murder are not particularly reliable because they depend on editorial decisions frequently designed to sensationalize the phenomenon in order to increase circulation. No resources are being allocated to examine the prevalence of this phenomenon. Neither the number of serial murders nor the extent to which they are increasing has been documented.

As Kiger (Egger, 1990a) notes, "Without accurate quantitative assessments of the extent of serial murder, we will be unable to develop informed typologies, theories, and policy decisions. Indeed, we run the risk of creating a social problem, the magnitude of which may be greatly exaggerated" (p. 36).

Such a quantitative assessment is currently under development by Kim Egger but is not yet complete. Preliminary data analysis of her data set of identified serial killers spanning the years 1900 to 1999 reveals some basic information. There were 1,246 serial killers identified during this period, worldwide. During the same period, 18,361 suspected victims were identified, for an average of 14.735 victims per killer. There were 236 serial killers in the United States during this time, accounting for 3,130 victims, for an average of 13.262 victims per killer. For more information on victims, see Chapter 4. The sexual preference of these killers was found to vary, with all of the following represented:

- Heterosexual
- Homosexual
- Bisexual
- Pedophile
- Unknown

FBI and CNN Disagree on the Numbers

The FBI Behavioral Sciences and Investigative Support Unit at the National Center for the Analysis of Violent Crime attempts to keep track of serial murderers. According to an official summary provided by this unit to *CNN Special Reports,* there were 331 serial murderers and almost 2,000 confirmed victims of serial murder between January 1977 and April 1992. But an independent examination of the FBI's supporting data commissioned by CNN found a very different picture. The FBI data had been collected from major newspaper wire services and other publications. After removing a number of duplicated cases, the total number of serial killers listed in the FBI's own supporting data was only 175. After adding in serial murderers missing from these data, the total number of known serial killers during this period was 191 and the actual number of confirmed victims totaled 1,007. This independent analysis reduced the number of serial killers by 140, or 42 percent, and reduced the number of victims by almost 1,000, or almost 50 percent (CNN, 1993).

A spokesperson for the FBI admitted to CNN that the numbers were "[v]ery squishy. Very unreliable numbers. It's hard for anybody to come up with accurate numbers" (CNN, 1993).

During the same television special first aired on CNN in early 1993, the FBI also estimated the number of active serial killers at any one time in the United States. One agent stated, "25, 35 or 40 serial killers active at a given time is not out of the ballpark" (CNN, 1993). Another agent estimated, "Probably fifty to a hundred out there in society" (CNN, 1993).

A New Phenomenon?

There is a general impression that serial murder has emerged only in the last few years. However, this perception cannot be supported. Hickey's (1985) historical literature review refutes the notion that serial murderers are a product of contemporary society. Hickey (1985) found 117 serial murderers as far back in U.S. history as the early 1800s and concluded:

> First, the data unequivocally contradicts the assumption that serial murderers are a recent phenomenon. Regardless of their typologies, serial murderers can be traced back 200 years. Secondly, the emergence of serial murderers to the public view is made possible by our advancing technology, but they probably have always existed and operated in the United States. (p. 11)

An Increase in Serial Killers?

Zahn (1981) found an increase (from 24 to 30 percent) between 1976 and 1978 in the percentage of homicide cases in the United States in which there was no known victim–offender relationship. Zahn suggests this trend may indicate an increase in stranger homicides.

Dietz (1986) states, "Claims to the contrary notwithstanding, there is no empirical evidence that the frequency of serial killers is increasing or is higher in the

United States than in other countries" (486). He argues that although detection of serial killers may be increasing, rates are not known, and the study of trends or comparisons is not yet possible.

Smith (1987) describes a number of serial killers from southern and southeast Asia, Europe, and England. Smith concludes: "One thing appears certain, serial killing represents a world-wide problem which isn't going away" (Smith, 1987, p. 4).

Norris (1989) argues that the number of serial killers has increased since 1960. Masters (1985) also finds a "rash of cases" (p. 251), beginning in the early 1960s. He concludes that these murderers "are becoming less rare and may well come to represent a type of 'motiveless' criminal who belongs predominantly to the twentieth century" (Masters, 1985, p. 251). Wilson and Seaman (1983) concur, finding such crimes rare prior to 1960. However, few serious researchers would appear to support Linedecker's (1990) claim that there were fewer than twelve serial killers in the United States between 1900 and 1950.

Norris (1988) agrees with the earlier estimate of Holmes and DeBurger (1985):

> In 1983 alone, according to the FBI, approximately five thousand Americans of both sexes and all ages—fifteen people a day and fully twenty-five percent of all murder victims—were struck down by murderers who did not know them and killed them for the sheer "high" of the experience. The FBI calls this class of homicides serial murders and their perpetrators recreational or lust killers. (p. 15)

However, this reference to FBI figures for 1983 is apparently referring only to Norris's analysis of the *Uniform Crime Report*, not to actual statements by FBI officials. Norris provides no reference citation within his text and no list of references or bibliography to his work.

Elliott Leyton (1986) states in his book *Hunting Humans: The Rise of the Modern Multiple Murderer* that in the early 1980s the multiple-murder rate in the United States was on a "meteoric rise" (p. 22), at a time when the homicide rate was beginning to abate. In a footnote to this statement, Leyton readily admits the unreliability and unavailability of statistics for multiple murder, the fact that these numbers fail to reflect those not captured, and the unreliability of reporting police jurisdictions. This footnote certainly tends to weaken Leyton's own argument for a "meteoric rise" or a dramatic increase in multiple murders. (Others mentioned herein who provide the same basic argument for an increase could also be held accountable to Leyton's footnote, to a lesser or greater extent.)

International: A Global Phenomenon

> Q: Did you ever think of the pain you were causing your victim? When you were killing boys, didn't you ever stop to think of your own son?
>
> A: It never entered my mind.

> —Transcript of Russian Judge Leonid Akubzhanovof's interrogation of the serial killer Andrei Chikatilo, convicted of killing fifty-two girls, boys, and young men (Krivich, 1993, p. 270)

Serial murder is not unique to the United States, although the United States produces more serial killers than any other country. Simon (1996) claims that the
United States accounts for 75 percent of the world's serial killers, but he provides
no data or references to back up this claim. Hickey (1985) found forty-seven cases
of serial murderers in other countries (p. 3). Franklin (1965) provides numerous
examples of European murderers who today would be referred to as serial, such as
Bela Kiss (early 1900s, Hungary); Henri Desire Landru (1919, France); Peter Kurten
(1929, Germany); Dr. Marcel Petiot (1941, France); Gordon Cummins (1942, England); and John Reginald Christie (1950, England). Of course, the most famous
serial murderer was "Jack the Ripper," who operated in the late 1800s in London,
England.

The following are examples of foreign serial killers. This section is not intended
to be exhaustive but, rather, to give the reader information about some of the better
known serial killers outside the United States. Following this brief summary are
some examples of identified or suspected serial killings in which the killer has not
yet been identified.

Colombia

Colombian police were first alerted to a possible serial killer operating in the country when they discovered the remains of thirty-six bodies in the western city of
Pereira in 1997. In October 1999, Luis Alfredo Garavito astonished Colombian
police by admitting that he had killed 140 children between 1994 and 1999. Most of
his young victims were between eight and sixteen years of age and came from
poor families; their parents were street vendors. These victims were left on their
own, unattended, in parks and at traffic lights, as their parents approached
motorists to sell their goods. Most of the victims were found with their throats slit,
their bodies mutilated, and forensic evidence of having been tied up.

Garavito apparently used a variety of disguises to lure his victims. He reportedly
posed as a monk, a charity representative, or a street vendor like the children's parents. He would persuade his victims to walk with him to remote rural areas, where
he would tie them up before torturing and killing them. As of October 1999, police
had recovered 114 skeletal remains of the victims. Garavito is also suspected of
killings in Ecuador, where he had lived previously (BBC, October 30, 1999).

Ecuador, Colombia, and Peru

Garavito might almost be considered an apprentice killer when compared to
Pedro Alonzo Lopez. While Garavito may have exceeded one hundred victims,
Lopez exceeded three hundred. Lopez may well be modern history's worst murderer, a serial killer of 350 children. Lopez became known as the "Monster of the
Andes" in 1980, when he led police to the graves in Ecuador of fifty-three of his
victims, all girls between nine and twelve years old. Three years later, he was
found guilty of murdering 110 young girls in Ecuador, and he confessed to an
additional 240 murders of missing girls in nearby Peru and Colombia.

Lopez killed on a regular basis, murdering two or three girls a week over a three-
year period. He said that at age eight he knew he was going to be a killer; he

explained: "I was the seventh son of thirteen children of a prostitute in Tolima, Colombia. My mother threw me out when I was eight after she caught me touching my sister's breasts, and I was taken in by a man who raped me over and over again. I decided then to do the same to as many girls as possible" (Laytner, 1998, p. 19).

Ironically, given Colombian criminal law, Lopez is now a free man. After eighteen years in captivity (less than one month for each girl he murdered), he was released in 1998 for his good behavior while in prison.

Russia

Andrei Chikatilo, quoted earlier, a former university professor known as "Citizen Ch" or the "Monster of Rostov" in the Russian press, confessed to having killed and mutilated twenty-two boys, fourteen girls, and nineteen women (a total of fifty-five victims) between 1978 and 1992 in or near the city of Rostov-on-Don in Ukraine, Russia. Chikatilo's first victim was a nine-year-old girl in December 1978. However, it was not until June 1982 that one of the killer's victims was discovered—a thirteen-year-old girl who had left her village to buy cigarettes, bread, and sugar—and not until October of that year that police saw similarities between three of Chikatilo's victims and organized a special work group of investigators to solve these three killings. Chikatilo became a suspect in these murders in 1984 and 1987, when he was placed at or near the scene of some of the crimes. There were no witnesses to these murders and almost no physical evidence, except for a semen sample. Chikatilo was placed under surveillance in 1990 and arrested on November 20 of that year. Nine days later he began confessing to his horrible crimes. He was described by Russian police as having no remorse for his victims, only pity for himself. He was convicted of killing fifty-two people in October 1992 and was executed on February 14, 1994 (see Conradi, 1992; Cullen, 1993; Krivich, 1993; Lourie, 1993).

Another Russian serial killer, Anatoly Onoprienko, from the Ukraine, killed fifty-two people between 1989 and 1996, many of them in small family groups. Though he has confessed to the fifty-two murders, Onoprienko claims he was not reponsible for his actions but was "programmed by a higher force to kill." According to Stepan Bilitski, a court deputy, however, "He is as sane as you or I. A man who was mentally sick could kill one person but then would get caught. To kill so many takes cunning. There is no doubt that he knew what he was doing" (Wroe, 1999, p. 6).

Onoprienko's confession revealed that he had been a lawless drifter throughout Europe. In his first killing, he murdered his landlady in 1989, at age thirty, shortly after leaving the army and moving to the southern Ukranian port of Odessa. Throughout the summer of 1989, he continued killing, shooting couples in cars and stealing their money and jewelry. For the next six years, he traveled throughout Europe, to Germany, Hungary, Greece, Yugoslavia, and Sweden. Onoprienko refuses to talk about this part of his life, but police suspect he may have killed in all of these countries. When he returned to the Ukraine in 1995, his known killings stood at thirteen victims. Within five months, this death toll would stand at fifty-two. Onoprienko shot all of his known victims.

India, Turkey, Thailand, and Nepal

Charles Sobhraj does not call what he does murder; he calls it "cleaning." By his own confession, he has "cleaned" many times. During one year, 1976, with no obvious motive, he befriended and then sadistically killed at least eight travelers on the drug trails through Thailand, Turkey, and India. After his conviction for one of these killings, he escaped from a high-security prison in Delhi and may have orchestrated his own recapture in order to avoid being sent to Thailand, where he would almost certainly have received the death penalty for his murders. He is currently serving life imprisonment in an Indian prison. Thailand and Nepal still have a number of outstanding murder charges against Sobhraj (see Thompson, 1979, for a fascinating account of the crimes and travels of Sobhraj; also see Lane & Gregg, 1992).

South Africa

On August 27, 1994, Norman Afzal Simons, twenty-nine, who is suspected of being a serial killer dubbed the "Station Strangler," was charged in Cape Town, South Africa, with killing ten people, bringing to twelve the total number of murder charges he faces. This serial killer is believed to have killed twenty-one boys and one young man over an eight-year period in and around Cape Town. In June 1995 Simons was convicted of murdering a young boy.

   South African police had assembled a team of three police psychiatrists to help track Simons. These psychiatrists helped a team of detectives compile a psychological profile of the killer. Simons is called the "Station Strangler" because several of his victims were attacked near railway stations. Most of the victims were children, who, since 1986, have been found buried in shallow graves after being sodomized and strangled. A note found on one of his victims read, "One more, many more in store" (Reuters, August 10, 1995).

Singapore

John Martin Scripps was serving a thirteen-year sentence in Hertfordshire, England, for heroin trafficking when he escaped during a weekend home leave in October 1994. His first murder is believed to have occurred when he allegedly used butchery skills he had learned in prison to chop up his victim, a South African tourist, Gerald Lowe. His victim's remains, minus the head, were found in several black plastic bags floating in Singapore harbor. At his trial, Scripps denied that he had killed anyone, but a number of police agencies believe him to have been an international serial killer. Shortly after this murder, Scripps flew to Thailand, where he is believed to have killed two Canadian tourists—Sheila Damude, a forty-nine-year-old schoolteacher, and her son Darin, age twenty-three. Their passports were found in Scripps's possession when he was arrested in Singapore. He is also suspected in the killings of two British nationals, one in Mexico and the other in San Francisco. He was found guilty of the Singapore killing and executed on April 19, 1996 (*The Herald [Glasgow]*, October 3, 1995).

Australia

Australian police arrested a truck driver, Ivan Milat, for the "backpacker murders" in late June 1994. He has protested his innocence and fired his lawyer during a court appearance at which he was again refused bail.

Two women backpackers, the latest of seven backpackers slain in an Australian forest, were the first to be found. The forest had been chosen as the site of the Australian national orienteering championships on September 20, 1992. Without the help of volunteers who assisted police in looking for the missing women, they would still be two names on the missing persons list.

On October 5, 1993, the next body was found close to where the first two victims had been found. It was that of a young man who had been missing since December 1989, when he had set off to hitchhike with his girlfriend to a conservation festival in Melbourne. The girlfriend's body was later found nearby. For the next two months, police coordinated a search of the forest with more than four hundred volunteers. They found the remains of three more young persons who had been stabbed and shot to death.

After the discovery of the last of the seven bodies, the Australian government offered a $500,000 reward, and a local paper added another $200,000 to the reward ("Backpacker murders," January 23, 1994). Milat was ordered to stand trial in early December 1994 after a seven-week pretrial hearing. He was found guilty of the seven murders in June 1994 (Millikan, 1994).

United Kingdom

England has had its share of serial killers, including the Yorkshire Ripper, Peter Sutcliffe; London's Dennis Nilsen; and, of course, the infamous Jack.

Peter William Sutcliffe was first arrested for carrying a hammer in 1969 and was convicted of going equipped for theft. During that same year, he was accused of attacking a woman in the red light district of Bradford, England, with a weighted sock, but he was not charged with this crime. There is no record of Sutcliffe's criminal activities for the next four years. He was married in 1974 and, approximately eleven months later, began a series of twenty attacks on women for which he was eventually charged. He tried to kill two women during 1974 and killed a third in Leeds in October of that year. He used a hammer in each attack, so that police began to suspect a serial killer. The British media dubbed these attacks the work of the "Yorkshire Ripper," after "Jack the Ripper," the infamous Victorian-era serial killer in London. In November 1975 another woman was murdered, and by March 1978 Sutcliffe had killed a total of eight women and had tried to kill five others.

Between 1975 and 1981, Sutcliffe (sometimes referred to as the "harlot killer," as most of his victims were prostitutes), who was working as a truck driver, is believed to have killed thirteen women and injured seven others. Some believe Sutcliffe to have committed four other murders and seven additional assaults (Yallop, 1982). He was arrested in the company of a prostitute on January 2, 1981, for theft of a car license plate, but at the time of the arrest the arresting officers were not really sure who was in their custody (David Baker, arresting officer, May 31,

1994, personal communication). Following his arrest, Sutcliffe confessed to being the Yorkshire Ripper.

It was not until after his arrest that Sutcliffe ever saw a psychiatrist. He was diagnosed as suffering from paranoid schizophrenia. During his trial in London, Sutcliffe stated: "They [the police] had all the facts for a long time. . . . But then I knew why they didn't catch me; because everything was in God's hands" (Davies, 1981, p. 6). He was convicted of thirteen homicides and sentenced to life in prison (see Burn, 1984; Doney in Egger, 1990a; Jouve, 1986).

Prior to his arrest, Dennis Nilsen had never been incarcerated or suspected of a crime. He had worked as a police officer for a year for the London Metropolitan Police Force. It was only when Nilsen complained to his landlord of blocked drains in his flat in the north of London that he came to the attention of police, who soon found the drains clogged with body parts of Nilsen's victims. When confronted with this evidence, he quickly confessed to his crimes. He had murdered fifteen men in his flat between 1978 and early 1983. All of his victims were either drifters, homosexuals, or prostitutes. Only seven of the fifteen victims were ever identified. Nilsen kept his victims in his flat for days and sometimes weeks, posing them and holding one-way "conversations" with them. He was found guilty on six charges of murder and sentenced to twenty-five years to life in prison (Masters, 1985).

The neighbors of Frederick and Rosemary West on Cromwell Street in Gloucester were surprised to learn that they had lived with a serial killer in their midst for quite some time. In late February 1994, police began a search for human remains that would last 114 days and would result in the unearthing of twelve female corpses from two houses in the western English city of Gloucester and a field nearby. West, fifty-two years of age, was charged with eleven of the murders, which included that of his first wife, Catherine, and two daughters. His current wife, Rosemary, was charged with nine murders. Two other adult accomplices were charged with sexual assault on some of the deceased murder victims.

The remains of nine women were found buried in the garden, in the cellar, and under a bath at 25 Cromwell Street in central Gloucester. The search then moved to a nearby house at 25 Midland Road and to a country field outside the city close to where West had once lived. Police finished searching 25 Midland Road late in May 1994. The last body found, exhumed from the field earlier, was that of a pregnant woman.

Frederick West died while awaiting trial. The criminal trial of his wife, Rosemary, began in mid-1995. She was found guilty of ten murders and two rape offenses ("The West case," Associated Press, February 6, 1995).

According to a health workers' union representative, it was bad management of health services that were seriously short of funds that enabled nurse Beverly Allitt to attack children she was caring for. Warning signs were apparently overlooked or ignored. Allitt was known to have incurred self-inflicted injuries and feigned illness while a student at the hospital. Her frequent absences should have been investigated, and her family doctor should have been asked if she was suitable for appointment as a nurse. By several criteria, she was unfit to begin work as a nurse. But information about Allitt was either unavailable to hospital management or lost in the hospital bureaucracy. Hospital authorities made "a serious error of judgment" when they recommended Allitt for employment.

Allitt, twenty-five, was sentenced to thirteen consecutive life sentences for the attacks, which included four murders. She is still detained at Rampton Special Hospital in Nottinghamshire, England.

Another medical professional in London may have killed as many as 150 of his patients. Dr. Harold Shipman, fifty-four years of age and a father of four, was convicted on March 31, 2000, of murdering fifteen of his elderly and middle-aged female patients by administering lethal doses of the drug morphine to them. He was also convicted of forging the will of one victim to make himself the beneficiary of an estate worth $643,000 in U.S. dollars. Shipman was given fifteen concurrent life sentences, as there is no death penalty in England. His number of victims would make him the worst serial killer in modern British history. In at least fifteen instances police found that Shipman's victims had died after receiving house calls from him, sometimes only five minutes after he entered their homes. Police sources have indicated that they have identified an additional twenty-three alleged cases of murder connected to Shipman and have investigated 136 deaths altogether. Unfortunately, all of these victims were cremated (Moseley, 2000).

Another medical doctor involved in serial killing was Michael Swango, who pled guilty in 2000 to killing four hospital patients at Ohio State University Hospital and a Veterans Affairs hospital in Northport, New York. The FBI believe Swango may have killed as many as sixty people in hospitals across the United States and in Zimbabwe (see Chapter 4 for more details).

Robert Black is now referred to as Britain's worst child killer, but in 1982 he was simply a truck driver, not under suspicion for anything. His birth certificate has a blank space under the column headed "Name and Surname of Father." Black's mother did not know who his father was. Eighteen months after his birth, Black was placed in foster care with a widow, who died when he was thirteen years old. At age sixteen he was convicted of indecent assault on a six-year-old girl. By the age of twenty he had amassed a large collection of child pornography.

During the summer of 1982, a videotape showing a young schoolgirl reading poetry to her classmates was seen by millions of television viewers across the United Kingdom. The police were trying to jog the public's memory in the belief that someone, somewhere might hold a vital clue to the whereabouts of the missing child. A few days later, the schoolgirl was found brutally murdered; she was probably already dead when she was seen and heard on television. The police then made another plea to British television viewers: "Help us find her killer." This was the beginning of a murder investigation (referred to as an "inquiry" in Britain) that would become the biggest manhunt ever by British police. The investigation lasted nine years, utilized unparalleled manpower resources, and cost an estimated £5 million to conduct ("Long trail to find Black," *The Independent,* May 20, 1994, p. 3). The investigation involved both Scottish and English police and, initially, four separate police forces.

In March 1986, after the third young victim was found dead (four weeks after she was reported missing) seventy miles from her home near Leeds, members of fifteen police forces attended a Scotland Yard conference looking into a series of child murders and abductions across the country. The Nottingham police force then joined what was to become the largest computerized murder investigation ever in the United Kingdom.

In July 1990, Black abducted a six-year-old girl and dragged her inside his van. A neighbor who saw the incident noted the van's license number and alerted police. When police located and stopped the van, they rescued the young girl and arrested Black. The victim's hands had been tied behind her back, two pieces of plaster were stuck over her face, and a bag had been placed over her head ("Serial killer loses appeal," February 21, 1995).

Black was convicted of abduction and assault in August 1990 and was subsequently found guilty of kidnapping, murder, and improper burial of three young girls, ages five, ten, and eleven. He was also convicted of kidnapping a fourth girl. Black committed these crimes between 1982 and 1986. On May 19, 1994, Black, forty-seven, began serving a minimum of thirty-five years in prison for these murders. Police believe he may be responsible for between thirteen and seventeen other murders of young children.

Italy

Donato Bilancia is suspected by Rome police of having killed six prostitutes and two security guards in 1998. At the time of Bilancia's arrest, in May 1998, he also became a suspect in five other killings. The prostitute victims were found near train stations with bullets to the head or neck (Goodfellow, 1998).

France

When Christine Malevre first admitted to killing thirty people, she received five thousand letters of support and a book contract, and she became a heroine to many people in France. Malevre, a twenty-nine-year-old nurse who specialized in dealing with the terminally ill, said she "accompanied" her victims to death because it would have been "inhumane" to do otherwise. However, following two separate psychiatric reports, officials are charging her with premeditated murder and are considering her a serial killer. These reports found her to be "a person without any true compassion," who had a megalomanic desire to be in a "position of power" over her patients (Lichfield, 1999, p. 17).

Serial Killers Outside the United States Who Have Not Been Caught

The United States is not the only country in which police have difficulty catching serial killers. The following cases are examples of unsolved and apparently serial murders outside the United States.

Europe—Identified but Not Caught

Detectives in three countries are hunting a convicted murderer suspected of another eight killings. Dieter Zurwehme, who is reported to be cunning and outwardly charming, is wanted in connection with the deaths of couples in Koblenz, Germany, and Toulouse, France. In both of these cases, the couples were bound and gagged, then shot or stabbed. The Dutch police are also assisting in the manhunt. Zurwehme, who is fluent in Dutch, German, and French, was freed from his sentence for killing an estate agent's wife near his hometown of Bochum.

United Kingdom

Detectives of the South Yorkshire police force in England are still hunting the killer of an unidentified woman found beaten and naked in a ditch. The police fear she could be the fifth victim of a serial killer. The body, with clothes and jewelry missing, was found wrapped in a blanket.

Chief constables and senior detectives met on August 9, 1994, to discuss possible links between the murders of four women who were all strangled during the previous nine months in an area known as the Midlands, north of London. Three of the women were prostitutes. They all had had jewelry removed, and their bodies were left naked or seminaked in isolated areas. Police believe the fourth victim could have been mistaken for a prostitute.

The killings, referred to by the British press as the "Midlands Ripper Slayings," are being compared to the Yorkshire Ripper case because the first four victims were known or believed to be prostitutes who regularly worked red light districts. One of the victims discovered in May 1994, the nineteen-year-old mother of a young boy, was found naked in a shallow grave in the Peak District in Derbyshire. She had disappeared from the Sheffield red light district of Broomhall, and was last seen getting into a dark-colored hatchback. This fourth victim, however, was later excluded from this series of killings (anonymous South Yorkshire police officer, personal communication, September 21, 1994).

The police jurisdictions of Leicestershire, West Midlands, Lincolnshire, and Lancashire have not formally linked their investigations together. These murders remain unsolved ("Police chiefs rule out," August 10, 1994).

Canada

Between 1995 and 1999, twenty-one women disappeared in the Vancouver, British Columbia, area. Many of these women are thought to have been prostitutes. No bodies have been found.

Information on the unsolved murders of six women in southern Ontario, Canada, shows that some were stalked, kidnapped, and driven to remote areas where they were murdered between early spring and late summer, from 1982 to 1983. Although a sixth victim was not abducted, there are similarities between her murder and those of the other five.

Over the years, detectives have cautiously, in private, admitted the possibility that several of these killings might be linked. *Toronto Star* reporters found that as many as four other murders also could be connected to this possible series.

The bodies of five of the women were discovered in lovers' lanes—wooded areas down back roads frequented by teenagers. No effort was made to conceal the bodies. In at least three of the slayings, the victim's clothing was folded neatly and her shoes were placed side by side at the murder scene.

Most of the victims were transported many miles from where they were abducted. Five of them either vanished or were killed on a weekend; the sixth was murdered on a Friday; five of the crimes took place at night, the sixth in the early evening. Two of the women were stalked after getting off a bus; a third was apparently waiting for a bus; a fourth was hitchhiking at the end of a bus line. The killer or killers kept personal effects from some of the victims—clothing, a shoe, jewelry. The detectives who worked on the six murders said the similarities pointed out by the *Toronto Star* reporters might warrant further investigation.

Staff Sergeant Les Graham, head of Halton's Criminal Investigation Bureau, said police had looked at connections but came up with nothing. "One thing's for sure, the killer had to know the location of that lovers' lane before taking her there," he said (Pron & Duncanson, 1994).

In all six murders examined, the women were out alone at night. Of the six victims, one was strangled, a second was believed to have been strangled, two were stabbed, and one was bludgeoned. The cause of death was not established for the sixth. Despite the similarities, police forces involved have made no concerted effort to establish a task force or pool information (Pron & Duncanson, 1994).

Mexico

In the Mexican border town of Juarez, located only three miles from El Paso, Texas, with a population of 1.5 million and an arid desert geography, a massive homicide investigation has been conducted at various levels since 1996. The victims were women and young girls found beaten or stranged to death in the gullies and ditches of Juarez's desert outskirts since 1993. Many of the victims had been sexually assaulted. Many of them were abducted from, or last seen leaving, the large factories, called *maquilas,* where thousands of young people come to work daily. This investigation, focusing on a six-year murder mystery that has left 187 women dead, may be reaching at least a partial solution. Police received a break in the case when a fourteen-year-old girl was attacked, raped, and left for dead by a bus driver. The girl survived the attack and was able to name her assailant, Manuel Guardado. Guardado, when confronted by police, implicated four other bus drivers in the killing and astonished the police by explaining that the murders were being coordinated by Omar Latif Sharif, who was in prison serving a thirty-year sentence for murder. Sharif paid these bus drivers $1,200 per victim and required them to deliver the panties of the victims to prove the killings. Nearly one-third of the victims were found without their panties. No other victims have been found since the bus drivers were arrested. However, the bus drivers have implicated themselves in only twenty killings and are now saying that their confessions were obtained by torture. It is likely that other serial killers have also been operating in the Juarez area.

Poland

Fear swept Warsaw in June 1993 when law enforcement officers hunted a deranged killer and hundreds of people telephoned police to turn in their neighbors. The killer is believed to have bludgeoned six women in recent attacks, killing one and leaving three hospitalized, unconscious, and in critical condition. Each of the women was hit on the back of the head with a blunt instrument. Several were struck as they entered darkened staircases of their apartment buildings in the city center.

Until the attacks were made public by the Warsaw police, there was no campaign to warn women about two similar waves of assaults, on April 9 and May 18, 1993, when seven women were attacked. Two of these victims died, according to newspaper reports ("Callers turn in neighbors," June 18, 1993).

Sweden

In July 1993 police in Stockholm announced they were investigating a string of homosexual murders and warned gay men to be on their guard against a possible serial killer. Detectives are working on seven separate and still-unresolved murder cases involving gay male victims and dating back to 1990. Although police are not linking all the killings, they say that several bear strikingly similar hallmarks ("Stockholm gays warned," July 9, 1993).

Becoming an International Phenomenon

Serial murder is definitely an international phenomenon. In addition to South Africa, Australia, and the United Kingdom, serial killers have recently been reported operating in Germany, China, Japan, Austria, France, Russia, Nigeria, Bonsai, Italy, and Hungary. Few countries have escaped the horror of the serial killer.

Although the United States has reported many more serial killers than other countries, more and more serial killers are being identified across the globe. In particular, areas of the former Soviet Union are acknowledging the presence of a number of these killers, either currently or in the relatively recent past.

Essay by the Author

SERIAL KILLING OF THE LAMBS IN OUR DREAMS: CONCEPT OF THE "LESS-DEAD"

The perverted, dominating, horrific mega-intellect of the serial killer Dr. Hannibal Lecter, as portrayed by Anthony Hopkins, packed movie houses across this country. Of those who fell under the spell of Jonathan Demme's *Silence of the Lambs*, many failed to feel the slaughtering of their senses as Dr. Lecter's hypnosis took its toll. As rookie FBI Agent Starling revealed in her recurring nightmare of the spring slaughter of her innocence, symbolized by the death of lambs on her uncle's farm during her youth, her submission to this psychopathic interrogator reflected movie audiences' voyeuristic fascination with evil.

It was not only the brilliance of Anthony Hopkins that transformed this serial killer from a cruel, sadistic animal to an antihero. Acting skills notwithstanding, the public is preprogrammed to identify with or even laud the role of the serial killer in our society. For some, the victims of serial killers, viewed when alive as part of a devalued stratum of humanity, become "less-dead" (since for many they were "less-alive" before their death and now become the "never-were"), and their demise is experienced as the elimination of sores or blemishes cleansed by those who dare to wash away these undesirable elements. Just as the psychopathic serial killer depersonalizes his victims, society, in a sense, dissociates these victims from the human race because of the irritant symbols they represent. Victims become those who "had it coming" or whose fate is in some way preordained. We publicly abhor this violence while privately excusing the killer's acts as utilitarian or his motives as explained by terrible parenting or childhood trauma.

Victims, in this view, become relatively unimportant, and the multiple nature of the killer's acts and his ability to elude the police become the central focus of this phenomenon. Those who view with nostalgia the rapid decline of patriarchal society may see these killings as a reassertion of male potency and domination. Others may experience them as a safety valve for their own impulses to do violence. Some will secretly admire the killer for his ability to outdo the typical murderer who slays his wife or her husband. For many, the serial killer is a symbol of courage, individuality, and unique cleverness, a figure who allows them to fantasize rebellion or the lashing out at society's ills. For some, the serial killer may become a symbol of swift and effective justice, cleansing society of its crime-ridden vermin. The serial killer's skills in eluding police for long periods of time transcend the very reason he is being hunted: The killer's elusiveness overshadows his trail of grief and horror.

As we clamor to read the page-turners of Thomas Harris, Stephen King, and David Lindsey, we incur a sort of moral "debt" that takes a toll on our humanity. This debt increases exponentially as our view of the multiple victims of serial killers relegates them to the status of the "less-dead." The interest on this debt is compounded by our fascination with the horror and gore of real serial killers such as Ted Bundy, Richard Ramirez (the "Night Stalker"), and John Wayne Gacy, or of unsolved cases like that of the "Green River Killer." Only when the "less-dead" are perceived as above the status of prostitutes, homosexuals, street people, runaways, or the elderly does our own vulnerability become a stark reality. Until that time, the killer's aberrant behaviors are imbued with a kind of rationality or logic born of our class consciousness. When we begin to identify with the killer's prey, we shun such feelings and, intellectually, come to see the behavior of victims, their lifestyles, as the central factor in their demise.

The serial killer is not in fact our hero, but the mirror image of our potential selves. He can be seen as just like us, except that his avocation happens to be killing. We may develop a twisted infatuation with the fact that this person has killed and killed and killed again. We may marvel at his ability to commit the unthinkable, even though we ourselves have harbored such thoughts. To commit murder time and time again, to satiate the killer's continuing taste for death, has resulted in society's own insatiable fascination with these acts.

Once caught, the serial killer does not look "abnormal" on our television screens or on the front pages of our newspapers. We label him insane or a "wacko," but deep down we see him as very much like ourselves, yet different. It is this difference yet similarity that captures our attention. His less-dead victims become less and less real. The similarity of their lives to our own and the nature of their demise, which should alert us to our own risk, lose clarity and focus as our self-manufactured reality defines our own status as the antithesis of the serial killer's prey.

As movie audiences unknowingly submit to the hypnotic strength of Dr. Lecter's presence, they begin subconsciously to think of this psychopath as "cool." The woman fulfilling the male role of the hunter, portrayed by the actress Jodie Foster, becomes a troubled soul in need of Dr. Lecter's superhuman expertise. The evil of the doctor becomes cool, and thus natural, and we seek to identify with this naturalness. We begin to ask ourselves, "How are we different from this person?" or "How are we alike?" Such stimulation of our id forces our buried homicidal thoughts to the surface of our personality. We marvel at this character who brings such thoughts into his personal reality. We become avid spectators of a reality in which these thoughts are acted out, again and again, with amazingly creative and horrific violence.

Victims, in this view, are only the grist for the hero's courageous acts, the result of our actor's heroism. Our hero, the super serial killer, is admired—not only Anthony Hopkins's acting, but the reality it represents. The film frequently reminds us to revile this creature, but this moralizing seems almost unreal, and we continue feeling admiration for his deeds. Our recreational focus, so to speak, is on these homicidal acts, as we become willing patients in Dr. Lecter's clinic of horrors.

The doctor's "treatment" results in a self-segregation from the reality of pain and death as the empathetic pathways of our common humanity are anesthetized to virtual numbness. Serial violence, in particular serial homicide, is indeed on the rise. This is not the result of a few abnormal outliers in our demography but, rather, of an aggregate psychopathology in the very essence of our being. Human beings are devolving into an ultimate immorality. Our humaneness is rapidly dissipating into an enjoyment of violence, an addictive-like drive toward our fate.

Our ability to feel compassion for serial murder victims is brutalized by the excessive brutality provided by a slick Hollywood screen. The wide-screen realism and appeal of a Hannibal Lecter are but a metaphor for our future morality, a morality in which less-dead victims are simply dropped from perceived reality, and Orwellian thought becomes a Disney-like fantasy. Descriptions of the horrific acts of serial killers lose their uniqueness as they begin to articulate a truer reality. Human skins to clothe and hide the remnants of our innocence will become unnecessary. Vestiges of our humanity will be lost in fantasies of childhood, soon forgotten in a world inured to violence and death. We are seeking the ultimate experiences of evil, and the bleating of the lambs in our dreams will become our future nightmares as we become the less-alive and grow deaf to the cries of the victims.

CHAPTER 4

Victims: The "Less-Dead"

Kim A. Egger

I were just cleaning up the streets.
 —Peter Sutcliffe, the Yorkshire Ripper

Serial Murder Victims

"In most cases," according to Egger (1984), "victims are selected solely on the fact that they crossed the path of the serial murderer and became a vehicle by which hypo-arousal occurred for his pleasure. Victims are self-selecting only due to their existence at a place and point in time."

Should the average person on the street be looking over his shoulder? Perhaps. Most serial killers choose their victims based solely upon their presence at a particular point in time at a particular place. However, the average heterosexual male is not likely to be targeted at random. The child in the park, the prostitute on the street corner, the homosexual male prostituting his body in clubs, the hitchhiker trying to find a ride along a stretch of highway—these individuals seem to be more vulnerable than the housewife doing laundry. But should that housewife feel secure from the threat of a serial killer? The simple answer is no. The presence of a person in a particular place at a particular time is apparently the only known precipitating factor for falling prey to a serial killer on the prowl. The definition of serial murder used by Steven Egger also strongly suggests other commonalities among victims. Levin and Fox (1985) appear to concur with this definition. They state: "Serial killers almost without exception choose vulnerable victims—those who are easy to dominate" (p. 75). "The serial killer typically picks on innocent strangers who may possess a certain physical feature or may just be accessible" (p. 231). Levin and Fox (1985) provide examples of these vulnerable and typical victims of serial murderers, who include prostitutes, hitchhikers, children, derelicts, and elderly women (pp. 75–78). An emerging trend is seen in the killer who murders robbery and burglary victims. The number of killers who repeatedly kill victims of robbery or home invasion seems to be on the increase. Although the psychological motivation of the "traditional" serial killer may be lacking, these killers do meet the criteria for serial murderers. These victims are increasing with the lack of traditional psychosocial constraints against the taking of human life by killers whose only motivation seems to be monetary gain and avoiding apprehension. Increasingly, then, the new definition of serial murder must include not only the known groups of victims but also these newly vulnerable targets—robbery and burglary victims.

Karmen (1983) in discussing susceptibility and vulnerability of victims, states:

> The vulnerability of an individual or group to criminal depredations depends upon an opportunity factor as well as an attractiveness factor. Extreme risks are run by people who appear at the "right time" and the "right place" from the offender's point of view. Hence certain lifestyles expose individuals and their possessions to greater threat and dangers than others. (p. 241)

Karmen provides examples of these high-risk lifestyles: homosexuals cruising downtown areas and public bathrooms, cult members soliciting funds on sidewalks and in bus stations, and released mental patients and skid row alcoholics wandering the streets at odd hours (pp. 241–242). The same could be said for hitchhikers, lost or runaway children, migrant workers, and single (especially elderly) women, college students, and hospital patients (see the definition in Chapter 1).

Maghan and Sagarin (1983), in discussing homosexuals as both victimizers and victims, note that "the offender's rage against society is deflected and targeted on those who are victimized as the offender is. Victimization appears to produce a rage that feeds an offender mentality, and offenders then choose victims who are the most vulnerable, closest (spatially and socially), and offer the greatest opportunities" (p. 160). Homosexual killers most often prey on homosexual victims, although bisexual and heterosexual males become victims as well. Whereas Jeffrey Dahmer, Larry Eyler, and Herbert Baumeister preyed upon males who were either homosexual or bisexual, John Wayne Gacy also victimized young heterosexual males who were seeking employment, or who were employed by him at the time of their deaths or had been in the past, as well as young male hustlers. Homosexual serial killers are feared out of proportion to their actual statistical threat. Homosexuals who become serial killers represent less than 5 percent of all known serial killers. As Michael Newton points out, however, "Ironically, while gay serial killers represent a tiny minority of [the] broader group, their ranks include some of the most prolific slayers in modern times" (Newton, 2000, p. 103). Newton goes on to cite the legacy of death left by such killers as Donald Harvey (37 convictions; confessed to over 50 victims), John Wayne Gacy (33 convictions), Dean Corll (27 deaths; died after arrest), Juan Corona (25 convictions), Patrick Kearney (21 convictions; confessed to 28), Jeffrey Dahmer (17 convictions), William Bonin (executed for 10 deaths), and Randy Kraft (16 convictions; suspected in the deaths of 51 more victims).

The latest man to prey on homosexuals was Herbert Baumeister in Indiana. A local businessman, married with children, he was not suspected of leading a dual life. But while his family was out of town, he preyed on young homosexual males.

Baumeister, who buried the violated corpses at his home in Hamilton County, went undetected for years. After committing sixteen murders, he committed suicide in Canada before he could be arrested. How many deaths did he cause? No one can say for sure.

But heterosexual males are responsible for the majority of serial murders. The typical serial killer is a heterosexual male, wrestling with his demons, who chooses to work out his problems by torturing and murdering woman after woman. Many of these female victims are prostitutes, a group of women who are especially vulnerable to predation by serial killers.

But why?

If one combines Karmen's (1983) discussion of vulnerability and Maghan and Sagarin's (1983) discussion of victim–victimizer, an extrapolation is possible in examining the victims of the serial murderer. If a number of serial murderers were victimized in childhood, as case studies and research suggests, and are thus vulnerable because of their childhood situation, they may in fact have chosen victims like their earlier selves or from the same general lifestyle. Karmen (1983) states, "One common thread [that] emerges from most victim/offender studies is that both parties are usually drawn from the same group or background" (p. 242). However, it must be noted that there were no serial murder victim–offender empirical studies found in the literature other than anecdotal material or conclusions based on very few serial murder cases. Therefore, no valid conclusions can be drawn from the literature regarding victim–offender relationships in this context. The literature suggests, however, that many of these killers were abused, neglected, or otherwise victimized in their childhood. This appears to indicate the possibility that a number of serial killers do victimize people who seem to be earlier versions of themselves.

Victims or victimizers, the simple fact is that, at this point, it is impossible to know whether or not victimization in childhood is a major contributing factor in the creation of a serial killer. Most criminals and their attorneys know that extenuating circumstances are effective tools for persuading juries to render more lenient verdicts. In jailhouses around the world, criminals are aware that stories of abuse in childhood, real or imagined, will gain sympathy—the more horrendous the abuse, the more sympathy their stories will engender. This situation has put the researcher at a disadvantage that may be impossible to overcome. Researchers relying solely on documented histories of criminals will be forced to ignore abuse that has not been certified by authorities or the health care community, even though they know that abuse can and does go undetected. Of all the abuses of children, physical abuse is the most likely to come to the attention of authorities, but it is well documented that sexual and psychological abuse can go on for years without being discovered. Without clear evidence of abuse, it is impossible to know the full impact of childhood victimization on the future serial killer's development and the role that it plays in victim selection and death rituals. Although it is clear that sexual, physical, and emotional abuse play a substantial role in deviant behavior, it may be impossible to create empirical models for its presence in the phenomenon of serial killers.

Some blame the mobility of U.S. society for making victims more available to serial murderers. "It's not unusual for people—especially if they're drug users—to just up and leave home," says Commander Alfred Calhoun of the Ouachita Parish sheriff's office in Monroe, Louisiana. "Many become victims because they're hitchhiking or wandering in deserted places" (Gest, 1984, p. 53). Robert Keppel contends that because many serial murderers are charismatic, they can convince their victims to go with them for some reason. "They pick people they can have power and control over, small-framed women, children and old people" (Lindsey, 1984, p. 7).

The belief that people "just up and leave home" has unwittingly been used by police to ignore the activities of serial killers. When the parents of teenaged boys in a suburb of Houston began complaining about their disappearance in 1970, police were quick to use this excuse to avoid further investigation of the complaint. As a result, by 1972, at least twenty-seven boys had died at the hands of Dean Corll. This pattern has continued. The victims of the Green River Killer continued to disappear while police failed to investigate their disappearance promptly. How many lives could have been saved if officers had followed up immediately? It will never be known. Larry Eyler's victims also died because of the belief that "people just up and leave home." This is only one of several failures of law enforcement to be aware of the warning signs of a serial killer at work in their jurisdiction. But the belief that "people just up and leave home" should be discounted until proven otherwise.

The psychiatrist Helen Morrison contends that the "look" of the victims is significant. She states, "If you take photos, or physical descriptions of the victims, what will strike you is the similarity in look." Morrison also theorizes that some nonverbal communication exists between victim and killer: "There's something unique in that interaction" (McCarthy, 1984, p. 10). Morrison believes that the victims of serial murderers were symbolic of something or someone deeply significant in the murderers' lives. Some psychologists have specifically said that the victims represent cruel parents on whom some murderers feel they cannot directly take revenge (Berger, 1984).

But psychological explanations such as this do little to explain the carnage. Ted Bundy, for example, did prey on young coeds who looked like the woman who had dumped him. But Bundy had long been practicing sexually deviant behavior. The resemblance between victims and the former girlfriend may have been intentional, or it may have had little to do with their selection. Kimberley Leech, Bundy's final victim, certainly did not resemble his former girlfriend. The victims' selection may, rather, have been due to the fact that they were easily lured away and then restrained.

Dr. Morrison says that the serial murderer does not distinguish between human beings and inanimate objects (Berger, 1984). This characteristic may be similar to what is seen in contract killers, whom Dietz (1986) describes as depersonalizing their victims (p. 115). Lunde (1976) found that sexual sadist murderers dehumanized their victims or perceived them as objects. He argues that this "prevents the killer from identifying with the victims as mothers, fathers, children, people who love and are loved, people whose lives have meaning" (1976, p. 61).

Typically, the serial killer does not think much about his victims, have any empathy for the victims' loved ones, or reflect any feelings of remorse. When asked about his victims, Ted Bundy responded, "What's one less person on the face of the earth, anyway?" When the Australian serial killer James Miller, charged with the murder of seven young girls and women, was asked about his victims during his trial, he stated: "They weren't worth much. One of them even enjoyed it" (Wilson, 1983, p. 81).

A number of researchers have found that children and young women are the prime targets for serial killers. These groups are certainly considered to be victim-prone, primarily because of their vulnerability. Children are frequently the victims of serial killers. Hickey (1991) found sixty-two serial killers, 31 percent of those he studied, who had killed at least one child. Arthur Shawcross, who murdered two children and was later released, changed his victim type to women. As indicated earlier, young females make up a majority of the serial murderer's victims.

The fact that serial killers turn their victims into objects is by itself of little help to the investigator or the researcher. It is obvious to even a casual observer that the victim is objectified and that the serial killer has no feeling for the person beyond that of his or her own needs. The depravity of the victims' deaths is ample evidence of this. Serial killers lack the normal capacity for feeling or conscience. Their ability to compartmentalize their "normal" life and their true self is more telling. Their lack of empathy or compassion for their victims is evidence of an absence of psychological development that is rooted firmly in their early development and experiences. The developing serial killer may also be aware that certain segments of society are objectified by the general public, so that when, for instance, a prostitute dies, the public is quick to blame her. How often does the serial killer hear that a dead prostitute "asked for it" by being out on the street or climbing into a john's car? Might this awareness help the budding serial killer rationalize and objectify his victims? Most likely it does.

A growing number of victims are falling prey to parolees. In an alarming trend, the number of killers who are released from prison and then kill again is increasing. Because of changes in United States criminal law, more and more one-time killers are released, and they kill again. One of the most frightening examples is Coral Watts, imprisoned in Texas and suspected of murdering twenty-two women in the Houston area. When Watts was in Michigan at the university in 1974, he began his reign of terror with nonfatal attacks on two coeds. He strangled them and left them for dead. The two women survived, but his next victim was not so lucky. Nineteen-year-old Gloria Steele was found stabbed to death. Police identified Watts as the suspect in the two nonfatal attacks, and he committed himself to a mental hospital. He pled guilty to the assault charges and served one year, after which he was released. He then began to kill in earnest. While he was under surveillance in Michigan for the so-called "Sunday Morning Slasher" crimes, he lost his job and moved to Houston, Texas, in 1981. Michigan authorities notified their Texas counterparts of his arrival, but to no avail. Watts began killing again. Caught fleeing the scene of a brutal attack on two women in their apartment, he was arrested later that day and charged with the nonfatal assaults and with burglary. Bargaining again, in exchange for pleading guilty to assault and burglary, and accepting a sixty-year prison sentence with a twenty-year minimum, he confessed to thirteen murders in the Houston area. Houston investigators believe he may have been responsible for the deaths of as many as twenty-two young women, but he was never tried for any of these deaths. Watts is to be released from his Texas prison in 2002. Michigan may attempt to extradite him for the Michigan murders, but without legal action, Watts will be released, and he will surely kill again. And he is not alone. Other men who were paroled and went on to kill include the likes of Charles Manson, Westley Alan Dodd, Donald "Pee-Wee" Gaskins, Hubert Gerald Jr., Richard Marquette, Arthur Shawcross, and Henry Lee Lucas.

Watts is not the only serial killer who is waiting for release. Christine Falling, who was convicted of murdering three children she was baby-sitting, is due to be released in 2007. And there are others. This is a trend that must be addressed, and quickly.

Society's Throwaways: A Low Priority for Law Enforcement

Steven Egger defines the "less-dead" as

> marginalized groups of society who comprise the majority of the serial killer's victims. They are called the "less-dead" because before their death, they "never were" according to society. In other words, this group is basically ignored and devalued by their own communities or members of their neighborhoods. The "less-dead" victims are not missed and basically ignored by society. Examples of the "less-dead" are prostitutes, the homeless, vagrants, migrant farm workers, homosexuals, the poor, elderly women and runaways. (Egger, 1994)

This attitude toward marginalized members of society is often reflected in conversations at the dinner table. I have heard, "They were asking for it," too many times and in too many places not to believe that this attitude is prevalent in American society.

This attitude goes beyond mere "table talk." A great deal less pressure is on the police when the victims of a serial murder come from the marginal elements of a community. The public is much less incensed over a serial murderer operating in their area when they feel little or no identification with the victims. In this case, the victims seem far from real, and little attention is paid to their demise.

When the victims are prostitutes, homosexuals, or the homeless, their deaths fail to capture the attention of the police or the media until the number of victims becomes too large to ignore. However, when the victims are people that the public perceives as "blameless," such as college students or young children, public outrage begins with the first murder and continues to build until the perpetrator is arrested. Although public outrage and police response should be immediate, regardless of the social standing of the victims, this is not the case. Few people care when a few black prostitutes die, or when young male homosexuals cruising the gay club scene disappear. They are not "like us," so their deaths do not matter. It is only when the public perceives the threat as striking near home that pressure is applied to law enforcement and politicians.

An example of this attitude is the case of a young woman who was murdered while out on the streets at 3:00 A.M. Many people commented that she should not have been out at that hour, as if she were somehow responsible for her own murder. Several days later, when the circumstances of her death were revealed, the attitude changed. The young woman was out that late because she had run out of disposable diapers for her sick child. The public then demanded a quick resolution to her murder. We somehow hold victims responsible for their own deaths. Although that assumption may be true in the case of some homicides, the victims of serial murder are not responsible in any way. Despite their occupation, sexual orientation, or social status, no member of any society deserves the atrocities that are perpetrated on the victims of serial murder.

The deaths of victims from the "less-dead" may receive little media coverage until the number of victims becomes intolerable. As can readily be seen from press and television news reports, victims and survivors receive little attention in mass media accounts of crime. Unless victims are well-known celebrities or people of power and wealth, the central focus of the media is on the crime and the offender. Victims are of little interest, and survivors are, for the most part, ignored or quickly forgotten; while the killer goes on to instant celebrity and the survivors are victimized again.

Since the majority of victims are the "less-dead," it is easy to forget that they were someone's child, someone's mother. It is easy to simply write them off, forget *who* they were, and concentrate instead on *what* they were. It is too easy to blame them for their fate. Some journalists and writers have taken the public, law enforcement, and politicians to task for this, but too few do so, and their efforts have little effect. And what of the victims' families? Continually being bombarded with the near-"celebrity" status of the captured serial killer must surely take a toll on their psyches. Their lives are forever changed. For the spouses and children of the murder victims of a serial killer, the pain never ends.

It would appear from the data available on serial murder investigations that the most frequent victim of a serial killer is the female prostitute. In the United States, nearly 78 percent of female victims of serial murderers are prostitutes (K. Egger, 2000). From the killer's viewpoint, these women are simply available in an area that provides the protection of anonymity, as well as adequate time in which to make a viable selection. It is probable that the serial killer selects prostitutes most frequently because they are easy to lure and control during the initial stages of an abduction. Potential witnesses to the abduction see only a pickup and transaction prior to paying for sex. They are programmed to see only what they expect to see when a woman gets into a car with a john. And who will miss one less prostitute plying her trade on the streets? It becomes too easy to blame her for her own fate. As Michael Newton (1992) points out in *Serial Slaughter:*

Worse yet are cases where police or members of the general public blindly over-look—or actively applaud—a killer's work. Authorities in San Diego, California, still reject Eddie Cole's confession to five local homicides, dismissing each case—including that of Cole's wife, found strangled to death in a closet, wrapped in a bedspread—as "death by natural causes." In Portland, Oregon, following the unsolved murders of several prostitutes, a police lieutenant voiced his opinion that violent death was an occupational hazard for streetwalkers. England's Yorkshire Ripper, Peter Sutcliffe, preferred to call himself "The Streetcleaner," purging his district of whores, and few complained about his crimes until Sutcliffe accidentally bagged an "innocent" girl on his fifth outing. Closer to home, similar feelings are echoed in Lake Elsinore, California, where some residents claim that a local prostitute-killer—as yet unidentified—is merely "cleaning up the trash downtown." Small wonder, in the face of such an attitude, that women's groups and gay rights activists complain of being short-changed by a legal system that evaluates a human life in terms of income, social status, sex, or race.

The serial killer is no doubt aware of such attitudes. With this underlying attitude, it is no wonder that prostitutes are the most common target of serial killers in the United States, England, and South Africa.

Dr. Steven Egger made a search of major newspaper reports of prostitutes as victims of serial murders, either unsolved or under active investigation, that occurred between October 5, 1991, and October 5, 1993. During this two-year period, he found that a total of 198 prostitutes were identified as victims of serial killers involving twenty-one different and distinct serial murder patterns, or an average in excess of nine prostitute victims per serial murder. No other group of victims was found that frequently in an identified group of serial murders during that period. For the female prostitute, lifestyle certainly plays a part in putting her at risk of being prey for a serial killer. In the United States, this pattern of victimization continues to hold true, whereas elsewhere serial killers are increasingly targeting children. Iqbal in Pakistan, who has been convicted of 100 murders of young boys (CNN, March 28, 2000), and the monsters in South America such as Pedro Lopez, who was responsible for as many as four hundred deaths of young children (Laytner, 1998), reflect the fact that serial killers are increasingly targeting larger and larger numbers of children. Children are at extreme risk in developing and third-world countries because of the socioeconomic pressures on populations that cannot provide adequately for their food, shelter, or safety. This socioeconomic pressure also appears to be creating serial killers. In Africa, a nine-year-old boy was arrested in the deaths of other young people (BBC, January 28, 2000). As human populations continue to increase without adequate socioeconomic resources, and children continue to be caught in the crossfire of war, the creation of younger serial killers may also be on the rise.

Most victims of serial killers are persons who are vulnerable—those individuals who are perceived as powerless or lacking in prestige by most of society. A lack of power or prestige readily defines them as easy prey for the serial killer. A careful selection of vulnerable victims does not mean that the serial killer is a coward; it only means that the killer has the "street smarts" to select victims who will not resist, will be relatively easy to control, and will not be missed. Such a selection protects the killer from identification and apprehension. In many cases, selection of a prostitute assures him that the killings may never be revealed. Even if such a victim's remains are found, she will be difficult for the police to identify, given her lifestyle and lack of close ties to her family or the community.

In a small number of cases, the victims of a serial killer knew their murderer. This fact may seem to contradict previous statements made in this chapter. But sometimes a personal or professional relationship becomes one of dominance and power. Perhaps the killer was the victim's doctor, or nurse, or wife, or husband, or parent. Dr. Michael Swango killed for years while suspicion swirled around him. Suspected in at least thirty deaths in several countries, he was finally convicted in 2000 for the deaths of three of his patients in New York. Genene Jones, a pediatric nurse in Texas, may have killed forty of her tiny patients, but she stood trial and was convicted for only one death. Marybeth Tinning murdered her seven infant children in New York, but their deaths were ruled SIDS (sudden infant death syndrome) by the medical examiner. Only when her adopted son died did authorities take notice. In the early twentieth century, Nannie Doss confessed to killing at least ten of her family members, including several husbands, her children, and a grandchild. These killers usually kill for a number of years, and their victim count continues to rise. They go unnoticed because of their choice of victims and their communities' disbelief that it could happen to them. Although these victims are not marginalized by society, they are just as much the "less-dead" as the victims of the Green River Killer, because they were in a subservient relationship with their killer. Like prostitutes, the homeless, or homosexuals, they were powerless to prevent their own deaths.

Who Are the "Less-Dead"?

Looking at data on 1,246 serial killers from 1900 to 1999, I found that in the United States, 65 percent of the victims of serial killers were female. Additionally, 89 percent of the victims were white, 10 percent were African American, and 1 percent were Asian or Native American.

Although prostitutes make up the majority of female victims—as much as 78 percent in some time periods—that does not mean they are the only women targeted. Elderly women and women who live alone are also routinely targeted. A growing number of victims are in their homes when they meet their deaths, when serial killers choose home invasion as their modus operandi. Women also often fall victim to their lovers or spouses, who may kill them for monetary gain. But men are not alone in killing for profit; women are quite capable killers in their own right.

Children are frequently targeted by serial killers because they are unaware of their vulnerability, easily lured away, and easily subdued. Some children are also at special risk of being murdered by their mothers, as the murderers Marybeth Tinning, Gayle Savage, and Waneta Hoyt have proved. Children are at special risk when parents are afraid to warn them of the real threat that adults and even other children can pose to their safety. The tragic Bulger case in England and the recent arrest of nine-year-old Hamisi Prince in Rwanda serve to remind us that children can and do kill other children. And in the third world and developing nations, children are killed in large numbers.

Male homosexuals are also at special risk. When male serial killers target other males, 48 percent of the victims will be homosexuals. As seen earlier, the number of victims of a homosexual serial killer is large. Because homosexuals are often marginalized in the larger community, serial killers seem to be able to operate for long periods of time, abducting and killing large numbers of victims, before law enforcement is forced to act.

Race plays a role in the selection of serial murder victims. Approximately 7 percent of victims are chosen simply because of their race. The white racist Joseph Paul Franklin attempted to kill and did kill black males, many of whom were with white females. Hubert Gerald, a black male, killed black females on the South Side of Chicago. Local police and even an FBI analysis failed to notice his activity until he confessed.

Physical health can play a role in victimization. Being hospitalized can put a person at risk if he or she is unlucky enough to be admitted where an "angel of mercy" is at work. With medical personnel continually moving through patient rooms and medications frequently being given, medical serial killers easily find victims. In England, the trial of Dr. Shipman shook up the medical community. In the United States, the reaction to Dr. Swango's conviction in 2000 led to the medical community's trying to excuse its behavior. The American medical community has refused to acknowledge its responsibility in allowing doctors and nurses to kill by ignoring and discouraging personnel who report suspicious activities. The mere fact that Dr. Swango was allowed to keep his medical license after he was convicted of poisoning emergency medical personnel serves to warn the public of the tolerance given to doctors who commit crimes.

At least 2 percent of victims are chosen because of their location. They are in the right house, or working in the right shop, or living in the right alley, or shopping in the right mall, or working the right street corner. They are chosen simply because they happen to be in or live in the place where the serial killer is hunting—where he feels most comfortable and safe in killing. This means that despite the statistics describing the most frequent victims, we are all at risk. If we are in the path of a serial killer, we can easily become his next victim unless we are aware of our vulnerability.

One of the main theses of this book is that the most frequent victims of serial killers are the persons Steven Egger calls the "less-dead, " and that those who fit this description are at the highest risk. But despite the validity of this construct, we are all at risk. Any of us who is in the path of a serial killer can easily become his next victim unless we are all aware of the risk. The exception proves the rule. Cases like that of Jerry Marcus, described in Chapter 10, illustrate this vulnerability. Marcus preyed on women he dated, as well as an occasional stranger. His sweet, kind manner hid a rage that cost several women who trusted him their lives. Marcus's victims are not alone. Children, lovers, friends, and patients continue to be killed by someone they know and trust.

The Killing Fields: Where Do Serial Killers Hunt?

The hunting grounds of the serial killer will vary a great deal among killers. However, many serial killers tend to select their victims from the same general areas where they feel comfortable, have control over those frequenting the area, or are assured that the area is infrequently patrolled by local police. They hunt in areas where they will not be noticed or appear different from others. They seek anonymity.

Different areas that serial killers search for their prey reflect different types of victims sought out by the killer. The red light districts of larger urban areas are probably the most favored hunting grounds, given the large number of prostitutes who fall victim to serial killers. Here the killer can blend in with all the other johns and have relatively little fear of drawing special attention from witnesses. Many serial killers have lured and abducted their victims from business establishments providing short-term services to people in transit, such as convenience stores or service stations near interstate highways. These locations appear to provide attractive hunting grounds to the serial killer, given the almost guaranteed anonymity in places where stranger-to-stranger interaction is commonplace and witnesses remember little of their brief time spent there. From the killer's perspective, one unique and attractive characteristic of these points of prey is that stranger-to-stranger interaction is the expected norm. No one takes any notice. The so-called I-70 Killer, who remains at large as of 2001, found businesses near interstate highways to be a perfect killing ground for all the same reasons. A similar environment can also be found on many large college campuses. Danny Rolling, Edmund Kemper, and Ted Bundy found these sites perfect.

Shopping malls, city parks, pools, fairs, parking lots—all are locations with large numbers of people paying little attention to their personal safety, making them easy places for stalking and abducting victims. Adam Walsh was abducted from a department store when he was out of his mother's sight for only a few moments. Westley Alan Dodd stalked his young victims in parks and attempted to abduct his final victim, a young boy, from a movie theater. We feel secure in these places, and we forget to be aware of our surroundings and the people around us. Because of the methods serial killers adopt, we are all at risk. The home is not always the sanctuary that it seems to be, either. Several children have been abducted from their yards or from the front of their homes. That small children are being killed by their caregivers or parents continues to be revealed. The unexplained death of an infant is devastating, and all consideration must be extended to the grieving parents. But SIDS has been the bane of modern medicine. Physicians need to be especially aware of the particular threat to infants from their mothers or caregivers. More than one murderous mother has been able to kill her children as a result of a lack of vigilance by the medical community. These serial killers have been identified only when the number of deaths stretched the bounds of believability.

Home invasions committed by serial killers seem to be on the rise. This is especially frightening because we all have a sense of security when we are in our homes. The Boston Strangler would gain entry and then rape and murder his victims. Richard Ramirez terrorized southern California with his nighttime invasions of Los Angeles homes. In Sacramento, California, Richard Chase went from house to house during the day, looking for an unlocked door and killing whoever was home. This trend seems to be increasing as the twenty-first century begins. Thus, we are all vulnerable.

Outside Houston, Texas, abductions of young women and children from a stretch of highway have continued without an end in sight. Female motorists who have broken down alongside the road have been targeted. The cases of children abducted from their neighborhoods and young women abducted from their workplaces emphasize that none of us is truly immune to the threat of a serial killer.

Investigative Value of Victim Information Quickly Dismissed

Criminal law in this country defines a criminal offense as one against the state. It is the state, rather than the victim, that prosecutes the charged offender. The criminal justice system emphasizes crime control and prosecution, focusing on the crime and the criminal offender. Little formal attention or recognition is paid to the victim, other than collecting evidence to strengthen the state's efforts in prosecuting the offender. The needs, comfort, and convenience of victims or, in the case of serial murder, of the surviving relatives and loved ones, very rapidly lose importance or priority. Once the physical evidence or information gathered begins to point toward a suspect or a type of suspect, the victims or survivors quickly become only names on a police report for entry into a master name index file, to be retrieved at a later date only if they are considered valuable in the prosecution of a defendant.

Criminologists have only recently turned their attention to crime victims. Much of their research has focused on lifestyle and victimization, victim characteristics, and victim precipitation (the ways victims contribute to their own victimization). Seldom have criminologists studied victims' or survivors' responses, or ways to provide assistance to them. The criminal investigation literature, ironically, depicts a similar lack of interest in the victims or survivors.

In the investigation of several homicides believed to have been committed by the same individual, survivor information may be the most important information collected. This is because in many serial murder investigations, physical evidence from the crime scene is scarce or nonexistent. In most of these homicides (as was noted earlier), the victims and the killer had not been acquainted prior to the fatal encounter. In other words, the survivors may be the only major source of information on the basis of which the investigation can proceed and be developed.

As Ford (Egger, 1990a) has indicated, in the investigation of gay murders committed in the Indianapolis, Indiana, area in the early 1980s, the Central Indiana

Multiagency Investigative Team initially discounted the value of a victimological approach to the investigation. Ford argues that this early exclusion of a valuable investigative strategy was a major problem in the team's effectiveness.

Early attention by investigators to the targeted victims is essential in a serial murder investigation, which typically reveals an elusive killer. Sufficient analysis of targeted victims and their networks inevitably yields greater insight into the victim's role in the crime setting. It also permits inferences regarding the killer's decision-making process in selecting intended victims.

Ford argues that an applied victimological approach requires that five general tasks be accomplished in order to assemble social characteristics of victims and circumstances of the crimes:

1. Identify category or type of victim.
2. Delineate victim social networks.
3. Determine personal factors contributing to risk.
4. Describe situational factors affecting risk.
5. Identify routine victim activities and expected behaviors related to contact with predator (adapted from Egger, 1990a, p. 116).

Ford, a sociologist who was the only non-sworn member of this Indiana investigative team, argues for the importance of analyzing the ecology of possible contact settings (between killer and potential victims) in order to help narrow the focus of the investigation to promising areas for locating witnesses, including surviving victims.

Much of the research on serial murder has concentrated on finding similarities among such murders. With few exceptions, the victims of serial killers have been all but ignored. However, one of the greatest similarities among serial killers is their consistency in choice of victims. As indicated in the serial murder definition offered earlier, the victims of serial murderers often are vagrants, the homeless, prostitutes, migrant workers, homosexuals, missing children, single women out by themselves, elderly women, college students, or hospital patients. In other words, the serial killer preys on people who tend to be vulnerable or those who are easy to lure and dominate. In part, these victims' vulnerabilities may lie in the locations that they frequent, or in their lack of power, or in being considered the "throwaways" of our society. Frequently, they are not missed or reported missing by others. A good example of this is seen in the arrest of Joel Rifkin in New York on June 28, 1993. When police chased and stopped him for not displaying a license plate, they found a decaying female corpse in the back of his pickup truck. After a lengthy interrogation, Rifkin confessed to having killed seventeen prostitutes during the past three years. On the basis of this confession, the police investigation then concentrated on finding and identifying Rifkin's victims. But this was difficult because there were few records of these victims being reported missing. In instances where bodies of these victims had been found, they were yet to be identified when Rifkin was arrested. No one had missed these victims until Rifkin stumbled into the hands of a New York state trooper.

Little else is known about the victims of serial murderers other than that they are commonly murdered by a stranger (unless the murder takes place inside the family). In a preponderance of known cases, the victims seem to be young females, presumably chosen to satisfy craving for dominance of the mostly male serial murderers. The victims are sometimes young males, as in the cases of John Wayne Gacy, Elmer Wayne Henley, and Jeffrey Dahmer. It has been estimated that 50 percent of unidentified bodies in county morgues or medical examiners' offices across the country are those of young children or adolescents (C. Wingo, personal communication, July 1983). Unfortunately, we do not know how many of these bodies represent victims of serial murder.

In a number of cases it appears that the victims were selected solely because they crossed the path of the serial murderer and became a vehicle for his hypo-arousal and pleasure (S. Egger, 1984a). Victims may be self-selecting only because of their presence at a certain place and point in time. This, and possibly the physical appearance of the victim, which may hold some symbolic significance for the killer, are apparently the only known precipitating factors for their selection. The definition used by Egger identifies lack of prestige, lack of power, and membership in a lower socioeconomic group as common characteristics of serial murder victims. Levin and Fox (1985) seem to agree that "serial killers almost without exception choose vulnerable victims—those who are easy to dominate" (p. 75). "The serial killer typically picks on innocent strangers who may possess a certain physical feature or may just be accessible" (p. 231).

Predatory-stranger offenses may be particularly dependent on the availability of vulnerable victims at a particular geographic location. Many criminologists consider victim precipitation—the extent to which the victim's actions contribute to his or her demise—a major cause of, or certainly a contributing factor in, homicide. However, the extent to which victim precipitation occurs in serial murder can only be speculated about, since very little information is usually available regarding the interaction between the killer and the victim prior to the point of fatal encounter.

A number of high-risk lifestyles place one in a victim-prone status: homosexuals cruising downtown areas and bathrooms; cult members soliciting funds on sidewalks and in bus stations; and released mental patients and skid row alcoholics wandering the streets at odd hours (Karmen, 1983). In some instances, it may simply be that an individual is out alone. Females out by themselves are particularly vulnerable, given the high proportion of female serial murder victims. Prostitutes are at particular risk of being targeted by serial killers. For women, there appears to be strength in numbers in reducing the risk of a serial murderer attack.

In many cases, serial murderers may be attacking mirror images of themselves. If sexual child abuse and neglect are contributing factors in the production of a serial killer, then the killer may be choosing victims who resemble his earlier self or who have the same general lifestyle. Many victim/offender studies indicate that both parties usually come from the same group or background (Sagarin & Maghan, 1983).

Some blame the mobility of American society for making victims more available to serial murderers. We are indeed a transient culture. Robert Keppel, chief investigator in the attorney general's office in Washington, D.C., contends that since many serial murderers are charismatic, they can convince their victims to go with them for some reason: "They pick people they can have power over and control over, small-framed women, children and old people" (Lindsey, 1984, p. 7).

Regardless of the reasons, serial killers are primarily white males in their twenties and thirties. They are continually prowling for victims who, statistics show, are more likely to be white and female. The following table* describes a few of the characteristics of victims of serial killers in the United States. Also shown are some of the known motives of serial killers. These statistics are based on data from 1900 through 1999.

American Serial Killer Victim Characteristics

Victims	Percentage	Race	Percentage
Female	65	White	89
Male	35	Black	10
		Asian	1

Motive or Basis for Victim Selection

Motive	Percentage	Motive	Percentage
Selected on basis of gender	40	Killed for profit	7
Selected on basis of age	6	Selected on basis of health or physical condition	3
Selected on basis of race	2	Selected on basis of residence	2
Selected on basis of specific characteristics	1	Selected on basis of occupation	1
Changing criteria	13	Unknown criteria	12

Source: Preliminary data, K. Egger, 1999. These statistics replicate the findings of Newton (2000).

*For those who are concerned with statistics, the data set from which these preliminary results are taken includes identified and solved cases only. Unsolved cases such as the Green River Killer investigation are excluded from these results. There are differences in the factors used for U.S. data versus worldwide data that account for the apparently contradictory results.

These trends can be summarized in the following manner:

• Serial killers are most likely to choose their next victim on the basis of sex alone. This is the primary factor in victim selection 40 percent of the time. Killers in this category overwhelmingly select women.

• Serial killers will change their victim criteria 13 percent of the time. Arthur Shawcross, as an example, first killed two children and after his release from prison began killing women.

• It is impossible to determine the victim criteria in 12 percent of the known cases.

• For-profit killing is a primary motive in victim selection 7 percent of the time. Margie Barfield, Rhonda Bell Martin, Herman Drenth, and Herman Mudgett all found ready sources of money by killing family members.

• Victims selected on the basis of their age (6 percent) include not only children but also the elderly. Killers such as Westley Alan Dodd specifically targeted children, whereas the killers Carlton Gary and Edward Kaprat, and the French team of killers Thierry Paulin and Jean-Thierry Mathurin have targeted the elderly.

• Victims who are chosen because of their health or physical condition (3 percent) most often fall prey to medical serial killers. Britain's Dr. Shipman is believed to have killed over two hundred of his patients. The American nurses Donald Harvey, Lynn Majors, and Richard Angelo all found their patients perfect victims for their murderous cravings. Other serial killers have targeted the physically handicapped.

• Race is another characteristic that can lead to being targeted by a serial killer. In 2 percent of cases, race is the primary reason for being victimized. White racist killers like Joseph Paul Franklin and Richard Clarey randomly targeted African American males. The De Mau Mau gang consisted of African American males who targeted solely white victims. Other serial killers prefer to prey upon their own race.

• Where a victim lives is the primary criterion in 2 percent of cases of serial killers. The homeless have been repeatedly been victimized by men such as Charles Sears, Vaughn Greenwood, and Bobby Joe Maxwell. Calvin Perry, Henry Lee Moore, and Sylvester Mofokeng of South Africa based their victim selection on the location of their victim's residence.

• A victim's occupation is the primary concern in only 1 percent of serial killings. Prostitutes are specifically targeted, as are topless dancers and female college students. Victims targeted by occupation are overwhelmingly female, although male prostitutes are just as likely to be targeted by these serial killers.

Just as victims of serial killers share certain traits, the serial killers themselves also share certain traits. The majority of serial killers are heterosexual white males.

Worldwide Serial Killer Sexual Characteristics

Sexual Preference	Number of Cases	Sexual Preference	Number of Cases
Heterosexual	973	Bisexual	19
Pedophiles	85	Homosexual	48
Undetermined	127		

Source: Preliminary data, K. Egger, 1999.

Over half of all serial killers use manual means to kill their victims, who are strangled, beaten, and stabbed. The lack of a weapon does not stop these killers. Others murder their victims with any available weapon; slightly more than 20 percent of the time, victims are killed by a handgun.

All of the statistics and the research on the kinds of people serial killers select for targets and where they hunt do not answer the question that is most immediate for most of us: How do we avoid becoming the victim of a predatory serial killer?

The simplest answer is to avoid being out alone in parking lots, malls, public parks, and the other usual hunting grounds of the serial killer. We need to be aware, at all times, that there is a legitimate threat out there, not only from serial killers, but from other predators, such as rapists, pedophiles, and robbers. We also need to be aware that our home is not a sanctuary but is another common target of predators and of a growing number of serial killers. Home invasions have increased over the past decade as a way of satisfying the serial killers' needs. And above all, we need to keep in mind that although the "less-dead" are the most common targets of a serial killer, more and more serial killers are targeting mainstream victims.

But the best answer to the question is simply to cease creating these monsters so that succeeding generations do not have to deal with them. How do we do this? We need to ensure the safety of all children, not only from outsiders but from their own families as well. We have seen that children are especially vulnerable to the murderous desires of a parent. We as a society need to recognize that children deserve special protection from physical, emotional, and sexual abuse by adults, including their parents. We need to remember that serial killers were once children who needed protection, help, and comfort and didn't get it.

If we want to avoid victimization, we need to protect the next generation from being victimized. We can do that by providing economic, academic, and social support for all children, regardless of their socioeconomic standing.

We also need to be aware of the social environment in which our children are growing up. We need to take an honest look at the popular culture of our modern society and the role that it plays in the embryonic serial killer's development.

CHAPTER 5

Serial Murder As a Growth Industry: A Brief Analysis

It's something you can't get anywhere else. I mean if you like the truth, if you like something a little different, a little bit more fresh, a little bit more bloody, well we got the meat.

> —Hart Fisher, author and artist of the comic book *Jeffrey Dahmer: An Unauthorized Biography of a Serial Killer,* discussing the popularity of his comic book (CNN, 1993)

Serial murder is important to the press, the electronic media, screen writers, and movie producers, as well as to comic book artists. It sells newspapers and books and draws viewers to TV screens and movie theaters. The media have played a role in the public's understanding of and continued interest in serial killers and their victims since the time of Jack the Ripper (Caputi, 1987). The true-crime section of most large bookstore chains is always kept well stocked by the publishers of this genre. True crime sells books. In effect, the media spend a great deal of resources in glorifying the serial killer.

Not all members of the media continue to glorify the killer and devalue the victims. True-crime writers such as Gary King, Jack Olsen, and the team of Thomas Guillen and Carlton Smith provide a different and more balanced approach. King pointed out in an essay some of the deficiencies of other writers and the devastating consequences of sanitizing accounts of serial murderers. Olsen strives for accuracy while creating for the reader a good "feel" for the time and place of the serial killer's crimes. These two authors convey to their readers the reality of the serial killer's work and the nightmare that the victims and their families must endure. In addition, authors Guillen and Smith provide the reader with a very detailed account of the procedure of the investigation of the so-called Green River Killer.

Published accounts of violence have existed in the publishing world since the beginning of the industry. The public appetite for detailed accounts of crime sells. True accounts of serial murder have a seemingly endless audience of readers, and that popularity carries over into fictionalized accounts of serial murder as well. Gary King, the author of several true-crime books, has openly criticized the sloppiness of his fellow writers. His perception is that during the writing process the serial killer has been elevated to "hero" status. He further argues that the tendency of writers to sanitize the serial killer and his crimes does a disservice not only to readers, but to the survivors as well. It also minimizes the horrible acts committed by the serial killer against his defenseless victims and against the larger society. King's *Driven to Kill* is a nightmarish look into the case of Westley Alan Dodd's murders. King includes portions of Dodd's diary so that the reader can accurately gauge the merciless state of mind of this serial killer. The current trend in true-crime writing is, however, weighted against the opinions of Mr. King.

Many theorists of serial murder believe these killers' reason for killing is to achieve a sense of power over their victims. In effect, the serial killer's search for power receives an intensified and additional fulfillment through the mass media's celebration of his horrific acts. This fulfillment through celebrity continues with a sensationalized criminal trial in which the killer's attorney invariably attempts to show that the killer was insane at the time of his killings. Subsequent fame or, more correctly, notoriety builds through television movies of his life and his crimes. Much earlier in this transformation process from an evil and deranged killer to celebrated antihero, the instant true-crime paperback, providing the reader with graphic descriptions of the serial killer's crimes, can be found on the "just published" shelves of major bookstore chains across the country. Serial killers thus achieve renown by being celebrated by the media and true-crime writers. It appears that more and more men and women are becoming students of the darker side of the soul, and that the exploits of serial killers exert a singular power and fascination that attracts us like an addiction, never to be satisfied. Unfortunately, fodder for such fascination continues to be forthcoming in our society.

In media reporting of a possible serial murder, one of the first things journalists ask is whether a profile has been done on the killer. Most fictional accounts include either an FBI agent or a local psychiatrist who develops a profile of the serial killer. Police procedurals and more elaborate murder mysteries are now being written in a formulaic format requiring that when a serial murder is suspected, a profiler better appear somewhere in the first seventy pages of the novel. Unfortunately, these fictional accounts are far from the reality of a serial homicide. In the first place, a series of murders may run to double digits before someone begins to suspect that all these murders were committed by the same killer. Second, when multiple agencies are involved, it normally takes time to for these agencies to agree to work together on the homicides. If multiple law enforcement jurisdictions are involved, friction among agencies is almost always the case. For the novel to be closer to reality, the author would allow the killer to kill with impunity because of this mobility, or to kill in different jurisdictions. Further, a forensic profiler would appear later in the story, when the profile might or might not assist the detectives in identifying the serial killer.

The continual rise in the violent content of television since the 1950s has prompted comment by former attorney general Janet Reno. Ms. Reno, speaking before a Senate committee in 1997, suggested that if the television networks were unwilling to "police" themselves, perhaps the government should step in. This caused a great commotion in the television industry. The attorney general's comments were decried as attacks on the First Amendment rights of the artistic community, and they drew promises by industry leaders to oversee themselves. To date, this has occurred in only limited measure.

The existence of a market for television programming containing high levels of violence is evident in any program guide for any given week. Serial murder has become popular fare for television viewers, and hardly a month goes by without a made-for-television movie about the subject.

Television has been quick to create miniseries or docudramas about violent crimes and biographies of serial killers. Ted Bundy, John Wayne Gacy, Wayne Williams, and Aileen Wuornos have all found themselves the subject of these television programs. Big-name stars are often enlisted to play the serial killer: Mark Harman played Bundy, Brian Dennehy played Gacy, and Jean Smart played Wuornos. In contrast, the victims in these television programs are usually played by forgettable actors or actresses because the "star" of the program is, in fact, the serial killer.

The television news media have also followed this trend. In 1993 CNN produced a special report on serial murder, over the course of two hours introducing the serial killer to the American viewing public. The likes of Donald Harvey, Christine Falling, and Westley Alan Dodd recounted their crimes, with veiled references to their motives. Although this special was informative and thoughtfully done, it offered no answers, and those that may have been offered were lost on the cutting-room floor.

Any suspected case of serial murder immediately finds its way into the living rooms of thousands and sometimes millions of viewers. The more heinous the crime, the greater the interest taken by the media, and the more the public clamors to hear details. And in many cases, serial murder falls into the news media category "If it bleeds, it leads."

When asked why Hollywood is infatuated with the genre of serial murder, DreamWorks marketing chief Terry Press replied, "It's not just Hollywood. People everywhere are intrigued by them [serial killers]. There is, frankly, a morbid fascination with people who carry out multiple murders. It's more than horrific. You get into the psychology of Why?" (Broeske, 1998, p. 1). When serial killers are considered by the general public, the question is always, "Why?" People are fascinated with determining the reasons for these horrific killings. They are not satisfied with the mere presence of a serial killer in a fictional thriller or a movie. They want to be able to understand why these people kill, and kill, and kill again. They are entertained by the media's glorification of the killer's violence.

In a *Time* magazine article entitled "I Deserve Punishment," the reporter pointed out the media role in the glorification of violence and the serial killer:

In a society increasingly fascinated with violent crime, the Ted Bundy story captured the public imagination. Five books and a television mini-series were produced about the boy-next-door killer. With network-TV broadcasts of the murderer's last interview and scenes of crowds gathered outside the penitentiary, even his execution became a media circus. Whether Bundy intended it or not, his final encounter with death renewed his nightmarish grip on the nation's attention. (*Time*, July 7, 1989)

But the roots of the glorification process are deeply ingrained in the American psyche. The United States has long made legends of outlaws. American history is full of the folklore of killers. Many of the so-called heroes of yesteryear, including the lawmen and guinslingers of the old West, would fit the modern definition of serial killer. The legends of Wyatt Earp, Billy the Kid, and Butch Cassidy and the Sundance Kid all contribute to this mystique. One of the key elements of the personality of the serial killer appears to be that he kills for an intrinsic motive. Simply, he enjoys killing. Many of the "heroes" of the West displayed this trait. All forms of the media have contributed to this portrayal of serial killers as clever, daring, sexy, and elusive. Folklore has romanticized Bonnie and Clyde, Al Capone, and John Dillinger in stereotypical portrayals repeated in account after account and film after film, while the American public passsively takes it all in. This is in contrast to the portrayal of the victims of serial killers, who are glossed over in broad strokes as hapless, one-dimensional characters of little or no value or interest.

Serial killer films also provide a cautionary tale, warning the viewer to beware, despite the very low probability that viewers will ever encounter a serial killer. Michael Gingold, managing editor of *Fangoria,* notes: "These killers are in the public consciousness. . . . When you see a movie where Freddy Krueger is coming at teenagers in their dreams, you don't really think it can happen. But with serial killers, there is this 'this thing could happen to me'" (p. 1). The movie industry exploits the public's fascination with the serial killer as well as the public's fear of these killers. While we must remember that movies are meant to entertain, it does not seem a worthy goal of this industry to place fear in the viewing public. Nevertheless, in many instances this occurs.

For the moment, we need to forget the psychological reasons for these films. The real motive is money. These films make big money. *The Silence of the Lambs* grossed $130 million in its U.S. theatrical release and won five Oscars, including Best Picture. Given the financial success of this film, other profit-makers followed. *Scream,* released in 1996, grossed $103 million domestically. A sequel grossed $96 million.

But it was really *Silence of the Lambs* that made serial killing at the movie houses respectable. The film established almost a formula for success. According to the formula, we have reprehensible killings. Forensic experts discuss these crimes without a great deal of graphic photography (just enough!). The killer is pursued. The villain or villainess is complicated and sexually twisted. The investigator is usually, but not always, with the FBI. And frequently a bonding is shown between the villain and the hero or the villain and the intended victims (Broeske, 1998). Such a formula led to *Basic Instinct* (1992), which grossed $118 million domestically, and *Seven* (1995), which grossed $100 million domestically. *Hannibal,* a sequel to *Silence of the Lambs* showing in theaters internationally in early 2001, appears to be following this successful and profitable formula.

In commenting on *Silence of the Lambs,* David Canter, a pioneer profiler in England, has noted the way in which the myth of the serial killer is generated:

> The character of Hannibal Lecter, the gruesome and brilliant multiple murderer created by the novelist Thomas Harris and interviewed [in the film] by a novice FBI agent, draws on the interviews that were conducted by real FBI agents with murderers and rapists, but the fictional creation has as much to do with reality as the fictional Dr. Jekyll and Mr. Hyde of a previous century. (Canter, 1994, p. 65)

The selling of the modern-day serial killer to movie audiences is accomplished in several ways. One of the most important elements is the casting of the actor who plays the killer. Casting Sir Anthony Hopkins in the role of Dr. Lecter in *Silence of the Lambs* brought strength, humor, intelligence, and a certain amount of sympathy to the character. Brad Pitt, playing the role of the serial killer in *Kalifornia,* brought sheer sexiness to the film. This strategy not only brings in the audience; it also automatically makes the serial killer the hero in the audience's eyes. No matter how many murders this "hero" has committed, he is forgiven because of the impact the actor has on perception of the character. This pattern has existed in films since the first sympathetic portrayal of the tortured soul of a vampire or a werewolf.

These "heroes" are in reality the sociopaths or psychopaths of our century. Dr. Park Dietz, a psychiatrist specializing in criminal psychiatry, points out that we as a society could not be doing more to create sociopathic individuals.

> We are doing everything we can to manufacture them. We have a society that does what it can to prevent the development of conscience, to prevent the development of morals, to link sexuality with violence. . . . I literally can't imagine a better way to produce such people than to use the formula that is used in a large number of films today. Of having a scene that arouses every red-blooded American boy and then mutilating the woman. (CNN Special Reports, 1993)

Television viewers are constantly bombarded with true-crime as well as fictional accounts of serial killers. The accuracy of the true accounts is always questionable, because a great deal of information about the serial killer and his victims must be presented within half-hour or hour-long formats—allowing, of course, time for commercial messages. We no longer have public executions or flayings, but we have macabre and extremely violent films, such as *The Texas Chain Saw Massacre* or *Natural Born Killers* (I walked out after the first four minutes of this film, which depicts six or seven horrible slayings in the same amount of time). It may be, for those who would pay to view a public execution or a private showing of a "snuff flick," that viewing fictional accounts of serial killers on the big screen, or television news reports consisting of pictures of crime scenes and recitations of police accounts of horrific acts, may satisfy the thirst for suspense, entertainment, or thrills that for many is lacking in the single-murder fictional whodunit or the drive-by shooting in our urban slums. And after the credits roll across the screen or the crime scene fades to a commercial, viewers are left with the warm feeling of being survivors.

The development of the serial killer as hero, or more correctly as antihero, involves the public's desensitization to violence and devaluation of serial killers' victims. Extremes become less and less extreme, filmmakers seek out ever-increasing levels of violence, and the desensitization process continues. This cycle of violence is maintained for one reason: profits. In many ways, many of the box office receipts collected in the last twenty years can be considered blood money. When true-crime writer Jack Olsen was asked if this pattern would ever change, he responded: "Maybe it would be nice if we did that. But when did anyone in America ever do anything nice when it would cost them money?" (*CNN Special Reports*, 1993).

Serial Killers in the Arts and Music

The serial killer has also become a hero in our art and our music. Artists have long chronicled the darker side of human nature. The serial killer with some artistic talent can also find an audience for his work. For example, John Wayne Gacy's paintings received a special showing. However, the recent creation of serial-killer collector cards and comic books has struck a new low in the art world. Sadly, there is a market for these pieces of "art."

The American market for this kind of art appears to reflect a darkness in the country's soul. This darkness is apparently growing if the recent trend in pop culture and film is any indication. The comic-book presentation of the killings of Jeffrey Dahmer, for instance, completely disregards the lives of the victims and the continuing ramifications faced by the survivors. Response to that darkness will continue to be carefully and thoughtfully packaged by the artistic community as long as it is popular in the marketplace.

Music is another medium that exploits the development and glorification of heroic qualities in the serial killer. The Beatles wrote a song about Bobby Maxwell, suspected of killing ten homeless men in the Los Angeles area in the late 1970s, called "Maxwell's Silver Hammer." Charles Manson used the Beatles' song "Helter Skelter" as part of a twisted rationalization for his crimes. Warren Zevon wrote the song "Excitable Boy" parodying the murder and dismemberment of the subject's girlfriend, an act reportedly inspired by the crimes of serial killer Edmund Kemper. The Alice Cooper band devoted an entire album, called *Killer*, to murder. The rock group The Police included a song titled "Murder by Number" on one of their most popular albums. While music is hardly the sole causal factor in the process of depersonalizing violence, it does reinforce the message that the victim, or any individual, is irrelevant, and that the serial killer is somehow a hero, daring enough to stand up to "the system."

Serial Killers in News Reporting

For some, violence and the mass media feed off one another. The psychiatrist Park Dietz stated, "The psycho killer public relations industry depends on real offenders for its fodder, and the real offenders draw ideas, inspiration and hope of historical importance from their pubic relations industry" (CNN, 1993). Unfortunately, such a public relations industry expends most of its resources concentrating on the offender, and little time is left to remember the victims. Whether in news reporting or in fictional stories, the victims are all but ignored except to tally their number. Frequently, news reporting provides horrific detail of a serial killer's acts without acknowledging that the victims were human beings. It is as if we have forgotten or do not want to be reminded that the victims were mothers, fathers, daughters, or sons who were loved and cherished by their families.

As discussed more fully in Chapter 14, one of the major problems in the investigation of a serial murder can be the adversarial nature of the relations between the media and law enforcement during such an investigation. Competition among media for press and television news coverage can be very disruptive to the investigation. Reporters often want all their questions answered by investigators, not recognizing that some information must be held back to protect the integrity of the investigation and the rights of the suspect to receive a fair trial. It would seem that some reporters are not aware of the reasons that information is being held back and in other instances don't necessarily care. They just want their story and their byline in what is frequently a very competitive field.

Marsh (1989), in his content analysis of newspaper crime coverage in the United States from 1893 to 1988, provides a number of findings related to journalists' coverage of serial killers. On page 511, for example, he notes:

- The vast majority of crime coverage by newspapers relates to violent and sensational crimes.
- Because newspaper reporting overemphasizes violent crimes and at the same time fails to address adequately either personal risk or prevention techniques, some people's fears of victimization become exaggerated.

In other words, reporting of crime, in particular serial murder, does not generally reflect an accurate picture of this phenomenon in society. Serial murder headlines in newspapers or lead-ins to television news programs attract readers and audiences. They don't inform. If news stories were to inform, they would identify the very low probability of the general public's encounter with a serial killer. Crime reporters would emphasize the fact that serial murderers are responsible for only a very small percentage of all the homicides committed in this country every year. Unfortunately, such information, if reported by journalists, receives very little or no column space or airtime in most news reports.

It should also be noted that the reporters themselves may become instant celebrities when they "break" a particularly abhorrent or outrageous crime story. Fisher (1997) notes an account by Ann Schwartz of the *Milwaukee Journal*, who broke the Jeffrey Dahmer story:

> As the news spread, the paper received calls from around the country. We found our stories all over the world, and they ran in the *Los Angeles Times*, the *New York*

Times, and the *International Herald Tribune.* We saw our bylines in French, Spanish, and German. Reporters from out of town papers called the newsroom and spoke to whoever picked up the phone, as if he or she were an expert on the case. If you worked for the *Journal* you must know something about Jeffrey Dahmer.

"Who wants to do *Larry King*?" a secretary yelled out. Reporters lunged for their phones. We got calls from *People* magazine, a producer from *Geraldo,* a Canadian talk show, and a publishing company looking for someone to write a book in a month. (p. 23)

It should also be noted that journalists who have reported on a serial killer story frequently go on to write a true-crime book on the killer. Unfortunately, in many cases the pressure to get these books to press quickly often means that they are full of erroneous information.

"Mutants from Hell"

It is self-serving, though comforting, to think of serial killers as different from us. We think, "They are different, and that must be why they do what they do. It's certainly not something we could do!" Such thoughts are, however, fallacious. These so-called monsters, these "mutants from hell," may actually exhibit very human life forces rather than the diabolical and mysterious riddles of unique, atavistic creatures. They terrify us not because they are from hell, but rather because they are extreme examples of the potential of humankind.

Serial killers often long for recognition and an end to their tormenting nightmares of childhood. In many instances, a serial killer who has been caught and who has confessed has rarely been given attention prior to his apprehension. Most serial killers who have confessed to the police thoroughly enjoy the attention they receive from the police, and especially from the news media, now clamoring to interview them and write their story. This is why so many of these killers are willing to grant interviews to the press. In addition, an interview with a journalist frequently means there is a book deal somewhere in the near future. And since society hungers for insight into a serial killer's life—a description of his handiwork and the splatter of blood—true-crime books continue to enjoy a strong market in our society.

The Profile That Isn't

Like any news medium, television news reporting provides its viewers with summaries of facts, theories, concepts, and situations. Reporters are constantly striving to simplify and provide brief explanations to complex problems whether they're reporting on the Bosnian war or on a serial murderer. These reporters have a limited amount of airtime to make their point before the next story or commercial, and their reporting is structured within this framework.

Television reporters and to some extent newspaper journalists are infatuated with the term "profile." To them, the term "profile" belongs in any reporting of crime where the criminal is yet to be arrested. A "profile" means a summary about the offender for the public. It includes criminological research on why these people commit such crimes. It is shorthand for the criminal's background, his motivation, the type of victims he selects, and how the police will eventually catch him. Experts who shy away from using this shorthand receive little attention. They take too long to answer reporters' questions and generally don't have all the answers. Reporters want answers, and they want them to be simple and straightforward.

The problem with this simplistic approach by the mass media is that there are no simple answers, and even complicated answers frequently provide only a partial picture. Also, many of the answers are no more than someone's theory about a person's motives or the reason something happened. Although reporters may treat these theories as fact, it must be remembered that they are only someone's opinion. And opinions are frequently wrong.

Sound-Bite Answers

Not only do reporters and journalists want profiles that are easily understood by their readers or audience; they want them to sound nice. They want comments that are slick and polished, that provide wide appeal. The thirty-second sound bite is what the mass media are constantly seeking. If it's good enough, it can be used to advertise the upcoming story and give the reporter more airtime and exposure. For the television reporter or journalist, a good sound bite means that his or her career is on an upward swing.

Reporters seek out experts on serial murder in order to ask them questions. They expect these experts to provide simple and understandable answers to what are frequently complex questions. For instance, when a reporter asks a researcher why serial murderers continue to kill, the researcher is hard pressed to come up with a short, simple answer. He or she may respond that serial killers kill for a variety of reasons relating to the killer's childhood and background and may begin to describe different backgrounds and different childhoods. The researcher may add that criminologists and forensic experts do not yet have all the answers to the motivation of the serial killer. But this is not the type of response the reporter is seeking. If, on the other hand, the researcher responds by saying that these serial killers have become "addicted to their killings," and that this is why they continue to kill, the reporter has a satisfying sound-bite answer. Such an answer may sound great on the evening news, but it provides very little in the way of an adequate explanation of serial murder.

The FBI and Serial Murder Mythology

The FBI, a large, bureaucratic mechanism, tends to function as a monopolist organization when it comes to serial murder. Notwithstanding the fact that only a small number of FBI agents have ever conducted a homicide investigation, the FBI is portrayed by much of the press and electronic media as the experts on the phenomenon of serial murder, and as the central police force tracking and arresting these killers all over the United States. Many true-crime books feature FBI agents hunting down the serial killer or providing uncanny and extremely accurate psychological profiles of the killer for the local police. This myth is perpetuated by media promotion of individual technocrats skilled in psychological profiling or of expert crime analysts poring over crime reports at the Behavioral Science Unit of the Bureau in Quantico.

Crime journalists have become so well versed in FBI mythology that their questions focus on the point in time that the FBI experts are called into the case. Sometimes reporters do not understand why the FBI is not initially involved in a serial murder investigation. They buy into the myth described in Chapter 1 that since some serial killers cross state lines, the FBI has jurisdiction over all serial murder investigations. It frequently takes a great deal of time and effort to convince these reporters that the local law enforcement agency has jurisdiction over the investigation of a serial murder. Although it is true that the FBI frequently assists local law enforcement agencies in a serial murder investigation, serial murder is still a local problem, to be dealt with by local authorities.

As implied earlier, media manipulation and the resulting media perception that FBI agents are experts in homicide, and more specifically serial murder, investigation builds a large base of power for the Bureau. Such a power base forces the media focus in any major homicide investigation away from local law enforcement agencies to the FBI agents assisting those who, day to day and hour to hour, actually conduct the investigation.

This power base also means that any writer interested in developing a crime novel or true-crime story of a serial killer will seek assistance from the experts at the FBI. This can be seen in the recent work of David Lindsey *(Mercy)*, Thomas Harris *(Silence of the Lambs)*, and Patricia Cornwell *(Body Farm)*. These works, all best-sellers, provide advocacy for the false notion that FBI agents investigate homicides. For someone to question this fallacious assertion is to bring the equally fallacious retort from any layperson that if the victims are killed in different states, the FBI takes over jurisdictional authority.

The FBI does little to disabuse the public of this mythology. To do so would call the cost-effectiveness of the FBI into question and refocus media attention on the more accurate target of local law enforcement's effectiveness or ineffectiveness in identifying and apprehending the serial murderer.

Thus, FBI agents continue to ride the wave of publicity that surrounds a serial murder investigation. These agents speak as experts to the media, even though their knowledge may be based solely on a training bulletin from the FBI Academy. Some of these agents have even had the audacity to characterize the movie *Silence of the Lambs* as an accurate portrayal of a typical FBI investigation into a serial murder.

A Violent Culture

American culture as a whole has cultivated a taste for violence that seems to be insatiable. We are a people obsessed with violence, and consequently our entertainment industry is driven by such violence. The violence of our contemporary popular culture, reflected in movies, television programs, magazines, and books of fact or fiction, has made the shocking reality of this violence seem a routine risk that we all face. Our own sense of humanity is anesthetized, almost to the point of unconsciousness. We sit in front of the television set and obliterate our sensitivity to the humanity of the serial killer's victims. Instead, we desire to learn more about the killer. The killer becomes our total focus.

In the same way, we want to hear or read about the torture and mutilation deaths of female victims almost as if such acts were an art form. The serial killer becomes an artist, in some cases performing a reverse type of sculpture by taking the lives of his victims with a sharp knife. Pick up a paperback mystery or a police procedural. Many that sell are about the hunt for a serial killer. We as a society enjoy serial killing, albeit vicariously.

Elliott Leyton, a wise observer of cultures, stated: "If we were charged with the responsibility for designing a society in which all structural and cultural mechanisms leaned toward the creation of the killers of strangers, we could do no better than to present the purchaser with the shape of modern America" (Leyton, 1986, p. 295).

PART II

CASE STUDIES OF SERIAL KILLERS

To acquire information on serial murderers, I used a case study approach. Case studies are generally the preferred strategy when questions of *how* and *why* are being posed, when relevant behaviors cannot be manipulated, and when we are trying to understand a complex social phenomenon (Yin, 1984).

Case studies of criminals are common in the psychological literature and have a long history (see Abrahamsen, 1973; Bjerre, 1927; Lunde, 1975; Wertham, 1949). Though less well known and with a briefer tradition, past criminological/criminal justice literature does provide a precedent for the case study approach (Chambliss, 1972; Cressey, 1932; Klockars, 1974; Shaw, 1930; Sutherland, 1937). The research conducted for the case studies presented in this volume differs in two respects from earlier criminological/criminal justice research. First, the earlier research dealt with what might be considered quasi-natural behavior—with serial murder as an idiopathic, psychopathological phenomenon. In other words, the origin or cause of the behavior was thought to be unknown. Second, and more important, the earlier research focused primarily on etiological concerns as opposed to questions of crime control or the administration and operation of such control. In this book, by contrast, case study methodology is used in a somewhat modified form, and for an applied purpose.

Investigating serial murder through this case study approach has involved an exploratory effort concerned primarily with describing the serial killer and verifying the description through various data sources. Selected case studies of serial murderers have been provided as examples for the reader.

A multiple-case (embedded) research design was used. Seven cases were selected for documentation and analysis. External validity is frequently cited by critics as a major problem for case studies because they offer a poor basis for generalization. However, case study research does not rely on the statistical

111

generalization of samples to the entire population (as in survey research) but, rather, on the analytical generalization of a set of results to some broader theory. Further, as Katz (1982) argues, "Statistical evidence of representativeness depends on restricting a depiction of qualitative richness in the experience of the people studied" (p. 139).

The multiple-case design used a replication logic rather than a sampling logic: Each case was not a "sample" of the total phenomenon. Such a universe has yet to be defined, and it is not the objective of a case study to assess the incidence or prevalence of a phenomenon. Each case that I documented and analyzed served as a separate exploration into the phenomenon of serial murder. Yin (1984), in discussing multiple-case studies, suggests that in following a replication logic, "a major insight is to consider multiple cases as one would consider multiple experiments" (p. 48). However, it must be emphasized that this research design is not causal or predictive, as is the case with classic experimental studies; rather, it is exploratory and developmental.

Selected Cases

My decision to select the cases of seven serial murderers for documentation and analysis was based on four criteria: (1) ease of access to information, (2) currency of the murderer's arrest or conviction, (3) geographical representativeness, and (4) the murderer's mobility. First, the fact that a great deal had been written about a murderer or case was a significant factor in data collection. Second, the fact that the arrest and/or conviction of the murderer had occurred within recent history was important to the relevance of subsequent conclusions and recommendations of the study. Third, the different geographical areas of the country in which the murderers operated constituted a significant factor in determining whether differences in "linkage blindness" varied by region. Fourth, it was important to include both "megastat" (killing over time in a single area) and "megamobile" (killing in different geographic areas) serial murderers within the sample because they appear to be two different types of serial killers.

The serial murderers selected for case study were as follows:

1. John Wayne Gacy
2. Henry Lee Lucas
3. Kenneth Bianchi and Angelo Buono Jr.
4. Theodore Robert Bundy
5. Jerry Marcus
6. Joseph Miller
7. Jeffrey Dahmer

A protocol, or guide, for conducting each case study facilitated between-case comparisons. This guide was organized according to Gibbons's (1965) dimensional categories developed for role-career typological research. However, for the purposes of this volume, modifications to these categories were made to better fit serial murder case study research. The dimension of "role career" was eliminated. "Recall of events" (by the murderer) was added to the dimensions because a preliminary review of the cases revealed that serial murderers apparently have unusually acute memories. Each dimensional category was considered to be self-defining by means of its category label or in traditional social science terminology. The following schematic was used as a guide in collecting data on each case study:

DIMENSIONS
1. Social environment
2. Family background
3. Peer group associations and personal relationships
4. Contact with defining agencies
5. Offense behavior
6. Self-concept
7. Attitudes
8. Recall of events

Part II concludes with the results of a cross-case analysis of the seven case studies. These are presented in Chapter 13.

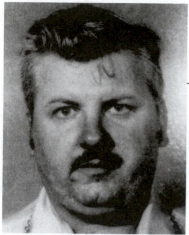

John Wayne Gacy (1978 photo).
© *Associated Press AP.*

CHAPTER 6

John Wayne Gacy

— A CASE STUDY

As I walked into death row in Menard Penitentiary, John Wayne Gacy began spitting out a long stream of profanity at me between the bars. His utterance became almost a scream as it ended with "expert!" I turned to face the man I had read about and written about but never met. My answer to him was straightforward, "No, John I'm not the expert. You are the expert. An expert serial killer." From the other cells came laughter and catcalls. It seemed not even the condemned liked a serial killer.

—Author's notes, Menard Penitentiary, Illinois, April 14, 1993

Social Environment

John Gacy grew up in a working-class neighborhood on the northwest side of Chicago. Little is known about his childhood. By the end of grade school he reportedly daydreamed a lot and was resistant to his teachers. His sister described him as a normal person, like everyone else. The only unusual thing she could recall about her brother's younger years was that he occasionally had blackouts. The problem, she said, was diagnosed when he was sixteen years old as a blood clot on the brain, which was thought to have resulted from a playground accident five years earlier. Gacy was treated and apparently cured (*New York Times*, January 10, 1979, p. 14).

However, episodic blackouts continued into Gacy's adult life. He sometimes complained of shortness of breath and pains in his chest. His childhood problem had been diagnosed as syncope, a brief loss of consciousness caused by transient

115

anemia, leading to probable psychomotor epilepsy later on. Once, after a seizure, he was hurriedly given the last rites by a priest. But the cause of his malady was never determined with certainty, and his friends tended to regard it as heart trouble.

Gacy was always interested in being a police officer. In fact, he often played policeman as a boy.

Gacy attended a vocational high school, where he took business courses. His grades ranged from good to excellent. He was enamored of uniforms, according to his brother-in-law. Both his sisters stated he was active in a civil defense organization that enabled him to go to accidents and fires with a flashing blue light on his car. Then he transferred to another vocational high school. After two months he dropped out of school and moved to Las Vegas, Nevada, where he worked for a brief time for a mortuary before returning to Chicago.

He worked for a shoe company in Chicago and in 1964 was transferred to Springfield, Illinois, to manage the company's retail clothing store. In 1966 he moved to Waterloo, Iowa, to manage three fried chicken restaurant franchises, which were owned by his father-in-law. His father-in-law reportedly considered him a "braggart and a liar" but encouraged the move so that his daughter and grandson would be nearby (Sullivan & Maiken, 1983, p. 261). Gacy's falsified resume at the time indicated that he had managed several stores in Springfield, Illinois, and that he held a college degree in accounting and business.

In Waterloo, Gacy was active in the Junior Chamber of Commerce (Jaycees). He recruited many new members and served as chaplain for the organization. After the local paper referred to him as "Colonel" in a story about his organizational activities, Gacy liked to be called "Colonel."

Gacy frequented the bar at a local motel and a Waterloo nightspot that featured strippers. According to his friends, he constantly bragged about his sexual prowess with women. Yet Gacy never showed any affection toward his wife in public and on several occasions reportedly offered her as a sexual favor to other men in return for their performing fellatio on him.

Gacy's wife described him as a "police freak" (Sullivan & Maiken, 1983, p. 263). He had an intense curiosity about emergency vehicles, which he sometimes followed at high speeds with his portable red light flashing. He liked to be known as having influence with the police; in fact, several times a month he would take free fried chicken to local police and firemen.

Upon his release from prison in Iowa, where he had been sent for sodomy with a juvenile, in 1970, Gacy returned to Chicago to live with his mother in an apartment on the northwest side of the city. Through a family friend, he got a job as a cook in a downtown Chicago restaurant that was a gathering spot for city policemen and politicians. It was here that he met Chicago policeman James Hanley, whose name Gacy later modified as his street alias. Gacy briefly dated a waitress from the restaurant but was soon seen associating with homosexuals.

Four months after his return to Chicago, Gacy reportedly borrowed money from his mother and bought a house in Norwood Park Township, an unincorporated area northwest of Chicago. Shortly thereafter he formed his own construction company, which he operated out of his home; the company specialized in remodeling work at retail stores and subcontracting work on larger construction projects.

During this time, Gacy was active in politics in the Chicago area. For example, he was a Democratic party precinct captain in the township. In 1976 he organized a fund-raiser for President Carter's reelection campaign; the event was attended by over five hundred people. Gacy was also involved in organizing the annual Polish Constitution Day Parade in Chicago. His second wife subsequently stated she felt that Gacy often used his local political involvement to buy his way out of trouble.

Gacy's neighbors described him as a likable man who frequently volunteered to perform as a clown for children at charitable events. One neighbor stated that he seemed short-tempered at times and that he often threw large parties. His former baby-sitter said many people, mostly teenagers who worked with him, were "always going in and out of the house" (*New York Times*, December 3, 1978, p. 11). The head of the Norwood Park Democratic organization stated:

> The John Gacy I'm reading about in the newspapers is not the same John Gacy I knew. He was always available for any job: washing windows, setting up chairs for meetings, playing clown for the kids at picnics and Christmas parties, even fixing somebody's leaky faucet or rehanging a crooked door. I don't know anyone who didn't like him. (*Newsweek,* January 8, 1979, p. 24)

Gacy was characterized by many as a civic-minded building contractor. He claimed he had made $200,000 a year prior to his arrest in 1978 for murder. He was known as an excellent cook but as an untalented construction worker.

Gacy was described by those who employed him as a very gregarious man who put a lot of energy into getting the job done. He was obsessed about keeping track of his time and kept notebooks that recorded what he did minute by minute, even logging such trivia as the precise moment he mailed a letter (Berger, 1984). He kept an extremely neat and clean house, even doing his own housekeeping.

He stated that he began dating at age sixteen and had his first experience with sexual intercourse at age eighteen. He claimed that his first homosexual experience occurred after his first wife's pregnancy, when, he said, he got drunk with a friend who then performed fellatio on him. Gacy told his second wife in 1972 that he was bisexual, but she was convinced that he was rapidly becoming homosexual. Less than two years after they were married, Gacy announced to her on Mother's Day that this occasion would be their last to have sex together. It was. His wife stated later that she frequently found her bikini underpants in the garage. Gacy had begun bringing young men to the garage late at night, sometimes spending hours there with them (Sullivan & Maiken, 1983, p. 73).

Family Background

John Wayne Gacy was born on March 17, 1942, at Edgewater Hospital in Chicago, Illinois. His parents, John and Marian Gacy, were both factory workers. He grew up in a working-class neighborhood in northwest Chicago. He had two sisters, one two years older and one two years younger.

He was reportedly strongly influenced by his mother. When he was a newborn, she gave him daily enemas for no apparent reason (Berger, 1984). After she found a bag full of her underpants under the porch where John played, she made him wear a pair of her underpants to embarrass him. When his father learned of this, he whipped John with a leather strap.

Although Gacy was reportedly a hard worker, he rarely succeeded in pleasing his father. When he failed to meet his father's standards, his father called him stupid. His father was of Polish ancestry, a hard worker, a perfectionist, a stern parent, and a good provider, according to Gacy's younger sister. Their father was also a drunkard who beat his wife and had a Jekyll and Hyde personality, according to his children. Apparently John's father got drunk almost every night. When Gacy tried to defend his mother against his father's beatings, his father called him a mama's boy or a sissy. His father reportedly never showed his own emotions, except once, when Gacy was sentenced to prison in Iowa on a sodomy conviction. At that time, his father cried.

Gacy left home during his second year of high school. Apparently his departure was prompted by a specific incident: His father, who had loaned him money to buy his first car, was tired of all John's driving around and removed the distributor cap. Gacy became angry, left home, and moved to Las Vegas, Nevada.

Later, after returning to Chicago in 1964 and being transferred to Springfield, Illinois, by his employer, a shoe company, he met a woman whom he dated for nine months and then married in 1965. The couple had a boy and then a girl. According to neighbors, Gacy was a loving and attentive father. In Springfield, he was viewed as a hard worker who was heavily involved in the Junior Chamber of Commerce.

Following Gacy's move with his family to Waterloo, Iowa, and his subsequent conviction for sodomy, his wife divorced him. After a divorce hearing in Waterloo in September 1969, he told prison friends that as far as he was concerned his children were dead. After returning to Chicago, Gacy tried to arrange visitation rights with his children. However, his former wife never answered his letters, so he told his mother to get rid of the pictures of his former wife and children and to consider them dead.

Gacy's father died on December 25, 1985, while Gacy was in prison in Chicago. In subsequent years he sometimes cried on Christmas Day, remembering his father. Gacy told a friend that prison officials had not informed him of his father's death until a month after it happened. He stated he was still very angry about that.

Gacy's sister commented that John was the sort of brother and son who could not do enough for his family, who stayed in close touch by telephone, and who visited once or twice a year. The family knew of his sodomy conviction in Iowa, she said, but considered it an incident in his life that he had paid for (*New York Times*, January 10, 1979, p. 14).

After purchasing the house in Norwood Park, Gacy moved there with his mother in 1971. According to a former employee of Gacy's, he, as well as several other men, lived with the Gacys in 1970 and 1971. The former employee admitted that he had slept in John Gacy's bedroom while living there.

In May 1971, Gacy became reacquainted with a high school girlfriend who had two children and was going through a divorce. They were married in July 1972, after Gacy's mother moved to an apartment. While his mother shared the house, Gacy reportedly didn't like her answering the telephone and talking to his potential business clients as "John's mother" (Sullivan & Maiken, 1983, p. 278). After his mother left, Gacy invited his wife's mother to move in with them. A year later, Gacy subsequently complained, he needed a court order to evict his mother-in-law. Gacy's relationship with his second wife deteriorated rapidly when, shortly after their marriage, he began to associate more and more with young boys. After he declared his bisexuality less than two years after their marriage and stated he would no longer have sex with her, Gacy and his wife lived separately in the same house. They were divorced on February 11, 1975. The next day, one of Gacy's male employees moved into the house. In Gacy's second interview with the police, he said he had been divorced twice and was now enjoying the single life.

Peer Group Associations and Personal Relationships

John Gacy was described as a good, friendly, and generous man by his neighbors in Norwood Park. At Christmas, Gacy gave his neighbors hams or baskets of fruit. He also showed genuine kindness toward their children. However, his boastful personality turned them away. They were invited to the huge parties he held but many chose not to attend. To some, it seemed that John Gacy was striving for a social status that he would never attain.

In Springfield, Illinois, Gacy was nominated by the local Junior Chamber of Commerce as "Man of the Year." In Waterloo, Iowa, where he had been convicted of sodomy in 1968, there was disagreement over Gacy. His friends said he was a real go-getter, did a good job, and was an excellent Jaycee. Others described him as a glad-hander type who showered people with affection as a way of getting more attention himself. A man who defeated Gacy for presidency of the local Junior Chamber of Commerce stated, "He was not a man tempered by truth. He seemed unaffected when caught in lies" (*New York Times*, January 10, 1976, p. 14).

An associate in the construction business characterized Gacy as a workaholic who talked a big line. One of his employees stated that a lot of Gacy's workers quit because "[t]hey don't like the aggravation. John is so much of a perfectionist, it gets to where he's nitpicking" (Sullivan & Maiken, 1983, p. 68). Moreover, Gacy developed a reputation among some of his associates, friends, and employees as a man who did not always tell the truth. An employee commented, "John is a funny person. He's a bit of a bragger, and he lives in a fantasy world. Now, how much is fact and how much is fiction is up to the individual to decide, but he claims that he does work for the syndicate. He's said he has set up people before" (Sullivan & Maiken, 1983, p. 70).

Gacy told the police, who had him under surveillance for murder, that he had attended bisexual parties and that he saw nothing wrong with what went on there.

He said that he thought people should do whatever they wanted as long as it didn't infringe on another person's rights and no force was used. However, he made it clear to the police on a number of occasions before and after his arrest that he was not a homosexual. After he was arrested, Gacy told police he had had his first sexual relationship with a man when he was twenty-two years old. Later, the police learned that members of the homosexual community thought Gacy was a policeman and a "chicken-hawk," that is, an older man who seeks out young men and boys.

An employee who lived with Gacy for two months stated that he had to sleep with his pants on because Gacy often entered the bedroom in the middle of the night and tried to have sex with him. On one occasion when Gacy and he were celebrating Gacy's birthday, John locked him in handcuffs to show him a trick. Gacy then stated, "The trick is you gotta have the key" (Sullivan & Maiken, 1983, p. 142). He then began to swing the man around the room on the handcuff chain. They fought, and the man ultimately recovered the key and freed himself.

On the day Gacy was arrested, he apparently knew he would soon be behind bars. He went to say good-bye to people he considered his friends. To a young man from whom he always bought gas he said, "We've been friends. You're like a brother—I can't take much more" (Sullivan & Maiken, 1983, p. 151). Gacy then slipped a bag of marijuana into the youth's pocket. To an employee he commented, "This may be the last time you'll ever see me" (p. 152). Gacy also bid good-bye to another employee and to his lawyer. Then he wanted to go to the cemetery to say good-bye to his father's grave. But Gacy was arrested before he got there.

Contact with Defining Agencies

John Gacy's first known contact with the criminal justice system occurred on May 2, 1968, in Waterloo, Iowa, when he was given a polygraph examination by the police in response to accusations brought by two young boys who stated he had sexually assaulted them. The polygraph examiner found indications of deception in the tests, although Gacy continued to deny any guilt. He was indicted by a grand jury later that month. In July 1968, he took another polygraph examination, with the same results, after which he admitted having had homosexual relationships with one of the boys but claimed that he had paid the boy.

In September 1968, Gacy was arrested for paying a boy to beat up one of the youths who had accused him of sexual assault and for being implicated in a lumberyard break-in. On September 12, at his court appearance, he was ordered by the court to submit to a psychiatric evaluation at the Psychiatric Hospital of the State University of Iowa.

During Gacy's seventeen days at the psychiatric hospital, he was observed by the staff, was given psychiatric interviews, and underwent physical and psychological tests. In his report to the court, Dr. Eugene F. Gauron stated:

Gacy would twist the truth in such a way that he would not be made to look bad and would admit to socially unacceptable actions only when directly confronted.

He is a smooth talker and an obscurer who was trying to whitewash himself of any wrongdoing. He had a high degree of social intelligence or awareness of the proper way to behave in order to influence people.

The most striking aspect of the test results is the patient's total denial of responsibility for anything that has happened to him. He can produce an "alibi" for everything. He alternately blames the environment while presenting himself as the victim of circumstances and blames other people while presenting himself as a victim of others who are out to get him. Although this could be construed as paranoid, I do not regard it that way. Rather, the patient attempts to assure [*sic*] a sympathetic response by depicting himself as being at the mercy of a hostile environment. To his way of thinking, a major objective is to outwit the other fellow and take advantage of him before being taken advantage of himself. He does things without thinking through the consequences and exercises poor judgment. (Sullivan & Maiken, 1983, pp. 271–272)

According to Gacy's discharge summary, he did not seem to feel remorse for his actions. He was evaluated as competent to stand trial. The psychiatrists' diagnosis was that Gacy had an antisocial personality and was unlikely to benefit from medical treatment.

Gacy pled guilty to the charge. The probation officer's presentence investigative report recommended that Gacy be placed on probation. The judge disagreed and, on December 3, 1968, sentenced Gacy to ten years' imprisonment.

While he was in prison, Gacy told other inmates he had been charged with showing pornographic films to teenagers. Also during his incarceration, he was assigned to food service; reportedly the prison food improved and the kitchen was kept spotless. Gacy also became involved in the Jaycees as director of the prison chapter, served as chaplain, and played Santa Claus at Christmas. He was awarded the chapter's "Sound Citizen Award" and helped build a miniature golf course on the prison grounds. Subsequently Gacy applied for early release under supervision, but the parole board denied his request.

Following the denial of parole, Gacy completed his high school education, began taking college-level classes, and became more involved in the Jaycees. In March 1970, a psychiatric evaluation of Gacy was ordered by the parole committee. The prison psychiatrist diagnosed him as a "passive aggressive personality" and recommended parole, stating, "The likelihood of his again being charged with and being convicted of antisocial conduct appears to be small" (Sullivan & Maiken, 1983, p. 276). After twenty-one months in prison, Gacy was paroled on June 18, 1970, to Chicago, Illinois.

Police records show that on two occasions before June 1971 he engaged in homosexual activity, thus violating his parole (Sullivan & Maiken, 1983, p. 277). However, Gacy was never formally charged with parole violation. In August 1975 and December 1976, Chicago police questioned Gacy about the disappearance of two young men. Then, in January 1976, police officers placed Gacy's home under surveillance for two weeks during the investigation of the disappearance of a nine-year-old boy. Accusations of kidnap and rape were also placed against Gacy in December 1977 and March 1978 in Chicago (*New York Times*, January 8, 1979, p. 16).

On December 12, 1978, Gacy was contacted by telephone by the Des Plaines Police Department regarding the disappearance of a fifteen-year-old boy from outside a pharmacy in that city the day before. Gacy had been to the pharmacy twice on the previous evening, giving the owner advice on rearranging his display shelves. After leaving his notebook at the pharmacy, he had returned a second time to pick it up. The missing boy worked at the pharmacy; shortly after Gacy left the pharmacy the second time, the boy told another employee he was going outside to talk to a contractor about a job. He never returned.

The Des Plaines police pursued the missing persons report on the boy in a nonroutine fashion after a preliminary investigation indicated that he was probably not a runaway. Gacy became a suspect in the disappearance after the police examined his record and learned of his sodomy conviction in Iowa, his charge of battery in Chicago in 1978, and his charge of aggravated battery and reckless conduct in a Chicago suburb in 1972. He was interviewed at his home on December 12 and asked to come to the police station to fill out a witness form because he admitted seeing, but not talking to, the missing boy at the pharmacy. Gacy stated he would come to the station later that evening. Then he was put under surveillance and eluded the officers. At 11:00 P.M. he called the Des Plaines police, asking if they still wanted to see him. When they replied in the affirmative, he said he would be there in an hour. However, a vehicle registered to Gacy was reported by the Illinois State Police to have been stuck in a ditch alongside the northbound lane of the Tri-State Tollway approximately thirteen miles south of Des Plaines at 2:29 A.M. the next morning. Gacy arrived at the police station at 3:20 A.M., but the officer he was supposed to see had left. He was told to come back later that morning.

Subsequently, Gacy returned to the station and was interviewed. When he was asked to make a written statement regarding his activities at the pharmacy, he complied. He was then asked to wait for the police lieutenant's return. In the meantime, the police and the Cook County state's attorney's office obtained a search warrant for his house based on probable cause of unlawful restraint. Gacy remained at the police station while the police searched his house looking for evidence of the missing boy.

The search of Gacy's house revealed a high school ring; a number of erotic films and pornographic books; a switchblade; a starter pistol; handcuffs; a wooden two-by-four that was three feet long with holes cut in each end; a hypodermic syringe; an empty, small brown bottle believed to have contained chloroform; and a customer photo receipt from the pharmacy where the missing boy had disappeared. Two driver's licenses were also found. The police took a section of carpeting believed to be stained with blood, and they discovered a trap door in a closet that led to a crawl space under the house. The ground in the crawl space was covered with something that appeared to be lime, and it showed no evidence of recent digging. The officers noticed a strong odor in the house but could not determine its origin.

Thereafter Gacy's pickup truck and car were confiscated. He signed a Miranda waiver form on his lawyer's advice and was released by the Des Plaines police at 9:30 that evening. Although he was placed under twenty-four-hour surveillance by the police, he managed to elude surveillance officers on three separate occasions on December 15, 1978. He drove at high speeds and often in a reckless manner. During this time, officers arrested a friend of Gacy's in Chicago for reckless driving. It turned out that Gacy and another friend were passengers in the vehicle.

On December 16, Gacy began to converse with the police surveillance team as they followed him around the Chicago area. The officers ate with Gacy at restaurants where he stopped. On one occasion, at a Chicago restaurant, Gacy said to the officers, "You know, clowns can get away with murder" (Sullivan & Maiken, 1983, p. 90). He repeated this statement to another police surveillance team on the same day.

Before long, the police began to see a pattern in Gacy's travels around the Chicago area. He was leading his surveillants to places that the Des Plaines detectives had just checked out, apparently to learn what the investigators had found out. On December 17, Gacy invited the surveillance team to his house for dinner. After dinner, he tried to elude the officers. On December 19, he accused the surveillance officers of trying to tape-record their conversations. Gacy also told the officers that he was prepared with bond money and that he expected to be allowed to call his attorney if they arrested him. Later that day, a surveillance team was invited by Gacy to his house for a drink. While there, they attempted to read the serial numbers on Gacy's television, which they suspected belonged to a missing boy. They again detected a strong unidentified odor in the house. On December 20, Des Plaines police and the state's attorney's office learned that on December 22 Gacy's lawyer would be filing a lawsuit against the police for harassment.

On December 21, 1978, Gacy had a late-night conference with his lawyers that lasted until 8:00 A.M. the next morning. He was then followed around Chicago while he met with various friends, who later told the officers that Gacy was saying good-bye to them. Police observed Gacy giving one of his friends a plastic bag; they suspected it contained marijuana. Gacy was arrested on the same day on a marijuana charge. Also on that day, one of the officers who had been in Gacy's house before determined that the strong odor he smelled in the house was the same as the odor he had smelled many times at the county morgue. That evening, another search warrant was obtained to search Gacy's house again.

Early the following morning, on December 22, 1978, after the police had discovered dead bodies buried in the crawl space, Gacy began confessing to a number of murders of young boys. He stated that the body of the missing boy they were searching for had been in the attic of his house when the police first interviewed him at home. Gacy had taken the body in his car later that evening to the Des Plaines River bridge of the Tri-State Tollway and dumped it into the river. This is why he had been late in coming to the Des Plaines police station on the following morning.

After hearing this, the officers took Gacy to the Des Plaines River bridge, and he showed them where he had dumped the body of the missing boy and four other boys he had killed. Gacy was then taken to his home, where he showed the officers where he had buried one of his victims in the garage. On December 22, 1978, Gacy was charged with the murder of the missing boy for whom the Des Plaines police had been searching. Gacy was denied bail and was transferred to the medical wing of the Cook County jail.

By December 29, 1978, police had recovered twenty-six bodies from under Gacy's house and one from his garage. On January 3, 1979, Gacy was interviewed by the police and the state's attorney's lawyers in the Cook County jail. At this time, he elaborated on his earlier confessions and was questioned regarding the identification of his victims. The following week, Gacy was indicted by a Cook County grand jury on seven counts of murder and one count each of deviate sexual assault, aggravated kidnapping, and taking indecent liberties with a child. At his arraignment on January 10, Gacy entered pleas of not guilty to all charges and was ordered to undergo a behavioral-clinical examination to determine his fitness to stand trial. On February 16, 1978, the examining psychologist found him mentally fit to stand trial. The psychologist, A. Arthur Hartman of the Cook County Court forensic unit, stated that Gacy was

> [v]ery egocentric and narcissistic with a basically antisocial, exploitative orientation. One reflection of this is his development of a technique of "conning" (his own term) or misleading others in his business or personal dealings. He has a severe underlying psychosexual conflict and confusion of sexual identity. (Sullivan & Maiken, 1983, p. 252)

Hartman's diagnostic impression of Gacy was of a "psychopathic (antisocial) personality, with sexual deviation and a hysterical personality and minor compulsive and paranoid personality elements" (Sullivan & Maiken, 1983, p. 252).

The Cook County state's attorney's office also requested an evaluation of Gacy by Professor Frank Osanka, a sociologist from Lewis University in Glen Ellyn, Illinois. Professor Osanka reviewed all the files on Gacy, including taped interviews, but did not interview Gacy. He concluded:

> The explanation of episodic psychotic states simply cannot explain multiple murders, committed essentially at the same location, in essentially the same methodological manner, hiding the remains in essentially the same methodological manner, over a period of eight years by a man labeled acceptable and successful by his neighbors and in his business. [Gacy] suffered neither with a mental illness nor mental defect which prevented him from appreciating the criminality of his behavior or from conforming his conduct to the requirements of the law. (F. Osanka, personal communication, March 8, 1980)

Meanwhile, Gacy's defense lawyers employed a psychiatrist, who concluded that Gacy was insane at the time of his alleged crime. The psychiatrist, Dr. R. G.

Rappaport, stated that Gacy had a "borderline personality organization with the subtype of psychopathic personality and with episodes of an underlying paranoid schizophrenia" (Sullivan & Maiken, 1983, p. 253). Rappaport supported his diagnosis of psychopathic personality by attributing the following characteristics to Gacy: "Unusual degree of self-reference, great need to be loved and admired, exploitative, charming on the surface and cold and ruthless underneath, noticeable absence of feeling of remorse and guilt, and a history of chronic antisocial behavior" (Sullivan & Maiken, 1983, p. 253).

The state's attorney's office of Cook County employed psychiatrists from the Issac Ray Center at St. Luke's Medical Center in Chicago to examine Gacy. The psychiatrists found the following:

> For at least the last fifteen years, Gacy had demonstrated a mixed personality disorder, which included obsessive-compulsive, antisocial, narcissistic, and hypomanic features. He abused both alcohol and drugs. The crimes he committed resulted from an increasingly more apparent personality disorder dysfunction, coupled with sexual preoccupations within an increasingly primary homosexual orientation.
>
> Narcissistically wounded in childhood, by a domineering and at times brutal father figure and [by an] inability to physically participate in athletics, Gacy continued to fail to master psychosocial milestones, in part because of a series of apparent psychosomatic disorders. Increasingly obsessed with his sense of failure (constantly emphasized by his father), he dedicated himself to a career of productive work, which brought him positive feedback. Simultaneously, however, his rage at his presumed powerlessness, due to a pervasive, defective self-image, began to merge with sadistic elements in a slowly unfolding homosexual orientation. This began to center upon young men with whom he re-enacted the projected helplessness and sense of failure that he himself continued to experience. His sadistic, homosexual conquests were much more gratifications through the exercise of power than erotic experiences motivated by unmet sexual needs. Murderous behavior became the ultimate expression of power over victims rendered helpless. With each murder victim he was presented with undeniable evidence of his crimes (a dead body), yet he continued with the same patterns of behavior. Ultimately he came to justify murder as socially acceptable because of the degraded nature of his victims (human trash) and his increasingly egocentric conviction that he would never be apprehended because of his own cleverness in concealment and a disordered belief that his murderous behavior was of assistance to society. (Sullivan & Maiken, 1983, pp. 255–256)

On April 23, 1978, a Cook County grand jury indicted Gacy on an additional twenty-six murders, making a total of thirty-three. All charges against Gacy were consolidated for the purposes of criminal trial, and a compromise on a change of venue for the trial was reached between the prosecution and the defense. Jurors were selected from the community of Rockford, Illinois, in late January 1980, and the trial was held in Chicago beginning on February 6, 1980.

Gacy's criminal trial lasted six weeks. His lawyers' strategy and defense, as well as the major issue at the trial, was that John Wayne Gacy had been insane when he committed the crimes and could not control his conduct. The final rebuttal witness for the defense, Dr. Helen Morrison, a psychiatrist, diagnosed Gacy as having mixed or atypical psychosis. Despite his high IQ, she said, Gacy had not developed emotionally; his entire emotional makeup was that of an infant. She concluded that Gacy had been suffering from mixed psychosis since at least 1958. When asked under cross-examination if she thought that Gacy would have killed his victim if there were a uniformed officer in the home with him at the time, she replied that she did.

On March 11, 1980, Gacy was found guilty on all indicted charges. Two days later, he was sentenced to death. Fourteen years later, on May 10, 1994, John Wayne Gacy was executed by the State of Illinois.

Offense Behavior

Little is known regarding the circumstances of the deaths of Gacy's thirty-three victims between 1970 and 1978. Although Gacy confessed to committing these killings, he provided very few details of these murders. Most of his criminal behavior has been determined on the basis of information provided by the surviving victims of his assaultive crimes. Using this information, police officials and psychiatrists have hypothesized or extrapolated from this behavior to his homicidal acts.

Gacy's first known criminal offenses occurred in Waterloo, Iowa, when he was twenty-four years old. In Waterloo, he was a member of the Merchants Patrol, a cooperative security force whose members guarded their own business establishments at night against break-ins. Male employees from the restaurants he managed went on patrol with Gacy and broke into businesses, stealing auto parts and funds from vending machines. Gacy would monitor the police radio to determine if police patrols were nearby.

Gacy also organized a social club in the basement of his home, where young boys employed at the restaurants he managed were allowed to play pool and drink alcoholic beverages in exchange for monthly dues. Gacy had many of the boys perform fellatio on him when they won at pool; he intimidated and coerced them or else convinced them that he was conducting scientific experiments for an Illinois commission on sexual behavior.

In the summer of 1967, Gacy took a sixteen-year-old boy to his home to watch some films, shoot pool, and have a few drinks. Gacy's wife was in the hospital after giving birth to their second child. When the boy refused to perform fellatio on him, Gacy attacked him with a knife and cut the boy on the arm. Gacy quickly apologized and insisted the boy stay and watch some pornographic films. After showing the films, Gacy chained the boy's hands behind his back and tried to sexually attack him. When the boy resisted, Gacy began choking him. The boy pretended to black out. Gacy revived him and agreed to take the boy home.

During 1967 and early 1968, Gacy frequently forced a fifteen-year-old boy, who was a part-time employee, to submit to oral sex. Gacy often got the boy intoxicated on alcohol before performing these acts. He told the boy that he was conducting experiments, and he usually paid the boy. Later, after being indicted for sodomy, Gacy paid one of his employees to assault one of the boys who had gone to the police with his parents and, according to Gacy, had spread lies about him.

Within eight months after being released from prison in Iowa, Gacy twice violated his parole, according to police records. In November 1970, he had a homosexual encounter with a twenty-year-old male in his mother's apartment. In February 1971, Gacy was arrested on a complaint of disorderly conduct filed by a nineteen-year-old male who claimed Gacy had sexually attacked him. However, Gacy filed a similar complaint against the boy, and the charges were dismissed.

In the late fall of 1971, Gacy struck an employee on the head with a hammer. When the employee asked why Gacy had hit him, he replied that he didn't know but that he had had a sudden urge to kill the man.

In June 1972, a twenty-four-year-old man told police that he had been picked up by Gacy, who offered him a ride. Gacy identified himself as a county police officer, showing the young man a badge and telling him he was under arrest. Gacy then told the young man that if the youth performed oral sex on him, Gacy would let him go. Gacy drove the man to a building in Northbrook, Illinois, where the man resisted. Gacy then clubbed him and pursued him in his car, knocking the man down. The man finally escaped to a nearby gas station. The complainant later identified Gacy as his assailant, and police arrested Gacy on June 22, 1972. Gacy told the police that the complainant was threatening him and trying to extort money from him. After finding marked money given by Gacy on the complainant, the police dropped the charges against Gacy.

Prior to Gacy's arrest by the Des Plaines police, he had been arrested by Chicago police on July 15, 1978, on charges of battery. The victim, a twenty-seven-year-old male, had been walking at 1:30 A.M. when a man driving a black car stopped and asked him if he wanted to smoke some marijuana. The victim got into the car. Shortly thereafter, the man held a rag over his mouth and he lost consciousness. The victim awoke at 4:30 A.M. with burns on his face and rectal bleeding. He later identified the car and gave police the license number. After several court postponements of the case, it was still pending when Gacy was arrested by Des Plaines police.

Meanwhile Gacy's employees, one after another, disappeared. One boy disappeared after only a week in Gacy's employ. Another boy was found drowned in a river sixty miles south of Chicago. Gacy sold the car of one former employee to another employee, stating that the owner had left for California. When asked about the constant turnover of employees, Gacy would respond that the boy had gone back home or had been fired. The transitional nature of his business meant that victims would appear and disappear with little notice. It was reportedly very common for Gacy to offer money to his former employees in exchange for oral sex.

One of Gacy's employees told the police that he had been down in the crawl space under Gacy's house on two occasions. Once he helped Gacy spread lime. On another occasion he dug some trenches. Gacy had told him he was going to lay some tile because of all the moisture. When the employee started digging away from the area Gacy had plotted out, Gacy became very upset.

Gacy was known to have marijuana in his house. He used the drug frequently and often provided some to his employees. He also reportedly abused alcohol. But apparently he was not habituated to either marijuana or alcohol. When the police found human bodies buried in the crawl space under his house, they also found other evidence of his criminality: a television and radio belonging to one of the missing boys, a foot-long vibrator with fecal matter on it, and pieces of plywood stained with blood.

On the basis of autopsies and the examination of bodily remains, forensic pathologists deduced that most of Gacy's victims were Caucasian males in their teens or twenties. In most cases, it was impossible to determine the cause of death. Clothing and clothlike material were found in the throats of some of the victims, indicating they had been suffocated. Gacy claimed that none of his victims had been tortured and that they all had been strangled.

He stated that he killed all but one of his victims by looping a rope around the victim's neck, knotting it twice, and then tightening it, like a tourniquet, with a stick. Many of the victims were handcuffed at the time. He stated that others put the rope around their neck themselves, anticipating that Gacy would show them an interesting trick. On more than one occasion, Gacy claimed, he had killed two boys in one night. He reportedly read the Twenty-third Psalm to one of his victims as the boy died. Gacy also stated that one of his victims was a masochist, so he chained the youth to a two-by-four with his wrists and ankles together. Gacy stated, "Since he liked pain, I did the ultimate number on him." When asked how he got the idea for the restraint board, he answered, "From Elmer Wayne Henley, the guy in Texas" (Sullivan & Maiken, 1983, p. 197).

Gacy claimed he lost count of the number of victims buried in the crawl space under his house. He either soaked the bodies in acid or put lime on them and buried them under a foot of earth. He told the police that one of his victims was buried in the garage and that the last five victims had been dropped into the Des Plaines River off a bridge southwest of Chicago.

In addition to his male employees, Gacy preyed on homosexuals and male prostitutes who frequented Bughouse Square, a park in north Chicago. He would cruise the area in his car late at night picking up youths. Gacy often convinced boys whom he picked up that he was a policeman. He stated that he had had sex with one hundred people he had picked up in this area and that he had paid all of them. He had a schedule: Between 1:00 A.M. and 3:00 A.M. he had sex. All but two of his victims had died between 3:00 A.M. and 6:00 A.M., according to Gacy. He referred to most of his killings as involving the "rope trick." One of Gacy's intended victims survived the "rope trick" by physically forcing Gacy to release the stick. The survivor did not report the incident because he thought Gacy was a police officer. Gacy told the police that his first killing took place in January 1972 and that his second occurred in January 1974. He said he had killed no one while his mother-in-law lived with him. Police determined that Gacy had killed five people in less than a month in June 1976. He stated that he had killed for two reasons: Either the victim raised the originally agreed-upon price for sex, or he posed some sort of threat—such as telling Gacy's neighbors about his sexual activities (Sullivan & Maiken, 1983, p. 225).

Gacy's murders appear to have been well planned and thought out in advance. He eliminated most traces of his victims and disposed of their remains in a methodical manner. He even prepared the graves of his future victims in advance.

Self-Concept

Gacy was very concerned about other people's perception of his sexual identity. Although he had engaged in homosexual relationships since his early twenties and probably prior to that, he always talked about being bisexual because he did not want anyone to consider him a homosexual. He was certainly aware of his homosexual desires when he told his second wife that they would no longer engage in sexual intercourse. After his arrest in Des Plaines and during his confession, he wanted his captors to know that he was bisexual, not homosexual. He stated, "After all, I do have some pride" (Darrach & Norris, 1984, p. 60).

Gacy also told police that the pornographic books taken from his house were not his. He claimed he would not spend money on that type of reading material and only used the books to stimulate some of his victims.

Gacy seemed to rationalize everything he did. After the fact, his actions were always inflated when he described them to others; or if his actions could be seen in a negative light, he would twist the truth so that he would be viewed as having committed no wrongdoing. He seemed to have an excuse and a ready explanation for everything. Gacy told his family he had been mentally ill. On Christmas Eve, 1978, he wrote to his family, "Please forgive me for what I am about to tell you. I have been very sick for a long time (both mentally and physically). I wish I had help sooner. May God forgive me" (Sullivan & Maiken, 1983, p. 199).

Whether he truly viewed himself as he portrayed John Gacy to others is difficult to determine. His psychological and psychiatric evaluations indicate that he did.

Gacy appears to have regarded himself as an important person and a good businessman. He always discussed his management and sales experience in Iowa in glowing terms. He also frequently exaggerated his actual experiences in business.

Gacy had always wanted to be in control of a social situation or an organized activity. He was the boss of his business and frequently mentioned this in conversation. While he was a member of the Junior Chamber of Commerce in both Springfield, Illinois, and Waterloo, Iowa, he sought leadership roles and always held some sort of official position. He was later characterized by friends and others as a person who manipulated situations and people to his advantage and tried to place them under his control. The county attorney in Waterloo attributed Gacy's prominence in the community to a "[u]nique ability to manipulate people and ingratiate himself" (Sullivan & Maiken, 1983, p. 264).

Gacy also wanted to be considered a celebrity. Whenever he felt it was appropriate, he claimed to be part of a criminal syndicate in Chicago. In Iowa, he seemed to enjoy being addressed by his friends as "Colonel." He is remembered by many in Iowa as always talking about his money and connections. And he was proud of his political activities. According to his first wife, his political work was extremely important to Gacy. In his home, he prominently displayed his political trophies, including an autographed picture from President Carter's wife.

Even after being arrested and jailed for murder, he acted important. For example, he asked the jail chaplain to have the Chicago archbishop visit him. He also falsely claimed to have received a social visit from the Cook County sheriff (Sullivan & Maiken, 1983, p. 238). People later realized he frequently lied about his previous status and accomplishments. However, he seemed to believe his own falsehoods.

Attitudes

In Iowa, Gacy had his car equipped with spotlights and siren. His membership in the Merchants Patrol allowed him to patrol in uniform with a shotgun. Gacy was always interested in ambulances, fire engines, and police cars. His first wife stated that he used to follow these vehicles when they were speeding to an emergency. While under police surveillance, he took great pride in eluding the police. In Chicago, he convinced the homosexual community that he was a policeman. He frequently carried a police badge, and a number of such badges were subsequently found in his house. Even as a boy, he had wanted to be a policeman. Later, his attitudes toward law enforcement officers and what they represented seemed to place him above them, yet he identified with them as persons who could control others. Even his prison inmate friends noticed that he closely identified with the guards because he, himself, enjoyed being boss.

Following his arrest, Gacy seemed to feel no remorse or concern for his victims. During his confession, he showed no emotion while speaking continuously about his murderous actions. Indeed, he discussed his victims with the police in an almost clinical fashion. He stated that he killed his victims, "[b]ecause the boys sold their bodies for twenty dollars" (Sullivan & Maiken, 1983, p. 173). Gacy gave his police audience the impression that he felt he was ridding the world of some bad kids. Dr. Helen Morrison, a psychiatrist who examined Gacy, quoted him as saying, "All the police are going to get me for is running a funeral parlor without a license" (Berger, 1984, p. 11).

Little has been written regarding Gacy's religious beliefs. Although he had a Polish Catholic heritage, his activities in the church appeared to be for social or political gain only. He was the chaplain for all three chapters of the Junior Chamber of Commerce to which he belonged. His reading of the Twenty-third Psalm to one of his victims might have been a way of absolving himself of any sins he feared he might be committing—or it might simply have been added torture to the victim.

John Gacy enjoyed the limelight that his crimes brought to him. In his first formal confession to a group of police officers, Gacy spoke as if holding court, frequently leaning back in his chair and talking with his eyes closed. He had overcome his fatigue and spoke with a renewed air of confidence. Just as he wanted, the room belonged to him (Sullivan & Maiken, 1983, p. 176).

It is reported that following his arrest, Gacy kept a scrapbook on his case (*Newsweek*, November 26, 1984, p. 106). He complained about how his former friends were now treating him and how the press was libeling him. However, to those around him, he appeared to be enjoying all the attention. Regarding his former associates and friends, he wrote:

> When things were good and I was giving, everyone was on my bandwagon, but as soon as I am accused and suspected, they run and hide. May God have mercy on them. If it wasn't for God's will, I would have never given or helped so many people. Oh, I am no saint or anything like that, just one of God's children. I do not take the right to sit in judgment on others or myself. (Sullivan & Maiken, 1983, p. 237)

Gacy thought the press misinterpreted everything he said or took it out of context.

Recall of Events

When he was first asked by the police how many people he had killed, Gacy responded, "I told my lawyers thirty or thirty-five but I don't know, there could be thirty-five, forty-five—who knows" (Sullivan & Maiken, 1983, p. 178). He never spoke of his victims by name, other than the ones the police already knew about or suspected when he was first arrested. He said he couldn't remember their names. He provided relatively sketchy information regarding the actual killings, stating that he couldn't remember. Prior to his trial, Gacy was tested on an alcohol-electroencephalogram. The psychiatrists found the results of the test, as well as the fact that Gacy blacked out within an hour after drinking six ounces of whiskey, to be significant. They concluded that in Gacy's repetitive murder pattern, there is

> a psychological mechanism or repression, in which he attempts to spare whatever conscience he had from awareness of and responsibility for his actions, [that] could explain the "patchy recollection." [However,] the defendant's degree of intoxication could be so extreme that recollection of some or all of the details of what transpired could in fact be missing—e.g., "a blackout." (Sullivan & Maiken, 1983, pp. 254–255)

In his opening statement to the jury, a state's attorney's lawyer for the prosecution referred to Gacy's wife's assertion that he had a memory like an elephant. Examples of this assertion are (1) Gacy's pinpointing of the precise location on the river bridge where he dumped some of his victims and (2) the detailed recollections in some of his statements to the police. Contrived or real, Gacy's lack of memory or his patchy memory of his crimes is still debatable.

The Demise of John Wayne Gacy

Gacy was executed in 1994. Yet until the very end he continued to maintain his innocence. Joseph Kozenczak, who chronicled the investigation that led to Gacy's confession and subsequent conviction in *A Passing Acquaintance* (1992), states that at the time of his book, Gacy had been on death row for eleven years and most of his appeals in the courts had been denied (p. 187).

During his time on death row, Gacy kept busy maintaining his innocence. He continually referred to himself as another victim. In his correspondence with me, Gacy stated that "[n]early 80% of what is known about me is from the media, it is they who made this infamous celebrity fantasy monster image, and now they have to live with that as I have not granted any interviews in over ten years to media people" (personal correspondence, March 6, 1991). Near the end of his stay on death row, Gacy did grant media interviews in which he still maintained his innocence.

In his one and only letter to the author of this volume (further correspondence seemed fruitless, although I did write to him again about a month prior to his execution and received no answer), Gacy included a two-page "fact sheet" entitled "They Called Him the Killer Clown: But Is JW Gacy a Mass Murderer or Another Victim?" This "fact sheet" was sent to all who corresponded with Gacy between the late 1980s and his execution in 1994.

John Wayne Gacy was consistent in maintaining his innocence. One writer who interviewed him in February and March 1994 found him to be obsessed with his innocence (Wilkinson, 1994).

In 1991, Gacy's obsession was published in book form as *A Question of Doubt: The John Wayne Gacy Story,* by John Wayne Gacy, C. Ivor McClelland, editor. The 216-page book was spiral bound on 8½-inch by 11-inch paper. In the preface to this first-person account of Gacy's initial contact with the Des Plaines police through his trial, conviction, and sentencing, he states, "he is the man waiting to be strapped to a gurney with an IV of lethal injected drugs coursing through his system—*who has never told his story.*" Gacy concludes the preface by saying, "These are the first words that John Gacy has spoken. This is *my side of the story*—the story of THE THIRTY-FOURTH VICTIM" (Gacy, 1991, p. ii). But it is hard to imagine that anyone would consider John Wayne Gacy a victim.

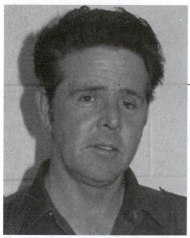
Henry Lee Lucas. From the author's files.

Henry Lee Lucas

—A CASE STUDY

Social Environment

Henry Lee Lucas has been described as always living at a very low economic level. The house he lived in until age fourteen was apparently a two-room shack that had no electricity until 1951. It had no flooring and was furnished with only the bare necessities. Lucas mentioned the fact that he frequently stole the food that his family ate.

Lucas was in the first grade for the first three years of his schooling. His first-grade teacher remembers him as "a very humble little boy who was a little slow and a little dirty" (personal communication, anonymous, 1985). He finished the fourth grade at age fourteen. He never finished the fifth grade, and his last known exposure to formal education involved vocational training while in prison.

When not "doin' all the work for the family" (interview, July 7, 1984), Lucas spent his childhood playing with knives and terrorizing animals. He claimed to have learned how to have sex with animals from his mother's live-in boyfriend. He experimented by killing cows, sheep, goats, dogs, and cats.

His goal in life was to travel. "I wanted to travel and have adventure" (interview, June 5, 1984). Lucas made numerous attempts to run away from home and at age fourteen was successful. In fact, he traveled thousands of miles and never returned. He stated, "I ain't got no roots" (interview, June 22, 1984).

His main concern in life was survival. He stated, "I don't leave witnesses" (interview, June 5, 1984). For Lucas, having no witnesses guaranteed his survival. In

133

order to survive, he kept moving and he kept killing. He was always on the move when not incarcerated. "Remaining in one place causes me to have thoughts of escape. It becomes more of a pressure—not bein' able to get up and go" (interview, July 18, 1984). He boasted of sometimes traveling twenty-four hours a day, keeping himself awake with amphetamines, marijuana, and PCP. For years he lived among the rootless, the searching, the homeless, and the roamers of this country, living out of his car, stealing, and murdering hitchhikers and stranded travelers. All but three of his victims were strangers.

Lucas spent a great deal of his life behind bars. Although he did not talk kindly of his keepers in prison, his discussions of prison life never conveyed the intensity of hatred with which he described his home life. For Lucas, prison was where he got his degree in criminality. He stated, "It was a learnin' to do crime" (interview, June 24, 1984). Apparently he spent many years in the Michigan prison as a records clerk. During this time, Lucas studied crimes committed by the inmates and learned how to commit them himself. He described living at Jackson Prison in Michigan as being like living in a big city.

Because Lucas spent most of his life in institutions of correction (starting at age fourteen), he never learned to live by the rules of society. If the rules benefited him, he followed them. If they did not, he broke them.

The last year of his travels seemed to signal his capture, for he was apparently trying to settle down. For almost a year he continued to return to Stoneburg, Texas, from his murderous trips. With Becky Powell, the fifteen-year-old niece of his traveling companion, Ottis Toole, he lived there in a trailer. They lived as man and wife until Lucas killed Becky and dissected her body in a farmer's field the day after his forty-sixth birthday in 1982.

Family Background

Lucas has been described by a psychiatrist as having a poorly developed moral sense owing to undesirable ancestry. Lucas's family consisted of his father and mother, a brother, three half brothers, and four half sisters. He was reportedly closest to one of his half sisters who lived in Tecumseh, Michigan. His home was a two-room cabin with dirt floors located in a mountainous area of Montgomery County, Virginia. The first fourteen years of his life were spent there, living with his mother, a man he remembered as his father (records indicate the man was not his real father), his older brother, and his mother's boyfriend.

According to Lucas, his parents "lived together, but my father didn't have no legs and he stayed drunk and my mother, she drank and was a prostitute. And, that's the way I growed up, until it was time to get out on my own" (interview, June 22, 1984). Lucas remembered that his father usually was either drinking or trying to sell pencils, his mother was either not around or having sex with different men, and his brother was gone most of the time. His mother, the head of the family, dominated everyone.

He described his mother as a Cherokee Indian of muscular build, weighing 150 to 160 pounds. His mother "didn't work, she'd rather sell her body. [She] believed just in sex. Didn't try to provide for anyone" (interview, October 25, 1984). Lucas said the worst thing he remembered about his family was being forced to watch his mother having sexual intercourse with various men.

He claimed his father never argued with anyone, and Lucas had a good relationship with him. Lucas remembered his grief at his father's death in 1949, and his mother saying, "Good riddance."

Lucas remembered his brother as being stronger and bigger. He claimed his mother would not allow him to play with his brother. Reported to have once suffered a nervous breakdown, his brother joined the navy when Lucas was fourteen years old.

Authorities describe Lucas's mother as a bootlegger who drank heavily. According to her daughters, she cleaned homes and restaurants to support them. She was fifty-one years old when she gave birth to Lucas. Her grandaughter remembers her as a dirty old woman who was not nice to be around.

The man Lucas called his father, Anderson Lucas, had worked for the railroad and lost his legs when he reportedly fell under a train. He was described by one caseworker as being illiterate and as having a bad reputation as a bootlegger.

From as early as he can remember, Lucas was apparently confused as to his own gender. "I grew up from four years old, best I can remember, 'til about seven years old as a girl. I lived as a girl. I was dressed as a girl. I had long hair as a girl. I wore girl's clothes" (interview, June 22, 1984). His half sister in Maryland still keeps a childhood picture of Lucas with long curls and dressed in girl's clothing.

In the first grade, at age seven, Lucas had his hair cut after his schoolteacher complained about its length. Lucas claims that his mother's attitude toward him changed after this; she beat him and forced him to carry heavy objects, steal, cut wood, carry water, and take care of the hog.

Lucas recalled no good times in his childhood because if he had fun, he "would get beat for it" (interview, June 22, 1984). In fact, he said that a scar on the back of his head resulted from his mother striking him with a two-by-four. He reported that he was unconscious for eleven hours following this beating and that his skull was fractured.

Lucas referred to his childhood as one of constant abuse or neglect:

I don't think a human being alive that can say he had the childhood I had. Bein' beaten ever day. Bein' misused ever day. Havin' to cook my own food, havin' to steal my own food. Eatin' on the floor instead of the table. Bein treated like what I call the hog of the family. It's a lot harder than what people can imagine. Growing up with hatred, without any kind of friendship, without any kind of companion to be around or anything. The best thing was leavin' home. (interview, November 30, 1984)

Lucas's accomplices in crime could be described as his substitute, self-made family. He was very close to Ottis Toole, who had been a pyromaniac as a child and later became a homosexual and an admittedly sexually sadistic killer. Lucas stated that in their sexual relationship, he was the passive participant. He treated Ottis

Toole's niece and nephew, Becky and Frank, like his own children. Ironically, he exposed these two children to his killings just as his mother had allegedly exposed him to her sexual relationships. Lucas stated, "I would avoid actually killing anyone in front of them, and a lot of times they would sneak around to see what I was doin' and I would catch 'em and I would scold 'em for it" (interview, February 2, 1985). For Lucas, the fact that these young children witnessed some of his horrific deeds was not particularly important.

Peer Group Associations and Personal Relationships

Lucas's half sister, in describing her brother, stated, "He always seemed like he wanted someone to love. He never seemed to be able to keep a friend for some reason" (personal communication, anonymous, 1985). Apparently he was reluctant to initiate any conversation with other boys and girls while in school. In retrospect, those who knew Lucas as a boy characterize him as either socially inept or hostile.

His appearance, owing to an empty eye socket and the subsequent artificial eye, apparently caused children to shun him or avoid direct contact with him. This restriction of peer relationships was intensified by his mother, who Lucas claimed would not allow him to play with other children, including his own brother.

The lack of any significant peer relationships, combined with his treatment at home, resulted in an overwhelming hatred. Lucas referred to it frequently. For example:

> I've hated since I can first remember, uh, back when I was a little kid I've hated my family and anything. Anytime I went out, uh, to go play [with other children] or some show, or something, I never could get anybody to go with me. I never could make friends and I just hated people. Nobody would accept me 'cause of my left eye. [I] looked like garbage! No girls would go out with me. No boys would have anything to do with me. They just wanted to stay away from me. (interview, June 22, 1984)

Upon leaving home, Lucas stated, "[I] didn't believe in association with anybody" (interview, August 14, 1984).

With the exception of a young woman Lucas wanted to marry prior to his mother's death, Lucas claimed to have had few relationships in his life. His few true relationships were with Becky Powell; Ottis Toole; a lay minister in Stoneburg, Texas, who provided him with housing; and the lay sister who visited him in the Williamson County jail. In describing his attempts to establish relationships, he stated, "I tried married life and it didn't work. I tried to go back with my family and that didn't work. I went to Florida, met Ottis and just started travelin'" (interview, June 22, 1984).

According to Lucas, Becky "more fit into my kind of life. She accepted everything I done. I could tell her things. She understood. This took off the pressure that was there. Before, I had the urge to destroy anything within my reach. Becky took some of the pressure away." In describing his relationship with her, he said, "Yeah, uh it's, uh weird. My love for her was like a daughter—you know, a father to daughter. I never thought of her as sexual." He had sexual intercourse with her only three times, in order to satisfy her. "I loved her, but I don't think she felt love," he said (interviews, June 22, 1984; February 8, 1985).

Psychiatrists who talked to Lucas characterize him as poorly socialized, with an exaggerated need to feel powerful and important and to manipulate others. They describe his mind set as putting trust in no one except himself. Lucas's relationships are interpreted by psychiatrists as self-aggrandizing and exploitative.

Contact with Defining Agencies

Lucas's first documented contact with law enforcement officers was at age fourteen or fifteen. His first contact with correctional personnel was in 1952, when he was incarcerated at Beaumont, Virginia. During this period he was assigned to a correctional case worker. His first documented contact with correctional psychologists was when he was in prison in Michigan. His first known psychiatric diagnosis, made in July 1961, involved his transfer to Ionia State Hospital.

Although Lucas appeared to enjoy playing detective in "solving" his crimes, which he refers to as "my cases," he appeared to have little regard for law enforcement in general. He stated, "The police didn't know who done it. They never would have knowed who done it. They'd never know who done it unless I'd told 'em." He frequently reiterated, "Unless I tell 'em, they'd never clear these cases." He characterized many of the hundreds of law enforcement officers who had interviewed him by stating, "I've seen better kids play cops than that!" (interviews, June 5, 1984; June 22, 1984; July 18, 1984).

All officers who traveled to Georgetown, Texas, to interview Lucas about his suspected homicides were thoroughly briefed by the Texas Rangers on ways to handle Lucas and specific procedures to follow. Lucas was shown a picture of the victim when alive or a number of pictures including the victims. He was told the state, jurisdiction, and date of the incident. If Lucas remembered the victim, he would describe the crime in great detail. He has a phenomenal memory for details. In 113 separate instances, Lucas led law enforcement officers back to the scenes of his homicides, unassisted.

Lucas described his interviews with police officers,

> I have to give 'em every detail . . . how it happened, where it happened at, the description of the person, what was used, uh every type of, uh, where the body was left, parts of bodies missing. I have to tell them what parts are missing, if they've been shot, I have to tell them that. If they were stabbed, cut, whatever. They don't give me no details. (interview, June 5, 1984)

From January 1, 1952, when he was incarcerated in juvenile detention in Richmond, Virginia, to June 11, 1983, when he was arrested in Stoneburg, Texas, Henry Lee Lucas spent over twenty-one years living under the control of various correctional authorities. In other words, 70 percent of his life during these thirty-plus years was spent under someone else's control. Lucas contended he was beaten and even shot at by "law enforcement" in prison. He threatened to kill himself while in prison in Michigan and is reported to have attempted suicide by cutting his left wrist. Prison authorities did not consider this a serious suicide attempt. Lucas stated that he was trying to change and get help in prison by talking to doctors and prison officials. During his first confession in Stoneburg, Texas, Lucas claimed that he had begged prison officials in Michigan to help him but got no assistance. Between the times he diligently reported to his parole officer in Maryland following his first release from prison in Michigan, he was traveling across the country and leaving the remains of his murder victims in a number of states.

Lucas consistently maintained that he requested not to be released from prison when he was paroled in 1975. He claimed he killed four people on the day he was discharged. In fact, five murders committed by Lucas have been confirmed by the Texas Rangers during the remainder of 1975. One of those murders was committed on the same day Lucas was married.

The results of psychological testing conducted while Lucas was incarcerated reveal that he read at the sixth-grade level, spelled at the fifth-grade level, and understood mathematics at the fourth-grade level. Institutional psychological examinations conducted in Michigan show Lucas to have a total average of 65 on the Standard Achievement Test and an IQ of 89 as determined by the Army General Classification Test. He placed in the 60th percentile on the Revised Minnesota Paper Form Board. Lucas was also administered the Minnesota Multiphasic Personality Inventory, the Figure Drawing Test, and the Rosenzweig P.H. Study. A summary of the interpretation of Lucas's performance on these tests, written by psychologists on July 14, 1961, is as follows:

> While contraindicating any underlying psychotic process as well as incapacitating neurotic qualities, test results are suggestive of a basically insecure individual who has a relatively well crystallized inferiority complex and who is grossly lacking in self confidence, self reliance, will power and general stamina. There is also some evidence of a preoccupation with sexual impotence, the same which is believed to exist as only another reflection of his deflated impression of personal qualities in general. According to Rosenzweig P.H. Study he was found more value oriented than he is need oriented, but due to his lack of will power and self confidence he does not characteristically engage in behavior which is aimed at an implementation of his values. The anxiety and hostility caused by threats to the ego are usually directed intropunitively toward himself or inpunitively toward the frustrating situation. *He does not have the courage to blame others for mistakes or misfortunes or to engage in aggressive social behavior* aimed at alleviating some of his discomfort [emphasis added]. (Ionia State Hospital, July 14, 1961).

The clinical psychologist who provided the interpretative summary qualified his diagnostic impression on account of the absence of pertinent and general background information on Lucas. In fact, prior to writing the summary, he had never seen Lucas. He stated that his report should be considered a working hypothesis.

The following psychiatric diagnoses, which were made while Lucas was incarcerated, were provided to law enforcement officials in 1984 in the form of narrative reports:

July 14, 1961—Psychiatric Clinic Ward, Jackson Prison (2nd admission)—DSM II—301.81. *Passive-aggressive personality* with a significant inferiority complex and general lack of confidence, self reliance, will power and perseverance. DSM II—295.0. *Schizophrenia, simple type, chronic, severe.* Transfer to Ionia State Hospital recommended, prognosis fair. (Ionia State Hospital, July 14, 1961)

August 10, 1961—Ionia State Hospital—DSM II—295.90. *Schizophrenia, chronic undifferentiated type,* sex deviate, sadist. (Ionia State Hospital, August 10, 1961)

January 28, 1965—Ionia Staff Conference on Lucas. "The patient's affect during the staff interview was definitely inappropriate. He is *potentially dangerous* [emphasis added]." (Ionia State Hospital, January 28, 1965)

November 17, 1971—Center for Forensic Psychiatry—DSM II—301.81. *Passive aggressive personality.* Found competent to stand criminal trial for kidnapping. "It is not felt that there is much outside an incarceration setting which would be effective in modifying the defendant's presently erratic social behavior." (Center for Forensic Psychiatry, November 17, 1971)

At Lucas's murder trial in San Angelo, Texas, a psychologist for the defense testified that Lucas was a chronic schizophrenic who belonged in an institution. Three other psychiatrists for the prosecution disagreed, finding Lucas sane enough to stand trial (*Houston Chronicle*, April 7, 1984, p. 1). "I need medical help, there's no doubt about it" was the layman's diagnosis offered by Lucas himself (interview, February 8, 1985).

Lucas was transferred to the McLennan County jail in Waco, Texas, on April 12, 1985, by authority of the state attorney general and the McLennan County district attorney, who had convened a grand jury in Waco to investigate (1) two homicides Lucas had confessed to in the county, and (2) the conduct of the Lucas Task Force coordinated by the Texas Rangers. On April 14, 1985, the *Dallas Times Herald* charged in a five-page article that Lucas had committed very few of the murders he had confessed to and that law enforcement agencies across the country had provided Lucas with information on homicide cases so that he could confess to them. The paper also charged that in many instances the Lucas Task Force was aware that Lucas was confessing to murders he did not commit. The Texas attorney general publicly stated that Lucas probably had not committed all the murders to which he had confessed. The Texas Rangers and numerous law enforcement agencies across the country have disputed the charges made by the newspaper and the attorney general.

The grand jury completed its investigation in late June 1985 and issued a no bill on Lucas for the two homicides he had confessed to in McLennan County. It should be noted that the officers who took the confessions from Lucas never testified before the grand jury. Members of the Lucas Task Force did testify before the grand jury, only after strongly insisting that they be allowed to testify. No charges against the task force were issued by the grand jury.

Upon completion of the grand jury deliberations, Lucas was transferred to the Texas Department of Corrections death row facility near Huntsville, Texas. He stated at this time that he no longer wished to talk to law enforcement officials. Lucas sued the Texas Rangers, charging that they had drugged him to elicit confessions, did not provide him with an attorney during questioning, and did not advise him of his rights prior to questioning. Ironically, by state law, the attorney general had to defend the Rangers against these charges. The charges were never upheld.

Lucas talked to people in his death row cell and conducted interviews. On the advice of his attorney, he saw no law enforcement personnel; and corrections officials were advised not to allow police officers to talk with Lucas. He proclaimed his innocence until his death, of natural causes, on March 12, 2001.

Offense Behavior

Although his first deviant act, labeled as such, was theft, Lucas killed animals for his own sexual gratification in his early teens and began using alcohol at age nine. He also became fascinated with knives in the first grade. In fact, they became one of the tools of his "trade." The knife was his favorite weapon because it was silent and quick, its target the throat and chest area of his victims.

Lucas stole numerous automobiles during his criminal career. Also, many of his killings were the result of burglary, theft, and armed robbery. His most frequent target for robbery was the twenty-four-hour convenience store.

His criminal career was diffuse and intermittent, yet involving ever-increasing forms of aggression. His first homicide victim was a seventeen-year-old girl in Virginia in 1951. His second was his mother, nine years later.

> It was just an impulse thing that if I wanted to kill somebody, I'd go and kill 'em. I wouldn't plan it, how I was gonna do that. Then I would sit and plan how to get rid of the body. Whether I would just dump it out on the road or whether I would leave it partially clothed or would leave anything around the body or whether I'd leave the body cut up, how I would leave the body, ya know. (interview, February 8, 1985)

In describing his acts of killing, Lucas stated,

> We [Lucas and Toole] killed them every way there is except one. I haven't poisoned anyone. . . . We cut 'em up. We hanged 'em. We ran 'em down in cars. We stabbed 'em. We beat 'em, we drowned 'em. There's crucifixion—there's people we filleted like fish. There's people we burnt. There's people we shot in cars. . . . We strangled them by hand. We strangled them by rope. We strangled them by

telephone cord. We even stabbed them when we strangled them. We even tied them so they would strangle themselves. (*Avalanche Journal,* June 3, 1984, p. 1)

All these methods, except hanging and crucifixion, have been confirmed by the task force. Lucas talked about some of his victims being used for target practice. A synopsis of two confirmed homicides by the task force reveals one victim being shot while standing at a car wash and another being shot while hanging up clothes in her back yard. Both were shot as Lucas and his accomplices drove by in a car.

Lucas claimed that he and Ottis Toole were members of a death cult, which resulted in many of his murders. A religious book on Lucas (Call, 1985) and a religious pamphlet about him (Larson, 1984) provide details of his activities in this cult. However, law enforcement officials have been unable to substantiate any of Lucas's claims regarding the existence of such a cult.

Lucas admitted to being a necrophiliac, although the term itself had to be explained to him. "In most of my cases, I think you'll find that I had sex with them after death; uh, the other way I'm not satisfied" (Terry interview, August 11, 1983).

Lucas stated, "I've had people in houses, I've had people in stores, I've had people in banks" (interview, June 5, 1984). During his confinement in the Williamson County jail in Texas, he continued to claim a total of 360 victims.

One reason Lucas gave for his killings was, "I didn't leave no witnesses. I've never left witnesses" (interview, June 5, 1984). In his opinion, in addition to his felony murders, a witness was whoever was on the street or in the area. "After the first few, ya know, I just felt the next one was covered. I'd just kill that one so they couldn't say I was there. If I came into contact with somebody, I couldn't afford to let 'em live" (interview, February 2, 1985).

Lucas claimed to have been drinking prior to most of his killings. Indeed, an argument with his mother in 1960, which led to her death, began in a tavern. Also, he reportedly used amphetamines, PCP, LSD, and marijuana. He stated that the drugs kept him relaxed and kept him awake so he could travel a lot. "Drugs allowed me to stay on the road, to get out of the victim's neighborhood" (interview, June 5, 1984). For Lucas, being on drugs increased his degree of awareness.

Lucas and his accomplices used many vehicles in their travels. Several old cars were purchased in Jacksonville, Florida. When a car they were using broke down, they would hitchhike or steal another car. Sometimes they would briefly use the cars of their murder victims.

He was constantly moving around the country, taking care not to be seen, not to leave behind clues, and rarely repeating in the same area the ways in which he murdered. Lucas talked of a "force" that kept him moving and traveling with no specific destination. It was as if he had heeded the advice of Harry King, the Boxman, who stated, "The only way you can beat the law is by moving all the time. The law is easy to beat as long as you keep moving. But you have to continuously move" (King & Chambliss, 1984, p. 91).

Many of his victims were subjected to what the task force referred to as "overkill." Lucas explained this by referring to the "force," which caused him to mutilate and frequently dissect the bodies of his victims. He and his accomplices claimed to have carried the head of one victim through two states.

Very little physical evidence has been found to link Lucas to the crime scenes of his murders. A partial latent fingerprint was found in a robbery murder he committed at a motel in Louisiana. Victims' hair has been found in cars used by Lucas. Blood matching his blood type has been found at crime scenes. Lucas's blood type was ABO-A, AK-1, HP-2, and he was a nonsecreter (*Regional Organized Crime Information Bulletin,* February 1984). This blood type is found in fewer than two-tenths of one percent of the population. Also, a composite drawing made by a police artist from witnesses' descriptions of an abduction closely resembles Lucas.

Lucas contended that he constantly changed the way he killed in order to confuse law enforcement personnel. By the time one of his murders was discovered, he might be two or three counties away, killing in a different way. Sergeant Bob Prince, a Texas Ranger in charge of the task force, states, "Lucas has sixteen homicides within a fifty-mile radius of Georgetown [Texas]. If you laid these cases out on a table and asked investigators not familiar with Lucas to evaluate them, the officers would undoubtedly talk about numerous different killers instead of just one" (interview, November 30, 1984).

Self-Concept

Lucas frequently spoke of being driven by hatred, which he attributed to the way he was brought up by his mother. "When I first grew up and can remember, I was dressed as a girl. And I stayed that way for two or three years and then after that I was treated as, uh, what I'd call the dog of the family" (interview, June 5, 1984). This, the beatings by his mother, and being forced to watch her have sexual intercourse caused, according to Lucas, a deep hatred that he couldn't get rid of.

Killing and sexually experimenting with animals at age nine, he stated that he "never thought about killing anyone 'til I was fourteen years old. Everything I had was destroyed" (interview, June 22, 1984). When asked if he ever really thought about himself, Lucas replied, "Once in 1970. I knew what I was gonna do" (interview, February 2, 1985). He thought someone would eventually shoot him but, he said, he didn't care.

Many detectives who questioned him reported that Lucas was not reliable. He admitted to certain crimes and then denied them. He confused places and dates. In some respects, he bragged about his murders. "Well, most of your other people leaves evidence. I don't. I've never left evidence in any of my cases" (interview, June 22, 1984). During a subsequent interview, Lucas claimed to have left evidence on purpose.

Lucas stated he was trying to "show people I can do anything I want to. Outsmart everybody else. It's your responsibility to catch me. Anything I wanted to do, I could do. Outsmart a burglar alarm. Get around electric alarms. No kind of safety device I can't get out of" (interview, August 14, 1984).

He was apparently impotent. In discussing sexual relations, he always referred to not getting anything out of it. He attributed this to a stab wound to his groin while in prison; the wound required surgery. After that, he stated, "I could only get a feeling but no liquid" (interview, June 22, 1984). He saw himself as sterile.

Lucas stated that at one time he had a problem, "but I wasn't sick," although he never described what the problem was. In reference to his past killings, he stated, "From fourteen years old all I can say is I killed. I just lived a criminal life." As to specific killings, "To me, it's as if I haven't killed anyone, yet I have. . . . It's like bein' two people. I could see myself commit 'em, the crime, but I couldn't feel myself committin' it." Lucas further states, "It's like living in two different worlds. You want to do what is right, and yet, ya can't do it" (interviews, February 2, 1985; March 22, 1985).

Attitudes

Although frequently claiming to the contrary, Lucas seemed to enjoy his "celebrity" status. He knew he had something others wanted—information. Lucas was now in the limelight, no longer going unnoticed. When he spoke, a great many people were willing to listen.

Lucas later claimed remorse for killing his victims. However, a big smile crossed his face whenever he was identified as having committed a homicide and he cleared another of his "cases." This might indicate pride that he got away with a murder for so long, or it might indicate pleasure that he had, as he called it, "solved his case."

To value human life seemed beyond his capability. When asked why more of his victims weren't males, he replied, "That's somethin' I very seldom do, unless it's an emergency and [I] have to do it." For him, the victim was an object: "only one that ever bothered me was Becky." As for his mother, "No, 'cause I didn't kill her, she died of a heart attack after I hit her with the knife." He didn't take any responsibility for his mother's death because she was beating him with a broom when she was killed. He viewed it as self-defense (interviews, August 14, 1984; February 8, 1985).

Lucas did not like to admit that some of his victims were young children. He blamed most of these deaths on his accomplice, Toole. He claimed to have believed that one four-year-old victim was fifteen years old.

He seems to have traveled from one victim to the next. "I'd go from one to the other and wouldn't think about the last one I'd killed. I never had no feeling for that person at all" (interview, August 14, 1984).

Most of his female victims were, in his opinion, prostitutes. "Most of the girls I've met on the highway has turned out to be prostitutes. [They] has been either out sellin' theirselves to truckers or people on the highway and I, uh, have always since I was a little kid hated prostitutes" (interview, June 22, 1984).

Lucas claimed to have studied law enforcement. On the one hand, he showed concern for law enforcement problems; on the other, he showed disdain for law enforcement agencies. "I've turned a lot of law enforcement, as far as people know it today, upside down. It took years of practice, years of understanding criminal law" (interview, June 22, 1984).

When asked how he had changed since his arrest in 1983, he responded, "I've changed from what I used to be. I was a killer. Let's put it plain out. The type of life I lived. I mean that thing was nothin but crime. I didn't do nothin else. It got so killin' somebody meant nothin' to me" (interview, March 22, 1985).

When asked why he had changed, he responded:

Seein' what I've done. It's my own personal feelins. What I've seen what I've done. Stuff like 'at. That's caused me ta change. Since I've learned about the families. I've learned about the sufferin' they went through. How much sufferin' I've caused. It hurts! It would cause anybody to change. Seein' the misery 'cause of what I've done. I'd never dreamt of that before. (interview, March 22, 1985)

Recall of Events

Lucas's memory is described as including an excruciatingly intense wealth of detail. Law enforcement authorities found that Lucas had a remarkable recall for road numbers, mileages, and landmarks. They frequently took Lucas into the countryside and let him direct them to the crime scene. In one instance in Texas, Lucas was being driven past a commercial building when he said that he and an accomplice had killed a man and woman in an armed robbery of "that liquor store over there." The officer noted that the building was not a liquor store, but later he learned that it had been one when the proprietors were killed in a robbery. In another instance, a rural crime scene was so remote that the officer could not find his way back to it. Lucas led the officers directly to the crime scene.

When questioned about his memory, Lucas stated, "Yeah, I can't recall how I do it, really. . . . there's so many of 'em, they just seem to come back clear as crystal. It's like something in a movie, like watching a movie over and over" (interview, March 22, 1985). Lucas confessed to his murders because "The Lord told me to" (interview, June 5, 1984). As for his phenomenal memory, "That was done by Jesus Himself. That was from a light comin' into my cell and, uh, asking me to come forth with my confessions. And, uh, I have been able to uh, go back to the bodies, and give complete descriptions of the bodies through Him. And that's the only way I can do it" (interview, June 5, 1984).

It is possible that Lucas was suffering from delirium tremors from alcohol withdrawal and was hallucinating. Another explanation of his recall ability is referred to by psychologists as "hypernesia," that is, an unusually exact or vivid memory. Lucas's ability to remember his victims could also be attributed to an "eidetic" memory, which causes mental images that are unusually vivid and almost photographically exact.

The Aftermath and the Lucas Controversy

On April 19, 1985, a federal district judge in Austin, Texas, ordered Lucas to be transferred from the Williamson County jail in Georgetown to San Antonio to appear before a grand jury in that city the following week. On the previous Friday,

Lucas had been taken from Georgetown to Waco, where he testified before a grand jury just prior to the judge's order. Two days following the trip to Waco, on Sunday, April 14, the *Dallas Times Herald*'s front-page headline asked, "Mass murderer or massive hoax?" The extensive reporting and investigative journalism in the pages that followed certainly helped the *Herald* in its battle with the local and fierce competition from the *Dallas Morning News*. In all, the *Herald* devoted five full pages to the story, which charged that Lucas had perpetrated a hoax to embarrass authorities and keep himself off death row. The article, written primarily by Hugh Aynesworth (who at one time had talked Lucas into signing a contract giving Aynesworth exclusive rights to Lucas's life story), went into great detail regarding Lucas's travels and his alleged victims. For the task force, it was the end of their work with Henry Lee Lucas.

The Lucas Task Force and, more important, the Texas Rangers, were to become targets of criticism by the news media and the attorney general of Texas, who under the Texas constitution was charged with defending the Rangers in a civil or criminal court of law. The Lucas Task Force had been a unique organization during its seventeen months of operation. Never before in the history of law enforcement had the coordination of hundreds of homicide investigations been conducted in over thirty states on one suspect and his accomplices. A person might think that for such an endeavor there might be a margin for some error, but the charge that all of it had been a hoax was hard for many to believe. A Texas newspaper was indeed making news by charging literally hundreds of police agencies in twenty-seven states with falsifying information for the purpose of increasing their homicide clearance rates! What could possibly be the motive of the Texas Rangers, the Williamson County sheriff's office, and law enforcement agencies from all over the country in perpetrating such a hoax? Others would ask a different question. What could possibly be the motive of the attorney general of Texas in making such charges against the Texas Rangers, one of the oldest and most respected police agencies in the United States?

Henry Lee Lucas was indeed a serial killer, having been convicted of eleven homicides. He probably did not kill 360 people. However, it is very difficult for a social scientist to question the clearances of all 162 homicides attributed to Lucas in thirty states.

Briefly, the evidence used by the reports of the *Dallas Times Herald*, which the attorney general relied on almost exclusively, reveals little of a probative nature. Much of the evidence is based on the recollections of Lucas's half brothers and half sisters, who have searched their memories as far back as eight or nine years. Other evidence is based on the weak assumption that Lucas could not have driven 11,000 miles in a month or an average of 367 miles per day. The documentary evidence of payroll records comes from the Jacksonville, Florida, roofing company records at the time when Lucas and Toole were working there. It is suspected that their employer falsified time sheets in collusion with Lucas and Toole. Further, the dates of Lucas's endorsements on his payroll checks (which could easily have been forged) were also crucial to the newspaper's charges, because these dates coincided with those of some of his killings that took place hundreds of miles away.

Henry Lee Lucas (left), the author (right). From the author's files (1984).

As a result of the Texas attorney general's staff investigation, a report was issued on the task force and alleged homicides committed by Lucas. This report was never made public. After the Texas Rangers prepared a four-volume, extensively documented response to this report, the attorney general's report was substantially modified and revised. The Texas Rangers' report was not made available to the public by order of the Texas attorney general. Such an order appeared to be self-serving and placed the Texas attorney general in a position reflecting a conflict of interest.

The Texas attorney general's *Lucas Report,* issued in April 1986, was, in effect, an indictment of law enforcement investigators in thirty states and, more directly, an attack on the various judicial systems that found Lucas guilty of ten or eleven homicides. It is also interesting that the report relied almost exclusively on the investigative reporting of the *Dallas Times Herald* for documentary evidence. Over

80 percent of the evidence in the report came directly from the newspaper's article of April 14, 1985.

To illustrate the contextual flavor of this report, the following comments are taken from Attorney General Jim Mattox's transmittal letter in the introduction to the report (Mattox, 1986, pp. i–ii). Comments in brackets are those of the author of this volume.

> Questions about Henry Lee Lucas will be debated for decades. This report is not offered as a final answer. There may never be a final answer. . . .
>
> [W]e find numerous discrepancies between Lucas' confession and obtainable evidence regarding his whereabouts. . . .
>
> [Staff] conducted interviews with law enforcement officers around the country. [There is no evidentiary documentation to these interviews in the report, and other reliable evidence strongly indicates that the majority of law enforcement agencies that believe Lucas to have been the killer of the victims were never contacted by the attorney general's staff.]
>
> [T]here is a notable lack of physical evidence linking Lucas to the crimes to which he confessed. Luas did not [sic] lead authorities to any bodies of victims. [This statement is patently misleading, according to numerous law enforcement agencies, because they have video and audio tape evidence that Lucas did lead them, unassisted, to the sites of some of his killings.]
>
> We have found information that would lead us to believe that some officials "cleared cases" just to get them off the books. [Nowhere in this report is the term "some" quantified.]

Authorities remain convinced of Lucas's involvement in at least one hundred homicides (Newton, 2000).

Lucas's partner in death, Ottis Toole, died of AIDS in a Florida prison on September 15, 1996.

Lucas's Last Words

The last time I interviewed Henry Lee Lucas was in May 1998. He was scheduled for execution the following day. It was visiting day on death row, and it was hard to conduct a conversation amid the din of the other inmates' discussions with their lawyers or loved ones.

Lucas admitted he was fighting for his life and was trying to get his death sentence commuted to life. He told me and my wife and collaborator, Kim, that he had not killed anyone and that the only reason he had confessed was to make law enforcement look bad. The following day, Lucas's sentence was commuted to life imprisonment by the then-governor of Texas, George W. Bush.

On March 12, 2001, Henry Lee Lucas died of natural causes.

Hillside Strangler Kenneth Bianchi.
© *Bettmann/CORBIS.*

CHAPTER 8

Kenneth Bianchi

— A CASE STUDY

Social Environment

Kenneth Bianchi had numerous problems throughout his childhood owing to various maladies and illnesses, many of which were reported to be psychosomatic. His mother was apparently very overprotective (see the Family Background discussion that follows). In his teens, Bianchi frequently purchased hard-core sex material in adult bookstores in Rochester, New York. He sometimes borrowed the family movie projector and showed pornographic films to friends at their homes, telling his mother he was showing family movies. Bianchi smoked marijuana a few times but was never seriously habituated. His first sexual experience probably took place in his early teens.

His teenage marriage right after high school lasted only eight months. After it was annulled, Bianchi attended Monroe Community College in Rochester, where he took police science and political science courses. His grades were generally high C's. Then Bianchi dropped out of college and took qualifying tests for the U.S. Air Force. He registered high on the electronics tests, but did not enter the military. Instead, he worked as a bouncer at a bar for a while, and then he obtained a job with an ambulance service.

After his mother remarried, Bianchi decided to travel to California. His mother had arranged for him to stay with Angelo Buono, his forty-seven-year-old half cousin, who ran an auto upholstery business out of his home in Glendale, California, a suburb of Los Angeles.

In early 1977, Bianchi moved in with a young woman from Bellingham, Washington, who later bore him a son. Their finances were tight, but Bianchi bought a Cadillac even though he couldn't afford the payments. He simply ignored the bills until the car was repossessed. In May 1977, Bianchi's girlfriend went to Las Vegas with a friend and was allegedly raped during her stay. She did not report the incident to the police or to Bianchi. It wasn't until later, when Bianchi had caught venereal disease from his girlfriend, that he learned of the rape. When she was examined by doctors, they discovered she was pregnant.

In March 1978, three and a half weeks after Bianchi's son was born, his girlfriend broke up with him and moved with her baby back to her hometown of Bellingham, Washington. In May of that year the couple decided to give the relationship another try, and Bianchi moved to Bellingham. As his girlfriend was breast-feeding their son, Bianchi limited his sexual relations with her. He stated later that he went out with other women during this time. He also apparently masturbated frequently. After his arrest, police found a briefcase belonging to him that contained hard-core pornography, several stained pairs of undershorts, and a heavily stained towel.

When Bianchi arrived in Bellingham, he was hired by a uniformed private security firm. That summer, Bianchi left his security job and went to work for a department store for higher wages. Bianchi was reportedly popular with some of the security firm's clients, and the firm subsequently rehired him in a supervisory position.

Reportedly, throughout high school Bianchi had been obsessed with becoming a police officer. He took police science courses at Monroe Community College in Rochester. However, he was repeatedly rejected when he applied and reapplied for police positions in New York and in California. In Los Angeles he participated in police ride-along programs twice in the latter part of 1978. He was never satisfied with any of his jobs because he intensely wanted to do police work. His security job in Bellingham was the closest he ever came to doing police work. Prior to his arrest in 1979, he had reportedly held eleven jobs in previous last seven years (*New York Times,* April 24, 1979, p. 16).

Family Background

Kenneth Alessio Bianchi was born in 1951 to a young teenage girl in Rochester, New York. After Bianchi's mother became pregnant, she married a man who was not the father. She was allegedly an alcoholic. The Monroe County, New York, adoption report stated, "She [Bianchi's mother] appears to be a pathetic creature of limited intelligence" (Schwarz, 1981, p. 123). After the birth, his mother placed Bianchi in a foster home. When he was a few weeks old, a private adoption proceeding was initiated by Francis and Nicholas Bianchi. He was legally adopted by them in 1952 and given their last name when Bianchi reached his first birthday.

Bianchi's adoptive parents were both born in 1919 and were of similar backgrounds: first-generation Americans raised in Italian Catholic families. They both left high school in their second year to take full-time jobs. As a child Nicholas had a stuttering problem, which he never fully overcame. In December 1941, the two were married. Francis learned shortly thereafter that she could not bear children and had to undergo a radical hysterectomy. Ten years later when Ken was adopted, she very quickly became an overprotective mother. Between December 1951 and May 1952, she took him to the doctor eight times, but nothing was found to be wrong with him other than a minor respiratory infection that was responding to treatment. Shortly after the adoption, the Bianchis moved to a larger apartment with a fenced-in yard so their son wouldn't wander into the street.

Doctors had evaluated the Bianchis for the adoption agency. The agency's report described the doctors' evaluations:

> He [the doctor] thinks she [Francis Bianchi] will always be excitable but doubts that this will affect the baby in any way. He thinks that her love for him will compensate [for] any emotional upset, as her love is true and not artificial. Her attitude and emotional stability may improve after she is through the menopausal period, which was induced by the operation. (Schwarz, 1981, p. 127)

The family moved to Los Angeles in 1956 because of Ken's asthma. In January 1957, Ken fell from a jungle gym at the school playground and struck his nose and the back of his head (Schwarz, 1981, p. 127). He also began to have petit mal seizures, and when he was upset he would roll his eyes. His mother thought he had epilepsy, but the doctors felt that his various problems were psychological. This angered her. Moreover, the doctors thought the eye rolling was simply a habit. In 1958, the family moved back to Rochester, where Ken was admitted to Rochester General Hospital because he frequently urinated in his pants. His mother had done everything she could to stop Ken from doing this. She had gone so far as to spank him before he went to the bathroom to ensure that he urinated enough not to dribble in his pants later.

Ken was diagnosed as having diverticulitis, a horseshoe kidney, and transient hypertension. Although these were physical findings, the doctor also stated that Ken had many emotional problems. In fact, the hospital report indicated that there was no problem with Ken until his mother came to visit him in the afternoon. Then he would complain about everything for his mother's benefit. Hospitalization was a trying experience for Ken, and the attending physician wondered if his social or home environment was adequate. The hospital staff and investigating social workers suggested that Ken and his mother see a psychiatrist, but his mother refused.

In a parent–teacher conference report, Ken's third-grade teacher described his mother as a very nervous person who was easily upset. The teacher said that as a result, Ken was also nervous and wet his pants.

Ken's parents had been reported numerous times to the Rochester Society for the Prevention of Cruelty to Children because of concern over Ken's emotional state. On September 15, 1962, the society issued a report on its investigation of the Bianchis. The report apparently focused primarily on Ken's mother. She was found to be "[d]eeply disturbed, socially ambitious, dissatisfied, unsure, opinionated and overly protective . . . guilt ridden by her failure to have children . . . [and who had] smothered this adopted son in medical attention and maternal concern from the moment of adoption" (Schwarz, 1981, p. 130). The report also focused on Ken's mother's frequent attempts to have him tested because of his constant urination. Each test involved the probing of his genitals.

Ken's mother often kept him home from school for fear he would develop an illness and his urination problem would worsen. Ken was seen at DePaul Clinic in Rochester in 1962. Part of the clinic report stated:

> The boy drips urine in his pants, doesn't make friends very easily and has twitches. The other children make fun of him and his mother is extremely angry at the school because they do not stop the other children. The mother sounded as if she were very overprotective of this boy. When the boy fell on the playground in kindergarten early in the school year, she kept the boy home the total year. She indicated that she has become so upset because people keep telling her to take her child to a psychiatrist. She does not think he needs a psychiatrist and she went into great detail about how the doctors these days are just out for money and she does not trust any of them.
>
> The mother is obviously the dominant one in the family and impresses one as a quite disturbed woman. Mrs. Bianchi tends to displace her anger especially on doctors and hospitals and project the blame for the boy's problem onto other sources. (Schwarz, 1981, pp. 132–133)

The DePaul Clinic report also more specifically addressed Ken's behavior:

> Dr. Dowling reports that Kenneth is a deeply hostile boy who has extremely dependent needs which his mother fulfills. He depends on his mother for his very survival and expends a great deal of energy keeping his hostility under control and under cover. He is eager for other relationships and uses a great deal of denial in handling his own feelings. For example, he says that his mother and father are the best parents in the world. . . . To sum up, Dr. Dowling said that he is a severely repressed boy who is very anxious and very lonely. He felt that the only outlet whereby he could somehow get back at his mother was through psychosomatic complaints. Dr. Dowling felt that without this defense of the use of his somatic complaints he might very well be a severely disturbed boy. (Schwarz, 1981, pp. 133–134).

Bianchi testified at his cousin Angelo Buono's murder trial in 1983 that he had lied about his mother while he was being examined by psychiatrists in 1979. He claimed that his statements about child abuse were "exaggerated and extended (*Los Angeles Daily News*, August 18, 1982, p. 1). Bianchi had told psychiatrists that his mother had held his hand over a flame as punishment for playing with matches. Bianchi claimed that he was encouraged by his attorney to lie about his mother in order to bolster a potential insanity defense plea.

Bianchi reportedly did not spend much time with his father, who worked a great deal of overtime during Ken's childhood. When Bianchi was fourteen years old,

his father died suddenly at work. After this, Ken reportedly underwent a prolonged period of grief.

Shortly after Bianchi graduated from high school in 1971, he got married. But he
quarreled with his wife constantly, and after eight months she left him and filed for
an annulment. Bianchi later referred to the marriage as being "dumped on"
(Schwarz, 1981, p. 40).

Peer Group Associations and Personal Relationships

The prosecutors at Buono's trial characterized both Bianchi and Buono as having
sex-oriented, manipulative personalities (*Los Angeles Daily News*, October 17, 1983,
p. 1). Bianchi had read a lot of hard-core pornography, and Buono reportedly had
been involved in a number of perverted sexual acts. Also, Bianchi had very obviously manipulated his girlfriend from Washington, convincing her that he had
cancer and going to his "chemotherapy appointments" without her. (He had
apparently stolen some medical records and altered them with his own name.)
Buono, though not appearing manipulative, had given his wives the strong
impression that he wanted to totally control them.

When Bianchi was arrested in 1979, his live-in girlfriend stated, "The Ken I
knew couldn't ever have hurt anybody or killed anybody, he wasn't the kind of
person who could have killed somebody" (Barnes, 1984, videotape). His boss at
the security firm considered him an excellent security guard (Levin & Fox, 1985,
p. 148). A number of his friends in Bellingham offered to be character witnesses for
him. Almost everyone who knew him believed him to be innocent.

A Canadian border guard who worked with Bianchi in the County Sheriff's
Reserves program in Bellingham described Bianchi: "He was a little off. Always
talking about psychology and stuff, but in a way that made you know he didn't
know what he was talking about. Nice guy, though. Wouldn't want him as a
cop. I wouldn't have trusted his backing me up. Not aggressive enough. Just
a nice guy. A bit of a nut, but not the kind to murder anyone" (Schwarz, 1981,
pp. 117–118).

Bianchi met his live-in girlfriend in Los Angeles in 1976, and they lived together
on and off for about two years. In the summer of 1978 they argued often, and the
girl moved to Bellingham, Washington. Bianchi moved there shortly thereafter,
and they resumed living together. After Bianchi's confessions to murders in Washington and California, the girlfriend became convinced that Bianchi had a multiple
personality. She stated, "How else could he have killed those women and then
come home to me as though nothing had happened? Maybe he could have fooled
me once or twice, but for three years!" (*Bellingham Herald*, January 1, 1980, p. 1).

A former girlfriend of Bianchi's testified at Buono's trial that she had lived with
Bianchi in 1976. She said that she broke up with him in late 1976 and for more than
a year after that Bianchi harassed her by stealing items from her apartment, cutting
up her sandals with a razor blade, ripping up her nightgown, and pounding on the
outside walls of her apartment.

Contact with Defining Agencies

When Bianchi joined the Sheriff's Reserve program in Bellingham in March 1978, he was the first private security officer to be accepted by that organization. He was scheduled to attend a meeting of the reserve on the night two girls disappeared in Bellingham. The Bellingham police subsequently learned that he did not attend the meeting. When they found out that Bianchi had been out in a security vehicle that night and that he had been made aware of missing keys from the home that the missing girls were supposedly going to house-sit, they became suspicious. Then the police learned that Bianchi had called a neighbor and told her not to go near the house that night because work was being done on the alarm system. Nothing appeared to be wrong in the house, although someone had evidently been there recently. When the strangled girls' bodies were found in their car on the following day, the police immediately arrested Bianchi. He surrendered willingly, stating he had killed no one.

Kenneth Bianchi had very quickly become a suspect in the Bellingham case. Although he consistently and calmly maintained that he was innocent, the police found long blond hairs believed to belong to one of the victims and pubic hairs matching those of Bianchi in the Bellingham house that the victims were supposedly housesitting. His attorney requested the assistance of psychiatrist Donald Lunde, to whom Bianchi recounted a love-filled, joyous, and tranquil childhood. Bianchi's recollection did not match medical and psychiatric records from his childhood. Lunde was forced to conclude that Ken was repressing much of his past and might not remember committing the stranglings (Levin & Fox, 1985, p. 149).

By now his attorney was skeptical not only of Bianchi's alibis, but of his sanity. Yet Bianchi resisted his attorney's argument to enter an insanity plea. Dr. John Watkins, an expert in hypnosis, was called in to try to restore Bianchi's memory. During one of the hypnosis sessions, Dr. Watkins discovered the emergence of a second personality, called "Stevie Walker." Bianchi's second personality, who appeared sadistic and boastful, proudly talked about committing murders in Bellingham and Los Angeles. He stated that Angelo Buono, his cousin, had killed with him in Los Angeles. Based on Watkins's discovery of this second personality, Bianchi's attorney concluded that Bianchi was not legally sane at the time of the murders. After videotapes of Watkins's interviews with Bianchi were shown to Bianchi, he agreed to allow his attorney to plead not guilty by reason of insanity.

Because of this change of plea, the judge in Bellingham called in Dr. Ralph Allison, an expert on multiple personalities and altered ego states, as an independent advisor to the court. Allison hypnotized Bianchi and was also confronted with Bianchi's second personality, Steve, who boasted of the murders. Through hypnosis, Dr. Allison took Bianchi back to his childhood and learned that the second personality, or alter ego, had been invented by Bianchi when he was nine years old. Allison concluded that Bianchi was a dual personality, who was not aware of his crimes and who was incompetent to stand trial.

The prosecutor, who disagreed with the conclusions regarding Bianchi's dual personality, requested that Dr. Martin Orne, a psychiatrist at the University of Pennsylvania Medical School, be called in to examine Bianchi. Rather than attempting to authenticate Bianchi's multiple personality, Orne devised tests to determine the authenticity of Bianchi's hypnotic trance. Orne told Bianchi before hypnotizing him that it was rare in cases of multiple personalities for there to be only two personalities. When Bianchi was hypnotized, another personality surfaced. This one was called "Billy." On another occasion, Orne asked Bianchi, while hypnotized, to talk to his attorney, who was not actually in the room. Bianchi complied with Orne's request, even shaking the hand of his attorney who was not there. When Bianchi's attorney was asked to enter the room, Bianchi asked, "How can I see him in two places?" (Barnes, 1984, videotape).

On the basis of (1) the third personality, which had been suggested by Orne prior to hypnosis, (2) the fact that a hypnotized person ordinarily does not question the existence of two of the same people, and (3) other tests, Orne concluded that Bianchi was faking hypnosis and thus faking his multiple personalities. Indeed, books on psychology had been found in Bianchi's home, including one on hypnotic techniques. This seemed to support Orne's conclusion; however, there was no real proof that Bianchi was faking a hypnotic trance and a multiple personality.

While checking his background in Los Angeles, investigators found a copy of Bianchi's academic transcript from Los Angeles Valley College. The transcript had an incorrect date of birth and listed courses that had been taken before Bianchi even moved to Los Angeles. It turned out that the original transcript belonged to a person named Thomas Steven Walker. Further investigation revealed that Bianchi had placed an advertisement in the *Los Angeles Times* requesting applications for a counseling position; applicants were to send in their resume and college transcript. When Walker sent in his transcript, Bianchi substituted his own name on the transcript and used the transcript to further his own career.

Even though an alter ego could presumably mimic a real identity, like that of Steve Walker, Bianchi first saw Walker's name as an adult, whereas "Stevie Walker" had appeared under hypnosis when Bianchi regressed back to the age of nine. Although it is possible that two Steve Walkers appeared in Bianchi's life by coincidence, it is more likely that Bianchi was faking hypnosis (Levin & Fox, 1985, p. 153).

On June 1, 1979, Dr. Saul Faerstein examined Bianchi at the request of the judge. At the end of his report to the judge, Faerstein discussed Bianchi's motivation and long-standing interest in the police:

> I would like to add one note of speculation which may shed some light on the motivation for these crimes. From his earliest years, Kenneth Bianchi admired and dreamed of becoming a law enforcement officer. He drew the figure of a policeman in a childhood Draw-A-Person test. He studied police science at junior college. He applied to law enforcement agencies for jobs in New York, California and Washington, but he was always rejected. Perhaps he saw his goal as the achieve-

ment of some victory over his mother, whom he saw as another authority figure. All these rejections by law enforcement agencies made him bitter. In the long string of murders he committed, he demonstrated that he had mastered the science of law enforcement and that he was a better policeman than any policeman on the force. He left no clues. He went undetected for over a year. So in the process of achieving his victory over the female authority figure by killing her surrogates, he also vanquished the male authority figure by eluding the police, sheriffs, and detectives. (Schwarz, 1981, p. 218)

Because the multiple-personality theory was no longer believable, Bianchi's lawyer negotiated a plea with the prosecutors in Bellingham, Washington, and Los Angeles County, California. His client would enter a plea of guilty to the murders in Bellingham and to five of the murders in California if he would not be given the death penalty. In return, Bianchi would testify against his cousin Angelo Buono in California.

Shortly after Bianchi entered a plea of guilty in Washington, Angelo Buono was arrested in Los Angeles on October 18, 1979, for ten "strangler" murders. The only substantial evidence against Buono was Bianchi's testimony. Buono was also charged with a number of nonmurder felonies and misdemeanors, including sodomy, pimping, pandering, and conspiracy to commit extortion and oral copulation involving an outcall prostitution scheme that Buono and Bianchi were accused of operating in 1977. In March 1980, two young women reportedly told a Los Angeles County grand jury that they had been engaged in a prostitution and extortion operation with Buono and Bianchi in 1977. Buono was arraigned on these nonmurder indictments on March 27, 1980. Buono was appointed private counsel by the court, because the regular public defender's office in Los Angeles County could not defend Buono on account of conflict of interest. They were representing Bianchi. Buono was eligible for court-appointed representation because prior to his arrest, while under police surveillance, he had given his home and business to his neighbor through a quitclaim deed. The first part of Buono's preliminary hearing in the summer of 1980 dealt with the nonmurder charges. The second part dealt specifically with the ten counts of murder. The hearing was closed to the press and media at the request of Buono's attorneys, which was granted by the presiding judge. On June 20, 1980, Buono was allowed by the judge to fire his court-appointed attorneys. The judge appointed new attorneys to defend Buono, and the second part of the hearing was delayed for ten days. On March 16, Buono was bound over for trial after the longest preliminary hearing ever held in Los Angeles County (involving 120 days of testimony).

Shortly after his arrival in California, Bianchi wrote a letter to Dr. Allison, one of the psychiatrists who had examined him in Bellingham, stating that he had not personally killed any of the "strangler" victims. When the Los Angeles district attorney's office confronted Bianchi with this change in his story, he reportedly said he had not told them initially that Buono did all the killings because he was afraid they would not believe him if he did not also implicate himself (*Los Angeles Times*, October 22, p. 1). In early October 1980, Bianchi's jailers seized some papers in his cell, including a forty-three-page document entitled "An Open Letter to the World" in which Bianchi denied participation in any murder. On October 2, just prior to the seizure of this letter, a woman who had been visiting Bianchi in jail was arrested in Los Angeles for attempting a "copycat" version of the two murders in Bellingham, Washington, to which Bianchi had confessed. She was charged by Bellingham authorities with the attempted strangling of a woman whom she had lured to a downtown hotel. The woman was also accused of sending a series of tape recordings to law enforcement authorities with a message that Bianchi was the wrong man and that more murders would be committed by the real killer. The woman told law enforcement officers and the press that Bianchi could not have committed the "strangler" murders because he was in bed with her on the nights that the victims were abducted and killed. She claimed that she had met Bianchi in 1977. Police, however, learned that the woman's first contact with Bianchi was by mail in January 1980. Police believe that this woman's actions were coordinated by Bianchi during her visits to him in jail in an effort to clear himself of all charges. The woman was later convicted of attempted murder in Bellingham and was sentenced to life in prison.

Prior to Buono's trial, which was scheduled for July 1981, the Los Angeles County district attorney filed a motion for dismissal of charges against Buono owing to Bianchi's lack of credibility as a witness. The judge, in an unusual move, denied the motion, and the prosecution of Buono was moved into the hands of the Office of the State of California Attorney General.

When the trial began in November 1981, jury selection took five months because of the highly publicized nature of the case. The trial lasted two years and two days, the longest trial at that time in the history of the United States. The prosecution's key witness was Kenneth Bianchi, who testified for a total of eighty days. He described how the abductions took place, how the victims were tortured and killed, and how the victims' bodies were discarded. His testimony, however, changed frequently. At one point he stated, "The strangulations I don't remember. I remember the women were alive and picked up and . . . dead and . . . dropped off" (*Los Angeles Times*, July 1, 1982). As to what happened in between these times, he said he did not know. At other times, he was graphic in his descriptions of the killings, but the descriptions changed with his further testimony.

On March 14, 1982, the California Supreme Court ruled that witnesses whose memory had been enhanced through hypnosis could not testify in criminal trials. This ruling effectively barred the testimony of some witnesses for the prosecution who would have linked Buono to some of the victims. The ruling, however, did not bar Bianchi's testimony because the presiding judge ruled that Bianchi had "voluntarily and consciously faked hypnosis "(*Los Angeles Times*, March 15, 1982, p. 3).

Late in the trial, in June 1983, the woman who had attempted the "copycat" killing in Bellingham testified for the defense. She had been found guilty of attempted murder in Washington. She stated that she and Bianchi had conspired to frame Buono for the "strangler" murders; they had planned to testify falsely that Buono confessed to the murders and told them he had an accomplice other than Bianchi. She further stated that Bianchi had directed her to go to Bellingham and commit a murder to show that the accomplice was still at large (*Los Angeles Times,* June 22, 1983, p. 1).

After 345 days and the testimony of over 400 witnesses, the case went to the jury on October 20, 1983. The jury found Buono guilty of nine out of the ten counts of murder. The not-guilty verdict was for the first victim. In this case, the body of the victim did not have the ligature marks of the other nine victims, and microscopic fibers from the chair in Buono's house were not found on her body, as they had been on the other victims. The verdicts of the jury included a finding of "special circumstances of multiple murder," which in California carries only two possible sentences: life imprisonment without parole, or death. Following his conviction, it was revealed that prior to the trial Buono's attorney had been offered a life sentence with possible parole for his client by the Los Angeles County district attorney's office if Buono would plead guilty. Buono had rejected the offer.

Buono requested that he be allowed to defend himself during the penalty phase of the trial. After the presiding judge determined that Buono's understanding of the law applicable to the penalty phase was too limited, he denied the request. The jury recommended life imprisonment without parole. On January 9, 1984, the judge sentenced Buono to life imprisonment without the possibility of parole. He is currently incarcerated in Folsom State Prison in California. Bianchi was returned to the state of Washington to be incarcerated in Walla Walla State Prison until his first parole hearing in a little less than twenty-seven years. If he is ever freed by Washington, Bianchi will face five consecutive life sentences in California. In late 1984, Bianchi legally changed his name. Later that year, he changed it again, to Nicholas Fontana.

Bianchi has been denied parole on a number of occasions since his convictions. On May 6, 1994, the U.S. Court of Appeals in San Francisco rejected Bianchi's challenges to his legal representation and guilty plea in the Washington killings. The court stated that it was not clear whether Bianchi was hypnotized during psychiatric examinations. Even if he was hypnotized, the court said, there was no proof that his memories of the murders were the product of hypnotic suggestion. The prosecution's case against him was strong, and he avoided a possible death sentence by pleading guilty. The court also said that Bianchi's claims of ineffective assistance by his court-appointed lawyer were far outweighed by the evidence against him (*San Francisco Chronicle,* May 7, 1994, p. A21).

Offense Behavior

Within two months, eleven females between the ages of twelve and twenty-eight were found strangled in Los Angeles County, California. Seven of the victims had been raped. Eight were found within a six mile radius of the city of Glendale. Two of the victims, ages twelve and fourteen, had been last seen together at a local shopping center in Glendale. Their bodies were found a week later near Dodger Stadium. Six of the victims were known to have been heavily involved in the nightlife of Hollywood Boulevard. One had been seen frequently in an area where prostitutes gather at Hollywood and Vine Streets. One was a local runaway who was well known on the streets of Hollywood. One had worked as a waitress in Hollywood. One had moved to Hollywood after being convicted of prostitution in the state of New York. One was a Hollywood resident and a chronic hitchhiker, and the last was frequently seen in the area trying to get into show business.

The nude body of the first victim was discovered alongside Forest Lawn Drive near Forest Lawn Cemetery. She was a nineteen-year-old part-time prostitute. She had been manually strangled. Almost two weeks later, a second victim was found on a roadside in Glendale. The fifteen-year-old girl was nude and had ligature marks around the wrists, ankles, and neck. She had been raped and sodomized.

Between October 18 and November 29, 1977, eleven victims were found dumped by their assailants in a similar manner. The victims were all found nude, strangled, and left in remote areas of the county. The majority had been sexually assaulted. Most of them bore ligature marks similar to those on the second victim.

On December 14, 1977, a twelfth female victim was found strangled and nude in a residential area east of Silver Lake (*Los Angeles Times,* December 15, 1977, p. 1). An autopsy revealed she had not been sexually assaulted. The victim had been employed by an outcall "modeling" service and was known to have worked as a prostitute. She had been reported missing shortly after 10:00 P.M. on December 13 after she failed to make her customary check-in call at 10:00 P.M. The victim had been sent to what turned out to be a vacant apartment in Los Angeles. Her abandoned auto was found nearby. It was learned later that the original call for modeling services had been placed from a telephone booth in the Hollywood branch of the Los Angeles City Library.

Almost two months later, a thirteenth victim was found. The victim, a twenty-year-old female who lived in Glendale, was discovered nude and strangled in the trunk of her car, which was found in a ravine near a highway in the Angeles National Forest. She had been last seen near her home on the afternoon of February 16, 1978, and was discovered at 9:45 A.M. the following morning. This was the last victim of what was now being referred to as the "Hillside Strangler."

On January 11, 1979, Kenneth Bianchi had lured two girls in Bellingham to an unoccupied house by offering them a house-sitting job. He met them there and forced them into the house at gunpoint. He bound them with rope, sexually assaulted them, and then strangled them. He then put them in their car and drove it to a deserted cul-de-sac, where he left the car. He was quickly linked to the girls' disappearance and arrested. When Bianchi's home was searched, a number of stolen items were found that had been taken from houses to which Bianchi had been assigned as a security guard.

Thus, almost a year after the last "Hillside" victim was found, following a double murder in Bellingham, Washington, and Kenneth Bianchi's arrest and subsequent confession, the task force in Los Angeles learned that ten of the thirteen victims attributed to the Hillside Strangler had been killed by Angelo Buono and Kenneth Bianchi. According to Levin and Fox (1985), by one account Bianchi and Buono were sitting around Buono's house one day when they began talking about what it would feel like to kill someone. They decided to try it. Except for the first victim, who was killed in Buono's automobile, the other nine victims had been kidnapped and taken to Buono's home in Glendale, where they were tortured and killed. One had been injected with a cleaning fluid and gassed with a hose from the oven. Another was tortured and burned with an electric cord before her death. Bianchi's girlfriend, who lived with him during the time the murders were committed, said that Bianchi had been gone a lot at night during this time.

The killers reportedly first asked each of the victims to go to the bathroom in order to avoid involuntarily urinating right after death (*Los Angeles Times*, November 15, 1983, p. 6). The victims were each tied by their arms, legs, and neck to a special chair in Buono's spare bedroom. Each was then raped, sodomized with various instruments, and strangled to death. Nine of the bodies were then tossed on roadsides and hillsides in Los Angeles and Glendale. The last victim was put into the trunk of her car, which was pushed down a ravine.

Bianchi told police that he and Buono would flip a coin to see who would rape the victims first before they were murdered. He also stated that many of the victims had plastic bags placed over their heads before they were slowly strangled to death by tightening a rope around their necks. He stated that on one occasion he took Polaroid pictures of Buono raping one of the victims (*Los Angeles Times*, March 2, 1982, p. 1).

Buono had promoted Bianchi as a casting director and location scout for Universal Studios, so Bianchi played this role with a number of the victims. However, in most cases the victims were apparently lured into going with Buono and Bianchi because the two were posing as police officers. Witnesses stated they had seen Buono with a badge and handcuffs. Police proved that Buono had owned a police-type badge by analyzing an impression left in a wallet found in his home. Bianchi was known by a number of people to have police badges. Also, the police learned that Bianchi had obtained an official Los Angeles County seal from an aide to a county supervisor. The blue and white Cadillac that Bianchi drove while in Los Angeles was impounded by the police with this seal still affixed to the windshield. Further, the daughter of the late actor Peter Lorre identified Buono and Bianchi as the men who posed as vice squad officers and tried to force her into their car on a Hollywood street during the fall of 1977 (*Los Angeles Times*, July 22, 1981).

Buono reportedly kept one woman a virtual prisoner in his home for three weeks in the summer of 1977. She testified at the trial that she was beaten by both Buono and Bianchi. She and another woman were apparently forced into prostitution by the duo. Although the women were not allowed to testify to the specific acts of prostitution, because these charges were pending against Buono and were to be tried separately by court ruling, police investigation has shown that the women did commit acts of prostitution under Buono and Bianchi's direction (*Los Angeles Times*, March 11, 1982, p. 8).

Following Buono's arrest, he talked of demolishing his home, where the murders are believed to have taken place. A search of his home at this time revealed that the house was completely bare of any fingerprints. Forensic experts testified at the trial that fibers found on two of the victims matched those found in Buono's house.

Following Buono's trial and his sentencing, those who prosecuted the case stated, "We still don't know how they did the strangulations and how they worked together" (*Los Angeles Daily News*, January 14, 1985, p. 10).

Self-Concept

Bianchi bragged about his killings as "Steve Walker," one of his alleged personalities. He also talked of hating women while under this alter ego. However, the clues to Bianchi's self-concept appear to be so contradictory that an effort to establish Bianchi's self-image would be a guarantee for failure. Although Darcy O'Brien's book *Two of a Kind* (1985) presents a reconstruction of many of the killings that Bianchi and Buono committed, a reconstruction is not an accurate rendition of what was said and done; it is only the author's best guess at what was said and done. Therefore, this material has not been used. No criticism of O'Brien's work is intended.

Attitudes

When Kenneth Bianchi pled guilty to the two murders in Bellingham, Washington, he stated, "I can't find the words to express the sorrow for what I've done. In no way can I take away the pain I have given others, and in no way can I expect forgiveness from others" (Schwarz, 1981, p. 239). Bianchi was sobbing and crying as he made this statement. Some people might contend that he was truly a sick man with a multiple personality and genuinely sorry for what he had done. Others might argue that he was crying out of frustration because he had been caught. Psychiatrists still disagree in their interpretation of Kenneth Bianchi.

Recall of Events

Bianchi was able to remember minute details about his victims. Yet he gave only limited details on the actual killings and frequently changed his recollection of these events. Buono never spoke of the killings and consistently maintained his innocence.

Afterword

Kenneth Bianchi now resides in the Washington Walla Walla prison. His first parole hearing will be scheduled sometime in the year 2010. As noted earlier, he has changed his name to Nicholas Fontana. If he is ever freed from prison in Washington State, he will face five consecutive life sentences in California.

CHAPTER 9

Ted Bundy (1980 police mug shot).
© Associated Press DOC.

Theodore Robert Bundy

— A CASE STUDY

Social Environment

Not a great deal has been revealed of Bundy's early childhood. According to his fourth-grade teacher, "Ted was neither good nor bad, happy, well adjusted and always eager to learn" (Larsen, 1980, p. 92). He talked of being a policeman or a lawyer when he grew up. According to Robert Keppel, a detective from Seattle who spent a considerable amount of time delving into his background, information on Bundy's early years was sketchy, "[m]ainly because the crucial people we talked to—his cousin, his mother—have this particular image of him where he could do no wrong" (Larsen, 1980, p. 99). Keppel reports that Bundy displayed babyish tendencies up to the fifth grade in school. He was a loner who didn't want to get involved with too many people at a time. He could do superior work in school when he wanted to and liked to foster the impression that he always did superior work. Keppel describes his character at this time as too good for any sort of discipline.

Bundy had been born out of wedlock, and his mother married when he was four years old. The Bundys were not financially well off, but neither were they poverty stricken. "Upper lower class" would best describe their socioeconomic level when Ted Bundy was growing up. Following his mother's marriage the family reportedly moved several times over a four-year period in Tacoma, Washington. While Bundy was adjusting to his new father, he was also dealing with the family's moves around the city. Bundy comments on this period in his life by saying, "Life

161

was not as sweet, but not a nightmare" (Winn & Merrill, 1980, p. 105). This was a difficult and sometimes lonely period of readjustment for Bundy.

On the surface, Bundy's teenage years could be characterized as fairly typical for a young man growing up in Tacoma, Washington in the 1950s and early 1960s. Following junior high school, he participated in Little League baseball and high school football. He was a Boy Scout and ran unsuccessfully for the student council in high school. He was also a member of the high school cross-country team. However, he tried these activities only briefly before moving on to something else.

During high school, he felt at ease in only two environments—the ski slopes and the classroom. Bundy found a lot of enjoyment in skiing and is believed to have stolen expensive ski gear. Although he was considered a scholar by many of his fellow students, Bundy graduated from Wilson High School with only a B− average.

At age thirteen, he was reportedly very naive about sex and shied away from any discussion of the subject. In high school Bundy never appeared interested in girls. He had one date in his three years of high school. Bundy later argued that he was "particularly dense, or insensitive, not knowing when a woman's interested in me. I've been described as handsome and all this shit or attractive. I don't believe it. It's a built-in insecurity. I don't believe I'm attractive" (Michaud & Aynesworth, 1983, pp. 55–56). Bundy's best friend in high school describes him as a very sensitive person.

He was considered very private and introverted. His IQ was tested at 122. He earned above-average grades but was not considered an outstanding student. Bundy's neighbors remember him during this time as serious, nice and polite, not a troublemaker, and rather quiet.

Bundy had three goals in life: (1) to get married and have a family life, (2) to be a lawyer, and (3) to get involved in politics. His heroes were Senator J. William Fulbright, Nelson Rockefeller, and, later, Governor Daniel Evans. After completing college he dreamed of going to law school and remarked, "But money's a real problem" (Winn & Merrill, 1980, p. 4). Within the following three years, he attended two different law schools and for a brief period became very active in politics.

During the summer of 1965, after graduating from high school, Bundy worked at a warehouse in Tacoma and purchased his first car, a 1933 Plymouth coupe. That fall he entered the University of Puget Sound in Tacoma. He purchased a 1958 Volkswagen during his first year of college. Bundy stated later, "I just love Volkswagens!" (Larsen, 1980, p. 111). In the fall of 1966, he transferred to the University of Washington in Seattle to major in Asian studies. In the summer of 1967, Bundy attended the Stanford Chinese Institute in Stanford, California. In the fall of 1967, he changed his major to urban planning and sociology and withdrew from the University of Washington with several incompletes in the winter quarter of 1968. Then he traveled to Aspen, Colorado, to California, and to Philadelphia to visit his grandparents. After returning to Seattle in the spring of 1968, Bundy committed numerous crimes of shoplifting and burglary and then became involved in politics as a volunteer in a campaign for the Republican nominee for lieutenant governor.

During his campaign activities, Bundy often got drunk. Meanwhile, he became the nominee's official driver and made a number of political contacts and acquaintances. According to Bundy, it was during this period that he lost his virginity at age twenty-two by being seduced by an older woman after he got intoxicated (Michaud & Aynesworth, 1983, p. 62).

He traveled to Philadelphia in early 1969 and attended Temple University, where he took classes in urban affairs and theatrical arts. Bundy returned to Seattle in the summer of 1969 and rented a room near the University of Washington. He reentered the university in the summer of 1970, graduated in the spring of 1972 with a degree in psychology, and promptly applied to a number of law schools. Although he was given high character references from his college professors, his academic record and his Law School Aptitude Test scores were not impressive, and he was rejected by the law schools. Then Bundy became very active in Governor Dan Evans's reelection campaign. In February 1973, Bundy reapplied to the University of Utah College of Law with a glowing character reference from Governor Evans, and this time he was accepted. At the last minute, late in the summer, he decided not to attend law school that fall and lied to the school that he had suffered serious injuries in an auto accident.

In late 1974 and early 1975, Bundy attended night classes at the University of Puget Sound Law School. However, he was not happy with the school and dropped out. In the spring of 1974 he applied again to the University of Utah and was accepted. He attended law school there through the fall semester of 1975. Later, in a Utah prison after being convicted of aggravated kidnapping, he stated that the two greatest goals in his life were to return to law school and to become active in the church.

In 1966, at age twenty, Bundy met his first real girlfriend while at the University of Washington. She was from a wealthy family in San Francisco. It was at her urging that he attended Stanford in the summer of 1967. That summer, his girlfriend broke up with him. Bundy's second romance began in September 1969 when he met a divorcée with a young child who was living in Seattle. After three months, they talked of marriage. Bundy changed his mind, but the relationship continued. He was sexually involved with his second girlfriend and after a while began sexually experimenting by tying her up with nylon stockings prior to having intercourse. On one occasion, he started strangling her during intercourse after tying her up. She stopped him, and the "experiments" ceased.

Ted Bundy worked at a number of jobs to pay his way through college: at the Seattle Yacht Club as a busboy, at a Safeway store stocking shelves, at a surgical supply house as a stockboy, as a legal messenger, and as a shoe salesman. His summer jobs included working at a sawmill and a power company in Tacoma. In 1968, Bundy was the office manager for the Draft Rockefeller headquarters in downtown Seattle. He was a work-study student at Seattle's Crisis Clinic in 1971; there he met Ann Rule, a volunteer, who later wrote a book about him, *The Stranger Beside Me* (1980). In 1972, he worked on Evans's political campaign. Posing as a political science graduate student doing research, he taped opponents' speeches and reported directly to the governor. He also worked as a counselor at a psychiatric outpatient clinic for four months that year. In October he began working as the assistant director of the Seattle Crime Prevention Commission and conducted some research on rape and white-collar crime. He resigned from this position in January 1973 when he was not selected for the director's position. In the same month, Bundy obtained a consulting contract with King County to study recidivism among misdemeanor offenders in the county jail. In April 1973, Bundy was given a political job as an aide to the chairman of the Washington State Republican party.

At this time, Ted Bundy appeared to be living by the rules of society. He held jobs in law enforcement–related positions. From early childhood he had been interested in a career in law enforcement. In April 1973, he caught a purse-snatcher at a shopping mall in Seattle. He was involved in politics and held responsible positions within the Republican party. During his teens he had saved a young girl from drowning. However, Ted Bundy had committed a number of thefts by shoplifting and breaking into homes. In 1973 he also became a voyeur, walking the streets of Seattle late at night.

By the early 1970s Bundy was considered a sharp dresser and a compulsively neat and orderly person. He was regarded as a young man with charming ways, good looks, and a steady social life when he wanted it. When he was arrested in Utah for evading a police officer in August 1975, he was attending law school, working part-time as a university security guard, and preparing to join the Mormon Church.

Family Background

Born Theodore Robert Cowell on November 24, 1946, to Eleanor Louise Cowell at the Elizabeth Lund Home for Unwed Mothers in Burlington, Vermont, until 1950 he lived with his grandparents, his mother, and her two sisters in the Roxborough section of northwest Philadelphia. In 1950, his mother had his last name changed to Nelson and moved with her son to Tacoma, Washington, to live with relatives. In May 1951, his mother married John C. Bundy, who adopted Ted and changed his last name to Bundy.

John and Eleanor had two boys and two girls, half brothers and half sisters to Ted. His mother worked as a secretary at the University of Puget Sound. His stepfather was a cook at an army hospital south of Tacoma. Ted did not get along well with his stepfather and refused to use him as a role model. He had memories of his grandfather in Pennsylvania, who was closer to being a father figure for him. Ted's mother was the dominant force in the family. Bundy stated that she, "paid all the bills and never used force or anger" (Larsen, 1980, p. 155). However, Bundy later commented sarcastically in a Tallahassee, Florida, jail regarding his mail, "And not one letter from my beloved mother" (Larsen, 1980, p. 262). He once stated that he grew up thinking his mother was his sister and that he was a late baby born to his grandparents (Rule, 1980, p. 27). Others dispute this (e.g., Michaud & Aynesworth, 1983).

As a boy, Ted had a paper route, was a member of the Boy Scouts, and was active in the Methodist Church with his family. He liked school and did well in his studies, according to his parents. Bundy said, "We didn't talk a lot about real personal matters, certainly never about sex or any of those things. My mom has trouble talking on intimate, personal terms" (Michaud & Aynesworth, 1983, p. 51).

It is not known when Bundy learned of his illegitimate birth. He was apparently never told by his parents. Bundy claimed he found out he was illegitimate at age thirteen when he discovered his birth certificate stating "father unknown." Others report that he learned this at age eighteen from his cousin, who taunted him about his birth. Rule (1980) states that he learned of his birth when he traveled to Burlington, Vermont, in 1969 and checked his birth certificate there.

Although Bundy consistently maintained that his illegitimacy was not important to him, it did seem to upset him. It further strained relations with his stepfather, frequently to the point of outright defiance. Bundy himself did not make the connection, however. Michaud and Aynesworth (1983) argue that there was an abrupt halt to his social development concurrent with the discovery of his illegitimacy. Michaud and Aynesworth (1983) offer evidence of this change, assuming his discovery of illegitimacy was just prior to high school, by quoting Bundy's comment about entering high school:

> I'm at a loss to describe it even now. Maybe I didn't have the role models at home that could have aided me in school. I don't know. But I felt alienated from my old friends. They just seemed to move on and I didn't. I don't know why and I don't know if there's an explanation. Maybe it's something that was programmed by some kind of genetic thing. In my early schooling, it seemed like there was no problem in learning what the appropriate social behaviors were. It just seemed like I hit a wall in high school. (p. 55)

After being found guilty on two counts of murder, Ted Bundy was married to Carole Boone in a Miami, Florida, courtroom during the penalty phase of his criminal trial in February 1980. They later conceived in a Florida prison, and his wife gave birth to a baby girl.

Peer Group Associations and Personal Relationships

Bundy has described his teenage years by stating, "Social relationships were not that important. I just felt secure with the academic life" (Larsen, 1980, p. 156). He reportedly insisted on showering privately while in junior high and endured a great deal of scorn and humiliation from his peers. During his first year of college, he "had a longing for a beautiful coed. But I didn't have the skill or social acumen to cope with it" (p. 93). Bundy's mother remembers, "He got good grades that first year [but] never got into the social life of the school at all. He'd come home, study, sleep, and go back to school" (Michaud & Aynesworth, 1983, p. 57).

During his second year of college, he worked at the Seattle Yacht Club and became friends with the pastry cook there. She sometimes fixed snacks for him, and he often borrowed money from her. She once loaned him money to go to Philadelphia and gave him a ride to the airport. He was dressed in expensive clothes and had expensive ski equipment. He was going to stop off in Aspen,

Colorado, to do some skiing. When she called to complain to his mother, she learned that his mother did not know what he was doing, that he never called home, and that she did not know where he was living.

A co-worker described Bundy as the office manager of the Rockefeller campaign in Seattle:

> Ted had control of what he was doing. He was really poised. He was friendly. He was always smiling. He was terribly charismatic. Obviously, he was someone who had a great deal of compassion in dealing with other people. (Larsen, 1980, p. 5)

Indeed, Bundy was noted for his attractiveness and charm. Levin and Fox (1985) suggest that his reassuring tone was developed and polished while he was working the hotline at Seattle's Crisis Clinic. Ted was described as charming, and he made friends easily at law school in Utah. However, he never was directly involved in the social circles of law students. Instead, his social contacts were with lawyers in the area and his law professors.

A former girlfriend stated, "If you know him, you can't help but have a great deal of affection for him as a human being" (Larsen, 1980, p. 5). However, she also noted that he was constantly on guard against anyone getting close to him. This girl's father said Bundy was "extremely moody on occasion. He can be very nice, pleasant, helpful, and then all of a sudden he'll sour on you. It'll look like he's really thinking hard about something" (Winn & Merrill, 1979, p. 99).

Bundy's first extensive involvement with a woman occurred during his first year at the University of Washington, in 1966. She was older, came from a wealthy family in San Francisco, and frequently paid for their dates together. For Bundy, the relationship was intense until she broke up with him in the summer of 1967. Ted's brother recalls that this "screwed him up for a while. He came home and seemed pretty upset and moody. I'd never seen him like that before. He's always in charge of his emotions" (Michaud & Aynesworth, 1983, p. 59). Bundy described this period as "absolutely the pits for me—the lowest time ever" (Michaud & Aynesworth, 1983, p. 59).

In 1968, he developed a close relationship with a divorced woman from Utah who lived near Bundy with her young daughter. They talked of marriage. The relationship lasted for five years.

Meanwhile, Bundy kept in contact with his former girlfriend in San Francisco, and by 1973 the relationship was reestablished to the point where the woman thought they were engaged. Bundy then refused to write or call her, stating, "I just wanted to prove to myself that I could have married her" (Larsen, 1980, p. 157). During this period, he had maintained his relationship with the woman in Seattle.

According to police research, Bundy outwardly made a good impression and was energetic, skillful, bright, moving from job to job, gaining his education and upwardly mobile. But he was committing petty thievery, used his boyish good looks and charm to exploit and manipulate, and lacked the inner discipline to finish any major task (Larsen, 1980, p. 100). Robert Keppel's profile of Bundy describes him as a "self-serving manipulator who lied at will, pinched goods from his employers, and stole his girlfriends' cars" (Winn & Merrill, 1980, p. 128).

After conducting a background check on Bundy and watching him in the court-room, the prosecutor in Aspen, Colorado, said:

> As long as he's functioning as a lawyer everything's real cool with Ted. Then when something reminds him that he's the prisoner, you sense those flashes of anger, hostility. He's always got to be the superstar. But he's only good in the first quarter of whatever game he's in. Then something happens. (Larsen, 1980, p. 206)

To the police in Utah Bundy was a "loner, always short of money, a leech and very moody" (Larsen, 1980, p. 153). While in Utah, Bundy was to some extent lead-ing a double life. He was becoming heavily involved in the Mormon Church but he never mentioned this involvement to his friends in the neighborhood where he lived. He sometimes had relationships with two women at the same time, as he did in 1973 when he was engaged to two different women. Rule (1980) notes that he was keeping two intense relationships going through visitations and corre-spondence while he was in prison in Utah.

Bundy's charm became well known. It was a decisive factor in both of his escapes. His charm affected the jailers, guards, secretaries, and officials at the Aspen courthouse and the Glenwood Springs jail in Colorado. For example, after a month of being incarcerated, Bundy was on agreeable terms with almost everyone around the jail in Glenwood Springs. He got along just as well with those who didn't trust him as with those who did.

Bundy was still a loner in some social circles. At the Crisis Clinic in Seattle, most of the students had strong liberal views. Bundy, however, was a strongly conserv-ative Republican. In Utah, the students and neighbors with whom he drank and smoked marijuana were also of a different political philosophy.

Because he could control and manipulate women, they were important to him and he was frequently in their company. Yet at the same time he was apart from them and never let them get too close.

Rule (1980) describes two Ted Bundys emerging in 1973:

> One, the perfect son, the University of Washington student who had graduated "with distinction," the fledgling lawyer and politician, and, a charming schemer, a man who could manipulate women with ease, whether it be sex or money he desired, and it made no difference if the women were eighteen or sixty-five. (p. 169)

Contact with Defining Agencies

Bundy was arrested in the early morning of August 16, 1975, by a Utah Highway Patrol sergeant for evading a police officer in a southern subdivision of Salt Lake City. Bundy had briefly tried to outrun the officer in his Volkswagen and later stated that he had been smoking marijuana and was trying to air out the car before being stopped. When he was stopped, he was cooperative and seemed almost too relaxed to the arresting officer. He was also placed under suspicion for possession of burglary tools based on the items found in his car: rope, two gloves, a mask made of panty hose, strips of torn sheet, a pair of handcuffs, a flashlight, and a box of black plastic garbage bags. Bundy was released later that morning from the county jail on his own recognizance.

The handcuffs found in Bundy's car caused the Salt Lake county sheriff's office to connect him with an attempted kidnapping that had occurred the previous November in Salt Lake City. The assailant in that case had used handcuffs and had driven a Volkswagen. Two days after his arrest, Bundy was charged with possession of burglary tools and the police began to investigate him further. They searched his apartment and took pictures of his Volkswagen. He was placed under police surveillance and frequently tried to elude his watchers, sometimes successfully. Subsequently, he sold his Volkswagen and canceled his gas credit card.

As part of its investigation, the sheriff's office contacted King County, Washington, whose officers had notified them a year previously that Bundy was a suspect in an investigation of missing women in the Seattle area and was moving to Salt Lake City. Contact was also made with police in Colorado, because ski brochures from Colorado were found in the search of his apartment. A small ink mark was found on one brochure describing a motel in Snowmass, Colorado, where the unsolved murder of a woman had occurred.

On October 1, 1975, Bundy stood in a police lineup. His hair was clipped short and parted in a new way. But the kidnap victim and two witnesses identified him as the kidnap assailant. He was charged with aggravated kidnapping and attempted criminal homicide. Bundy spent eight weeks in the Salt Lake City County jail and posted bond on November 11, 1975. On November 26, 1975, he was bound over for trial at a preliminary hearing and charged with aggravated kidnapping. Bundy was again placed under police surveillance while awaiting trial. Again he tried to elude the police and frequently seemed to be toying with them.

Prior to the trial, Bundy's attorney requested a psychological evaluation of his client. The psychologist found the following:

Good social presence, ego strength and good self-concept, positive self-identity. Bundy was highly intellectual, independent, tolerant, responsible and with normal psychosexual development. He had a healthy curiosity about his father. The worst thing was that he showed some hostility on tests. He is an extremely intelligent young man who is *intact psychologically* [emphasis added]. (Winn & Merrill, 1980, p. 154)

In late February 1976, Bundy was tried in a bench trial. During the trial, he frequently changed his appearance. For three days in a row he wore different clothing, changed his hairstyle, and wore different glasses. The prosecution's case rested primarily on the victim's identification of Bundy and her memory since the attempted kidnapping. Bundy was found guilty, and a presentence investigative report was ordered by the judge. Not satisfied with the results of the presentence report, on March 22, 1976, the judge delayed sentencing and ordered Bundy to Utah State Prison for a ninety-day diagnostic evaluation.

The diagnostic report issued on Bundy on June 22, 1976, contained a series of negatives and positives:

PLUS SIDE

High intelligence, no severely traumatizing influences in childhood or adolescence, few distortions in relationship with mother and stepfather, no serious defects in physical development, habits, school adjustment or sexual development and emotional maturation, adequate interest in hobbies and recreational pursuits, average environmental pressures and responsibilities, and no previous attacks of mental illness.

MINUS SIDE

When one tries to understand him, he becomes evasive, somewhat threatened by people unless he feels he can structure the outcome of the relationship, passive-aggressive features were evident, hostility toward diagnosis personnel. (Winn & Merrill, 1980, p. 163)

Bundy's test results on the MMPI reflected a somewhat different view of the man:

A fairly strong conflict was evidenced in the testing profile, that being the subject's fairly strong dependence on women, yet his need to be independent. Mr. Bundy would like a close relationship with females, but is fearful of being hurt by them. In addition, there were indications of general anger, and more particularly, well-masked anger toward women. (Winn & Merrill, 1980, p. 164)

The final diagnostic report was written by a Dr. Van Austin. Bundy was not found to be psychotic or suffering from schizophrenia. However, he was found to exhibit some characteristics of a personality disorder. Among the features of an antisocial personality disorder that were cited were lack of guilt, callousness, and a tendency to compartmentalize and rationalize his behavior. Van Austin concluded, "I feel that Mr. Bundy is either a man who has no problems or is smart enough and clever enough to appear to the edge of normal" (Larsen, 1980, p. 159). The doctor further stated that he could not predict Bundy's future behavior because there was much more to his personality structure that was not known.

On June 30, 1976, Bundy was sentenced to one to fifteen years in prison, with eligibility for parole in approximately fifteen months. He began serving his sentence in the Utah State Penitentiary in July. He was placed in medium security and given a work assignment in the print shop. Prison officials and guards considered him to be a respectful, pleasant, and cooperative prisoner. He had no problems with the inmates because he provided legal advice to them. Later that year, a search of his cell revealed escape contraband: a forged Social Security card, an Illinois driver's license, an airline schedule, and a road map. He was disciplined by serving fifteen days in isolation and then was transferred to maximum security as an escape risk.

In January 1977, Bundy was extradited to Colorado to stand trial for murder. He was incarcerated in the Pitkin County jail in Aspen. The judge in Aspen allowed Bundy to act as his own attorney and to appear in street clothes without any restraining devices. During this time, Bundy continually asked to have his jail security reduced on the grounds that it hampered his defense preparation. A deputy at the jail stated, "He's smart and very observant. He's making himself just as personable as can be to everyone around here. He's fine until he wants something" (Winn & Merrill, 1980, p. 180). In April, Bundy was moved to the Glenwood Springs jail forty miles from Aspen.

In April and May of that year, police and other prisoners warned jail officials that Bundy might try to escape because he had been practicing jumping off his bunk in his cell. On June 7, 1977, Bundy successfully escaped from a window of the courthouse in Aspen by jumping through a second-story window. He was caught in a stolen car after spending six days in the mountains nearby.

After being captured, Bundy resumed preparation for his defense. He worked actively as his own lawyer with legal advisors appointed by the court, he interviewed forensic experts, and his briefs on various motions to the court were considered superior. At a pretrial evidentiary hearing, he cross-examined his previous kidnap victim so that his kidnap conviction would not be introduced against him at the trial. Late in the year, he was granted a change of venue and his trial was assigned to Colorado Springs.

On December 30, 1977, Bundy escaped from the Glenwood Springs, Colorado, jail and disappeared. It was later learned that he had sawed through a light fixture in the ceiling of his cell. He traveled to Chicago, Illinois; to Ann Arbor, Michigan; and on to Tallahassee, Florida.

On February 10, 1978, Bundy was placed on the FBI's "Ten Most Wanted" list. The text of the FBI "Wanted" poster described him as an escapee from Colorado, wanted for questioning in thirty-six sexual slayings, beginning in California in 1969 and extending through the Pacific Northwest into Utah and Colorado. Below three different-looking photos of Bundy, the text of the poster read:

> Age 31, born November 24, 1946. Height: 5'11" to 6'. Weight: 145 to 175 lbs. Build: Slender, athletic. Caution: Bundy, a college-educated physical fitness enthusiast with a prior history of escape, is being sought as a prison escapee after being convicted of kidnapping and while awaiting trial involving brutal sex slaying of woman at ski resort. He should be considered armed, dangerous and an escape risk. (Larsen, 1980, p. 2)

On February 14, 1978, Bundy was stopped while driving a stolen car in Pensacola, Florida. When he resisted arrest, shots were fired by the police officer. He was subdued and placed in the Pensacola jail. At the time of his arrest, he was using a false identification and the police did not know his real identity. When his identity was learned, shortly after his arrest, he immediately came under suspicion for the January 15, 1978, murders of two women and the assault of others in a sorority house in Tallahassee. Police learned that on February 11 he had been confronted by a Leon County deputy in Tallahassee about stolen license plates in his car. Bundy had fled on foot and escaped the officer.

Shortly after his arrest, Bundy was interviewed extensively by Pensacola investigators. According to depositions given later in court by these officers, Bundy came very close to confessing to a number of murders. A few days after his arrest, Bundy was transferred to the Leon County jail in Tallahassee, Florida.

In March, police took blood and hair samples from Bundy. During that month, the court in Leon County denied Bundy's request to have access to a law library and members of the news media. In late April, Leon County secured a warrant to obtain impressions of Bundy's teeth to see if they matched bite marks on one of the victims in the sorority house murders. Bundy was again denied access to the press by the Leon County judge. During his previous periods of incarceration in jails in Utah and Colorado, Bundy had been in constant contact with the press either by phone, in correspondence, or at various press conferences. Many of his comments were controversial and probably prejudicial to his own case. The circuit court judge stated he was keeping Bundy from the press to guarantee "fundamental fairness and protect Bundy from Bundy" (Larsen, 1980, p. 272). Bundy, however, corresponded with reporters from all over the country during this time.

On July 27, 1978, Bundy was indicted on two counts of murder, three of attempted murder, and two of burglary in the crimes committed at the Chi Omega sorority house on January 15, 1978. This indictment was read to Bundy by the Leon County sheriff in front of television cameras. The sheriff was later reprimanded for this action by the Tallahassee Bar Association. Four days later, Bundy was indicted for murder in the death of a twelve-year-old girl in Lake City, Florida. He pled not guilty to each indictment.

When the judge denied Bundy's request to have a lawyer from Georgia represent him, Bundy moved to have the judge disqualified. He also filed a civil suit against the Leon County sheriff's office to improve his living and working conditions in jail. The civil suit was later settled out of court, and the lighting in Bundy's cell was improved and he was given periods of exercise. In December 1978, the Florida Supreme Court disqualified the judge in Bundy's case due to the "intolerable adversary atmosphere" between Bundy and the judge (Winn & Merrill, 1980, p. 285). In April 1979, the U.S. Supreme Court upheld Bundy's denial of a lawyer from Georgia and his conviction in Utah. Throughout his pretrial period, Bundy was repeatedly trying to exclude television cameras from the courtroom proceedings. Each time, the judge ruled against him.

On May 31, 1979, it appeared that a plea bargain had been struck between the Leon County prosecutor and Bundy's attorneys. Bundy would plead guilty to three counts of murder and receive three consecutive twenty-five-year sentences. On this date, however, Bundy claimed in open court that his defense counsel was ineffective and reneged on the negotiated plea. He stated, "There's only one hang-up with pleading guilty, and that is that you have to plead guilty" (Winn & Merrill, 1980, p. 296).

Tapes of the interviews with Bundy conducted by police officers in Pensacola after his arrest were played for the judge and depositions were given by the interviewing officers. After testimony from the public defenders, the judge ruled that Bundy had been denied his right to counsel during these interviews and ruled that the tapes and depositions were inadmissible evidence.

In May, the court requested psychological examinations of Bundy to determine his legal competency to stand trial. Emmanuel Tanay, a psychiatrist from Detroit, Michigan, and Harvey M. Cleckley, an authority on psychopathic and sociopathic personality disorders, were selected to examine Bundy. Tanay found the following:

> The pathological need to defy authority, to manipulate his associates and adversaries, supplies him with thrills. He takes pride in his celebrity status. His dealings with the criminal justice system are dominated by psychopathy. It could be argued he [Bundy] is effective in concealing his criminal activities—more accurate to say that he is of two minds on the issue—he attempts to conceal and reveal his involvement. (Larsen, 1980, p. 299)

Dr. Cleckley's testimony on Bundy was very similar to that of Dr. Tanay. Under the legal definition, both psychiatrists agreed that Bundy was competent to stand trial.

Dr. Tanay referred to Bundy's rejection of the negotiated plea:

> He has a deep seated need for a trial. It will allow him the opportunity to confront and confound various authority figures; judge, prosecutor and defense attorney. In a certain sense, Mr. Bundy is a producer of a play which attempts to show that various authority figures can be manipulated, set against each other. Mr. Bundy does not have the capacity to recognize that the price for this "thriller" might be his own life. (Larsen, 1980, p. 299)

In June, the court determined that Bundy could not receive a fair trial in Tallahassee and changed the venue of the trial to Miami, Florida. During the trial in Miami, Bundy was involved in the cross-examination of witnesses and eventually fired his defense team, proceeding as his own counsel with the defense team as standby counsel. He continually objected to the presence of television cameras in the courtroom but was overruled by the judge. On July 24, 1979, Bundy was found guilty and given two death sentences and three ninety-year sentences, which would run consecutively.

On January 7, 1980, Bundy was tried for the murder of a twelve-year-old girl in Lake City, Florida. On February 7, 1980, he was found guilty as charged. In open court during the penalty phase of the trial, he married a woman from Seattle to circumvent the authorities' denial of his request to get married. He received the death penalty and was returned to death row in a Florida prison, one of eight places he had been incarcerated since his arrest in Salt Lake City in 1975. He was executed by the State of Florida in 1989.

Offense Behavior

It must be remembered that Bundy was convicted only for the murders that occurred in Tallahassee and Lake City, Florida, in early 1978. He was never convicted for the murders he was suspected of having committed in Washington, Utah, Oregon, and Colorado. He did, however, confess to many of these murders just prior to his execution.

Eight abductions of females that occurred between January and July 1974 in the Pacific Northwest have been attributed to Bundy by law enforcement agencies. On January 31, a twenty-one-year-old young woman was taken from her basement apartment in Seattle. Bloodstains were found on her nightclothes. The top sheet on her bed and her pillowcase were missing, as well as some clothes. She had apparently been killed in her bed, dressed, and taken from her apartment. Twenty-seven days earlier, a young girl had been found viciously beaten and sexually assaulted nearby in a similar basement apartment.

On March 12, a nineteen-year-old girl disappeared without a trace on her way to a jazz concert at Evergreen State College in Olympia, Washington. On April 17, an eighteen-year-old girl left her residence hall on the Central Washington University campus in Olympia, Washington, to attend a meeting across campus and was not seen again. That same evening, two girls encountered a young man on campus near the library at two different times. On each occasion, the man solicited their help in carrying his books, claiming an injury to his arm, and led them to his Volkswagen in a darkened area of campus before they fled.

On May 12, a nineteen-year-old female student at Oregon State University in Corvallis, Oregon, took a walk across campus, and was not seen again. On May 31, a young woman disappeared from outside a tavern in Seattle. On June 11, an eighteen-year-old girl disappeared from a well-lighted alley on the way to her sorority house in Seattle. Shortly before this girl disappeared, a young man on crutches with a cast on one leg had been seen nearby having difficulty in carrying his briefcase and was offered assistance by another young sorority girl. The man waited while the girl entered a house on an errand. When she returned, he had disappeared.

On July 14, two more young women disappeared from the Lake Sammamish Recreation Area near Issaquah and east of Seattle, Washington. One of the missing women, who was twenty-three years old, had last been seen around noon in the company of a young man with his arm in a sling who called himself "Ted," according to witnesses. "Ted" told her his sailboat was in Issaquah and he needed help putting it on his Volkswagen in order to transport it to the lake. She agreed to help him and left with her bicycle. This man was seen on five separate occasions that day, asking females for assistance with his sailboat. The other missing female, who was nineteen years old, was last seen around 4:30 that afternoon on her way to the restroom.

All these missing females were single, had long hair parted in the middle, and were of similar appearance. The first six disappearances occurred in the late evening. The last two occurred in broad daylight. All the disappearances happened within a 250-mile radius of Seattle, Washington.

Fifty-five days after their disappearance, skeletal remains of the girls missing from Lake Sammamish were found in the foothills of the Cascade Mountains, four miles east of the lake near Interstate 90. The remains of a third person were also found but could not be identified.

On October 12, 1974, the skeletal remains of two girls were found along a deer path 130 miles south of Issaquah near the Oregon border, seventeen miles from Vancouver, Washington. One girl was identified as a girl from Vancouver who had last been seen in August. The other girl was not identified.

All the aforementioned disappearances occurred while Ted Bundy was living in Seattle, Washington. He was reportedly very familiar with the area east of Seattle, where six of the missing girls' bodies were found. As Robert Keppel noted, Bundy was a man who understood police jurisdictions and boundaries, who was familiar with their vulnerability—their imperfect exchange of information with one another (Larsen, 1980, p. 101).

Rule (1980) notes that Bundy was picked up at least twice by juvenile authorities in Tacoma for suspicion of auto theft and burglary. She states, "There is no indication that he was ever confined, but his name was known to juvenile caseworkers. The records outlining the details of the incidents have long been shredded—procedures when a juvenile reaches eighteen. Only a card remains with his name and offense listed" (Rule, 1980, p. 11).

According to Michaud and Aynesworth (1983), who interviewed him extensively in a Florida prison, when Bundy returned to Seattle from Philadelphia in 1968 he became involved in a great deal of property crime. He shoplifted and broke into homes. Apparently, he continued to steal and shoplift intermittently until he left Seattle in 1974.

Bundy's girlfriend in Seattle became suspicious of him during the disappearances of the girls in Washington and Oregon. He had a number of unexplained absences during the nighttime, and he frequently slept during the day. Moreover, Bundy would periodically hide in the bushes near her home and jump out and frighten her. She found surgical gloves in his jacket pocket, and she observed a package of plaster of paris and crutches in his apartment. She stated that Bundy kept a lug wrench under the seat of her car and a knife in the glove compartment. His girlfriend also claimed that she once found a bag of women's clothing in his room.

Bundy moved to Salt Lake City, Utah, in September, 1974. In the evening of October 18, 1974, a young girl disappeared while walking in the streets of Midvale, Utah, a suburban community near Salt Lake City. Her nude body was found a week later in Summit Park in a canyon of the Wasatch Mountains east of Salt Lake City. She had been badly beaten, strangled with nylons, and raped. The autopsy determined she had been killed elsewhere.

On October 31, 1974, a young girl disappeared from American Fork, Utah, after leaving a Halloween party. American Fork is approximately twenty-five miles south of Salt Lake City. Eight days later, on November 8, in Murray, Utah, just south of Salt Lake City and north of American Fork, a young woman was lured to the parking lot of a local shopping mall by a man who proceeded to attack her with a tire iron. She escaped unharmed. The man was driving a light-colored Volkswagen.

On November 11, 1974, a man posing as a police officer approached a young girl in a shopping mall in Salt Lake City in the early evening and stated that someone had been seen prowling near her car. He asked her to check the car to see if anything was missing. After she checked the car and found nothing missing, the man then led her to what he said was a police substation. Finding the door locked, he asked her to accompany him downtown to sign a complaint against the prowler, who had allegedly been arrested by his partner. He showed her his police identification and then led her to a light-colored Volkswagen with scratches and dents and a tear in the back seat. He drove her for a short distance in his car and then abruptly stopped and tried to handcuff her. She struggled and fled the car, at which time he tried to strike her with a tire iron. She resisted and, with handcuffs on one wrist, escaped into the street, where a passing motorist stopped and picked her up.

Half an hour later in Bountiful, Utah, just north of Salt Lake City, a young man stopped a woman backstage at a high school musical and asked her to come outside to the parking lot and identify a car for him. She declined, stating she was too busy with the musical. Thirty minutes later, the man again asked the same woman for assistance in the parking lot, and she again declined. The man was seen a few minutes later pacing near the rear of the theater. Toward the end of the musical, this same man sat down in the audience near the woman he had asked for assistance earlier. His hair was mussed and he was breathing heavily. A young girl who was attending the musical with her parents left the theater during the third act to pick up her brother nearby, and she disappeared. During a search of the high school the following day, a handcuff key was found just outside the school's south door.

On November 27, the body of the girl missing from American Fork, Utah, was found near a hiking trail on the north slope of Mount Timpanogos in the Wasatch Mountains. Like the girl found in Summit Park, this girl had been sexually assaulted, bludgeoned on the head, strangled with nylons, and stripped naked. These girls were found within twenty miles of each other.

On January 12, 1975, a young woman disappeared from a ski lodge in Snowmass, Colorado. She was there with friends on a vacation from Michigan and was last seen on the second floor of the lodge. On February 17, 1975, her body was found lying in the snow between Aspen and Snowmass Village. The autopsy revealed that she had received severe head injuries and had been raped.

In March 1975, four of the girls missing from Seattle and Ellensburg, Washington, and Corvallis, Oregon, were found on Taylor Mountain southeast of Seattle and ten miles east of where the Lake Sammamish victims were found. The victims' skulls had been fractured.

In March of that year, a young woman disappeared from Vail, Colorado, while on her way to visit a friend at a local bar. In April of that year, a young girl disappeared while riding her bicycle in Grand Junction, Colorado. Her bicycle was found under a bridge, her sandals nearby. On April 25, a girl disappeared on her way home from high school in Nederland, Colorado. On April 23, her body was found fifteen miles away off a county road. Her clothes were partially torn off, her skull was fractured, and her hands were bound.

In 1977, following his conviction and incarceration in a Utah prison, Bundy was transferred to Colorado, where he escaped twice. His escapes from the Colorado authorities were well planned. In each case he conned his captors into loosening security. His first escape from the Pitkin County courthouse in Aspen freed him for six days. He was arrested in a stolen car in Aspen after spending most of his time on foot in the mountains. His second escape, from the Glenwood Springs jail, left him free for forty-three days, during which time he took the lives of two college coeds and a twelve-year-old girl over a thousand miles away.

In early January, when Ted Bundy arrived in Tallahassee, Florida, by bus, he was traveling under a false identity. Each day he changed his appearance by parting his hair differently, wearing different glasses, and cutting off his mustache and then growing it again. He committed a number of property crimes: shoplifting of food, theft of a bicycle, theft of numerous credit cards from women's purses in libraries and restaurants, breaking into an automobile, and stealing a television, radio, and typewriter.

In the early morning hours of January 15, 1978, Ted Bundy killed again. He entered the Chi Omega sorority house in Tallahassee shortly after 3:00 A.M. and within approximately fifteen minutes had beaten five different girls as they slept in their rooms on the second floor of the house. He killed two of these girls by strangling them with panty hose. They had been beaten viciously about the head and body. One of the deceased had bite marks on her left buttock, and one of her nipples had been bitten off. A mask made of panty hose was found next to one of the victims. Bundy was seen leaving the sorority house and later was identified by a witness at his trial. One and a half hours later, Bundy struck again four blocks away from the sorority house. He attacked and beat a girl as she was sleeping in her apartment. The attack was heard in the adjacent apartment, and police were summoned. Bundy escaped and the victim survived. At 5:00 A.M. that morning, Bundy was seen in front of his apartment house, four blocks from the Chi Omega house.

From January 21 until his arrest in Pensacola on February 14, Bundy was busy committing a variety of crimes. On January 21, he stole a student's wallet and used the student's credit cards for the next ten days. By February 1, he had obtained a birth certificate of the owner of the stolen wallet. On February 6, he stole a Florida State University van and the license plates from another car. On February 7, he bought gas with a stolen credit card in Jacksonville. On February 8, he bought gas in Lake City and tried to pick up a fourteen-year-old girl by posing as a fireman.

The girl got the license number of the van. That night, he stayed at a motel in Lake City and left the following morning without paying the bill. That morning, he abducted a twelve-year-old girl from outside her school in Lake City. Her partially decomposed body was found on April 7, thirty-five miles from Lake City. On February 11, Bundy locked the door to his apartment, wiped it clean of fingerprints, and left by the fire escape.

The following day, he was stopped by a Leon County deputy near his apartment. The deputy observed a license plate in the car next to which Bundy was standing. Bundy fled before he could be questioned any further. That day he stole three different cars; the third one he drove west, leaving Tallahassee. On February 13, he was caught using a stolen credit card at a restaurant in Crestview and escaped. The next day, he was arrested in Pensacola. At a minimum, he faced sixty-seven felony counts in Florida for stolen credit cards, forgery, and auto theft. An inventory of Bundy's stolen Volkswagen included a bicycle frame, a portable television, stereo equipment, clothing, a sleeping bag, a notebook with student identification, over twenty stolen credit cards, and a number of photos of girls and women.

Bundy's girlfriend from Seattle claims that he called her on February 18 and confessed to the murders he had committed. In her book (Kendall, 1981), written under a pseudonym, she quotes him as saying:

> There is something the matter with me. It wasn't you. It was me. I just couldn't contain it. I've fought it for a long, long time . . . it got too strong. We just happened to be going together when it got under way. I tried to suppress it. It was taking more and more of my time. That's why I didn't do well in school. My time was being used trying to make my life look normal. But it wasn't normal. All the time I could feel that force building in me. (pp. 174–175)

> I don't have a split personality. I don't have blackouts. I remember everything I've done. Like Lake Sammamish. (p. 176)

Bundy readily confessed to the Pensacola police that he had stolen the television and credit cards. He also admitted to stealing three cars in Tallahassee. He told three Pensacola detectives that his "problem" had first surfaced in Seattle while walking on a street one night: A girl on the street ahead aroused a feeling he'd never had before. He wanted to possess her by any means necessary, so he followed her home until she entered the house and he never saw her again (Winn & Merrill, 1980, pp. 301–302). Bundy stated he had become a voyeur during law school in Seattle while walking the streets at night.

Bundy had an affinity for Volkswagens, because, he said, they went a long way on a tank of gas. He also preferred Volkswagens because the seat could come out and he could carry things more easily that way. When asked what he carried, he used the term "cargo." According to Bundy, "Sometimes the cargo was damaged and sometimes it wasn't" (Winn & Merrill, 1980, p. 302). He stated that he got along on little sleep and used to drive around at night in his Volkswagen. "Sometimes I felt like a vampire," he said, "just driving all night long" (p. 302). When investigators tried to elicit the number of victims Bundy might be talking about, he said, "We're talking about three-digit figures" (p. 321).

Prior to Bundy's confessions before his execution, law enforcement authorities believed he committed at least seventeen homicides coast-to-coast over a four-year period:

> 3 victims—Seattle, Washington
> 2 victims—Issaquah, Washington
> 1 victim—Olympia, Washington
> 1 victim—Ellenburg, Washington
> 1 victim—Corvallis, Oregon
> 2 victims—Salt Lake City, Utah
> 1 victim—Utah County, Utah
> 1 victim—Bountiful, Utah
> 1 victim—Aspen, Colorado
> 1 victim—Vail, Colorado
> 2 victims—Tallahassee, Florida
> 1 victim—Lake City, Florida

Law enforcement officers now believe Bundy committed many more. Robert Keppel states, "By my count he's been directly linked to twenty-three deaths in five states" (R. Keppel, personal communication, April 20, 1984).

Self-Concept

When Ted Bundy talked about his family with friends, the problems his illegitimacy had caused with his siblings and the problems he had with his stepfather seemed to reveal that the epithet "bastard" had left its mark. However, one day Bundy would write:

> In short, when I just came under attack by the legal system, I was 28, a bachelor, a law student, engaged to be married and enjoying the brightest period in my life. I had come to terms with many things and one thing I had come to terms with long ago was the circumstances of my birth. (Winn & Merrill, 1980, p. 104)

Bundy rarely revealed his negative self-image. During his interrogation by the Pensacola investigators after his arrest in Florida, this image briefly surfaced. When asked about the location of the little girl who was missing from Lake City, he replied simply, "But I'm the most cold-hearted son of a bitch you'll ever meet" (Winn & Merrill, 1980, p. 314). When asked if the little girl was dead, he responded, "Well, you gentlemen knew that you were getting involved with a pretty strange creature. And you have known it for days" (Winn & Merrill, 1980, p. 314).

He seemed to see himself as an active participant in his life, one who was in control of his environment and his destiny. He enjoyed exhibiting his confidence in himself to others. During his trial he stated that he had always wanted to be an attorney and now he was fulfilling that wish by defending himself and doing it fairly well. He compared the prosecutor in his trial with all his skill and training against a man with a year and a half of law school (himself), who could let the air out of the prosecutor's tires (Winn & Merrill, 1980, p. 321).

Against the advice of his attorneys, Bundy cross-examined his previous kidnap victim for four hours. It was just something he had to do. During the penalty phase of his trial in Miami, after being found guilty, he asked the judge for phone privileges. He was still fighting back, showing he was in control. He later stated to a psychologist, "I don't fear death, I don't fear anyone or anything" (Larsen, 1980, p. 151).

It is thought that Bundy had an inferiority complex when he was young. For example, when he first began dating, he refused to meet the parents of a girl he dated in Seattle. He referred to himself and his first real girlfriend from San Francisco as "Sears & Roebuck and Saks" (Larsen, 1980, p. 157). During his teens he appeared to be shy with strangers and reserved with his friends. He was looked on by many as a "loner." However, the same Ted Bundy later stated to his interrogators in Pensacola, "I feel like I'm in charge of the entertainment tonight" (Larsen, 1980, p. 231).

His application to law school was reflective of the image he held of himself. He started his application letter by stating, "My lifestyle requires I obtain knowledge of the law and the ability to practice legal skills" (Larsen, 1980, p. 37). He concluded the letter by commenting that law school would "give me the tools to become a more effective actor in a social role I have defined for myself" (Larsen, 1980, p. 37). Included in his application was a glowing letter signed by Governor Dan Evans of Washington, which Bundy had written himself.

After his escape and capture in Colorado, he wrote to a friend that he had no regrets except that he was foolish enough to get caught. He felt he deserved to be free and that his own knowledge regarding his innocence was sufficient. Bundy thought he was in control and understood himself. To his captors in Pensacola, Florida, he stated, "This story is one that I have always intended to give to you [the police], and a psychologist or psychiatrist. I'm a psychologist and it really gives me insight. I've got the answers and the answers are mine to give" (Winn & Merrill, 1980, p. 314).

However, on infrequent occasions Bundy admitted that he was not always in control. For example, following his arrest in Pensacola he said that after his first escape he seemed to have conquered his "problem." After his second escape he said the "problem" recurred, and he noted, "I guess I have a fool [himself] for a doctor" (Winn & Merrill, 1980, p. 303). He once stated that fantasies were controlling his life (p. 301).

Throughout his incarceration and criminal trials, Bundy continued to maintain his innocence of any murders. He constantly tried to reach the media to convey this message. Even though he seemed to enjoy being a celebrity, he sometimes contradicted himself regarding his own self-perception. He stated to a detective that it was important how people perceived him; he was not just a fiend, there was more to him than that (Winn & Merrill, 1980, p. 320). But he wrote to a magazine editor in Seattle, "I am still too young to look upon my life as history. I am at a stage in life, an egocentric stage, where it matters only that I understand what I am and not what others may think of me" (Winn & Merrill, 1980, p. 280).

Bundy's most appropriate role was as a defense attorney defending himself. It was what he had always wanted to do, and he was doing it now for himself. He wanted to bear the responsibility for his acquittal and for sustaining his innocence.

Bundy obviously felt in charge when attempting to strike a deal with his interrogators in Pensacola to escape the death penalty. He said he would talk, but only if they promised what he wanted: no death penalty, and incarceration in Washington. He stated: "I've got to take care of my own survival too. Ted Bundy wants to survive too. I'm not asking to be back on the streets, but I don't have a death wish either" (Winn & Merrill, 1980, p. 312). Some people might argue that he did have a death wish. Others might argue that Bundy loved the thrill of the chase and that his ultimate euphoria was to remain undetected, to do what no other man could do—and do it with impunity (Rule, 1983).

Ted Bundy may have expressed himself with the utmost clarity when he stated to his captors in Pensacola, "I realize I will never function in society again. I don't want to escape, but if I get the chance, I will. I want you to be professional enough to see that I never get the chance" (Winn & Merrill, 1980, p. 319).

Police believe that Bundy first killed in January 1974 in Seattle, Washington. He is suspected of committing rapes and aggravated assaults on young women somewhat earlier. He was incarcerated in eight different jails and prisons between his arrest in 1975 and his conviction for murder in 1979.

A few days before his execution, Ted Bundy began confessing his crimes. He told one interviewer, "I just liked to kill, I wanted to kill" (MacPherson, 1989, p. 198). In an interview with James Dobson, Bundy claimed that pornography had led him to kill:

> I'm telling you from personal experience, the most graphic violence on screen, particularly as it gets into the home; to children who may be unattended or unaware that they may be a Ted Bundy who has vulnerability to that, that predisposition to be influenced by that kind of behavior, by that kind of movie and that kind of violence. (Dobson, 1992, pp. 35–36)

To another interviewer, Bundy appeared startled by the hatred of those awaiting his execution. He stated, "I don't know why everyone is out to get me" (MacPherson, 1989, p. 196). The State of Florida executed Ted Bundy on January 24, 1989. For many, he still remains a very troubling enigma.

Attitudes

At first impression, Ted Bundy appeared to be a calm, self-assured, and charming man. He projected the image of an individual who was in control and cared little what others thought of him. However, his attitudes reflected a somewhat different person.

It is difficult to determine accurately what value Bundy placed on human life, because he never confessed to his murderous crimes. Only a few of his comments reflect his attitudes toward his victims, and they are anachronistic. For example, following his arrest in Florida he reportedly stated over the telephone to his girlfriend in Seattle, "I want to make it right with all the people I've hurt" (Larsen, 1980, p. 230). However, he would state a short time later that the girl he tried to kidnap in Utah was "lucky she got away" (Winn & Merrill, 1980, p. 302). Regarding the location of his twelve-year-old victim in Florida, he said, "I'm the most cold-hearted son of a bitch you'll ever want to meet" (Winn & Merrill, 1980, p. 314).

While he was in a Florida prison, Bundy told Michaud and Aynesworth (1983), "I feel less guilty now than I've felt in any time in my life" (p. 300). For Bundy, "guilt doesn't solve anything, it only hurts you" (Michaud & Aynesworth, 1983, p. 300). Other than the alleged statement to his girlfriend in Seattle Bundy reportedly never showed remorse for his actions or his victims, which he claimed numbered over one hundred.

Bundy's attitude toward authority is self-evident in many of his recorded statements as well as from occurrences in his early life. In grade school, he was characterized as being beyond any discipline from his teachers. When things went wrong for Bundy, he would blame an authority figure or the system, as he did when he failed to achieve success in law school or made sporadic attempts at various areas of study while in college.

He took a great deal of pride in outsmarting law enforcement officers. In fact, he bragged about losing the officers who had him under surveillance in Utah. He wrote to Ann Rule, "I have a standing policy from this point forward never to talk to a law enforcement officer about anything except the time of day and the location of the toilet" (Rule, 1980, p. 217). He frequently castigated his pursuers: "I never underestimate the inventiveness and dangerousness of such men [law enforcement officers]. Like wild animals, when cornered can become very unstable" (p. 219). He reportedly told a neighbor in Tallahassee, Florida, that he was a lot smarter than the police and could get away with anything he wanted (Winn & Merrill, 1980, p. 331).

Bundy referred to some police agencies as "Mickey Mouse" operations. He even saw himself as a threat to his prosecutor in Colorado. He said his self-confidence was threatening to this man, who "should never enter a courtroom" (Rule, 1980, p. 228). Moreover, he never really accepted the services of his defense attorneys. To him, they were inferior and not at his level of expertise.

He seemed to like to taunt the police. To the investigators of the Chi Omega house killings, he said, "The evidence is there. Keep digging" (Larsen, 1980, p. 232). He urged the investigators in Utah to search for straws to make the broom. Regarding the investigators in Washington, he stated, "They're not going to find any evidence there, because there is no evidence there to find" (p. 113). In continuing to proclaim his innocence, he accused the police of wasting taxpayers' money with all their conferences and task forces. The police, for Bundy, had their heads in the sand (Larsen, 1980). He claimed that the police and the prosecutor's charges against him were "grossly exaggerated, their accusations purely fictitious and totally without merit" (Larsen, 1980, p. 167).

Following his escapes from Colorado, he frequently poked fun at his former jailers and enjoyed describing in detail how he had outsmarted them. While incarcerated, he stated, "I'm not going to do what the man tells me to do" (Larsen, 1980, p. 208).

For him, judges were the adversary. In fact, he often came close to being held in contempt. He actually had one judge in Florida disqualified from his case, which pleased him immensely.

Bundy's view of the psychiatrists and psychologists who examined him was that they were determined to produce an analysis that would explain and rationalize his crimes. He was scornful of their tests, which as a psychologist he saw right through. He found their examinations to be "malicious, slanted and infernal" (Rule, 1980, p. 205).

Ted Bundy's attitude toward religion is a mystery. Although he affirmed his belief in the Church of Latter Day Saints by being baptized as a Mormon in Utah, when he was arrested in Florida he requested a Catholic priest. During his childhood he attended and was active in the Methodist church. He told a psychiatrist that he didn't believe in a life after death (Larsen, 1980, p. 151). In his letters to Ann Rule, however, he often wrote of his belief in God (Rule, 1980, p. 149).

Recall of Events

Whether Ted Bundy remembered his killings and his victims in any detail is not known. He alluded to killing over one hundred people in six states, yet he would not speak of the killings. He came close to discussing his murderous acts when speaking with authors Michaud and Aynesworth (1983) hypothetically in the third person. It is only their contention that he was in fact describing his killings. It is quite possible that he was simply fooling them, just as he had attempted to con everyone else throughout his life.

Bundy's Last Con

Ted Bundy was executed on Jaunary 24, 1989. Prior to his execution, he began confessing to his murders. Although a number of these confessions were taken seriously by law enforcement officials, Bundy was most likely trying one more con: a con to save his life. He did in fact kill a number of people. By confessing to these crimes, he was trying to avoid the death penalty. Yet many of his victims may never be identified. He also confessed to being driven by pornography as a young man. His motives remain a puzzle to criminologists, crime buffs, the media, and the general public.

Jerry Marcus. From the author's personal files.

CHAPTER 10

Jerry Marcus

—A CASE STUDY BY *Linda Lou Kreuger*

Social Environment

"I was a kid who had no real goodies in his life, so I would set out to cut grass, or do other odd jobs, in order for me to purchase some of the goodies that I desired so much" (Marcus, personal communication, August 1999). At the time in his life that Jerry Marcus was describing, he had no history of theft and worked odd jobs to get extra money. "My dad broke me from stealing. He made me get buck naked and he whipped me for hours for stealing $1.00 from his pants pocket. I always had flash-backs about when dad punished me, and I hated others when they took me for granted" (Marcus, personal communication, July 1999).

Jerry Marcus is black, and so were all of his victims. He did rob one of his mur-der victims after the fact, but the stolen property consisted of small, easy-to-carry items that he sold to a pawnshop for small amounts of cash. In each confession, when Marcus describes the robberies, they appear secondary to the kill. In the case of Lenore Wright, Marcus says he killed her for money that she owed him, but she had no cash on her person when the act was committed, evidence of a lack of plan-ning on Marcus's part.

Marcus's first and only known marriage, to Gwen Synegal, lasted approximately six years, but throughout the marriage Marcus was unfaithful. He separated from Gwen and their family between 1975 and 1979 and, during this time, left Tuskegee, Alabama, to attend school at Knoxville College in Knoxville, Tennessee. Also during

183

this time, he became intimately involved with two other women and had children with both of them.

Marcus did very well in school, was regarded favorably by his teachers, excelled in mathematics, and to this day is very literate. He is a good writer who currently works with other inmates at Parchman Penitentiary, teaching them to read and write. He participated in extramural sports in grade school and high school, and earned a football scholarship that enabled him to attend Knoxville College. He had many friends throughout his school years, most of them female.

When Marcus began his criminal behavior, he already had a juvenile history of animal abuse, window peeping, and playing with fire. Anger against women in general had been simmering beneath the surface of the docile personality that everyone had come to know and trust for many years. The first known time that Marcus's concealed aggressive behavior broke free of his own emotional control, he attacked and strangled Constance Collins, a student nurse on the Tuskegee University campus. Although the attack was unplanned and he did not complete the sexually oriented act, he did make his first successful killing on the campus, his site of employment. Feeding on the excitement of his unexpected success, Marcus killed his next victim approximately one year later, in 1971, demonstrating more aggressiveness and better planning in his technique, and this time completing the act of rape. He was never regarded as a suspect in either of these killings. Then, late in 1971, he was accused of assault with intent to ravish by two student nurses from Tuskegee University. When he was arrested, he expressed remorse but indicated that he would probably do it again. On March 12, 1972, the original charge of assault with intent to ravish was reduced to one of assault and battery. On March 17, 1972, Marcus was convicted and sentenced to six months in jail.

After his release, he quietly slipped back into society—marrying his high school sweetheart in late 1972, working to support his new family, going to school, and caring for his aunt, who had become ill. He appeared to be attempting to neutralize his criminal behavior, disregarding his previous actions as though they had never occurred and blaming others for the behavior that eventually led to his incarceration. "My dad never taught me the value of life, or the value of women [sic] lives, he just took things into his own hands, and did what he wanted when he lost self-control and respect" (Marcus, personal communication, June 1999).

In the Lowndes County justice court on April 20, 1987, Jerry Marcus was charged with the strangulation death of a woman whose nude body was recovered approximately five days after her murder. Already under suspicion for being seen with this woman, who had been reported as missing, Marcus then confessed to five additional murders over a sixteen-year period.

This case study is based on news media reports; case file documents from the initial arrest; and personal contact with Ruth Marcus, Jerry's mother, and Arthurlene Owens, Jerry's aunt, to fill in gaps in the original records pertaining to family issues and educational information. There have also been interviews and correspondence with Marcus to gain his own account of what occurred during his sixteen-year killing spree. This case was discovered through an inquiry made to Captain David Lindley of the Starkville Police Department in Starkville, Mississippi; he was involved in the initial investigation that led to the discovery and identification of the first victim, prompting Marcus to confess. In terms of the serial killer phenomenon, Stanford University psychology professor David Rosenham makes this observation: "The first murder would be like a good meal . . . all the other murders stem from the first one, like you or me trying to recapture that perfect dinner we experienced once in a little Parisian café or wherever. The taste, the smell, the moment. But, we can never quite recapture it" (Ressler, Burgess, & Douglas, 1985).

Family Background

Jerry Marcus was born on June 14, 1951, in Tuskegee, Alabama. His home life was sporadically unstable because his parents, Ruth and Eddie, experienced repeated conflict in their relationship, which affected the children. Marcus had three brothers, Edwin, Anthony, and Ronald, now deceased, and one sister, Beverly. As a young boy, Marcus played Little League baseball and then became involved in sports in high school, playing baseball and football and running track.

When questioned about his youth, Marcus indicated that he felt superior to other kids his age. Between the ages of eight and ten during 1959–1961, Marcus felt a "badness" deep inside his heart and mind toward others, except for his best friends and family members. These feelings of anger confused Marcus, because his family had always been religiously inclined. However, he admitted that he often skipped out on attending services and church school. Persuading neighborhood kids to give him a copy of the church bulletin, he would show this to his aunt and mother to prove that he had attended the services.

During this time, Marcus began to abuse animals:

> I tortured cats a lot, especially when they were pregnant, I would toss the cat around and around until it became drunk, then I would set its tail on fire. I got a kick out of that. When I played with fire, I felt amusement, what it would feel like to stick my finger in it, how it would feel to be caught in a fire with no way out. I poured hot water on stray dogs that came for a free meal around the house. When I tortured these animals, I felt pride, joy, happiness and being in total control of my naughtiness. (Marcus, personal communication, 1999)

By age twelve, in 1963, Marcus began to feel shame concerning his family and the abuse that he felt sure everyone knew about. Perhaps because he thought that everyone knew intimate details about him and his family's life, Marcus began to window peep. "I began window peeping at the age of 13. I admired looking at girls and women in their bras and panties" (Marcus, personal communication, 1999).

During the period 1964–1967, when Marcus was between thirteen and fifteen years of age, his mother separated from his father and took a job in New York State for an extended time. At this point Marcus moved in next door with his aunt to avoid his abusive father. Prior to this time, because of family problems, Marcus's mother had left the family home on several occasions to stay next door with her sister. Her husband, Eddie Marcus, told her that if she didn't come back he would kill all his children. When she returned to the family home, Eddie kept her locked up in the house for days. Marcus and his older brother Ronald each took two rifles and went to their father's house to get their mother back, but she shouted for them to go away or their father would kill them all. "I just wanted to take a brick and bust his brains out of his head. I hid one evening outside with a brick ready to kill my dad, but he never came outside" (Marcus, personal communication, August 1999).

When Marcus was fourteen years old and in tenth grade, he met Gwen Synegal, whom he considers the love of his life and one of the smartest and most intelligent girls he has ever met.

> I always felt intimidated by her smartness. She's the jealous type, dazzle, charm, a great sense of humor, easy to impress, wouldn't let me be me totally, a total mysterious woman towards "voodoo," shows a lack of passion, stubborn to the core when angry, a very attractive lady. She never wanted me to attend Knoxville College but to work at a gas station for the rest of my life. I could never please or satisfy her desires. (Marcus, personal communication, July 1999)

They were married in 1972, soon after Marcus was released from the assault and battery conviction. When Marcus married Gwen, perhaps he was attempting to deflect suspicion for the kidnapping and attempted rape of the students that had occurred on the Tuskegee campus in 1971. But Marcus was remembering the Collins killing in 1970, the Sturdivant killing in 1971, and the fact that the shadow of guilt was never cast his way. Perhaps he felt some remorse and guilt, and hoped that the normality of marriage with a wife and children would help him control his desire to dominate and overpower women. This obsession had already escalated from lying about attendance at religious events, extensive animal abuse, and window peeping as a teenager to abduction with forcible rape and murder as an adult.

Marcus and Gwen's relationship was not approved of by either family, and they separated in 1975. After Marcus's father passed away on June 15, 1977, they got back together briefly before splitting up for the final time. In subsequent police reports, Marcus talked about Gwen and how she practiced voodoo and was a witch. He made no reference to himself as participating in her activities. He feared her and noticed that she saved nail clippings and hair that she trimmed from his head; she also kept large Clorox bottles filled with water in all the closets. Gwen supposedly "deprived" Marcus of sexual activity for weeks at a time; this was when he started "dating other ladies behind her back." According to police reports from the original arrest in Starkville, Mississippi, during questioning Lynn Bishop (Marcus's girlfriend when he was arrested for the Davis murder) said that Jerry was "crazy . . . a nut on having sex . . . would get what he wanted if the girl wouldn't let him" (Starkville Police Department, Marcus case file, 1986). There is no written evidence that Gwen was aware of the incidents that occurred in Tuskegee. After her initial interview with the authorities in 1986, she has refused to comment further.

In 1969, when Marcus graduated from Tuskegee Institute High School, he was considered to be a sharp student, quick to answer questions and excelling in mathematics. He was also a good singer and an artist for the yearbook. "I was a creative child and I valued everything that I'd worked hard for without a handout from family members or others. I took my education more serious than playtime" (Marcus, personal communication, July 1999). After high school there was no money for him to attend a "big" college. When he asked his father for financial support, he was told that he wouldn't get "one red cent" because he had run away from home to live with his aunt during high school. So his aunt came up with the money for his fees, and Marcus enrolled in Alexander City State Junior College to study health and physical education. He commuted with John Bentley, a classmate from high school who had a car, and his cousin, Earnest Brown, who also attended class there. They commuted in this fashion until Marcus and his cousin met the Wise family and moved in with them, paying $50 a month for room and board. However, this didn't last long because within Marcus's first year of college, in the fall of 1969, he dropped out to move back to Tuskegee. His aunt had suffered a stroke and was forced to leave her job at John Andrew Hospital. Marcus cared for her until she became mobile again in 1971.

During 1971, Marcus began working at John Andrew Hospital on the Tuskegee Institute campus as a janitor in the operating room. At this point he decided to become a surgical technician, after watching the doctors and nurses at work in surgical procedures. "There's no procedure that I didn't have an input in it. I had gotten so good that one of the doctors on staff stated, 'Marcus, I'm going to have you operating soon.'" It was during this time that Marcus had access to medical supplies, stealing needles and phenobarbital that he claims to have provided to the two student nurses who accused him of assault and battery (Marcus, personal communication, 1999).

Marcus's mother and maternal aunt were very loving and supportive, and remain so today. However, this was not true of his father. Although Marcus did well in many other areas, he and his mother experienced both physical and mental abuse from his father, a known alcoholic. Marcus's parents never had a sound marriage, and his father used to mentally, physically, socially, and spiritually abuse his mother beyond physical and emotional recognition. Marcus indicated that although he loved his father, he was whipped a lot and struck with his father's fists as well. "There were numerous occasions when I wanted to end my dad's life, but my plans never went through because my mom truly loved him no matter now bad he beat her up or mistreated her, she always went back to him knowing how he is when he's drinking a lot" (Marcus, personal communication, August 1999).

When Marcus began killing his victims, perhaps he was reliving his resentment toward his mother's tolerance of abuse from his father and her inability to protect him as a child. "My uncaring dad, my role model didn't provide me with a safe place from poverty, neglect, drugs, and violence" (Marcus, personal communication, June 1999). It is interesting that even though Marcus loved his mother and his aunt very much, he became a repeat killer of women. Perhaps he was subconsciously modeling after his father in his rage toward both parents—his father for the repeated physical and mental abuse that affected the entire family, and his mother for being unable to control the abuse and for her willingness to be punished repeatedly. During his youth, Marcus was unable to help his mother or himself; the more hatred he developed toward his father for abusing his mother, the more of this hatred he transferred to girls. "The more I killed and got away with, the more I wanted to see them suffer the way my mom did by the hands of my dad. I saw all the bad things that my dad did to my mom, so by him teaching me how bad he treated mom, I knew it was wrong, but I had to find out by experimentation how it would feel to actually hurt a female physically the way my dad did" (Marcus, personal communication, June 1999).

Peer Group Associations and Personal Relationships

Other than comments made by one teacher and one previous employer, the records do not mention any specific male associations for Marcus. When he was questioned in a personal interview at Parchman Penitentiary about male friends, he indicated that he didn't have many (Marcus, personal communication, November 1999). Even though he was involved in sports throughout his educational history, apparently he did not belong to any type of fraternal organization. He played football and was active in high school sports, but there is no mention of him having any male friends within his own age group other than his commuting to Alexander City State Junior College with a former high school classmate and a cousin (Marcus, correspondence, 1998).

Even though Marcus grew up within a troubled family environment, he was successful in his attempts to gain a good education, was involved in sports, and had the attention of many women in different walks of life. He married his high school sweetheart in 1972, shortly after his release from six months in jail for the assault and battery of two student nurses on the Tuskegee University campus. It is unknown if Gwen Synegal was aware of this incident before she married Marcus. Until the summer of 1975, he lived at his mother-in-law's house and worked for Carver Super Service Station.

Marcus indicated that he traveled often to Pensacola, Florida, on "fishing trips"; and during 1974–1975, he drove Gwen's boss on several trips to New Orleans, Louisiana. It is possible that additional murders occurred during these trips; however, there is no solid evidence of this.

In September 1975, Coach Marian Quinn of Knoxville College sought out Marcus to play football on his team. As a result, Marcus became a student at Knoxville College in Tennessee and remained there until 1979. Quinn and Marcus had attended the same high school in Tuskegee and played ball together there. Marcus separated informally from Gwen at this time; she did not accompany him to Knoxville but stayed in Tuskegee, Alabama. During 1975, while he was attending Knoxville College, Marcus became involved with Lynn Bishop, who was also a student at the college. She graduated in 1978 and moved back to Starkville, Mississippi, pregnant with Marcus's son. Then, in 1979, after Lynn Bishop left the college, Marcus met Lennise Gillette, who was also a student there, and they conceived a son. Marcus then dropped out of college to work full-time on campus as a custodial supervisor. He lived alone at the Wesley House, which was considered a living area for "indigents." During this period, Marcus and Gwen divorced after a brief reconciliation in 1977. Marcus continued working at Knoxville College, and Lennise became pregnant again with a second son.

During 1983, Marcus was fired from his job at Knoxville College after he gave out the master key for the basketball locker room and items were stolen. He was formally charged with aiding and abetting, but the charges were subsequently dismissed. As far as the college administration knew, Marcus had never been in any type of trouble before. It is important to note that the loss of this job coincided with the killing of Francine Davis, whom Marcus had met when he filed for unemployment benefits and food stamps. Within a few weeks of losing his job on campus and having committed this killing (as it was learned later), Marcus left Knoxville College during January 1984 without completing his degree and with no plans to return.

When Marcus left Tennessee, he traveled to Los Angeles with an unidentified male companion. From Los Angeles the two took a bus to Houston, Texas, and then split up, with Marcus staying at the Salvation Army while searching for work in that area. By June 1984, Marcus had hitched a ride to Waugh, Alabama, and found a factory job as a steel worker, which he held until July 1985. During this time, he became heavily involved with alcohol and drugs and lost his job after not showing up for work. This was his second major job loss.

Early in 1986, Marcus moved back to Tuskegee and started doing construction work on the Tuskegee campus, building the Chappie James Aerospace Center. But he was laid off from this job early in 1987 due to bad weather conditions, so he moved to Starkville, Mississippi, to live with Lynn Bishop and her mother. This was his third major job loss. Perhaps he was fearful of being connected with the Yvette Chambers murder of May 1986, because for the first time in his career of hidden violence he was being questioned as a suspect. When Marcus returned to Starkville, he met and befriended his final two victims, Wydeane Ellerbee and Dorothy Davis (Starkville Police Department, 1986).

"He had quite a few girlfriends in high school. He was a leader and always showed me the utmost respect," said Thomas Calhoun, a former coach and teacher of Marcus. "He was like a son to me. He came to me with his problems, we talked about them and once I gave him some money when he needed it. I was very surprised when I heard about everything that had happened. Marcus was never violent, even when he played football" ("Town dumbfounded by murder charges against Marcus," *Birmingham Post-Herald*, April 23, 1987).

Contact with Defining Agencies

Except for a few traffic tickets, Marcus had a clean criminal record until after he graduated from high school in 1969. The Macon County courthouse records indicate that Marcus was arrested in 1971 for the kidnapping and attempted rape in an alleged attack on two Tuskegee students. He was admitted to Brice Mental Hospital in Tuscaloosa, Alabama, where he remained for approximately two months. The hospital staff found that Marcus demonstrated a personality trait disorder manifested by ambivalence, poorly controlled hostility, guilt, and frustration with irritability. He was considered legally sane and competent to face trial. Although a jury found Marcus guilty of assault with intent to ravish, the Alabama Court of Criminal Appeals reversed the ruling on the grounds that the confession was improperly allowed as evidence; thereafter, Marcus was recharged with assault and battery and convicted to serve six months in jail because he had no prior criminal record. After this arrest, he was reported to be remorseful over the charges but said that he might do it again. "I pray to God and I cry too" (Starkville Police Department, 1987).

When questioned about this incident, Marcus said that he had been falsely accused. He indicated that he was procuring needles and phenobarbital from John Hopkins Hospital for the students who accused him of assault with intent to ravish. Marcus said that when he grew afraid that he would lose his job and that his aunt would find out about the thefts, he refused to steal anything else for the students, and that they retaliated by accusing him of assault. After spending six months in jail on these charges, Marcus felt that his life and reputation had been destroyed forever. "So, I began to hate girls because two other girls had falsely accused me of doing something that I didn't do. I had too many girls to take or make them do anything on the sex side" (Marcus, personal correspondence, July 1999).

Marcus had a second contact with the police when the Tuskegee Jobs Corps filed a missing persons report for Yvette Chambers on May 8, 1986. At that time she was considered missing, having last been seen with her boyfriend. He was questioned on May 12, 1986, and indicated that he had seen Chambers getting into a car with Jerry Marcus on May 4, 1986. Marcus was questioned on May 14, 1986, and told several different stories about his contact with Chambers. On June 17, 1986, the police attempted a polygraph exam of Marcus to determine his truthfulness concerning involvement with Chambers's disappearance. Statements taken by the polygraph examiner revealed that Marcus had smoked marijuana and had drunk alcohol the night before the exam, thereby tainting the results. One wonders if Marcus realized these actions would invalidate the test.

In the spring of 1986, Lenore Wright's body was recovered in Alabama. Marcus was considered a suspect and was questioned again, but there was not sufficient evidence to charge him. During questioning, he wrote in his first confession that Wright had struck her head in a fall while entering her house and that he had left her unconscious on the bed. In the second confession, Marcus revealed that he had lost his temper and strangled the victim. But, as Marcus indicated, he drove to Wright's house carrying her body. Here the story takes a more sinister turn, revealing for the second known time Marcus's ability to plan and his attention to detail. He claimed he deposited the body in a darkened area in the rear of the house and moved his car to a parking lot nearby. He then returned on foot, dragged the body into the house, deposited it face down on the bed, and turned on the gas stove in the kitchen in the hope that an explosion would occur and conceal his crime. Photos of the crime scene reveal that Marcus may have positioned the body on the bed, removing Wright's shirt and unfastening her pants.

On April 10, 1987, while Marcus was being questioned in Tuskegee, Alabama, about the Wright murder, the body of Dot Davis was recovered in Starkville, Mississippi. This occurred approximately eleven months after the Chambers killing and the Wright murder, which occurred approximately fourteen days after the Chambers killing. This demonstrates a significant "cooling off" period, reminiscent of the fourteen years that passed after the Collins killing in 1971 and the Sturdivant killing in 1972. The police questioned Marcus about the Wright killing for four or five hours on April 11, 1987. Then, for lack of evidence, he was released.

On April 16, 1987, Marcus was brought in and questioned again. This time he modified his confession concerning the Chambers murder, indicating that although he had attempted to blame her boyfriend for the killing, he was the one who was really responsible. This behavior suggests that Marcus was experiencing confusion and disorganization, as he confessed to the Chambers killing when he had more recently committed the same act with Lenore Wright and then Dot Davis.

Then, on April 17, 1987, the body of Wydeane Ellerbee was recovered, almost one year after her murder. This occurred one day after Marcus was questioned about the Chambers killing and approximately seven days after the Davis killing. He was questioned about the Ellerbee murder because of the similar circumstances. All the pieces of the puzzle were starting to come together when Marcus was formally arrested on April 16, 1987, after confessing to the murder of Dot Davis. On May 16, 1987, Marcus was indicted for the murder of Dot Davis. He then confessed to six additional murders in three different states.

In the Marcus case, there does not appear to have been any conflict between law enforcement jurisdictions. This may be a result of the small size of the southern communities within which the murders were discovered. The various law enforcement officials worked well together. In fact, there is evidence of contact between the state's attorney's office, forensic investigators, county sheriffs, and so on, all of whom worked closely to coordinate activities in the investigation. A recent telephone interview with Captain Lester Patrick of the Tuskegee Police Department revealed that a major part of the investigative information on the Marcus case was destroyed during a fire at the Tuskegee Police Department in 1987. Thus, most of the information obtained on this case, including a copy of the actual closed case file, was gained from Captain David Lindley of the Starkville Police Department. Lindley, a police lieutenant, was the lead investigator of the Marcus case, and the incidents of recovery and arrest were well covered by the local media.

In the case file, there is no reference to the victims other than the missing persons report and brief interviews with the parents of the two victims whose bodies were recovered in Starkville, Mississippi. Alternative strategies for pursuing the killer were not considered, since this sort of crime was uncommon in the area. The case was handled in a coordinated manner by all participating jurisdictions, including the Knoxville County Sheriff Department; the Oktibbeha County Sheriff's Office; the Lowndes County Sheriff's Department; the Starkville Police Department in Mississippi; the Tuskegee, Alabama, Police Department; and York Police Chief Jeff

Bunt. Art Miller, public information officer for the Knox County Sheriff's Department in Tennessee, explained to reporters at the time, "We don't want to rush things because rushed homicide investigations are like hastily cooked meals—they're not very good." Miller continued: "If Lowndes County or other agencies develop any information, this department will step out smartly and give this information our fullest attention. It takes lots and lots of man-hours to piece together a coherent story of the information that Marcus says he has" (Starkville Police Department, 1987).

Offense Behavior

When officials began questioning Jerry Marcus, he was believed to have a clean criminal record with the exception of a few traffic tickets. However, documents from the Macon County courthouse in Alabama told otherwise, revealing that he had been arrested in 1971 and indicted in 1972 on charges of assault and battery in an alleged attack on two Tuskegee women believed to be nursing students at John Andrew Hospital. Although the jury found Marcus guilty of assault with intent to ravish, the Alabama Court of Criminal Appeals reduced the charge to assault and battery, and Marcus was released after spending six months in jail. Even though no media attention has been paid to this serial killer, it is suspected that Jerry Marcus began his killing spree of women in 1970 and continued intermittently until 1986, an estimated seventeen years. Marcus was a quiet type of man who did not appear to have any more problems than anyone else; he would willingly do anything that was asked of him, and he was nonviolent even when participating in sports involving aggressive physical contact, such as football. Because of this history of nonviolent behavior, even though Marcus was in the proximity of each of the murders he was never seriously considered a suspect until he met Lieutenant David Lindley of the Starkville Police Department in Starkville, Mississippi, and was questioned regarding Yvette Chambers's missing-person report.

Marcus continued living at the locations (Tuskegee, Alabama; Knoxville, Tennessee; and Starkville, Mississippi) where he had committed murders over extended periods, moving from one location to the next only to return to the same area where his murderous behavior originated. Additionally, he killed one victim in the basement of his mother's home, burying her body in the backyard, and killed two other victims at the Tuskegee Institute, where he was employed. This places Marcus in all three offender groups (Hickey, 1986). He traveled to reach victims (traveling serial killer). He killed victims at home (local serial killer). He killed no strangers—only co-workers, neighbors, fellow students, and/or girlfriends with whom he was intimately involved over an extended period of time—and he returned to the same kill site repeatedly with more than one victim (place-specific serial killer). Marcus is unique because he killed only women with whom he was intimate, those who trusted him, and those who he felt were in a subjugated role in relation to him.

Research indicates that killing close to home or work provides a degree of invisibility for the serial killer. Neighbors or co-workers tend to be familiar with the coming and going of certain individuals and generally disregard their actions because they are so familiar. This information coincides with a statement that Marcus made when he was initially arrested: "You see, once you've committed crimes and never suspected, the mind tells you no matter what I do, I will do it without being seen" (Starkville Police Department, 1987). In fact, a hand-written notice from the original file indicates that Marcus returned to the kill sites with different women while they were still alive. In light of the maps of the murder scenes drawn by law enforcement officials and Marcus, it appears that he may simply have felt more comfortable killing in the country areas outside the perimeter of the actual towns. These locations were popular "make-out" sites for the entire community. In Tuskegee, Alabama, Albert Park was the site for Marcus's assault and battery of the nursing students in 1971, his murder of Margaret Sturdivant in 1971, and the site where he played tennis with Francine Davis hours before killing her in 1984. When Marcus was questioned about his tendency to return to the same site with different women, he said, "Returning to the same locations with other girls made me feel safe from society, I felt safe from the police, I honored my selfish tendencies at those places, I had my own territory to do what I wanted to without interference from the law or others" (Marcus, personal communication, June 1999).

Although Marcus belongs to the category of male serial killers who kill women, his known killings would not be considered heinous because he did not abuse or torture his victims before or after the act. He apparently did not collect trophies such as clothing or body parts, and there is no evidence that he bragged about his kills to other individuals. Even though Marcus indicated that he robbed several of his victims of jewelry, small amounts of money, and some stereo equipment, the value of the stolen goods was minimal. And he did not mutilate the victims' bodies. In one confession he mentioned that although he did kill the victim, they had not had sex "because she was on her period." In another confession Marcus described the cleaning up and redressing of the victim, which could be considered as positioning even though the body was not disturbed or physically positioned. Evidence indicates that he was capable of killing with or without sexually compromising his victims. When questioned about his feelings toward his victims and women in general, Marcus seemed to differ from the norm of serial killers. During the times when he interacted with his victims, rather than being stimulated and excited he considered his respect for women and himself to be at its lowest point because of his lack of moral values and self-respect. In fact, Marcus claims that he kept teaching himself to become dangerous when alone with a girl as they smoked marijuana and drank alcohol. According to Marcus, his unsatisfactory lifestyle drove him to do more bad than good toward those girls (Marcus, personal communication, June 20, 1999).

Early in 1969, Marcus dropped out of City State Junior College and returned to Tuskegee to care for his aunt, who was recovering from a stroke. He was detained for six months between 1969 and 1970 for the assault and battery of two Tuskegee Institute nursing students. In mid-1970, he began working for the John Andrew Hospital in Tuskegee as a custodian in the surgical area. This is when the known killings began.

Marcus was off duty and driving through the campus of Tuskegee Institute when he spotted Constance Collins, a student nurse whom he recognized from the hospital, as she was walking by Tatum Hall. He stopped and asked if she wanted a ride to work. Recognizing Marcus from the hospital, she accepted the ride. Marcus drove her to the Emergency Room area; but as he stopped the car, the situation took a deadly turn when Collins attempted to get out of the car and Marcus grabbed her arm, pulling her back into the car and asking where she lived and if he could call her. Collins panicked and started fighting back, screaming for help as Marcus restrained her from behind while covering her mouth with his hands. He told her to stop screaming, that he would let her go, but she continued to fight back and scream. Marcus panicked and slid his hands down from her mouth to her neck, choking her to death right outside the Emergency Room entrance. Then he drove away from the hospital, traveling aimlessly on Montgomery Highway until he eventually pulled off onto Peterson Street. When he spotted an abandoned, hut-like building at the end of the street, he dumped her body, fully clothed in her gray nursing uniform, onto the ground and drove away. Marcus returned to the site approximately one month later and found everything gone, including the body. At that point he threw away her books, which he had been carrying around with him. Although in his written confession Marcus indicated that he killed Collins on a "sex urge," the victim was not sexually assaulted. Apparently he reached such a state of panic when she would not cooperate that he redirected his passion, drawing from the murder itself all the sexual pleasure that he craved. Marcus was never considered a suspect.

The next confirmed victim was Margaret Sturdivant, another nursing student. As she walked home from class and work carrying her books, dressed in her gray student nursing uniform, Marcus offered her a ride. She accepted because she had seen him working on campus. With little warning, Marcus felt his heart start to race; he says he could almost taste the adrenaline as it started pumping into his bloodstream. He detoured from her route home and drove to the local park, where he persuaded her to leave the car. Perhaps he attempted to appeal to the altruistic nature of any student nurse when he began discussing problems he was having at work and with other women. Sturdivant was tired and simply wanted to go home to her family, but Marcus became physically aggressive. She resisted, kicking him in the groin while attempting to flee. Then she tripped and fell with Marcus on top of her, attacking and raping her. She again attempted to attract attention and to cry out for help, but Marcus forcefully pushed her face into the loose dirt and suffocated her. He held her face down in the dirt until he was sure she was dead; then he hid her body in the nearby woods, discarding her clothing. Sturdivant's body was recovered on November 22, 1971. "I can still see her face buried in the ground as I tried to calm her down. When I turned her over, she wasn't breathing, so I disrobed her and left her body in the woods. I always remembered when my dad got mad at mom, and he tore her clothes off her to disgrace her publically [sic] in front of me and my brother" (Marcus, written communication, July 1999).

Following this episode, Marcus's urge to kill was apparently satiated until October 1984, when he went on the hunt again in Five Points, Tennessee. He met

Francine Davis through a male friend known as "Hotdog." Davis worked at the food stamp office and knew of Marcus. He had lost his job on campus and was living on food stamps and unemployment compensation. Davis and Marcus became sexually intimate for several months before her life ended. Early one weekend morning, Marcus went over to Davis's house so they could go to the park and play tennis. Afterward they stopped at the home of a friend of Marcus's, where he showered while Davis waited for him. Then they returned to Davis's apartment so she could shower. While she bathed, Marcus "cased" her apartment. He found an envelope with his name on it and, looking inside, discovered what appeared to be some of his food stamps and some cash. Marcus realized that while he had been showering, Davis must have taken the items. Initially he was hurt rather than angry at her for taking his stamps and cash, but then he redirected this hurt back at her. The longer she stayed in the shower, the angrier he allowed himself to become. When Davis came into the room wrapped in a bathrobe, Marcus turned on her, seizing her by the arm and spraying Mace directly into her face. Davis attempted to pull away from him, crying, "What do you want, what do you need? Don't kill me . . . ," but he threw her onto the floor. As his hands fumbled at his waist, he realized he was not wearing a belt. His eyes flitted around the room. Suddenly he saw what he was looking for. Jerking a narrow black cord away from the back of the television set, he wrapped it around her neck and choked her. Then he pulled the cord away from her neck, her body limp in his hands, and carried her into the bathroom. Marcus's head was spinning, but he remembered the effort of strangling Constance Collins and again wondered if he had really killed his victim. He held Davis's head under water, still furious with her but determined to make sure she would never reappear to accuse him of attempted murder. "I put her head under the water and held it until the bubbles quit coming up. It took a long time" (Marcus, written communication, June 1999). Then he pulled her body from the tub, dried her off somewhat, and put her in her bed to make it appear that she had died while sleeping. He also wrote a suicide note implicating her former husband, Arthur; took a few pieces of gold jewelry and a boom box; and left the apartment. After that, he went to his girlfriend's house for the night. The next day, he sold the stolen items at a local pawn shop and left town for Tuskegee, Alabama.

Soon Marcus began worrying about being suspected of the Davis killing and became upset about breaking up with his girlfriend, Lennise Gillette. Then, on October 31, 1984, the body of Francine Davis was recovered from her apartment. What makes this killing different from the previous incidents is that Marcus modified his modus operandi by using Mace prior to strangulation and by drowning the victim after the initial attack. It is apparent that he had known this victim for an extended period, was aware of her relationship with her former husband, and set up the murder scene with a picture of the former husband and a "suicide' note. Davis was the first victim from whom Marcus stole items; when questioned, he indicated that she had stolen money from him (Marcus, personal communication, June 1999).

Approximately two years later, on May 8, 1986, a missing persons report was filed by the Tuskegee Job Corps Center concerning Yvette Chambers, who had last been seen with her known boyfriend, Carl Washington. On May 12, 1986,

Washington was questioned. He indicated that he had last seen Chambers on Sunday, May 4, at 4:00 or 4:30 P.M., when she got into a vehicle with other male subjects, one of whom was Jerry Marcus. When Marcus was questioned on May 14, he told several different stories. The initial story indicated that he had picked up both Chambers and her girlfriend Janice on May 5, at 4:00 or 4:30 P.M. They drove around to get some beer and marijuana, hung around the lake until about 7:00 P.M., and then drove back to the Job Corps, dropping Janice off and returning to the store to get more beer and food and also picking up some more marijuana. This interaction occurred in the same local park where the Sturdivant killing had occurred in 1971, approximately fifteen years previously, as well as where Marcus had played tennis with Davis before killing her in 1984.

By the afternoon of the same day of the initial confession, Marcus had changed his mind. In his second sworn statement, he indicated that he had dropped Chambers off at a hair salon and had gone to pick up his girlfriend, Lynn Bishop. The story remained the same until after the beer and marijuana, when Chambers and Marcus drove to a club in Hardway, Alabama, and Marcus went inside, leaving Chambers inside the car for approximately thirty minutes. When he came back outside, both Chambers and his car (Lynn's car) were gone. After about fifteen minutes Chambers returned with another male in the vehicle, whom Marcus told to get out. This man was not identified. Marcus got into the car and started driving Chambers back to Tuskegee on Highway 80; then, without warning, he pulled off of the road and started slapping her. She attempted to get away but Marcus started tearing off her clothes, forcing her back into the car. She spit in his face and bloodied his nose during the struggle. Marcus then reached into the backseat of the car and retrieved a belt, which he tightened around her neck. As he started getting out of the car, dragging Chambers by the neck, he heard something pop. After that, she didn't move anymore. He panicked, pulling her body upright and shaking her to provoke some response. Getting none, he dumped her body in the trunk of the car and started driving across the bridge. Marcus then began having second thoughts. He pulled the car over to the side of the road and removed the body from the trunk, throwing it over the Highway 80 bridge. He heard a dull thump and the splash of water as the body made contact. Then jumped into the car and drove back to Tuskegee. As he drove into the campus of the Tuskegee Institute, he began to calm down and headed to a service station, where he threw the clothes he had torn off Chambers's body into a Dumpster. Then he drove home. In this case, Marcus had not succeeded in having any sexual contact with the victim; he had killed her by accident prior to the planned rape as he pulled her by the neck out of the car.

On June 17, 1986, the confession was modified again. At this time, Marcus said Chambers had revealed to him that Washington planned to kill her and that she feared for her life. Marcus then dropped Chambers off at the Chicken Coop restaurant, telling her he had to pick up his girlfriend from work. After he took Lynn Bishop home, he went out again, supposedly in concern for Chambers's safety. Spotting Chambers and Washington together, he followed them to the bridge on Highway 80. Marcus then indicated that as he drove by their car he noticed the passenger's door was open and Chambers and Washington were arguing. So he turned the car around and returned to the scene, not knowing whom he could trust to tell that he had seen Washington and Chambers fighting, then discovering that they were gone. He then indicated that he did not think Chambers was wearing any clothes and he thought that Washington's shirt was halfway off. In addition, Marcus commented that Washington "do drink a lot." On approximately May 27, 1986, Chambers's body was recovered from under the bridge on Highway 80, and a postmortem examination was performed on the body. Markedly decomposed, it was identified by a yellow metal cap with a star over the upper right incisor and a yellow metal cap with a central window over the upper left incisor. Positive identification was confirmed by means of dental records and X rays. The cause of death was undetermined, partially owing to advanced postmortem decomposition.

Then, on May 30, 1986, while Marcus was attempting to cover up his previous contact with Chambers, he apparently had the urge to kill again. This time his victim was Lenore Wright. During the brief time between the Chambers killing and that of Lenore Wright, something must have triggered Marcus's homicidal behavior. Perhaps it was fear; perhaps it was frustration in being considered a suspect in a killing he had committed many months previously and knowing that he had committed additional killings since that time. Perhaps some internal trauma resurfaced relating to his parents' violent relationship and his own moving out of the family home years earlier. Perhaps leaving behind his girlfriend and the children he had conceived with her in Knoxville, Tennessee, pushed him over the edge. Perhaps it was his inability to complete his degree at Knoxville College and the scandal surrounding the loss of his job with the Recreation Department there. Whatever the causal factor, Marcus was beginning to realize that he was no longer "invisible." He could almost hear the cell door slamming shut behind him for crimes he had committed that were far more serious than anyone knew.

When Lenore Wright's body was recovered in the spring of 1986, and during later questioning about this victim, Marcus wrote two separate confessions. The first, written in early April 1987, stated that he and Wright were just friends; the second, written approximately four days later, indicated that he and Wright were "secret lovers." In the first confession, Marcus said that he and Wright ate at Kentucky Fried Chicken and then drove out to the lake to smoke marijuana and drink some beer. When Marcus told Wright that his girlfriend was coming to town and that they planned to get married, Wright put her feet on the dashboard and, kicking, broke the windshield. Marcus then described what he considered to be a "seizure," during which he grabbed her mouth and held her jaw until she calmed down and "went into a little sleep." He then started up the car to drive away, but she started kicking again so he restrained her, calming her until they returned to her house. Marcus then helped her out of the car, but she fell and struck her head, which rendered her unconscious. Then he carried her into the house and put her into bed. Although he claims to have smelled gas, he abandoned her there, indicating that she had a male friend who would be coming back to the house soon and would help her. Marcus saw the police at Lenore's house two weeks later when he and his girlfriend, Lynn, were driving by.

In the second confession, Marcus demonstrated less concern for the victim's well-being. He related how he and Wright were together at the lake but indicated that after she became angry and broke his windshield, he lost his temper when he realized it was going to cost about $400 to have it repaired. So he wrapped his hands around her neck and choked her until he thought she was dead. As in the first confession, Marcus stated that he started driving away after choking Wright but that she began to regain consciousness, so he stopped to strangle her again. At this point, his story takes a more sinister turn, revealing for the second known time his ability to plan and his attention to detail. This time, Marcus stated that he drove to the rear of Wright's house, a concealed area surrounded by trees, and deposited the body on the back porch. He then drove his car about a block away to the parking lot of an apartment complex, left it there, and returned returning to Wright's house on foot. When he was unable to open the back door, he went to the front and let himself in. Heading to the rear of the house, he opened the back door and pulled her body through the doorway to the front of the house. In this confession, he stated that Wright sustained her head injury as he dragged her up the porch steps rather than when she fell from the car. Marcus stated that he then placed her body on the bed, removing her shirt to clean up the blood from the head injury. Again, he mentioned the gas, but this time he claimed to have turned on the gas stove, hoping that the house would blow up and cover up his crime. Then he modified the confession again, indicating that they had not had sex because Wright was "on her period." However, in an effort to clean her up he removed her pants and placed tissue between her legs, putting another pair of pants back on the body. He then wiped everything with bloody rags, which he put in a back room. As mentioned in another killing, Marcus talked about excessive blood at the scene; if this was so, it is possible that Wright was not dead when he left the scene. Perhaps to substantiate his truthfulness at this point in the confession, Marcus described the churchyard where he disposed of Wright's clothes; it could be seen from the back porch of her house. When questioned about this killing, Marcus indicated that he was under "Satan's curse" for bad things to happen to his female companions when they became disobedient to him. "Lenore did serious damage to Lynn's car (a broken windshield) and my anger intensified to punish her in her own home" (Marcus, written communication, July 7, 1999).

On June 17, 1986, Marcus was to be given a polygraph exam to determine his truthfulness concerning (1) whether he was responsible for the Chambers death in May, and (2) whether he was present when Chambers's body was placed below the bridge from where it was recovered. An actual polygraph exam did not occur, because of Marcus's written statement, his admissions, and his emotional and physical condition during the interview, including his indication that on the previous evening he had smoked four joints of marijuana and had drunk four beers, thus tainting the validity of the test.

On April 10, 1987, at about 11:00 A.M., Marcus picked up Dot Davis at her mother's home in Starkville, Mississippi. He was driving his fiancée Lynn Bishop's car, a 1984 blue Ford Tempo. They drove to the welfare office in Starkville and then headed out to Highway 389, buying some beer and parking near a fishing spot to drink it. Around 2:30 P.M. they returned to Davis's sister's house to check on her kids, and Davis received a phone call from her boyfriend. This call prompted her to urge Marcus to drive her to Columbus, Mississippi, so they could "party" at a club called Goldie's Disco in Catfish Alley. They drank some and then left to buy a pint of whiskey from the ABC package store; afterward they drove back to Highway 45 drinking, smoking, and killing time until dark. When they returned to the liquor store to get more beer, Marcus searched for $60 that he had put in the console of Bishop's car earlier. It was gone. When he asked Davis about the money, at first she denied any knowledge of the cash; then she said she needed the money and would pay Marcus back later. They drove off the highway onto a gravel road a mile or so from the crossroads, went under an underpass, and pulled onto a dirt road where they parked and had sexual intercourse. But all the time Marcus kept remembering the money Davis had taken, and, he says, his anger began building in that familiar way, leaving him breathless, better than sex, better than almost anything. He asked her about the money again. This time Davis made the mistake that cost her her life, saying, "You got your money's worth." Marcus gave her one more chance to stop his escalating passion to kill, saying, "Dot, let's not play games, I need my money." Davis must not have seen the rage in his eyes as she replied, "You'll get your money back, but not right now." Marcus felt she expected him to beg for his money back. He reached down for his belt on the floorboard and looped it around her neck from behind, taking her by surprise. Even though it was springtime, it was hot inside the car, and the driver's side door was already open when Marcus dragged her body out of the car by the belt around her neck. He held her down on the ground, pulling the belt tighter until blood started coming out of her nose and a foamy substance out of her mouth. According to Marcus, as quickly as the anger had escalated out of control, suddenly it was gone, replaced with panic. He picked up Davis's nude body, threw it into the trunk of the car, and drove away, skidding on the gravel road and throwing her clothing out the window. They were already in an isolated area, and after driving a quarter of a mile or so he stopped the car and dumped the body near the side of the road. As he drove away, he discarded the belt that he had used in at least three previous murders. Marcus then returned to Starkville and fell asleep in a service station lot. When he awakened the next morning, he attempted to file a false police report indicating that he had been robbed; this would furnish a cover for having Lynn Bishop's car out all night. On April 11, 1987, the police questioned Marcus for four or five hours concerning this report, but he was released for lack of evidence.

On April 16, 1987, Marcus was brought in and questioned again. This time he modified his confession concerning the Chambers kill, indicating that although he had attempted to blame Carl Washington for the kill, he himself was really responsible. This behavior illustrates the confusion and disorganization Marcus must have been experiencing as he confessed to the Chambers kill when he had more recently committed the same act with both Lenore Wright and Dot Davis.

On April 17, 1987, the body of Wydeane Ellerbee was recovered, almost one year after her murder on or about September 16, 1986, one day after Marcus was being questioned about the Chambers kill and approximately seven days after the Davis kill. Marcus was questioned about the Ellerbee murder because of the similar circumstances and because he admitted to having seen Ellerbee at the Turning Point Club in Tuskegee, Alabama at 10:30 or 11:00 P.M. in September 1986, commenting that she owed him $200. That night, Ellerbee asked Marcus to accompany her to a house to pick up some cocaine. He agreed and gave her $25 to purchase the drug while he waited in the car. When Ellerbee came back outside, she said there was just a little of the coke so she had done it herself. Did he know where they could find some more? Marcus took Ellerbee back to the house where he was currently living with his mother so he could call around to find more coke. When he was unable to located more drugs, Ellerbee became impatient, which prompted Marcus to ask her about the $200 she owed him. She pulled away from Marcus and turned, walking down the back steps of his mother's house; but he looped his belt around her neck from behind and pulled her toward him, choking her as he did so and dragging her into the backyard. He indicated that she was too heavy to lift, so he returned to the house and got a long black cord from the television set, remembering that he had used this type of cord successfully with Francine Davis. He tied it around Ellerbee's hands, dragging her down the wooden steps into a wooded area beyond the backyard behind his mother's house. Marcus then drove Ellerbee's car back into town, where it was recovered later. Then he retrieved his own car, returning home that same night.

The next day, Marcus returned to Ellerbee's body lying on the ground in the wooded area behind his mother's house. He attempted to dig a grave, but the ground was too hard. Lacking a better idea, he concealed the body with a cover that he took from the couch in his mother's house. Over the next few days, Marcus kept pouring dirt over the body to attempt to cover up the smell of decay that his mother had started to notice. He said that the only clothing he removed from Ellerbee's body was a gold top and underwear, which he threw in the trash and "buried" beside the body even though the ground was too hard to bury the body itself. Marcus killed Wydeane Ellerbee during September 1986 and was formally arrested on April 16, 1987, at which time he confessed to the suspected murder of Dot Davis. One month later, on May 16, 1987, he was indicted for the murder of Dot Davis. He confessed to six additional murders in three different states.

Self-Concept

On April 23, 1987, Marcus wrote a letter to Captain Lindley to help the authorities "pick up on killers or serial killers (stalkers)." In this document, he describes the sick mind and how such an individual will look good in the public eye and then become a schemer and a mastermind when he is alone. Marcus then describes himself as an athlete, "as cool as ever," in the fast lane, choosing the finest women. He indicates that the girls in high school were OK but that he preferred college girls because they had more to offer.

Marcus writes that when he was in high school he was very shy but that at night he became someone else as a "peeping tom." At this point the writing swings to the topic of teenagers, dirty magazines, sick minds, bisexuality, gay people, and straight people. It then heads in another direction: Marcus starts describing himself in the third person as a shy type, hanging around bars or clubs looking for prostitutes for sex. He warns the reader to beware of the shy type, because "these individuals could become a brutal person if rejection permits itself." He discusses anxieties and how they build up to be "dealt with prostitutes." When he finds someone who will trust him and go off with him, her life is in danger; especially if drugs and drinking are involved, the woman could easily be hurt or killed. At this point, he talks about college and how he became involved with women, drugs, and drinking, indicating that this was the start of his sick mind (even though earlier in the same document he talks about beginning as a peeping tom). Marcus writes that once the mind is poisoned by these things, it will automatically change into a "schemer or mastermind" influenced by money, women, and drugs; and when those people are "mastered," they become his victims.

In recent written communications from Marcus, his self-concept has appeared to redirect itself. Prison has taught him the "paradox" of giving to others, especially those in need. "Being here in prison for the past decade helped me learn to value myself by a more mature standard, that my worth is not determined by having all the material things that my heart desired, but by the way I'd helped my fellow man and others in the world" (Marcus, written communication, June 19, 1999).

Attitudes

During Marcus's initial arrest in Starkville, Mississippi, he demonstrated positive behavior in assisting the officers, writing lengthy confessions carefully in almost perfect handwriting, drawing maps to the locations of his kills, and leading officers to new kill sites. During this time, Marcus was observed to demonstrate the same humble, gentle behavior that everyone had known of him; however, this time the gentleness was frightening because authorities now know that it was this behavior that victims trusted, leading them to their death. This was the period during which Marcus wrote a long description of serial killers and what law enforcement officers should look for in these individuals. He drew two "medical" diagrams of the male body describing the organs, a human-anatomy "matching" test, and a list of "operations for patients in the operating room." He wrote the lyrics for a country music song vaguely describing a victim. There is a drawing of the Oktibbeha County sheriff, Dolph Bryan, and Lieutenant David B. Lindley; a self-portrait "to my dear friends, Mr. David B. Lindley and Mr. Dolph Bryan"; a few paragraphs describing "the life of Mr. J."; and a drawing of a professional wrestler, "Leaping Larry."

During his arrest, Marcus was submissive. He demonstrated no regret for being captured. As with many offenders, during this time Marcus seemed to see the light of religious salvation; in fact, he produced several religious drawings and writings during his initial incarceration in Starkville. As mentioned in the Family Background section, Marcus attended church when he was young and is still very religious. Most interesting is a story that he wrote describing the crucifixion of Christ, using vividly descriptive, somewhat violent wording. In the most recent written communications with Marcus he indicates that he has rededicated his life to God, having recently joined a religious group within the prison. "The living spiritual world has put my life back on the right track. I am whatever people want me to be as long as its part of 'God's Will.'" God has put me on a positive level mentally, spiritually, socially, and physically. I've asked God for His forgiveness, and to please give me His wisdom and understanding" (Marcus, written communication, June 19, 1999).

Throughout his life, Marcus has been regarded by others as a giving and conscientious individual. "He was the type who would try to do anything asked of him. I'm trying to figure out what went wrong," said Thomas Lee Calhoun, Marcus's former football coach and teacher. Marcus's girlfriend Lynn Bishop—in whose automobile he drove around with victims, killed victims, and transported at least one body to a dump site—refused to make any comment. Marcus had lived within Lynn Bishop's family for approximately three months in Starkville before he was arrested for the Davis murder. Lynn's grandmother Katie Jones indicated that she was surprised because Marcus had seemed like such a nice fellow, who hadn't said all that much and kept to himself most of the time. "He was a quiet man who helped with housework and didn't seem like a man who would kill women," said Jones. Maxey Peterson of Peterson Building and Construction of Louisville, Kentucky, indicated that Marcus was smart and a good worker. "He was an easygoing, quiet kind of fellow and I was always pleased with his work," said Peterson. "We had to lay him off because of bad weather, but I told him to come back. I had even called him and he was supposed to come back to work the day that he was arrested" (*Starkville Daily News*, April 22, 1987). The Lowndes County sheriff, Lewis Harper, said that Marcus had cooperated with detectives and described him as a "big man who is just as humble as he can be."

Recall of Events

Marcus provided the authorities with several handwritten confessions and details about his murders. Even though some of these accounts are contradictory, they are basically accurate statements in which Marcus seems to be attempting to relieve his guilt. The initial confession written on April 15, 1987, concerning the murder of Dot Davis, proclaimed his innocence and attempted to redirect the guilt toward her boyfriend. Within one day, on April 16, 1987, Marcus recanted this statement voluntarily, saying that he was unable to sleep until he could get everything out in the open and tell about killing Davis after having a sexual encounter. He also wrote lengthy confessions concerning the other victims.

Overall, Marcus had a very good ability to recall events. As illustrated in Francine Davis's murder, Marcus demonstrated a change in routine: In addition to strangulation, he drowned the victim and set up the scene so it would appear that her former husband had committed the crime. In this case, it appears that Marcus demonstrated fear of reprisal and tried to cover up the crime more than in the other cases. This is the only known killing in which he varied the MO of strangulation with his belt to the use of Mace and a black plastic-coated cable cord.

A Concluding Statement

Jerry Marcus murdered seven women: Constance Collins, Margaret Sturdivant, Francine Davis, Yvette Chambers, Lenore Wright, Wydeane Ellerbee, and Dot Davis. Although this killer was convicted many years ago, his case has not attracted widespread public attention. This could be so for many reasons: (1) The murders occurred in small communities, (2) Marcus is black and his victims were also black, and (3) Marcus was not a horrific killer. Yet he is the type of killer that should be feared the most: the type that is never suspected; the nice guy next door; a fellow student at college; the guy who worked maintenance in surgery; the one who respected his elders and his teachers and never rejected authority or discipline.

Research has demonstrated that Jerry Marcus is a serial killer of a different type, perhaps a type that hasn't yet been fully defined. He impressed everyone with his gentle personality and his willingness to help. Teachers, employers, and co-workers all noted his ability to listen and follow instructions. He dated and entertained women continuously without any of them ever suspecting that each date might be her last.

> As a youngster, I started living out my fantasies toward putting pain on something that had life. I used to hurt a lot, and I would try to shoot or kill anything that got in my eyesight. The anger from those college girls began to make me feel uncomfortable about girls, so I was riding around in my car hating every girl that I saw on the street. Something in the back of my mind said that it was O.K. to hate girls, so I began hating girls, and I got my first edge to pick one up, take her off somewhere, and punish her. I always felt insecure about myself, I had low self-esteem, and hated all the girls smarter than me. (Marcus, written communication, July 7, 1999)

Acknowledgments

I would like to thank Peter Wood, of the University of Mississippi Department of Sociology and Criminal Justice, who referred me to Captain David Lindley, Starkville Police Department, Starkville, Mississippi. It was Captain Lindley, who had been involved with the Jerry Marcus case, who indicated that no research has been done on the case and offered to send me a copy of the entire original closed case file.

Others who helped were Ken Jones, Public Information Officer for the Mississippi Department of Corrections, who gave me Marcus's address so that I could contact him by mail, and Rea Clark, the Alabama State's Attorney, and Dr. James R. Lauridson, forensic pathologist for the state of Alabama, both of whom talked with me at length.

Jerry Marcus's aunt, Arthurlene Owens, and his mother, Ruth Marcus, met with me and answered many of my questions. Eddie D. Mallard, Circuit Clerk, Tuskegee, Alabama, provided information about the community; Lieutenant Theodore R. Moon Jr. of the Tuskegee Police Department was also helpful, as was Ken Jones, who helped me gain access to Jerry Marcus within the Mississippi Corrections system.

Finally, I would like to thank Dr. Steve Egger, international expert on serial crime and my advisor in criminology studies and research, for reviewing my work and advising me along the way.

Joseph Miller. Peoria County, Illinois,
Sheriff's Office. From the author's files.

Joseph Miller

—A CASE STUDY BY *Donald W. Larson*

Social Environment

The life of the convicted serial murderer Joseph Miller seems to have been plagued by an array of debilitating relationships and situations. Not much is known of his extrafamilial associations or scholastic performance during his childhood; however, it is clear that his early adult life was arduous.

A single person is mentioned as having been important to Miller during that time: his wife, Marcia. The couple was first married in January 1972, when Miller was seventeen years old, and they spent their short time together living near Chicago. This initial marriage reportedly ended in divorce under unusual circumstances two years later. According to Miller, he had entered the U.S. Army in 1971 using the name of his stepfather, Donald Frank Tarczon; but military officials apparently discovered this misrepresentation and dishonorably discharged the man in August 1972 for having fraudulently enlisted. Miller later told an Illinois Department of Corrections interviewer that this was the basis for his divorce from Marcia, "since the Army told me that Donald Frank Tarczon didn't exist, and that was the name I was using, I wanted to be married under my own name." The couple was supposedly remarried shortly thereafter, with Miller choosing to use his given name (Illinois Department of Corrections, September 27, 1978).

Aside from the divorce episode, life with Marcia was apparently less than nurturing. According to Miller, she attempted to make up for shortcomings at home by having extramarital affairs. Miller seems to feel that he did not provide her with a productive relationship, and he expressed guilt at his self-reported inability to satisfy her sexually. "My wife was running around with other guys because I could not give her enough love and care and our sex life was terrible because of me," he recounted to a prison interviewer (Illinois Department of Corrections, September 27, 1978).

Later, Marcia played a pivotal role in the events surrounding her husband's arrest and conviction for the murders of two prostitutes near their home in the Chicago suburbs. According to Kenneth Gillis, a Cook County circuit judge and former assistant state's attorney who prosecuted Miller for these offenses, Joseph and Marcia had been staying at an apartment in Skokie, Illinois, during October 1977. When Miller confessed to the murders of the two women while serving time for an unrelated charge of taking indecent liberties with a minor child, he must have indicated in some way that Marcia had assisted him with the disposal of the body of one of the victims in October 1976. Gillis told a newspaper reporter that the officers investigating this homicide, as well as the murder of the second woman, in 1977, may have explained to Miller that Marcia could face charges for her alleged assistance, thereby leading to his confession in order to save her the possibility of a related trial and conviction (Smothers, 1993, p. A2). After Miller was sentenced to thirty years in prison for the slayings, he and Marcia divorced for a second time. Speaking of his former wife in 1978, Joseph Miller told a prison official, "She is out of my life. Although she told me she would wait for me, I don't believe her" (Illinois Department of Corrections, September 27, 1978).

Miller has apparently spent his entire life in the lower working class. Aside from the time he reportedly spent in the armed forces, his employment history was erratic. Miller claims, over the years, to have held a variety of jobs, usually semi-skilled, including work as a truck driver, a factory worker, and odd jobs in restaurants (Illinois Department of Corrections, 1978). Nothing suggests that Miller ever obtained any postsecondary or vocational education that might have helped him find a more lucrative or stable means of employment.

As a result, money was in short supply during the time Miller spent with Marcia near Chicago. Former prosecutor Gillis related that the couple were living in their automobile in 1977 when a concerned woman apparently took pity on them and offered the use of an apartment she owned for use as a summer getaway, an accommodation that included access to a swimming pool. According to Gillis, the benefactor did not request a specific lease or rent payment; she asked only that the Millers pay her what they could when they could (Smothers, October 6, 1993, p. A2).

Family Background

According to a Cook County, Illinois, birth certificate, Joseph Frank Miller was born at Cook County Hospital in Chicago on January 15, 1955. Although the middle name "Robert" and its corresponding initial are cited in his later life, it is apparent this is not Miller's given middle name. Miller's father is recorded as James Miller, a twenty-three-year-old newspaper-company salesman. Shirley Lorraine Watkins is listed as the mother; the document indicates that she was a native of Iowa and was eighteen years old when Joseph was born. According to the certificate, the boy was Shirley Watkins's first child.

During an interview conducted when he first entered the custody of the Illinois Department of Corrections in 1978, Miller explained that he did not know the whereabouts of his natural father. His mother married several times during his childhood, but it is uncertain whether Shirley Watkins ever married James Miller. One of Miller's stepfathers was apparently named Donald Frank Tarczon, a name that Joseph Miller would use at various times during later stages of his life. The future killer may have experienced problems with one or more of his stepfathers; one, he claimed, had a severe temper and exercised strict discipline within the household. Although Miller said he was afraid of this paternal figure, there is no specific mention of abuse (Illinois Department of Corrections, September 27, 1978).

Curiously, Miller recalled during the evaluation that when he was a child his mother repeatedly told him he had a twin brother. At some point in his later childhood, he said, he located a copy of his birth certificate and learned this was not the case. Miller told the interviewer, "I wonder why she told me that." When speaking of his family and childhood, Miller makes no mention of brothers or sisters, either step or blood (Illinois Department of Corrections, September 27, 1978).

It is apparent that Joseph Miller's early home life was fraught with neglect or, at the very least, lacked the attention the boy felt he deserved. He later recounted that he frequently ran away from home, usually to return within a short time. On one occasion, which reportedly took place when he was in ninth grade, Miller left home for a relatively long period; the actual length of time is not known. Basements of abandoned buildings, hallways in office and apartment complexes, and outdoor park benches served as Miller's living quarters during this absence from home. Nonetheless, regardless of the duration of these ventures, Miller said he always returned home. He thought his family would appreciate him more following his time away (Illinois Department of Corrections, September 27, 1978).

Peer Group Associations and Personal Relationships

An interesting aspect of Miller's nonfamilial social life during his adult years is his identification or associations with different religious groups and faiths. When he was initially processed into the Illinois prison system in 1978, Miller listed his religious affiliation as Jewish. Later, while serving his sentence, he is reported to have become involved with a Christian prison ministry organization. Members of this program helped Miller move from Chicago to Peoria, Illinois, following his release from the penitentiary in 1993; they even provided him with furnishings and linens, including a pillowcase that was later used during his final series of murders (D. Briggs, personal communication, February 9, 1996).

Contact with Defining Agencies

Miller claimed to have been a member of the U.S. military at two separate times. As noted, he first spent several months in the U.S. Army but was dishonorably discharged for having enlisted under an incorrect name and possibly for misrepresenting his age. In 1973 he supposedly joined the Marine Corps, but this time, he contends, he was honorably discharged because of a medical condition. According to Miller, doctors found that his heart was located to the right side of his chest (Illinois Department of Corrections, September 27, 1978).

The British psychologist and researcher David Canter, in his 1994 work *Criminal Shadows,* notes that serial murderers "do, though, quite often have convictions for theft and violence." He further suggests that some sexual murderers and/or rapists may have progressed from an earlier career of comparatively less serious sexually deviant offenses (voyeurism, indecent exposure, etc.) into one of decisively heightened violence and malignancy (p. 45). Joseph Miller seems to have matured in this fashion.

Like most serial killers, Miller has an extensive criminal history; most of his contact seems to have been with law enforcement agencies in the vicinity of Chicago. Arrest records show that he interchangeably used either his given name or the alias "Joseph Tarczon" while being processed. The sole record outside of Illinois is an arrest by the Petersburg, Virginia, police in May 1972 for grand larceny of an automobile. Miller was given a two-year suspended sentence for this act (FBI, Criminal History Record).

On January 15, 1973, the future killer was arrested for auto theft by officers of the Skokie, Illinois, police department. He used the name "Joseph R. Tarczon" on this occasion and was given one year of court supervision as a penalty. Several months later, he was sentenced to one year of probation after being charged with two counts of theft by the Chicago police. Miller's FBI arrest history shows this event was entered in that system on May 1973; however, the corresponding Illinois State Police record indicates he was arrested by the officers of the Chicago Police Department on December 16 with conviction and sentencing taking place in early January. Miller told authorities he was Joseph R. Tarczon on this occasion as well. The Chicago city police arrested Miller once again in February 1974 for criminal trespass to land; this record also indicates he referred to himself as Joseph R. Tarczon. Apparently, from this point forward, Joseph Miller gave arresting agencies his birth name. This strange change in nominal self-identity may loosely correspond with the killer's desire, as indicated with his discharge from the army, to be recognized as Joseph Miller.

Then, in 1975, Miller's illegal actions became more personal and more violent. His federally maintained history shows that on January 29 of that year he was arrested again by Chicago police and charged with sexual assault. In May the charge was reduced from rape to simple kidnapping, and Miller was yet again given probation, this time for five years. But the Illinois state record indicates that this arrest occurred on May 11, 1975, with an additional entry by the Cook County, Illinois, sheriff's office charging him with contributing to the sexual delinquency of a child on the same date. This time, Miller used his true name. A battery charge in Chicago followed in September 1976, and this led to an additional charge of probation violation for Miller. The Bloomingdale, Illinois, police department arrested Joseph Miller on April 10, 1977, for driving with a suspended driver's license and contributing to the delinquency of a child (Illinois State Police, Criminal History Record, FBI, Criminal History Record). According to Kenneth Gillis, it is possible that this event landed Miller in jail and led to his subsequent confession to the murders of two women near Chicago. The women were Ann Maxham and Martha Kowalski (Smothers, October 6, 1993, p. A2).

Miller was convicted of the Maxham and Kowalski killings and was sentenced to thirty years in prison, to be served at the Illinois River Correctional Center in Canton, Illinois. After spending only fifteen years behind bars, he was released on parole in April 1993. Miller was apparently paroled to the Chicago area but moved very soon thereafter to Peoria.

Joseph Miller's next documented contact with law enforcement authorities came in 1993, when he was arrested in Peoria County, Illinois, and eventually charged with a series of killings there.

At about 4:30 P.M. on Saturday, September 18, 1993, children walking along rural Cameron Lane in the central Illinois county noticed a dead body in the culvert adjacent to the roadway (Williams, September 19, 1993, p. A1; Moll, October 29, 1993, p. A2). Detective Lieutenant David Briggs of the Peoria County sheriff's police joined other officers at the scene a short time later. Lieutenant Briggs recalls that just as he and his associates were beginning to examine the immediate area, a crime scene technician called to him and announced that he had found another body approximately twenty-five feet from the first. Briggs said he initially thought the officer was joking (D. Briggs, personal communication, February 9, 1996).

The first body was later identified as that of Marcia L. Logue, a thirty-four-year-old white woman who had reportedly worked the Morton Square Park area in the city of Peoria as a prostitute on occasion. Logue's nude body was only slightly decomposed at the time of discovery. Two indications of foul play were immediately apparent: A cloth pillowcase had been stuffed in her mouth, and there were deep red creases encircling the skin of her ankles and wrists, indicating she had probably been bound. Helen E. Dorrence, another reported prostitute who frequented the same area in Peoria, was the second victim. Like Logue's, Dorrence's body was unclothed; but owing to more advanced bodily decay, detectives were unable to determine if she had ligature marks similar to those noted on Logue (D. Briggs & S. Schmidt, personal communication, February 9, 1996).

At approximately 8:30 A.M. on Sunday, September 26, 1993, a Peoria County sheriff's deputy patrolling the area of Christ Church Road was flagged down by two pedestrians. A foul odor had captured the attention of the couple, and they had peered into a ravine next to the roadway only to see what appeared to be a human foot protruding from vegetation layered at the bottom of the ditch. For the second time in just over a week, and within about two and one-half miles of the Cameron Lane scene, investigators found another nude female body dumped in a relatively remote locale (Williams, September 27, 1993, p. A1; Okeson, September 28, 1993, p. A1).

An autopsy was performed on the third body, and despite extreme decomposition she was identified as Sandra L. McMahill-Csesznegi. Csesznegi, who was forty-two years old when she died, had also been known to engage in prostitution activity in the Morton Square Park vicinity (D. Briggs, personal communication, February 9, 1996).

Coroner's juries ultimately ruled all three deaths to be homicidal. Marcia Logue had been beaten and stabbed several times; her body also showed signs of having been strangled, in addition to probable asphyxiation caused by the pillowcase stuffed in her mouth. Photographs taken during her autopsy depict severe reddish-purple bruising on her buttocks, and incisions revealed that the trauma extended approximately one inch beneath the skin. Along the sides and backs of her thighs there appeared to be numerous welt-like bruises of various lengths and severity (official autopsy photographs and records, 1993). One in particular was very distinct: It seemed to show a lengthwise geometric pattern and an uneven end. Asphyxiation due to possible strangulation was thought to have caused the deaths of Helen Dorrence and Sandra McMahill-Csesznegi. Peoria County coroner Herb Buzbee later told members of the media that Logue and Dorrence had also been subjected to sexual abuse and assault; McMahill-Csesznegi's body had been too decomposed to permit such a determination (Moll, October 29, 1993, p. A1; Williams, September 22, 1993, p. C1).

While the county authorities were attempting to piece together this growing series of unusual murders, their counterparts in the City of Peoria's police department learned of the disappearance of eighty-eight-year-old Bernice Fagotte. On September 4, 1993, a close friend of the elderly woman called the police and explained that mail and newspapers were accumulating at Fagotte's home in the city's West Bluff neighborhood. Fagotte had also reportedly missed several doctors' appointments. The responding patrol officers found no signs of natural death at her residence; however, they learned that Fagotte's 1991 maroon Oldsmobile Cutlass four-door was missing as well (Williams, September 18, 1993, p. A6).

Suspicions about the widow's fate intensified after crime scene technicians were summoned to examine her house and discovered what were later determined to be droplets of blood on a pillowcase found on her bed (Pyatt, Incident Report, October 5, 1993). Almost three weeks after the missing persons report was made, the maroon Oldsmobile was found parked unoccupied, with its doors locked, in the 1600 block of Dechman Avenue in the city's East Bluff area. The car was processed for evidence and inventories; technicians located a green tapestry rug in the vehicle and a large bloodstain on one of the interior seats. The amount of blood was such that the underlying foam cushion was also apparently soaked ("Car of missing woman," *Peoria Journal Star*, September 24, 1993, p. A6; Pyatt, Incident Report, October 5, 1993).

Following the discovery of Sandra McMahill-Csesznegi's body, a task force of city, county, and state law enforcement personnel was formed to investigate the killings. The break in the case came on September 28, 1993, when a caller to a devoted tip line advised that Joseph Miller, a white male living in the Pennsylvania Terrace apartment complex in downtown Peoria, might be a suspect. Having seen the news coverage of the bodies found near Peoria, a correctional officer at Illinois River reportedly approached a parole agent and pointed out that these murders were, as he understood it, similar in circumstance to the killings for which Miller had served time in his institution. The agent soon learned that Miller had been paroled back to Chicago but that he had requested and been granted permission to move to Peoria. Sheriff's detective Larry Hawkins was charged with pursuing this new lead (D. Briggs, personal communication, February 9, 1996; Perry, Computerized Leads Listing, October 18, 1993).

Over the course of the next twenty-four hours, Hawkins and other investigators explored the Miller angle. Progress was also being made in the Bernice Fagotte case, progress that would ultimately involve Miller as a suspect in her disappearance. A neighbor of Fagotte's was interviewed on the afternoon of September 29 by Peoria city detective Terry Pyatt. He learned that the neighbor had introduced Mrs. Fagotte to Joseph Miller and that Miller had been hired by the widow to perform odd jobs and yard work at her home. He described Miller as having become somewhat of a "pest" to Fagotte. The detective asked if the neighbor had ever been to Miller's apartment at Pennsylvania Terrace; the man reportedly had visited the apartment approximately two or three weeks before, only to have Miller dissolve their friendship when the neighbor accused him of having stolen a tape recorder. A photograph of the green tapestry rug found in Fagotte's car was shown to the informant, who immediately professed to having seen this rug, or one just like it, in Joseph Miller's apartment during previous visits there, but added that he had not seen the rug during his last visit, just weeks before.

Having connected Miller to the disappearance of the elderly woman, task force members obtained a search warrant and went to his apartment. Detectives Hawkins and Pyatt and another city officer were met at the door by a heavy man with brown hair and a mustache: Joseph Miller. Curious about the nature of the detectives' visit, Miller signed a consent form granting permission for a search of his residence; the detectives had chosen to attempt to get Miller's consent instead of immediately handing him the warrant. While lab technicians from the city and county police surveyed the apartment's interior, Miller voluntarily accompanied Hawkins and city police detective Rabe to the sheriff's office for questioning.

The clues needed to tie Miller to the deaths of Dorrence, Logue, and McMahill-Csesznegi, and to implicate him further in the disappearance of Bernice Fagotte, were located within the walls of Apartment 208 at the Pennsylvania Terrace tower. A single women's white tennis shoe was recovered, and several strands of white nylon rope were found in the bedroom. When detectives and laboratory technicians turned over the mattress of Miller's bed, they found a sizable amount of blood staining the material. Other bloodstains and spatters were located in the bedroom, on the bed's headboard, on an electrical outlet and surrounding wall adjacent to the bed, and on a pillowcase (Pyatt, Incident Report, October 5, 1993). Through DNA analysis and comparison, the remnant blood found in Miller's apartment that night was ultimately determined to have come from all of the three murdered women. The largest sample of blood, that found on the underside of Miller's mattress, was connected to Marcia Logue with an extremely strong statistical probability (S. Schmidt, personal communication, February 9, 1996).

Miller never completely confessed to involvement in the murders of the three women or the disappearance of Fagotte during the hours of interviews that followed his trip to the Peoria County sheriff's office. But when Pyatt showed him a Polaroid photograph of a knife recovered from the elderly woman's Oldsmobile, the suspect identified it as his property. Miller told Pyatt he used the knife to open paint cans, but he spontaneously added, "I know you won't find any blood on there, because there isn't any." Pyatt asked Miller why he thought police might expect to find blood on the knife, and Miller simply responded that he did not know. But Miller did say, "I knew you would be coming to talk to me because of those missing women," citing his past convictions as the reason for this belief (Pyatt, Incident Report, October 5, 1993).

The fact that his knife had been found in Fagotte's car led to Miller's arrest that day on suspicion of having at least burglarized the woman's home. The DNA test results that would eventually connect him to the murders were yet to come; but shortly after his arrest, a Peoria County grand jury indicted Miller on a charge of having burglarized Bernice Fagotte's home between August 26 and September 30, 1993 (Meidroth, October 27, 1993, p. A1). When the blood test results were returned from the state police crime lab, he was also charged in the deaths of Helen Dorrence, Marcia Logue, and Sandra McMahill-Csesznegi. The fate of Bernice Fagotte remained a mystery for nearly a year.

A change of venue moved Joseph Miller's triple murder trial from Peoria County south to Sangamon County, Illinois, in 1994. The trial lasted about one week, and Miller did not take the witness stand in his own defense. But the forensic evidence was overwhelming, and the man was subsequently found guilty of the deaths of the three Peoria women. A sentence of death was imposed in all three cases, as was a lesser sentence for the residential burglary charge. For the second time in his life, Miller was transferred to the custody of the Illinois Department of Corrections. This time, he was taken to a solitary cell on death row at the Menard Correctional Center to await lethal injection (D. Briggs, personal communication, February 9, 1996).

Despite the efforts of scores of police and volunteer searchers (a massive ground search conducted on October 16, 1993, was described as the largest such action ever undertaken in Peoria County), Bernice Fagotte's whereabouts were still unknown even after Miller's trial and sentencing (Moll, October 17, 1993, pp. A1, A12; Okeson, October 12, 1993, pp. A1, A2). After Miller's placement on death row, Lieutenant Briggs and the investigators learned that Fagotte's body was hidden in Springdale Cemetery, one of the largest cemeteries in the state, located near the Illinois River within the city limits of Peoria. The woman's skeletal remains were found there, well hidden under a blanket of leaves and grass; she had been strangled to death. No trial was held for the murder of Bernice Fagotte. Miller pled guilty to the charge of killing her and, as a result, was given a sentence of natural life in prison as a result (D. Briggs, personal communication, February 9, 1996).

Offense Behavior

The offenses reportedly committed by Joseph Miller in his early adult life were primarily property crimes. But his actions became more personal and violent in 1975, with arrests for sex offenses, battery, and contributing to the delinquency of a child. Former prosecutor Kenneth Gillis recalled, "There were a number of women—hitchhikers and prostitutes—who turned up dead or missing [around northern Chicago and nearby suburbs] at that time [the mid-1970s]. After we put Miller away, all of that ended" (Smothers, October 6, 1993, pp. A1, A2). Miller was convicted in 1977 for the murders of Ann Maxham and Martha Kowalski; it is certainly possible that he is responsible for additional deaths. However, given the metropolitan character of the Chicagoland area, it can also be assumed with reasonable confidence that Miller was not the only serial killer active in that area during that time. The failure to connect Miller to similar unsolved offenses may have resulted from the phenomenon that Steven Egger calls "linkage blindness." Linkage blindness occurs when, for any number of reasons, various law enforcement entities or practitioners fail to communicate among themselves information that might be crucial in the solution of unsolved crimes (Egger, 1990a, pp. 163–175).

Maxham and Kowalski both died of strangulation, and their bodies were dumped in remote, wooded areas. When Miller was interviewed by a Department of Corrections staff member at the beginning of his stay for these killings, he readily admitted the murders of the two women, whom he described as "prostitutes." He told the interviewer he would watch young women for several days before approaching them, then engage them in conversation and attempt to "date" them. During their rendezvous, he said, "[s]omething would snap and I began beating them" (Illinois Department of Corrections, September 17, 1978). Miller did not detail the nature of these beatings but said that following the attacks he would attempt to break the young women's necks. Usually, he was successful. Once the victim was dead, he supposedly would wash her in a tub of hot water; he "would clean them up as best I could." Miller said he then wrapped the bodies and took them to remote roadside areas, where he dumped them. He claimed that the last body he disposed of in this manner was dumped near his home in an attempt to "try and get some people to stop me" (Illinois Department of Corrections, 1978).

Interviews conducted during the 1993 investigation in Peoria County lend more detailed credence to Miller's paraphiliac tendencies. He can definitely be described, on the basis of this information, as a sexual sadist. On September 11, 1993, at approximately 7:00 P.M., a young woman reported she was approached by Miller, who was driving a mid-sized maroon car. He reportedly attempted to entice her into returning with him to his residence so he could tie her up and spank her. He allegedly offered to pay her $80 if she would bring a friend (Perry, Case Timeline, November 10, 1993). Detective Steve Schmidt, of the Peoria County sheriff's office, interviewed a woman who told him that Miller had taken her to his apartment for a similar session. The woman told Schmidt that Miller had spanked her with his hand while referring to her as "Daddy's little girl" (S. Schmidt, personal communication, February 9, 1996). It is probable that the deep bruising seen on victim Marcia Logue's buttocks was caused by this type of activity. Miller may have used a broken portion of a window shade adjustment rod to inflict the welt-like injuries evident on Logue's thighs. While searching his apartment, detectives found the warped plastic rod and submitted it to Mary Jumbelic, then the Peoria

County forensic pathologist. Dr. Jumbelic compared the features of this item to patterns seen in Logue's wounds and concluded that the welts were very likely caused by this particular instrument (S. Schmidt, personal communication, February 9, 1996).

Unlike the other victims, Marcia Logue had been stabbed. She had also been found with a pillowcase in her mouth. Not surprisingly, the largest amount of blood found in Miller's apartment, particularly on the bed mattress, was identified as having come from Logue. Detective Schmidt and Lieutenant Briggs speculate that Logue fought for her life while in Miller's residence. They believe she either passed out or acted as if she were unconscious while the killer was strangling her. When Miller released her neck, Logue probably became combative and started to scream; at that time, Miller may have shoved the pillowcase into her mouth in order to silence her. In all likelihood he probably then stabbed her repeatedly in order to hasten her demise (D. Briggs & S. Schmidt, personal communication, February 9, 1996).

Very little is known about the death of Bernice Fagotte, other than that she was apparently strangled. The detectives believe she was killed by Miller before the other three victims in Peoria County, possibly when she interrupted Miller burglarizing her home. Lieutenant Briggs speculates that the murder may not have been premeditated; he offers that Miller may have killed the elderly woman to prevent her from calling the police when she found him stealing her belongings. Briggs adds that the killings may have sparked some semblance of regret within Miller, because this was probably his first murder after being released from prison and because he seemed to prefer to target prostitutes, not senior citizens. Detective Steve Schmidt has a different hypothesis. He believes Fagotte's murder may have been "batting practice" for a killer who had only recently regained his freedom. Miller may have taken advantage of an unusually easy victim to test his own mettle and to see if he still had what it took to kill another human being (D. Briggs & S. Schmidt, personal communication, February 9, 1996).

Miller apparently preferred to dump his victims' bodies at remote outdoor areas, usually close to roadways. Maxham and Kowalski were left in this type of location, and the three younger victims in Peoria County all were deposited in culverts immediately adjacent to paved country roads. One could speculate that perhaps Miller did not or could not hide his victims farther away from the road on account of his heavy weight or a leg injury he reportedly suffered the first time he was in prison. The exception to this dump-site preference appears to have been the cemetery where Bernice Fagotte's remains were ultimately found. Briggs and Schmidt contend that Miller probably took the time and care to conceal her body more successfully because he knew he could definitely be connected to the woman as her hired hand (D. Briggs & S. Schmidt, personal communication, February 9, 1996).

Self-Concept

Joseph Miller does not seem to talk much about his own conceptual perceptions. The intake report written after he was first incarcerated in the Illinois Department of Corrections does include self-reported information about his background, as well as some of his apparent attitudes, but there is no introspective self-analysis or attempt to relate his current situation to past experiences. During interviews with task force detectives following his arrest in Peoria, Miller was relatively evasive when answering questions, and he reportedly offered almost no confessional information. This evasiveness, whether intentional or otherwise, was evident again when Miller met with a deputy U.S. marshal months after his arrest; this interaction is discussed in more detail in the subsequent sections.

Despite the fact that Miller never confessed to Peoria area detectives, some who interviewed him indicate that he seemed to relish the attention he was receiving. He was willing to talk for hours on end, but he would attempt to change the subject or otherwise avoid talking about the crimes he was suspected of having committed (S. Schmidt, personal communication, February 23, 1996).

Attitudes

Before Miller's trial for the Peoria murders began, he contacted Deputy U.S. Marshal Crystal D. Taylor and asked to speak with her at the jail. How or why Miller selected Taylor is unknown, but the fact that she is a woman may be significant. According to Lieutenant Briggs and Detective Schmidt, Miller seems to be more comfortable when he talks to a woman; they speculate that he probably feels threatened by the presence of another man (D. Briggs & S. Schmidt, personal communication, February 9, 1996).

Deputy Marshal Taylor spoke with Miller on the afternoon of February 1, 1994, while the man was still in the Peoria County jail. Her field report documents certain narrative aspects of their conversation, but Miller's statements and responses to Taylor's questions reveal very little about his self-concept. Most of the information he provided was disjointed and somewhat cryptic or incomplete. At times, he seemed to indicate that he felt responsible for the acts of which he was accused; but one can surmise that Miller's true concern, and his probable reason for contacting a federal officer, was that he feared his own death.

"They are going to fry me at the state level," Miller told Taylor. He went on to ask the officer about differences between the state and federal systems, and he inquired whether or not an act that occurred outside of Illinois would be considered a federal crime. Taylor explained that federal jurisdiction would depend on the nature of the offense. Miller then began a confusing dialogue about a woman hitchhiker he allegedly picked up while traveling in Missouri during the summer of 1993. He claims to have accompanied the hitchhiker to Illinois, where, he says, the pair had a fight and a "bad thing" happened. Some elaboration indicated that he reportedly strangled the woman and dumped her body somewhere in the vicinity of Quincy, Illinois, near the Mississippi River (Taylor, Field Report, February 1, 1994). No evidence has been found to substantiate this recollection, and it is thought that Miller was likely hoping to enter the federal system in order to avoid a state-imposed death sentence. Detectives relate that he definitely feared his date with the executioner (D. Briggs & S. Schmidt, personal communication, February 23, 1996).

Joseph Miller may harbor ill feelings toward women whom he considers to be prostitutes. He labeled as "prostitutes" the two women whom he was convicted of killing in the Chicago area (Illinois Department of Corrections, September 27, 1978). With the exception of Bernice Fagotte, all of Miller's known victims have been engaged in sex-trade activities.

Recall of Events

Either Joseph Miller suffers from a mental condition that affects his memory, or he intentionally responds to questions about his past with false, incomplete, or misleading answers. Attempts by criminal suspects to mislead interviewers are certainly not unusual; in fact, these actions are generally expected. This is definitely not a behavior that is exclusive to serial killers. In many instances, a person being interviewed regarding his or her involvement in a crime will be less than truthful in recounting the situation. Researchers, like criminal investigators, also face the possibility of intentional subject falsification. Professor Egger, who extensively interviewed convicted serial murderer Henry Lee Lucas, writes, "[T]hose conducting case histories on single criminal subjects are constantly warned by prison officials and other criminal justice professionals to beware of the 'snow job' or 'con job'" (Egger, 1990a, p. 137). In attempts to substantiate Lucas's recollections, Egger utilized a methodology based on "triangulation" of information sources. By interviewing other relevant parties, reinterviewing Lucas about previously discussed information, and thoroughly analyzing documentary evidence, Egger strove to reduce his susceptibility to misleading information (1990a, p. 137). Because the author of this case study has not been able to interview Joseph Miller, the analysis contained here must be based on documents and information collected from secondary sources.

Questions abound concerning Miller's accuracy in recalling events. For instance, there are sequentially unusual elements in Miller's background as he related his past to Department of Corrections interviewers in 1978. His account of his military service and the related change of name is a prime example.

When the killer was interviewed by Deputy Marshal Taylor, his recollections were strange. Referring to the Peoria killings, he said, "From the strangulation I'm convinced I did these three" (Taylor, Field Report, February 1, 1994). This is in stark contrast to Miller's refusal to admit to the murders during the interrogation following his arrest, but it may have been a tactical admission by Miller in order to attract the attention of federal authorities. The man also told Taylor that he experiences memory losses. Taylor wrote, "He would say that physically he can remember things, then when he would let his emotions take over he would do something 'bad'" (Taylor, Field Report, February 1, 1994). On several occasions, Miller makes reference to the "bad things" that he associates with periods of self-reported memory loss.

The Possibilities for Closure

Law enforcement officials do not know with certainty how many people Joseph Miller has killed. Former Cook County assistant state's attorney Kenneth Gillis indicated that Miller might have been responsible for additional deaths in the Chicago area. Detectives in Peoria have similar suspicions.

While the task force was investigating the Peoria murders, a list was compiled of missing local women. For the most part, the women who had been reported as missing were ultimately found alive, but a small number are still missing.

Joseph Miller is the only person who knows how many victims he has claimed. Given his past demeanor, it is unlikely that he will ever reveal the true extent of his actions.

Acknowledgments

Without the assistance of the Peoria County Sheriff's Department, this work would not have been possible.

I am particularly grateful to Lieutenant David Briggs and Detective Steve Schmidt, who gave up several hours of their time to walk me through the case files and who provided their recollections of the investigation. Their receptiveness to my project and their willingness to help exemplify a professional attitude that no doubt contributed to the successful investigation of the murders and the apprehension of Joseph Miller.

Chief Deputy Mike McCoy telephoned me only hours after recieving my letter requesting his agency's assistance with this research. He cordially facilitated my eventual meetings with Lieutenant Briggs and Detective Schmidt.

The entire Joseph Miller case file was provided for review with the permission of Sheriff Charles Scholfield.

The periodicals staff of the Peoria Public Library offered much needed assistance with locating the numerous newspaper articles covering the case.

Finally, I would like to thank my mentor and friend, Steve Egger, for his encouragement and editorial review. Steve's desire to blend criminal justice practice with academic investigation can only serve to strengthen our shared social responsibility in the future.

Jeffrey Dahmer (1991 file photo).
© *Associated Press AP.*

CHAPTER 12

Jeffrey Dahmer

— A CASE STUDY

Social Environment

Jeffrey Dahmer's morbid curiosity about death, bodies, bones, and flesh began at an early age. He started with a collection of insects preserved in jars full of chemicals. Then he began to collect dead animals that had been run over on the roads near his home. Once, while fishing with some other boys, he chopped up the fish he had caught into little pieces so he could see their insides. Another time, a group of boys walking in the woods behind the Dahmer home found the head of a dog impaled on a stick. They were so shocked at the sight that they took photographs, but they didn't tell the police until years later, after Dahmer had been arrested in his apartment in Milwaukee. Neighbors of the Dahmers also found frogs and cats impaled or staked to trees. A boy who grew up across the street from the Dahmer home said that young Jeffrey kept chipmunk and squirrel skeletons in a backyard shed and maintained a pet cemetery nearby, with small crosses to mark each grave.

When, on occasion, a neighborhood dog would disappear, no one suspected that Jeffrey was killing dogs for his autopsies. In 1975, when Jeffrey was fifteen years old, a neighbor boy walking in the woods behind the Dahmer home discovered a mutilated dog carcass. The head was mounted on a stick next to a wooden cross. The body, skinned and gutted, was nailed to a nearby tree. Apparently Dahmer's father had given him a chemistry set. According to Jeffrey's stepmother, "He liked to used acid to scrape the meat off dead animals." No one, including his parents, seemed to think this behavior warranted much attention or concern.

217

Most psychiatrists agree that cruelty to animals is one common childhood characteristic of the sadistic criminal. Many experts on serial killers agree that these killers often start out by torturing and killing animals as youngsters. Jeffrey Dahmer's behavior should have been a warning. Had this warning been heeded, a number of lives might have been saved. In 1978, he began experimenting with human beings.

Family Background

Jeffrey's parents were headed for divorce when he killed his first human victim. It became a bitter battle as Lionel and Joyce Dahmer fought over custody of Jeffrey's younger brother, David, who was then twelve years old. Because Jeffrey was already eighteen, he was not an issue in the custody battle. His father was the first to sue for divorce, charging his mother with "gross neglect of duty and extreme cruelty." Dahmer's mother countersued, filing the same charges against his father. In the court documents of the divorce, Jeffrey's father accused his mother of having an "extreme mental illness."

During the time Jeffrey's parents were arguing over custody of his brother, they divided the house, each living on one side. His father set up a warning system with a string of keys to alert him if his wife was trying to enter his half. Both parents pressured Jeffrey to side with them in the divorce. He later told Milwaukee police that his parents were "constantly at each other's throats" before they divorced.

Joyce Dahmer ultimately won custody of David. In August 1978, Lionel stopped by the house for a court-ordered visitation with David and found Jeffrey home alone. The house was a shambles and there was no food in the refrigerator. Joyce Dahmer had taken David and moved to Wisconsin, leaving Jeffrey with no money and instructing him not to tell his father where they had gone.

After his father had moved out of the house to a motel and his mother had left for Wisconsin with his brother, Jeffrey lured his first victim to his abandoned home and killed him. Dahmer may have been abandoned by his parents, but now he was someone very different. He now had a self-image: He was a killer.

Peer Group Associations and Personal Relationships

Apparently, Jeffrey Dahmer remained unattached during his childhood and never bonded with anyone. Further, there is no evidence that he ever developed an intimate, deep relationship. He seemed to trust no one.

In grade school, the other youngsters noticed that Dahmer never had any sympathy for others. When other students got hurt on the school playground, he would laugh or watch the scene without compassion.

By high school Dahmer was considered so weird that no one wanted to associate with him. He played on the tennis team but was not a popular student. He was very shy toward girls but was aggressive toward authority figures.

A neighbor remembers Dahmer's ritual as he walked to the school bus stop: four steps forward, two steps back, four steps forward, one step back—day after day, week after week. Little kids thought it was funny and stared at him. He seemed to be seeking attention everywhere he went. He reportedly faked epileptic fits in the classroom and at the nearby mall. He frequently drew outlines of nonexistent bodies on the floors at school.

One of Dahmer's former classmates, now a sociology professor, considered him a friend for a short time. However, "at sixteen years of age, he was lost," she said. "He seemed to cry out for help, but nobody paid attention to him at all. . . . He would come in with a cup of Scotch—not coffee, with something in it, Scotch whiskey: If a sixteen-year-old drinking in an 8:00 A.M. class isn't calling out for help, I don't know what is."

He spent most of his first semester drinking at Ohio State University in Columbus. He never made it through the second semester. A classmate remembers the last time she saw him. "He was passed out on a street in Columbus," she said.

After his failure with college, Dahmer joined the army and served in a medical unit in Germany. According to his roommate, "Jeff would drink his gin. He had an eight-track stereo with headphones, and he'd sit there and get plastered. He'd be on a two- or three-day drink. He wouldn't even leave his room to go eat." Dahmer was discharged from the army in 1981 because of his drinking.

Returning home from the army, Dahmer was arrested in a hotel lobby where he was drinking vodka and threatening people. On his way to jail, he kept insisting that the police stop the car and beat him up. In 1982, he moved in with his grandmother in West Allis, a suburb of Milwaukee. He began hanging out in gay bars and sometimes brought men home through a private entrance to his grandmother's basement.

Contact with Defining Agencies

For months after the grisly discovery in Apartment 213 in 1991, many people in Milwaukee would double-check the locks on their doors and windows before going to bed. Some would keep a log of phone numbers and addresses of where their children were supposed to be. Many would pay more attention to "things that go bump in the night." And, if they had them, many would load their guns and put them within easy reach.

Milwaukee police received numerous calls to check out suspicious strangers, day and night. A mind-numbing fear and paranoia seemed to envelop the city. Milwaukee had become a city of victims—victims of fear, horror, and disbelief over what had gone on behind the door of Apartment 213.

The breweries, beer halls, German restaurants, and various ethnic neighborhoods that had long been linked to this midwestern city in eastern Wisconsin on the shores of Lake Michigan were forgotten. When people heard "Milwaukee," they immediately thought of Jeffrey Dahmer. Of course, for some, who had been mesmerized by Anthony Hopkins's portrayal of Dr. Hannibal Lecter in the movie *Silence of the Lambs*, Milwaukee would become the "City of the Lambs," whose silence had been shattered by the screaming of innocent, slaughtered lambs in July 1991.

Since June 1978, Jeffrey Dahmer had beaten the system. When police in Bath, Ohio, stopped him, there was a dismembered body in garbage bags on the backseat of his car, but Dahmer merely told police he was taking the bags to the dump, and they let him drive on. In April 1988, a man reported that he had been drugged and robbed by Dahmer. Milwaukee police spoke to Dahmer but lacked evidence to pursue the charges. In March 1989, a friend of Anthony Sears reported him missing. The friend took police to the street corner where he had left Sears with another man. The other man was Jeffrey Dahmer, whose grandmother's house was nearby. But the police turned up nothing.

In February 1989, when Dahmer was released from the Milwaukee County jail, where he had been sentenced under work release for second-degree sexual assault and enticing a child for immoral purposes, he was on probation. Procedures required that his probation officer meet with him twice a month and make regular home visits. However, Dahmer's probation officer, who was supervising 121 clients at the time, requested that she be excused from making home visits with Dahmer. She argued that she had a heavy caseload and that Dahmer lived in a bad neighborhood. Her supervisors agreed to waive the home visit requirement with Dahmer. Jeffrey Dahmer was then free to pursue the creation of his "inferno" in Apartment 213. And when one of his victims escaped, the police unwittingly helped the murderer return the victim to the apartment and his death.

MILWAUKEE POLICE THOUGHT IT WAS JUST A LOVER'S QUARREL

Police Officer: Intoxicated Asian naked male. (Laughter) Was returned to his sober boyfriend. (More laughter)

Dispatcher: 10-4 64 and 65.

Police Officer: 10-4. It will be a minute. My partner is going to get deloused at the station. (Laughter)

  —Milwaukee Police Communications transcript, 2:00 A.M., May 27, 1991

The "intoxicated Asian naked male" became Jeffrey's Dahmer's twelfth victim, and his youngest. Dahmer later told the police that he had drugged the fourteen-year-old boy, who then fell asleep. Dahmer left the boy in his apartment and went out to buy some beer. When Dahmer returned, he saw the naked boy in the street talking to police officers. Neighbors described the young Laotian boy as naked and bleeding from his buttocks, staggering in the street. But Dahmer told the officers he would take care of his friend and that the boy was drunk. The officers then escorted Dahmer and the naked boy back to his apartment. The officers considered it a routine domestic dispute between homosexuals. But it became routine only for Dahmer, who, after the police left, strangled the young boy as he had his other victims.

On July 26, four days after Dahmer's arrest, Milwaukee police chief Philip Arreola suspended with pay the officers involved in the previous incident, pending an investigation. On September 6, Chief Arreola announced that he had fired two of the officers involved in the incident; they had been members of the department for six and seven years, respectively. Chief Arreola noted that the officers had failed to protect a child, failed to interview witnesses at the scene, and failed to consider impassioned pleas of a witness who later called the police. The Milwaukee County district attorney's office had already advised the Milwaukee Police Department that no criminal charges would be filed against the police officers involved. The two officers were reinstated to their jobs in 1995.

Escape from Apartment 213 — The Arrest

It was the night of the arrest. . . . I heard a knock on the door and the police were there with the last victim. They asked me where the key was to the handcuffs. My mind was in a haze. I sort of pointed to the bedroom and that's where they found the pictures and they yelled, "Cuff him" and I was handcuffed. And it was the realization that there was no point in trying to hide my actions anymore, the best route was to help the police identify all the victims and just make a complete confession.

    —Television program, *Inside Edition*, excerpts from Jeffrey Dahmer interview, February 8, 1993

Just before midnight on Monday evening, July 22, 1991, two Milwaukee police officers sitting in their squad car were approached by a short African American man with handcuffs dangling from his left wrist. The man, thirty-one-year-old Tracy Edwards, told the officers about a "weird dude" who had handcuffed him in a nearby apartment. The officers were reluctant to respond but eventually agreed to go with Edwards to the apartment to investigate.

Once inside the Oxford Apartment Complex, the officers noticed a heavy rancid odor. Jeffrey Dahmer opened the door for the three men. Dahmer was asked for the key to the handcuffs, and he told the officers the key was in the bedroom. One of the officers walked into the bedroom and looked into an open dresser drawer. He was horrified: There were Polaroid pictures of dismembered bodies, skulls, and a skeleton hanging from a showerhead.

Dahmer was immediately arrested. As the officers began to search the apartment, one of them opened the refrigerator door. He found a severed human head staring out at him. And the search of Apartment 213 had only just begun.

For the remainder of his life, Jeffrey Dahmer's home was to be a prison cell at the Columbia Correctional Facility in Portage, Wisconsin. Columbia, with its five guard towers rising as tall as the silos of nearby dairy farms, is the newest and most secure of the state's maximum-security prisons. "He's very glad that he's in there," his mother, Joyce Flint, age fifty-seven, told reporters in 1994. "He still has those thoughts," she said.

When Dahmer chose to plead guilty but insane, the nature of his criminal trial was changed. The question was no longer one of guilt but, rather, of responsibility. It was not for the court to determine the strange or perverted behavior of Dahmer or, for that matter, his bizarre motivations. The question was whether he had understood what he was doing and whether he knew the difference between right and wrong. Further, Wisconsin criminal statutes required that the court determine whether Dahmer could have stopped himself. The burden was no longer on the state to prove him guilty. It was now the burden of the defense to demonstrate his insanity.

Trial Judge Gram had warned the jurors that they were going to hear testimony unlike anything they had heard before. That was exactly what happened. During the first two days of testimony, the jury heard the reading of Dahmer's confession, in which he related how he skinned the victims, boiled and cleaned their skulls, and even ate the biceps of one man after seasoning it with salt, pepper, and A-1 sauce.

Dahmer's defense attorneys would have to prove that he was suffering from some form of mental illness at the time of his crimes and that he lacked the capacity to understand the wrongfulness of his actions or to conform his conduct to the law. The trial became a battle of psychiatrists. Those hired for the defense testified about Dahmer's mental illness, and those hired by the prosecution testified about his sanity.

Dahmer's intense sexual craving was described as a "cancer of the mind" by Dr. Fred Berlin of Johns Hopkins University, testifying for the defense. Berlin viewed Dahmer as "out of control. . . . The power of what was driving him basically took over." Berlin further stated, "I don't think the normal man could even force himself to walk around thinking about having sexual contact with dead bodies."

Dr. Park Dietz, testifying for the prosecution, stated that Dahmer suffered from a variety of sexual disorders, but that none would have made him unable to know right from wrong or unable to stop himself from killing. Dietz described Dahmer's sexual urges as "less than many teenagers experience in back seats with their girlfriends." (Dahmer wore condoms when having sex with his dead victims.)

Dr. George Palermo, a court-appointed psychiatrist, said Dahmer was "sick" but "not psychotic" and was "legally sane at the time of the offenses."

Dr. Frederick Fosdal, testifying for the prosecution, said Dahmer suffered from necrophilia "before, during and after" killing seventeen young males, but that the disorder did not prevent him from stopping. Fosdal stated, "He was able to refrain and had some control as to when he followed through on his sexual desires." Fosdal also noted that Dahmer appreciated the wrongfulness of his acts, was prepared to and did have the capacity to conform to the law, and could have controlled his behavior at the time of the acts.

Four of the testifying psychiatrists referred to Dahmer as a necrophiliac. Two of them classified him as having an antisocial personality disorder. One described Dahmer's behavior as clinically rare, unusual, and bizarre—behavior for which there was no current diagnostic category.

The jury heard from a total of twenty-eight witnesses before the attorneys provided their summation of the case. "He couldn't stop killing because of a sickness he discovered, not chose," Dahmer's defense attorney, Gerald Boyle, told the jurors. "He had to do what he did because he couldn't stop. This isn't a matter of choice," Boyle said.

Prosecutor E. Michael McCann described Dahmer as a sane, cowardly killer who sacrificed others for his own sexual pleasure and who was now "seeking to escape responsibility. Please, please, don't let this murderous killer fool you with this special defense," McCann told the jurors.

After twelve days of testimony, the jurors deliberated for a little more than five hours to find Jeffrey Dahmer sane on all sixteen counts of murder.

Jeffrey Dahmer's "thoughts" or fantasies drove him to a decade-long orgy of murder, necrophilia, and cannibalism. His orgy of death left at least seventeen people dead and scores of surviving relatives and loved ones crying for the execution of this serial killer. Fortunately for Dahmer, the State of Wisconsin does not allow the death penalty. However, he would not live long. On November 28, 1994, he was killed by another inmate.

Offense Behavior

On June 18, 1978, Stephen Mark Hicks, an eighteen-year-old white male from Coventry, Ohio, was last seen hitchhiking to a rock concert. Jeffrey Dahmer met him and brought him back to his home, where they had sex. When Hicks tried to leave, Dahmer struck him in the head with a barbell, killing him. Dahmer then smashed Hicks's body to bits with a sledgehammer, put the remains in plastic bags, and buried them in the woods behind his house.

Nine years passed before Dahmer killed again. However, this time he did not stop with only one victim. He killed and killed again.

In Milwaukee, Wisconsin, in November 1987, Steven W. Toumi, a twenty-five-year-old white male, was reported missing by his parents. He was already a victim of Jeffrey Dahmer, who had picked him up at Club 219 in Milwaukee and taken him to a room at the Ambassador Hotel, where the two got drunk and passed out. Dahmer subsequently claimed that when he awoke, Toumi was dead, with blood dripping from his mouth. So Dahmer bought a large suitcase at a nearby mall and put the corpse inside. Then he took the suitcase by taxi to his grandmother's, where he had sex with the corpse in the basement. Dahmer then dismembered the corpse, placed the body parts in plastic bags, and threw them in the trash. Toumi's remains were never found.

People who knew Jeffrey Dahmer in Milwaukee described him as a quiet, rather shy young man who didn't have much to say. Little did they know that he methodically assaulted and dismembered the corpses of his victims, placing their skulls on his death shrine in his apartment and their entrails and body parts in his refrigerator and freezer.

Like other psychopaths who became infamous serial killers in America, Dahmer appeared to be a very quiet person. But he was filled with a rage or force that controlled him. This rage was driven by a particularly dangerous chemistry: an antisocial trait, so that he flouted the law with impunity; a "borderline" personality that made him vulnerable to explosive rage when he felt he was being abandoned; and a bizarre sexual deviation that culminated in necrophilia.

Dahmer appears to have been both a sadist and a necrophiliac. Sadists find sexual pleasure in the suffering of their victims; the sexual thrill stops when the victims die. But for necrophiliacs, the thrill starts with the death. For Dahmer, the pleasure was in both the suffering of his victims and what he could do with them after their death.

After the New Yorker Joel Rifkin recently confessed to murdering seventeen prostitutes, a high school classmate said he was "quiet, shy, not the kind of guy who would do something like this." A friend of Juan Corona, who was convicted of killing twenty-five migrant farm workers in California in 1971, stated, "Juan kept to himself and never said much, for the most part." An army buddy of David Berkowitz, who was convicted of six "Son of Sam" murders in New York City in 1976 and 1977, described him as a man who "was quiet and reserved and kept pretty much to himself." "That's the way he was here, nice—a quiet, shy fellow," said Berkowitz's former boss. Westley Allan Dodd, who was executed in 1993 for the kidnapping, rape, and murder of three small boys in Oregon, was described by a neighbor as "a quiet young man who seemed so harmless."

Quiet and deadly—like a viper, waiting and ready to strike. When Jeffrey Dahmer picked up a young man in one of the gay bars he frequented in Milwaukee, the result was almost always death. Few young men escaped after entering number 213 of the Oxford Apartment Complex.

Neighbors said Dahmer always brought his guests in through the back door of the complex. Unbeknownst to the neighbors, all his guests would eventually leave through this door as well: their torsos floating in a chemical bath in a large blue barrel; their arms and legs in plastic bags; some of their skulls in cardboard boxes labeled "Skull Parts"; and some of their frozen heads in Dahmer's refrigerator. They would be carried out by police officers, hazardous waste removal specialists, and staff from the County Medical Examiner's Office. As Dahmer's guests left Apartment 213, their remains passed by a bright yellow tape that read, "POLICE LINE. DO NOT CROSS." For these victims, the warning came much too late.

As Dahmer's refrigerator was removed on a dolly, down the back steps of the Oxford Apartment Complex, Doug Jackson, a short black man, stood by watching from the neatly kept lawn of the complex. "My head could've been in that refrigerator," he said in a low, cracking voice. A few days earlier, Dahmer had invited Jackson to his apartment for a beer. His girlfriend had talked him out of going. He was very thankful.

Jeffrey Dahmer is what experts call a "megastat," "local," or "place-specific" serial killer. This type of serial killer finds his victims within the general area of a single city or county. Most of Dahmer's victims were lured from the immediate area of his home, where he killed them. However, Dahmer does not entirely fit into this category because he lured two of his victims from Chicago, fifty miles south of Milwaukee.

Dahmer's victims were lured into his lair, where he could control the situation and the assault of his prey. He didn't stalk them on the streets and then quickly slay them for the police to find. He needed time with his dead victims. Indeed, time was important to Dahmer—time to have sex with the corpses, time to dismember and fillet the bodies at his leisure, and time to select a trophy before disposing of the victim's remains.

As in the case of Dennis Nilsen, Britain's notorious and gruesome serial killer, Dahmer wanted company. Whether his urge to kill was driven by a longing for simple companionship or for sex, Dahmer killed for it. He wanted to be with the victims. He wanted to keep them with him. As his obsession grew, he began saving body parts. Wanting to remember their appearance, he took pictures of the corpses. They belonged to him.

Soon the offer of money for posing in the nude or for sex, the killing, having sex with the corpse, the dismemberment and examination of the body, the trophy selection, and the disposal became habit-forming for Dahmer. He was performing a ritual each time he convinced his prey to come with him to the slaughter. His reverse sculpturing of their bodies became the driving force of his existence: the search for his next work of art.

Most serial killers select easy prey, victims with little prestige or power in society. If they are reported as missing, the authorities spend little time looking for them. Often, victims are not missed for weeks or months. Some are never missed, because no one cares enough to note their absence. They are almost always strangers to their killer and are generally easy to dominate, lure, or manipulate.

The victims of serial killers are selected because of their vulnerability, but this does not mean the serial killer is a coward. In fact, it means he is smart! Choosing vulnerable victims reduces the time and effort of the selection, the lure, or the "con." For Dahmer, it provided more time for the control and the kill.

Dahmer was a gay man, and he selected his own kind. He understood their sexual frustration and their problems in meeting sexual partners. He knew how the rest of society felt about them. He knew that their parents had not sat down with them when they started dating men and warned them about certain kinds of men to avoid. Persuading his victims to go with him was seldom a problem, because he knew what they wanted. Only he wanted something more. Unfortunately for his victims, their death was required to fulfill his wants.

A victim's lifestyle is frequently the critical factor in falling prey to a serial killer. Prostitutes and gay men very often become the victims of serial killers. Dahmer chose gay boys and men from age fourteen to thirty-one. Most of them were African American.

Jeffrey Dahmer's mother, Joyce Flint (now deceased), who resumed using her maiden name after divorcing Lionel Dahmer, recently told reporters that she was worried that her former husband's book, *A Father's Tale*, published in 1994, would blame her for the gruesome deeds of her son. Dahmer's mother made her first public statement since her son's arrest: "We're still blaming mothers."

Advance publicity for Lionel Dahmer's book stated that it would examine "the origins of madness and role of kinship in the legacy of evil." In a television interview Dahmer's father suggested it was possible that drugs his wife took while pregnant could have helped shape the individual that Jeffrey became. His mother admitted she was treated for depression in 1978 and was taking prescribed drugs for the problem during the year Jeffrey graduated from high school. It was also the year he first killed.

The Victims: The Forgotten Ones

- **June 18, 1978** Dahmer picked up a hitchhiker, Stephen Mark Hicks, and brought him back to his home, where they had sex. When Hicks tried to leave, Dahmer struck him in the head, killing him. Dahmer then dismembered Hicks's body and buried him in the woods behind his house.

- **January 16, 1988** Dahmer met James Doxtator, a fourteen-year-old Native American boy, outside Club 219 and offered him some money to pose nude. Dahmer took the boy to his grandmother's, where they had sex. Dahmer then gave him a drink with sleeping pills in it, and, when the boy fell asleep, Dahmer strangled him. Dahmer dismembered the body with a knife and a sledgehammer, placed the remains in plastic bags, and put them in the trash.

- **March 24, 1988** Richard Guerrero, a twenty-five-year old Mexican American, met Dahmer near Club 219 and agreed to go home with him. After they had sex in his grandmother's basement, Dahmer drugged his victim with sleeping pills and strangled him. Dahmer had sex with the corpse, dismembered it, and threw the remains away.

- **September 26, 1988** The day after Dahmer moved from his grandmother's to an apartment at 808 North 24th Street in Milwaukee, he offered a thirteen-year-old Laotian boy money to come to his apartment, where he attempted to seduce the boy and laced his drink with sleeping pills. Somehow the boy managed to leave. When he passed out at home, his parents took him to the hospital, where the police were notified. Dahmer was arrested the next day for sexual assault. He pled guilty to the charge and was sentenced to five years' probation and one year at a correctional center in a work-release program.

- **March 25, 1989** Dahmer met Anthony Sears, a twenty-four-year-old African American, at the La Cage Aux Folles bar and offered him money to be photographed. The two drove to Dahmer's grandmother's, where they had sex, after which Dahmer drugged Sears and strangled him. Dahmer disposed of his victim as before; however, he kept the head, which he boiled so that only the skull remained. Dahmer painted his trophy with gray paint.

- **June 1990** Raymond L. Smith, a twenty-eight-year-old African American, met Dahmer at Club 219 and agreed to go to his apartment to be photographed. Dahmer drugged him, strangled him to death, and had sex with his corpse. Dahmer dismembered and disposed of the remains as he had before. He kept Smith's skull as another trophy.

- **Late June 1990** Dahmer offered money for sex and the chance to pose for pictures to Edward W. Smith, a twenty-eight-year-old African American whom he met in the Phoenix Bar. They returned to Apartment 213, where they had sex. Afterward, Dahmer drugged and strangled Smith. Dahmer disposed of Smith's dismembered body in trash bags. His only trophy was pictures of the dead man.

- **September 24, 1990** Ernest Miller, a twenty-four-year-old African American, was lured by Dahmer from in front of an adult bookstore. After taking a number of pictures of Miller, Dahmer drugged him and, when he passed out, cut his throat with a hunting knife. Dahmer placed the corpse in his bathtub, removed the flesh from the body, and photographed the skeleton. This time, his trophy was the entire skeleton. Dahmer put some of the flesh from the corpse in his freezer and later claimed he had eaten the flesh.

- **Late September 1990** The girlfriend of David Thomas reported him missing on September 24, 1990. This twenty-two-year-old African American died at the hands of Jeffrey Dahmer. His trophy this time was photographs, taken by Dahmer as he dismembered Thomas's corpse.

- **February 1991** Curtis Straughter, an eighteen-year-old African American, met his death after Dahmer lured him from a bus stop to his nearby apartment. Sex, followed by strangulation, more sex, and then dismemberment—it was becoming a ritual for Dahmer. He photographed the corpse and kept the skull.

- **April 7, 1991** Errol Lindsey's mother last saw her son when he left home to have a key made. This nineteen-year-old African American made a fatal mistake. He accepted Jeffrey Dahmer's offer of money to go to Apartment 213. All that remains of Lindsey is his skull and some horrific photos of his corpse.

- **May 24, 1991** The next victim Dahmer lured to his death was a deaf-mute, Tony A. Hughes. They met in front of the 219 Bar. Dahmer communicated with this thirty-one-year-old African American in writing, convincing him to go to Apartment 213. Another skull trophy was added to Dahmer's collection.

- **May 27, 1991** Like Dahmer's other victims, fourteen-year-old Konerak Sinthasomphone was lured with money; once in Dahmer's apartment, he was drugged with sleeping pills. However, in this case Dahmer left to get some beer before killing the young Laotian boy. Sinthasomphone awoke, and Milwaukee police officers found him staggering in the street near Dahmer's apartment. Dahmer told police that the boy was drunk and had done this before. He stated that he would "take care of his friend." The police escorted Dahmer and the boy back into Apartment 213, where the remains of Tony Hughes lay decomposing in the back bedroom. After the police left, Dahmer strangled the boy, photographed the corpse, and, after having sex with it, dismembered the remains and kept the skull.

- **June 30, 1991** Dahmer traveled to Chicago for his next victim. There he met Matt Turner, a twenty-year-old African American, at a bus station, after they had both attended the Gay Pride Parade in Chicago. Turner agreed to pose nude for money, and they returned together to Dahmer's apartment in Milwaukee. When Turner passed out from a drink laced with sleeping pills, his horrific fate was sealed. After dismembering the corpse, Dahmer placed Turner's head in the freezer and his torso in a fifty-seven-gallon barrel.

- **July 5, 1991** Returning to Chicago, Dahmer lured his next victim from Carol's Speakeasy by promising money in return for posing in the nude. Jeremiah Weinberger, a twenty-three-year-old Puerto Rican man, stayed in Apartment 213 with Dahmer for two days before deciding to leave. This triggered the deadly ritual again. Another head was added to Dahmer's freezer and a second torso to the fifty-seven-gallon barrel.

- **July 15, 1991** Jeffrey Dahmer found his sixteenth victim just around the corner from his Milwaukee apartment building. Oliver Lacy's remains would be found in Dahmer's apartment. Seven days later, police found this twenty-three-year-old African American's head in the refrigerator and his disemboweled body in the freezer. His heart was also in the freezer.

- **July 19, 1991** Joseph Bradehoft, a twenty-five-year-old white man, fell prey to Dahmer's lure of money for posing in the nude while they were riding a bus in Milwaukee. In Apartment 213, Bradehoft's head was added to Dahmer's gruesome refrigerator collection and his torso was stuffed into the fifty-seven-gallon barrel, which was getting full. Bradehoft was Jeffrey Dahmer's seventeenth and last homicide victim.

Self-Concept

It is difficult to understand what made Jeffrey Dahmer commit such horrendous acts against his fellow human beings. The crimes he committed were just not normal. After all, what normal person would systematically murder and mutilate seventeen victims? Our morbid fascination with him and his terrible acts may be a way of attempting to define him as separate and different from the rest of society. We seem to need the comfort of knowing that this serial killer is an aberration, that he is not one of us. To consider him normal would mean that anyone could be capable of these savage acts of terror and death.

Jeffrey Dahmer was sentenced to fifteen consecutive life sentences, plus an additional ten years for habitual criminality on each of the fifteen counts. The judge structured Dahmer's sentences in such a way that he would never again see freedom. He would have the rest of his life to contemplate his murders, away from society, behind bars.

Few disagree with the judge's wisdom in sentencing Dahmer—certainly not Jeffrey's mother, who, as noted, told reporters in 1994, "He still has those thoughts."

Attitudes: From Jeffrey Dahmer's 179-Page Confession

My consuming lust was to experience their bodies. I viewed them as objects, as strangers. If I knew them, I could not have done it. It's hard for me to believe that a human being could have done what I've done, but I know I did it. It would be me who has to stand before God and admit my wrongdoing.

I realize what I have done is my fault, but I have to question if there is an evil force in the world and if I am influenced by it. If I am to be honest with myself, I would have to admit that if I was set up in another apartment and had the opportunity, I probably would not be able to stop.

A power higher than myself had been fed up with my deeds and decided it was time for me to be stopped.

Recall of Events

Jeffrey Dahmer's recall of all his murders was very detailed and accurate. He wrote a 179-page confession that listed all his murders with descriptions of the victims and how he killed them. He also cooperated with the Milwaukee police and answered all their questions.

Dahmer's Demise

Jeffrey Dahmer was killed in prison by another inmate on November 28, 1994.

CHAPTER 13

Cross-Case Analysis

SIMILARITIES OF SEVEN SERIAL KILLERS

There are a number of similarities as well as differences between the seven murderers—Gacy, Lucas, Bianchi, Bundy, Marcus, Miller, and Dahmer—discussed in the previous seven chapters. The similarities among these serial murderers may give us a better understanding of these violent criminals who kill a number of victims in different locations over a period of time. However, in analyzing these serial murderers and identifying their similarities, readers are cautioned not to consider the results of this analysis as a definitive profile of the serial killer. This analysis is based on only seven serial murderers, who may not be representative of the entire population of serial murderers. As indicated in Chapter 1, there is currently no reliable empirical database on serial murderers from which to determine with any degree of accuracy the extent or prevalence of serial murder in the United States or in any other country. Therefore, the results of this analysis should be viewed only as a starting point from which to begin to describe empirically the similarities among serial murderers. Future efforts will require that a number of other case studies be conducted, focusing on selected geographical areas of the United States and on a variety of serial murderers who differ on such variables as gender, age, victim selection, methods of killing, length of time between killings, geographical locations of the killings, and type of "hunting grounds" where victims are selected. Even such an extensive research effort, of course, would be based on only those serial murderers who have been identified and apprehended. Missing from the database would be those killers who have not been identified or even suspected of committing a series of murders.

Given the limitations of an analysis based on only seven case studies, the information gained from this analysis still can be compared and contrasted with other research that has some empirical foundation, and can serve as a guide for future research efforts to determine the most commonly shared characteristics of serial murderers. This analysis, then, is only the beginning.

Social Environment

All the murderers were born into a working-class family or a family of lower socioeconomic status. Two killers, Bundy and Gacy, moved into a middle-class stratum; the others remained within their original social class. In educational achievement the subjects ranged from Bundy, who made an attempt at law school, to Lucas, who barely finished the fourth grade.

Bundy, Lucas, Marcus, and Dahmer all abused alcohol, and Lucas may very well have been an alcoholic. Lucas's parents were reportedly alcoholics, but there was no history of alcoholism in Bundy's family. Both Gacy and Marcus had fathers who abused alcohol. There is evidence that all seven of these killers had used marijuana, but none were habituated to the substance.

Bundy, Gacy, Dahmer, and Buono all maintained a neat, orderly lifestyle. Bundy's apartment was always spotless, and Gacy and Buono kept their houses very clean. Buono also was known as a meticulous worker. Gacy ordered his life to the extent that he kept a log of his activities during the day. Dahmer's apartment, though horrific, was kept orderly and neat.

All of the murderers first experienced sexual intercourse sometime in their teens. The sexual relationships of Bundy, Gacy, and Buono all involved some form of violence. They used bondage on their sexual partners, and Buono and Gacy were both sadistic and dominant in their sexual relations with others. Gacy, Bianchi, and Buono all read and showed a strong interest in pornography. Bundy claims to have been exposed to pornography.

All of the killers had experienced some form of childhood health trauma. Gacy was frequently beaten by his father and also experienced blackouts, which were never accurately diagnosed. Bianchi experienced urination problems and reportedly had severe respiratory infections. Lucas suffered the loss of his eye in an accident. Marcus was severely beaten by his father. Miller reportedly was subjected to severe discipline by two of his stepfathers, and Dahmer had to deal with his parents' acrimony during their divorce.

Bundy, Gacy, and Bianchi all had a strong interest in law enforcement going back to early childhood. Lucas claims to have "studied" law enforcement.

Bundy was considered a "loner" in high school, but Bianchi and Gacy reportedly had relatively normal social relationships in high school. Neither Buono nor Lucas ever attended high school. Marcus was seen as a loner during his high school years even though he participated in athletic activities.

Family Background

Bundy, Bianchi, and Lucas were all born to unwed mothers. Bundy was adopted when he was five years old, after his mother's marriage. Bianchi's mother relinquished him to a foster home, and he was adopted before his first birthday. Miller knew very little about his natural father. Lucas's real father is unknown. Bundy was apparently the only one of these four who was troubled by the circumstances of his birth.

Bundy, Bianchi, and Lucas all had dominant mothers. Bundy's mother paid the bills and spoke for the family. Bianchi's mother smothered him with her protectiveness and also administered his punishment, sometimes harsh. Lucas was beaten and neglected by his mother, who gave the orders in his family. Gacy was heavily influenced by his mother, whom he tried to protect when she was beaten by Gacy's father.

Gacy, Bianchi, Lucas, Miller, and Marcus all had parents with emotional problems. Gacy's father never showed his emotions except when he was intoxicated, as he was almost every night. When his father came home from work, he would start drinking until his anger surfaced and then would physically abuse Gacy's mother. Bianchi's mother was described as a disturbed woman who apparently experienced a great deal of guilt over her failure to bear children. She was extremely overprotective of Bianchi and became paranoid over his illnesses. Lucas's mother reportedly forced him to watch her engaging in sexual intercourse with a number of men. Until he was six or seven years old, she dressed him as a girl. Miller's early childhood showed evidence of child neglect, as he frequently ran away from home. Marcus had to deal with an abusive father who beat him and his mother.

All of the killers had been married and then divorced. Both Gacy and Miller were married twice, and Buono was married three times. Marcus fathered three children out of wedlock.

Gacy, Lucas, and Dahmer appear to have experienced some confusion regarding their sexual identity. Also, these murderers came from families with a history of alcoholism. Gacy, Marcus, and Bundy all experienced problems with their fathers.

Peer Group Associations and Personal Relationships

All except Lucas were apparently very manipulative of situations and people. Lucas could also be considered manipulative, but in a much less sophisticated manner as a result of his limited education and the severe economic deprivation of his childhood. On the surface, all of these men appeared harmless to most people. In five of these men, however—Gacy, Bianchi's "Stevie Walker," Marcus, Miller, and Lucas—it is apparent that a strong emotion of hatred lay just beneath the surface. All of these seven murderers had been unable or unwilling to establish lasting relationships with others.

Contact with Defining Agencies

Three of the men—Bundy, Marcus, and Lucas—had juvenile delinquency records; Lucas's early criminal activities were the most serious and consistent. Gacy, Dahmer, Miller, and Bianchi had no known juvenile records. All of these murderers appeared to be well informed about police procedures and practices. Bundy, Marcus, and Lucas appear to have understood problems of interjurisdictional communication among police and to have killed in more than one jurisdiction as a way of eluding detection. Bianchi and Buono were very conscious of the danger of leaving any physical evidence of their killings. When Bianchi killed on his own, however, it was a different story. Gacy seemed to understand that missing teenagers, especially young homosexuals, might not be actively sought and were apt to be investigated only in a routine fashion.

All of the men except Bianchi had known criminal records prior to their final arrests. Some had more extensive records than others. Gacy was on parole from Iowa, for sodomy, during his killing spree. Miller was on parole for two killings in Chicago, for which he served fifteen years. Marcus committed a number of criminal acts before and during his murder spree, including kidnapping and attempted rape (reduced to an assault and battery charge). Bundy had been convicted of attempted kidnapping and committed his three murders in Florida after his second escape from authorities in Colorado. Lucas committed his first killing at age fourteen and also committed a range of other felony crimes. Dahmer killed while on probation for sexual assault and enticing a child for immoral purposes.

All of the men except Buono, for whom psychiatric reports may never have been written, were referred to by psychiatrists or psychologists as having antisocial personalities. All have been labeled as sociopaths or psychopaths. Mental health professionals did not always offer consistent diagnoses of these men but in some cases disagreed strongly about an individual murderer. A common theme in the psychological and psychiatric evaluations of these seven men was that they were strongly resistant toward authority, were obsessed with controlling and manipulating others to their own advantage, and almost never shared their true feelings with others.

When arrested for the last time, only Bundy physically resisted the police. All the other men offered no resistance and submitted to authorities calmly.

Offense Behavior

Bundy, Gacy, and Dahmer used lures to attract their victims. Bundy used a faked injury, and Gacy used offers of homosexual relations for money. Dahmer offered his victims money to pose in the nude. Bundy, Gacy, Buono, and Bianchi all posed as police officers, using the force of official authority to persuade their victims to accompany them. All of the murderers carried some sort of deadly weapon most of the time. In all cases, automobiles were used to abduct victims and to transport their corpses.

Gacy's victims were all young Caucasian males. Bundy, Miller, and Bianchi and Buono killed only females, in most cases under twenty-five years of age and Caucasian. Lucas and his accomplices killed a number of males, but 75 percent of Lucas's victims were females, and over 90 percent were Caucasian, with a mean age of almost thirty-one but with an age range of eighty years. Marcus, the only African American serial killer under discussion, killed only black women, most of them under twenty-five years of age.

All killed over a period of at least a year, except Buono and Bianchi, who, when acting together, killed their victims over a four-month period. Lucas first killed as a fourteen-year-old boy. The others reportedly first killed in their twenties or thirties, except for Buono, who was in his forties.

Many of the serial murderers' victims were particularly vulnerable to assault or abduction because of their lifestyle or perceived powerlessness. Bundy's victims were young women who moved about by themselves or were alone in the late evening hours. Most of Gacy's victims were young homosexuals "cruising" for sexual contacts in areas known to be frequented by gay men. Dahmer found his victims in gay bars near his apartment. Bianchi and Buono approached many young women who had a history of prostitution and therefore were used to being accosted on the street. Lucas reportedly killed forty-two victims who were hitch-hiking when abducted. He also abducted many of his victims while they were traveling alone, at a distance from their homes. Miller's victims were prostitutes. Marcus placed his victims in positions of powerlessness prior to killing them.

All seven of the murderers used strangulation as their primary means of killing. Lucas strangled a number of his victims but also used a variety of other means, primarily a knife. Bundy and Lucas used "overkill" on their victims. Long after his victims were dead, Bundy continued to beat them, and many of Lucas's victims were mutilated after death.

While all murderers were very mobile, Gacy and Buono-Bianchi killed in only one location. Bundy and Lucas, however, killed in numerous police jurisdictions in many different states. Marcus killed in three different states. Taking Buono and Bianchi as one example, each of these men killed at least nine people. All of them also committed both property crimes and other violent crimes.

Self-Concept

All of these murderers seemed to see themselves as controlling others either through manipulation or by physical force. In many cases, they failed to recognize their own faults and tended to rationalize their behavior by blaming others. With the possible exception of Buono, who projected a macho image, all appeared to have concerns about their masculinity. Lucas and Gacy had problems with their sexual identity going back to childhood experiences. Dahmer seemed to fight against acknowledging his homosexuality. Lucas, emphasizing that his primary accomplice in murder was a homosexual, made a point of differentiating himself from this accomplice, although Lucas did admit to being the passive partner in homosexual relations with his accomplice. Gacy, when arrested, stressed to police that he was bisexual, not homosexual. Marcus described himself as "shy" and implied that he was very cunning in his murders. Miller, though never confessing to his murders, seemed to enjoy the attention he received from law enforcement after his arrest. All of these men seem to have been unwilling or unable to delay their own gratification.

Attitudes

Once they were arrested and in custody, Bundy, Bianchi, and Lucas tended to reveal their attitudes toward authority, symbolized for them by their captors. Bundy bragged to the police of his escapes and mocked his previous jailers. He taunted police into digging deeper to find evidence in his killings. Bianchi, faking hypnosis, patronized his examiners and showed pure defiance. Lucas acted on many occasions as all-powerful, controlling whether or not he would see people and choosing to whom he would confess. In his view, he, and not the police, was clearing the cases. Lucas bragged about turning law enforcement "upside down" (interview, June 22, 1984). Buono defiantly ignored almost everyone during his trial.

All except Buono seemed to enjoy their celebrity status and thrived on the attention they received. Bianchi's response to celebrity was sometimes difficult to determine, but he did not shun the limelight and usually seemed to enjoy the fact that he was known worldwide. Although Bundy complained constantly about the presence of television cameras in the courtroom, he constantly sought contacts with the media during his incarceration. When Gacy confessed to police and lawyers, he found himself the center of attention and seemed to want to retain this attention through his clinical, almost professional method of discussing his victims and how he had killed them. After his arrest, Gacy kept a scrapbook of newspaper clippings about his case.

Only Bianchi and Lucas ever showed any remorse for their killings. When Bianchi cried while speaking in open court in Washington, some felt he was truly sorry and a very sick man, but others saw his tears as merely expressing frustration over his circumstances. Lucas, after being "saved by the Lord," now claims to understand all the grief he has caused the relatives of his victims. However, few who have interviewed him, including this author, believe he is sincere. Many doubt that Lucas is capable of feeling remorse for the murders of his victims, including his mother and his common-law wife, whose deaths he rationalizes as accidents.

None of the murderers strongly professed a religious belief, except for Lucas, whose claims are widely discounted, and Marcus, who joined a religious group in prison. Bundy, who regularly attended a Methodist church as a boy, was baptized into the Mormon faith in his twenties. Yet, when arrested for the last time in Florida, he asked for a Catholic priest. Gacy's religious activities appear to have been undertaken only for social gain. Bianchi and Buono, both of Catholic heritage, reportedly professed no strong commitments to the Catholic faith.

Recall of Events

Buono has never discussed his killings and still maintains his innocence. Bundy only theorized about the person who committed the murders he is believed to have done. Bianchi remembered his victims under hypnosis, apparently faked, but was reticent to discuss the details of how they were killed. Gacy allegedly remembered some of his victims but may have repressed the memory of his killings or, perhaps, simply was incapable of remembering as a result of blackouts caused by alcohol use. He is recalled by his wife and relatives as having had a very good memory. Lucas's memory is a mystery. He has described his victims in graphic detail that has been verified by the police. He may have had what is known as an "eidetic" memory—an exceptionally detailed, vivid recall of visual images—or he may have had hypernesia, defined as the unusually vivid and complete recall of information, similar to a photographic memory.

Missing Persons Problem

In the Gacy, Bundy, and Lucas cases, a number of the victims had been reported missing to various law enforcement agencies.

PART III

THE INVESTIGATION OF SERIAL MURDER

In Chapter 14 the problems of investigating a serial murder are discussed. First, the four ways that a serial murder comes to the attention of law enforcement authorities are described. Then the seven major problems that law enforcement faces in investigating a serial murder are explained.

Chapter 15 presents an extensive discussion, as well as an update of information I presented in a previous book (Egger, 1990a) regarding the various law enforcement responses to a serial murder investigation. Fourteen different responses are highlighted and described in detail. The primary rationale for presenting this response taxonomy is to show how law enforcement agencies evaluate the types of responses that have occurred in the past in order to determine their best response in the current situation.

CHAPTER 14

Problems in Investigating Serial Murder

Defining the Problem

A serial murder investigation is generally initiated by an agency or group of agencies following the identification of a series or probable series of related homicides. This identification will typically occur as the result of one of four different situations.

First, a serial murder investigation may be initiated as an extension of a current homicide investigation when one or more additional unsolved murders are linked to the original case. The linking factors may be similarities in victims, crime scenes, attacks, geography, or any actions or situations that convince investigators that the homicides were committed by a common killer. Such was the case in Rochester, New York, where police publicly acknowledged in November 1989 a possible relationship among five of eleven homicides of female victims found since 1987. The police were in fact conducting a serial murder investigation at this time. On January 3, 1990, officers conducting helicopter surveillance of the site where a female homicide victim had been found that morning saw a car near the homicide scene. Following the car into Rochester, they learned it was registered to Arthur Shawcross, who immediately became a suspect because of his previous criminal record. The killings had begun in March 1988, one year after Shawcross was paroled from prison, where he had served fifteen years for the murder of an eight-year-old girl and a ten-year-old boy. Shawcross's interrogation by police led to his confession and subsequent conviction for eleven homicides.

Second, the suspicion from a non–law enforcement source that a serial murder exists may result in enough pressure on an agency or group of agencies for a formal acknowledgment of this possibility to be made, resulting in an active serial murder investigation. Such pressure may come from the news media, from politicians, from advocates for homicide victims, or from the relatives or loved ones of homicide victims. In the case of Donald Harvey, who was convicted of thirty-seven murders in Ohio and Kentucky, it was a local television station in Cincinnati that pressured police into reexamining a number of deaths occurring at Drake Hospital. Harvey had been a suspect in one death at the hospital and, under questioning, had confessed to the murder. No other murders at the hospital were being investigated when the television station reported that twenty-three other deaths of a questionable nature had occurred at the hospital during Harvey's employment there as a nurse. The situation strongly implied that Harvey was responsible. A law enforcement investigation of these deaths resulted in Harvey's confession.

Unfortunately, the third way a serial murder is identified is frequently through happenstance or a fluke, in which a serial murderer is revealed through routine police work in response to a seemingly unrelated criminal event. A suspect may be apprehended for driving a stolen vehicle, and very quickly the police learn they are dealing with a much more violent crime. This was the case when Ted Bundy was pursued in a stolen car and arrested in Pensacola, Florida. More recently, in the early morning hours of June 28, 1993, in Long Island, New York, two state troopers spotted a tan 1984 Mazda pickup with no license plates driving on the Southern State Parkway. The driver refused to pull over, and the officers pursued the pickup. The chase ended twenty-five minutes later when the Mazda slammed into a utility pole. The driver was unhurt and was arrested. Following the arrest, the officers noticed a very strong smell coming from the bed of the pickup, where they found the badly decomposed body of Tiffany Bresciani, a twenty-two-year-old woman from Manhattan. Within hours, the driver, Joel Rifkin, had confessed to the killing of sixteen other women. And, of course, the two Milwaukee police officers who, on the evening of July 22, 1991, checked out a reported assault and handcuffing of a man had no idea what they would find in Apartment 213 on North 25th Street. These officers found body parts of some of Jeffery Dahmer's seventeen victims.

A fourth situation in which serial murder is identified is one in which the criminal event under investigation is considered unique, singular, and nonsequential until the suspect alerts the police to multiple acts by confessing to a number of homicides. Within two days of Henry Lee Lucas's arrest in Montague County, Texas, for violation of parole and suspicion of killing an eighty-four-year-old woman, Lucas began confessing to the killing of scores of people across the country. He was subsequently convicted of ten homicides and still remains a very strong suspect in over one hundred homicides.

Whether a serial murder is identified by the police through investigative linkages, pressure from the outside, a fluke of routine police work, or a serial murderer's confession, the investigation of a serial murder poses numerous issues for the investigating agency or agencies. These issues involve questions of investigative tactics and strategies, the allocation of personnel to the investigation, the necessary expenditure of funds to meet the increased expenses of such an investigation, news media relations, the management of large amounts of information, inter- and intra-agency communication, and the organization of the investigative effort to include control and coordination. In other words, a serial murder investigation is a major undertaking. It is frequently complicated by the involvement of multiple jurisdictions, the scope of the investigation, and the resources necessary to carry it out.

Seven Major Problems of a Serial Murder Investigation

A review of serial murder investigations conducted in the United States, Canada, and England over the last decade, as well as recent investigations of serial murder in Australia, South Africa, Sweden, Poland, Russia, and Austria, reveals seven major problems common to such investigations:

1. Contending with and attempting to reduce linkage blindness
2. Making a commitment to a serial murder investigation
3. Coordinating investigative functions and actions
4. Managing large amounts of investigative information
5. Dealing with public pressure and limiting the adversarial nature of relations with the news media
6. Acknowledging and assessing the value of victimological information
7. Becoming aware of strategies employed in previous serial murder investigations in order to understand potential ramifications and select appropriate methods to apply in a given case

Linkage Blindness

Law enforcement investigators do not see, are prevented from seeing, or make little attempt to see beyond their own jurisdictional responsibilities. The law enforcement officer's responsibility stops at the boundary of his or her jurisdiction. Generally, the only exception is when hot pursuit is necessary. The very nature of local law enforcement in this country and a police department's accountability and responsiveness to its jurisdictional clients isolate the department from the outside world. I coined the term "linkage blindness" in 1984 to denote a major problem in the law enforcement criminal investigation function applicable to serial crime in general. Whereas it should be readily apparent to the informed reader that the concept of linkage blindness is applicable to all types of mobile criminal activity, examples here will be limited to that of serial murderers. Joel Norris (1989) uses the term "linkage blindness" somewhat differently to refer to the failure of professionals in disparate disciplines to relate causalities of behavior to one another's area of understanding and study. Norris also failed to understand the concept when it was first explained to him by the author in 1983 (see Darrach & Norris, 1984). True, the term does generally apply to faulty communication linkages among like players in similar circumstances with similar responsibilities. But the term was coined and applied specifically to the law enforcement criminal investigation function.

Intergovernmental conflict between law enforcement agencies is unfortunately a somewhat common occurrence. The reasons for these conflicts are as varied and as numerous as there are agencies; however, there seems to be a common basis for most of this conflict. The basis is a real or perceived violation of an agency's boundaries or geographical jurisdiction, or of the specific responsibilities of an agency to enforce specific laws over a wide geographical area. Agencies large and small continually practice boundary maintenance in order to protect their jurisdiction from intruders—other police agencies moving onto their turf. The problem with boundary maintenance, jurisdictional integrity, or turf protection is that the serial killer can take advantage of these situations and, in many instances, continue to kill until cooperative agreements or arrangements are made between the opposing agencies. If such agreements or arrangements are made, then resources can be combined and information can be shared in order to investigate killings that cross jurisdictional boundaries.

The National Crime Information Center provides officers indirect access to other agencies in order to obtain information on wanted persons and stolen property. However, the sharing of information on unsolved crimes and investigative leads is not a function of this extensive nationwide information system. Reciprocal relationships between homicide investigators are at best informal and are usually within relatively limited geographical areas.

Linkage blindness exemplifies the major weakness of our structural defenses against crime and our ability to control it. Simply stated, the exchange of investigative information among police departments in this country is very poor. Linkage blindness is the nearly total lack of sharing or coordinating of investigative information and the lack of adequate networking prevalent among today's law enforcement officers and their agencies. As a result, linkages between similar crime patterns or modi operandi are rarely established across geographic areas of the country. Such a condition directly inhibits a system of early warning or detection of the serial murderer preying on multiple victims, except where crimes are being committed within a relatively small geographic area so that possible connections can more readily be seen. A law enforcement agency operates on information, yet agencies fail to seek it out, use or process it from "outside sources," or share it with colleagues or their counterparts in other agencies.

The lack of interagency collaboration or sharing of information on unsolved homicides occurs for a number of reasons. Individual investigators may see any form of cooperation with another agency in investigating a murder as a threat to career enhancement. Investigators may also perceive such cooperation as a reduction of their role in the case, since dual agency responsibility may mean dilution of their control of the case. Investigators may see collaborative arrangements with other agencies as a challenge to their professional expertise. Such a challenge is then perceived as agency rivalry, creating a sense of vulnerability and fundamental distrust of "outsiders."

Budgetary considerations are generally foremost in the mind of a police administrator when contemplating interagency collaboration. Which facilities will be utilized and how will agency costs be apportioned? Less tangible resources, such as databases and accounting systems, are also a concern.

The loss of policy direction may also be of concern to a police administrator. Any form of collaboration will mean some loss of control of employees. Collaboration means compromise so that the investigation can move forward. The greater the compromise, the greater the resistance will be from police administrators.

The issue of accountability is another real stumbling block to effective interagency collaboration. Anxiety over accountability means that the affected agencies may hold one another accountable for the outcome of an investigation. Thus, accountability anxiety results from the infringement of agency turf.

Interagency collaboration also means that there will be a requirement to build and maintain a consensus regarding the specific strategies and tactics of the collaboration. This becomes especially difficult when agencies are dominated by professionals with different ideas and theories about how such a collaboration should work.

The individual self-worth of agency personnel is also an issue with interagency collaboration. As Bardach (1996) has noted, "the individual derives a sense of self-worth from the turf prerogatives accorded the institution with which the individual is associated" (p. 179). Thus, an attack, real or imagined, upon the institution's turf is taken as an attack upon employees' self-worth.

Empirical analysis, albeit retrospective in nature, reveals numerous instances of linkage blindness in the investigations of serial murder across the United States. It should also be noted that this failure in communication and networking is not a unique problem to this country, as evidenced by the Yorkshire Ripper investigation in England.

Once two agencies realize they are possibly dealing with the same criminal, there is a great deal of pressure, both externally and internally, to begin sharing information and collaborating in the investigations. Putting the point simply, sharing of information means a loss of control over this information by the participating parties. This loss of control must be weighed against the increased gains that will be derived in the progress of the investigation and the greater effectiveness that will result in identifying and apprehending the serial killer. The issue of control is especially acute when there is little or no history of information sharing between the two agencies as a basis for judging the gains that might be achieved.

The fact that linkage blindness exists across the various components of the criminal justice system, and more specifically among the thousands of law enforcement agencies in the United States, is not really debatable. The existence of linkage blindness has been documented in retrospective interpretations in an analysis of serial murder cases that I made in 1985 (S. Egger, 1985b). The problem has also become obvious to those journalists, researchers, and government officials who have examined numerous cases of serial murder. This is certainly true for the better known nationally recognized cases such as Bundy, Lucas, Gacy, and Ramirez, and also for those lesser-known or less publicized cases of Eyler, Gary, and Hatcher.

Police officers, and particularly homicide investigators, from Maine to Texas are quick to agree when it is explained to them that linkage blindness exists. However, numerous police chiefs, sheriffs, and police commanders respond with a negative and unfortunately opposite opinion, arguing that agencies (more specifically, their agencies) communicate with one another on a daily basis, frequently across hundreds of miles of geography. Those law enforcement administrators who are unwilling to admit this problem of communication and information sharing only serve to exacerbate the problem.

In discussing the mobility of serial killers and the difficulty of a multiple law enforcement agency investigation, Keyes (1986) describes what Bill Steckman, a homicide sergeant in Columbus, Ohio, was up against when he was facing the investigation of the ".22 caliber murders":

> [M]ost serial murderers moved from city to city, stalking their victims across city, county or state lines, over weeks, months and even years. Because different law enforcement agencies were involved—county sheriff's deputies, city police and the FBI, each concerned primarily with their own cases—detectives often didn't notice the patterns. Conflicting investigative methods, interdepartmental jealousies, and prosecutors overreacting to the political pressures of a fearful and outraged public, often gave serial killers the advantage. Among the most difficult criminals to apprehend; most often, when they were arrested, it was by accident. (p. 77)

Because of these conditions, it is difficult for me to provide an optimistic prognosis for controlling serial murder in this country. It is equally disheartening when one realizes that law enforcement's response to the phenomenon of serial murder is only symptomatic of the greater problem of serial criminality. The traveling criminal who repeats criminal acts in different law enforcement jurisdictions is indeed exploiting a systemic weakness, which frequently contributes to his or her continued immunity from detection or apprehension. The police can simply no longer ignore the fact that criminals are commuting to more distant locations and to other jurisdictions. Deutsch, Hakim, and Weinblatt (1984) found that in the early 1980s, information emerging from police departments indicated that criminal activity flowed among various sections of cities and between cities and their suburbs. During the same period, the researchers found criminals commuting to more distant locations and, more important, to other jurisdictions.

In a stranger-to-stranger murder lacking in physical evidence or witnesses, criminal investigators face a very large set of suspects, with small probability of including the offender. A review of serial murders occurring over the last few years reveals that most serial murderers are caught by chance or coincidence and not by ratiocination or scientific investigation. Law enforcement agencies today are simply not adept at identifying or apprehending the murderer who kills strangers, and moves from jurisdiction to jurisdiction, and crosses state lines. Why, in this age of information and rapidly advancing computer technology, are multijurisdictional crimes of murder so difficult for law enforcement to solve? The answer is linkage blindness.

According to Levin and Fox (1985), unless the serial murderer leaves a distinct or unique signature at the crime scene, the police may not recognize the similarity of the killings. They also contend that if a pattern does exist, it may go undetected because of the sheer volume of cases, particularly in large cities. For example, the Corll, Henley, and Brooks killings of twenty-seven young boys from 1971 to 1973 in the Houston, Texas, area was completely unknown to the police until they received a telephone call from Henley in August 1973. In this case, the police failed to thoroughly investigate missing persons reports or to correlate similarities in these reports (Levin & Fox, 1985, pp. 177–181).

Levin and Fox (1985) state:

> Seeing a common element in several reports of missing or murdered persons in one large city is difficult enough. Seeing it across city or state lines magnifies the problem. Some killers are able to kill on the move so that they are already hundreds of miles away before police discover the crime. (p. 182)

Goldstein (1977) refers to an acknowledgment by the New York City Police Department in September 1974 that it had failed to recognize the overall pattern in eight different murders and two assaults on women that occurred in the same hotel over a period of one and a half years. This pattern was discovered when the killer confessed after being charged with another murder that occurred near the hotel (p. 67). This failure to identify patterns in different homicides may be the reason that the police department in Houston, Texas, recently initiated internal changes in its homicide division in response to a homicide clearance rate of only 64 percent. Two new shifts of detectives were added within the division, which would overlap existing shifts and so would allow detectives more time to discuss cases and follow-ups with one another and possibly identify across-shift patterns.

Levin and Fox (1985) conclude that serial killers "may be hiding in the anonymity of large urban centers" (p. 186) or traveling across the country, and in either case the police will probably not detect their pattern of killing. This failure to detect a pattern is most certainly the result of a major law enforcement communication failure.

Lack of Commitment

Most law enforcement administrators are unwilling to make a public commitment to initiating a serial murder investigation. Since the public has been sold the concept that the police are responsible for the crime in their jurisdictions, chiefs and sheriffs are loath to admit that there is a serial killer running loose throughout their jurisdictions killing strangers at will. Given that employment stability for police chiefs can be tenuous, it is no wonder that they strive to put their best appearance before the public. Serial killers make the police look bad. To commit to trying to catch one can make the police look inept in the public's eye.

Commitment not only brings police abilities, however misperceived by the public, under close scrutiny; it also means that one agency may have to work with at least one other, and frequently more than one. As we have seen, police agencies don't work well together. They aren't trained to work together. As in all other vocations, the tasks at hand become habits that are hard to break.

When multiple agencies are forced to work together because a criminal offender is committing his crimes in a number of jurisdictions, the first question to arise invariably is "Who is in charge?" Unless this has been specifically worked out beforehand, determining who will lead the investigation takes a great deal of time. Mutual aid pacts are allowed in most states, as specified by state legislation. However, police agencies generally fail to take advantage of these laws until it is too late.

Commitment to a serial murder investigation means that an inordinate number of investigatory personnel will have to be reassigned to the effort. In addition, equipment will have to be dedicated, including vehicles, radios, and computers. Few agencies have the necessary contingency budget to allow for such extra expenditures without seeking additional funds from the policymakers of their respective governments. This can be time consuming and frequently a little embarrassing for the law enforcement administrator.

An additional consideration in committing to a serial murder investigation is that the mass media will undoubtedly cause a great deal of chaos for the investigatory personnel assigned to the case. In some cases, the media become almost frenzied in their search for information on the investigation. This was certainly the case in Gainesville, Florida, in late 1990, when five people were slain within seventy-two hours in that city. For some observers, this serial killing turned into a "media carnival" (Reynolds, 1992, p. 4). It has been reported that journalists used parabolic microphones to eavesdrop on members of the task force set up to investigate these killings. Michael Reynolds, a Reuters reporter, characterized his peers in Gainesville as exhibiting "brainstem behavior" and "[like] rats on methedrine, jabbering about semen and blood and missing nipples" (1992, p. 4).

Coordinating Investigative Functions and Actions

The reallocation of personnel to the serial murder investigation also requires that very skilled and experienced homicide investigators of supervisory and command level ranks must be reassigned. This means that ongoing cases and newly reported crimes will be responded to by less skilled investigators, supervisors, and commanders. Depending on the length of the serial murder investigation, this could eventually have a negative effect on the agency's clearance rate.

It must be remembered that a serial murder investigation is a major and complicated effort that requires a tremendous amount of coordination. Commanders must know the status of assigned personnel and be able to monitor their activities at all times. In other words, the left hand needs to know what the right hand is doing so that no mistakes are made and important pieces of information are acted on and not lost in the confusion of multiple tasks and different assignments.

Managing Large Amounts of Investigative Information

In a serial murder investigation, the amount of information and data that are generated is almost always unmanageable without the aid of the computer. However, as the most inexperienced student reviewing the literature of law enforcement and automated data processing will quickly realize, many police agencies operate with little computer literacy. In fact, most police departments use their computing machines simply as fast-retrieval file cabinets, not realizing the great potential of the computing machine of the twenty-first century. A fast electronic file drawer alone will almost certainly fail to provide timely and accurate information with the necessary speed for such an investigation.

In order to exploit the computer's ability to process information, the team of investigators must be able to cross-reference and retrieve aggregate data very rapidly. Command-level personnel who understand the need for such a capability may not be available to the agencies involved. Outside consultants may be required, but this has not always worked very smoothly in these sensitive and stress-filled investigations.

In addition, agencies may wish to use regional or state databases designed to assist them in a serial murder investigation. One such system is the Homicide Investigation and Tracking System (HITS) operated by the state of Washington. HITS provides three major services to law enforcement. First, it supplies information related to murder and predatory sexual assault cases, including incidents with similar characteristics, evidence, victimology, offender characteristics, modi operandi, associates, geography, and vehicles. It also provides identification of known murderers and sex offenders living in a particular community. Second, HITS permits analysis of murder cases to identify solvability factors, linkages, and statement verification. Third, HITS provides investigators with advice and the names of experts who could possibly assist their investigation (adapted from Keppel & Weis, 1993).

Public Pressure and Mass Media Pressure for Information

Most law enforcement agencies, though adequately prepared to withstand a great deal of public pressure to capture criminals and prevent crimes, are ill prepared to deal effectively with the mass media. The fact that serial murder investigations frequently involve more than one police jurisdiction only complicates the task of media relations. In some recent serial murder investigations, reporters have gone from one public source to another, seeking information about the investigation. Coordination with their counterparts in the other agencies involved is a topic that is almost always neglected in training courses in police–media relations.

The result of intense mass media pressure added to public pressure is that the press comes to be viewed as an adversarial and intolerant critic of the investigatory effort and all personnel assigned. A great deal of antagonism is therefore generated between investigators and journalists, resulting in poor and sometimes slanted reporting of the progress and effectiveness of the investigatory efforts. However, it must be remembered that, whereas at times the media seem to get in the way of an investigation, in the final analysis they are much more likely to have a positive effect than a negative one. The publicity generated by the media is likely to bring witnesses forward who are useful to the investigation.

The Less-Dead: Low Priority Leads to Low Clearance Rate

When a victim of a homicide comes from a powerless and marginalized sector of our population, there is little pressure to solve the case and apprehend the killer. As homicide investigators are assigned additional homicides to investigate, the "less-dead" victims receive less and less priority. Without public or mass media pressure, these less-dead victims become less and less important. If, as argued earlier, the less-dead constitute most of the serial killer's victims, law enforcement agencies are inadvertently placing a low priority on solving a homicide that has a fairly high probability of being part of a serial killer's pattern. Thus, because law enforcement differentiates the value of homicide victims, the serial killer remains free to kill and kill again. In the final analysis, when this occurs, society's throwaways are indeed thrown away. And as Mott (1999) has noted, higher proportions of highly vulnerable victims, such as prostitutes or hitchhikers, were found among the unsolved cases in her data. She found these highly vulnerable victims, dumped outdoors, were more likely to be found in the unsolved cases. Mott (1999) also found that "If the offender chooses victims who were more easily accessible [such as prostitutes and hitchhikers], and in turn, not as likely to be reported as missing, the timeliness of the investigation will be hindered, benefitting the offender" (p. 251).

Lack of Knowledge of Others' Experiences with Serial Murder Investigation: Documenting the Problem

Different law enforcement responses to serial murder have been employed over the last ten to twenty years. Unfortunately, most law enforcement agencies are not familiar with the experiences of their counterparts or the problems they have faced. Consequently, when an agency is confronted with a serial murder investigation, investigators are not aware of the various options, responses, or combination of responses available to them. Little research has been done in this area, other than mine, as documented in Chapter 15.

The following sections present examples of law enforcement agencies' problems with well-known serial murder cases.

The Ted Bundy Case

Many of Theodore Bundy's murder victims were reported missing to the police by friends or relatives. In most cases, the victims' disappearances were treated as routine missing persons reports by the police. In one instance in Utah, the police failed to officially file such a report when a victim's mother reported her daughter's disappearance.

It was not until the fourth victim was reported missing in May 1974 that the police established that there were some similarities among the disappearances of girls reported missing in Seattle, Olympia, and Ellensburg, Washington, and in Corvallis, Oregon. It was not until early fall of that year that the missing girls' skeletal remains began to be discovered.

The task force in Seattle, established in March 1975, was a delayed response to the problem of missing and murdered girls. No victims missing specifically from Seattle's jurisdiction had been discovered before that March. However, the girls disappearing from Lake Sammamish in July 1974 and the discovery of their bodies in September of that year should have been sufficient, coupled with all the other disappearances, to have warranted joint investigative action much sooner (see Larsen, 1980; Rule, 1980; Winn & Merrill, 1980). The task force, without access to computers until far into the investigation, had limited automated capability to cross-reference their information. When Bundy was arrested in Salt Lake City, he was one of the task force's top one hundred remaining suspects to be checked and entered into the computer.

Parents of the murdered girl in Utah County, Utah, asked the local sheriff's office to obtain assistance in their investigation from the Salt Lake City police. The sheriff's office refused, indicating that they didn't need any assistance. This agency had a reputation for not working well with other agencies in the state.

Following the Chi Omega sorority house murders in Tallahassee, Florida, officers from Washington and Colorado notified the Leon County Sheriff's Office to look for Ted Bundy as a suspect. This tip was apparently ignored by the sheriff's office. In addition, the sheriff's office provided little cooperation to Colorado police, who were interested in investigating Bundy's jail escape.

The John Wayne Gacy Case

By the time John Wayne Gacy's crimes were discovered, he was already in custody. Gacy had been separately linked to four of his victims who had been reported missing. However, this connection was not identified by the Chicago police because their computer files were not centralized so that any officer could have access to them. The Des Plaines police had connected Gacy to his thirty-third and last victim, who had been reported missing in Des Plaines, Illinois. Then, through their investigation, the Des Plaines police connected him to other missing boys, who turned out also to have been Gacy's victims. Nine of Gacy's victims were never identified by the police (see Linedecker, 1980; Sullivan & Maikew, 1983).

Four complaints had been lodged against Gacy in Chicago between 1971 and 1978 for homosexual assaultive behavior. One charge was still pending when he was arrested. However, since Gacy was never identified as a common link to the missing boys, this criminal information on Gacy was never connected to the boys' disappearances.

The Hillside Strangler Case

It was not until Kenneth Bianchi killed in Washington State that he became a suspect in the Hillside Strangler murders. He was arrested for a double homicide in Bellingham, Washington. The Bellingham police notified the Los Angeles County Sheriff's Office because Bianchi had a California driver's license and had recently moved to Washington (see Barnes, 1984; Schwartz, 1981).

The first three victims in Los Angeles County had been found within three separate law enforcement jurisdictions. The Los Angeles Police Department, the Los Angeles County Sheriff's Office, and the Glendale Police Department were each investigating a murder.

When homicide investigators from the sheriff's office viewed the body of the third victim where she had been found in Glendale, they immediately saw similarities with the death of the second victim, found in their jurisdiction (F. Salerno, personal communication, August 1, 1985). From this point on, the investigators from the Los Angeles Police Department began exchanging information with investigators in the other two jurisdictions. However, it was not until November 22, 1977, and the discovery of five additional victims, that these law enforcement agencies met formally to share information on the killings and decided to form a joint task force to investigate the murders.

Bianchi had been personally contacted in connection with the Hillside murders on at least three separate occasions, twice by the Los Angeles officers and once by a Glendale police officer. These contacts were in response to tips called in to the police. On a fourth and fifth occasion, Bianchi's name was reported to the police, but no officer responded to this information. In all these cases, the information on Bianchi was either evaluated as unimportant, cleared with no additional follow-up necessary, or lost among the thousands of tips given to police during late 1977 and in 1978.

The task force formed in November 1977 grew to involve 130 officers assigned full time from three police agencies at the height of their investigation in early 1978. The size of the task force is reported to have created internal communication and coordination problems among its members, who were working around the clock to solve the murders. Of possibly more importance is the fact that the three police agencies were physically separated, working in different facilities, working their own clues and leads separately, and providing only summary information, which was computerized without cross-referencing capability (F. Salerno, personal communication, August 30, 1985). Establishing linkages and common elements from all the data that were collected, transmitted, and stored in this manner became a difficult task.

The Henry Lee Lucas Case

No patterns in Henry Lee Lucas's homicides were identified prior to his arrest and subsequent confessions. However, he was strongly suspected of having committed homicides that occurred between 1978 and 1980 along Interstate 35 from Austin, Texas, to the Texas–Oklahoma border north of Dallas. A law enforcement conference was held to discuss these murders and share information among the various Texas jurisdictions involved.

The Lucas Task Force was formed after Lucas had been arrested and had begun confessing to the murders. Four major conferences were held, in Texas, Louisiana, and California, specifically to discuss Lucas and his killings. All of these efforts, however, were after the fact and came too late for a number of Lucas's victims (see S. Egger, 1985).

A Summary of Investigative Problems

In the Bundy and Gacy cases, the police responded to several reports of missing persons, most of whom were in their teens. While responding to reports on missing young persons in a routine and perfunctory manner does not necessarily relate to linkage blindness as I have defined it, it does suggest police unwillingness to look for linkages among such reports when they are considered routine, assumed to be reports of runaways, not really considered a law enforcement problem by the police, and not seen as potentially life-threatening. A similar problem was apparent in the Lucas case, although it was not well documented.

The Bundy and Lucas cases provide some examples of local and state agencies not sharing information or assisting one another. In the Bundy case, there were numerous examples of sharing across local and state jurisdictions. However, there were at least two instances of a refusal to share information, seek assistance from another agency, or cooperate with an investigation. The Lucas case illustrates the lack of sharing or coordination on a large scale, across numerous state as well as local jurisdictions. The difference here is that no patterns were identified to require interagency or interstate cooperation. However, the lack of such cooperation or a mechanism with which to communicate means that the patterns, apparent in some cases across broad geographic areas, were not identified until after Lucas's arrest.

In the Gacy and Lucas cases, all coordinated responses to the killings were after the fact. No patterns in Lucas's criminal behavior were identified until after his arrest. The police in the Gacy case did finally begin to discern a pattern in his behavior, but only after thirty-three deaths.

In the Hillside Strangler and Bundy cases, police responded with a multijuris- dictional task force operation. Both were delayed responses to a problem, with Seattle being the more delayed. Neither task force had adequate automated cross- referencing capability. And in the Hillside case, the task force was so decentralized that the problem of coordinating and sharing their information was undoubtedly magnified.

The subjectivity of hindsight is not necessarily a fair or reliable measure of the effectiveness or efficiency of the numerous law enforcement agencies responding to these four serial murderers. Also, an assessment after all the facts are known, combined with recommendations beginning with "They should have" or "If they had only," does not substantiate a cause-and-effect relationship and may facilitate very little change in the present state of intra- and interagency communications. However, if the examples of linkage blindness found in the police responses to these serial murderers are representative of the degree of the problem, workable solutions can be deduced. They are the next logical step.

Linkage Blindness: An Analysis

Interorganizational relations within the criminal justice system emerged as a major policy issue in the late 1960s and early 1970s. Recommendations of national commissions during this period attest to this concern.

- In 1967, the President's Commission on Law Enforcement and the Administration of Justice recommended more cooperation between criminal justice agencies at the local level (Johnson, 1977, pp. 5–6):
- In 1969, the National Commission on the Cause and Prevention of Violence called for local jurisdictions to establish criminal justice coordinating councils.

- In 1973, the National Advisory Commission on Criminal Justice Standards and Goals acclaimed those local areas that had adopted local criminal justice councils, then further recommended that all major metropolitan areas consider adopting this criminal justice linkage model.

Gray and Williams (1980) define "coordination" as the planned and self-conscious interdependence of two or more organizations. They note that coordination of functional and jurisdictional elements is an agreed-upon goal of the Omnibus Crime Control and Safe Streets Act of 1969, as amended (p. 138). However, neither the three commissions referred to above nor the Safe Streets Act refers specifically to coordination and communication between separate law enforcement agencies for the purpose of sharing information on unsolved crimes. The emphasis in these commission reports and this legislation is on communication and coordination among components of the criminal justice system (police, prosecution, courts, and corrections), and not on the interagency relations of law enforcement agencies.

Most references in the literature to the lack of communication, coordination, or networking among law enforcement agencies attribute this problem to the decentralized nature and local control of American policing. Vollmer concluded in 1936 that American police officers employed by various units of government operated under a highly decentralized plan of organization, with virtually no coordination among these governmental units (Vollmer, 1936, p. 236). Bruce Smith (1960) makes a similar observation:

> There is therefore no such thing in the United States as a police system, nor even a set of police systems within any reasonably accurate sense of the term. Our so-called systems are mere collections of police units having some similarity of authority, organization, or jurisdiction; but they lack any systematic relationship to each other. (pp. 20–21)

V. A. Leonard (1980) discusses governmental fragmentation and the police:

> The American system of government is based on a political philosophy of decentralized power and local control. As a result, governmental structures, including police agencies, have proliferated and often overlap one another. Semi-autonomous governments (for example, towns, villages, cities, and the like) have established a wide variety of police agencies with differing formal structures and functions. (p. 11)

In discussing the organizational scale of American law enforcement, Bayley (1977) states:

> The United States has the most decentralized police system in the world. Bruce Smith's famous figure is that there are 40,000 separate police forces in the United States. A more accurate figure may be 25,000. The United States does not really

have a system, in the sense of development in accord with a considered plan; it has abutting and overlapping jurisdictions predicated on separate units of government. Like Topsy, the American police just grew. The strength of this tradition has been seen recently in the prevalence of the slogan "Support your local police." (p. 232)

Colton (1978) refers to the fragmented nature of law enforcement work:

Although there are federal police services (e.g., the Federal Bureau of Investigation, the Secret Service, etc.) the guiding principle in the United States is that police work is generally a local function and that recruiting, training, and levels of compensation are provided by local control. (p. 8)

In discussing why American police operate differently from their counterparts in England and France, James Q. Wilson (1978) stated:

The essential problem is that whereas other nations have either a national police force (as does France) or at least a single police force for each city (as does England), police responsibilities in the United States are divided among local, state, and federal authorities, each with a constitutionally distinct basis for existence. Federalism, in short, creates a system of different and even rival police organizations sharing powers over common problems. (p. 58)

In advocating a regional approach to policing, McCauley (1973) states:

The demand for local autonomy and "home rule" has created rigid jurisdictional limitations. Traditionally, today's law enforcement officer has authority only within the confines of his territorial jurisdiction. Likewise, the responsibility for maintaining public peace and order is esoterically funneled, thus effecting a condition whereby law enforcement and the "national crime problem" are viewed as local problems. The implication, then, is that crime must be prevented and controlled primarily at the local levels of government. (p. 1)

Thibault, Lynch, and McBridge (1985) state that the large number of police forces in this country is an outgrowth of the federal system of government and the wish of local communities to have control over their police. As a result, they find certain organizational realities in American policing today:

1. Active competition between police organizations for calls, resources, and, at times, personnel.
2. De facto spheres of influence arranged by formal and informal agreements between agencies. For instance, while the state police have statewide jurisdiction, many will normally not answer calls in a village that has a police department; the village police, in the same light, will not go outside municipal limits except in pursuit of an offender.

3. Informal relationships, usually based upon how well certain officers or agency heads get along, determine the distribution of intelligence information, assistance to other departments during emergencies, and the success or failure of interagency projects. (p. 319)

In addition to the decentralization, fragmentation, or balkanization of police agencies, references in the literature also attribute the problem of linkage blindness to jealousy or competitiveness among agencies and, in some cases, among individual officers. In determining critical problems facing smaller police agencies, McCauley (1973) said that "interdepartmental conflicts and jealousies inhibit coordination and cooperation" (p. 4). He also noted: "Cooperation between state and local police is not always genuine" (p. 229). McCauley (1973) believed this less-than-genuine cooperation is a product of status manifestation resulting from differential compensation, standards, equipment, and working conditions between state and local police agencies.

Smith (1960) argued that the competition among law enforcement agencies results from personalities and leadership style. He stated:

The relationship between the varied types of police forces is difficult to explore in a system fashion. Partly it rests upon the personalities of the chief figures in the departments involved. As between forces in such specialized fields as narcotics suppression and liquor enforcement there is intense rivalry, based upon competition for informants and prestige. Numerous department heads imagine that interagency rivalry will develop a spirit among their own subordinates: rivalry thus becoming a device for leadership. (p. 23)

Strecher (1957) referred to both fragmentation and competitiveness among law enforcement agencies as contributing to coordination and communication problems. In his case study of the well-known Sam Shepard murder case of 1954 in the Cleveland, Ohio, metropolitan area, Strecher found that the administrative deficiencies in the investigation of Marilyn Shepard's murder occurred because of the jurisdictional overlapping and interagency rivalry of the law enforcement agencies involved. He stated:

The reaction of each of the assisting officials cognizant of the interagency rivalry and the distribution of legal power among rival officials, was to hasten into the investigative activity, assuming as large a role as possible without entirely supplanting any other organization. It is problematical, even if one competent official had assumed total responsibility for the inquiry, whether he could have elicited the cooperation of rival officials or their personnel. (p. 115)

Robert Daley (1983), a writer and former police commissioner of New York City, commented on the jealousy, competitiveness, and territoriality of police officers in a work of fiction (which, for many, is fact disguised as fiction):

Like politicians they fought over jurisdiction, over protocol. Like actors they fought for credit for a headline. Given the chance to make a major arrest, to break an important case, they were willing, figuratively speaking, to destroy each other. (pp. 125–126)

Law enforcement personnel deal in secrets every day. Indeed their business relied on secrets almost exclusively. Which was not say they were good at keeping them. Juicy tidbits were revealed to girl friends, to barmen and to the press almost as a matter of habit. Secrets were kept habitually—and with an almost religious fervor—only from each other. (p. 283)

Robert Keppel, who was involved with the Ted Bundy investigation in Seattle, Washington, and was a consultant to the Green River Killings task force, found evidence of direct and intentional resistance to cooperation and coordination among police agencies. After trying to link serial killings in Seattle with murder in other locales, Keppel discovered that some police agencies wanted no part of a serial murder investigation. One officer stated to Keppel, "I've had problems there in the big city. Stay away from us" (*Newsweek*, November 26, 1984, p. 106).

Obtaining forensic investigative services is difficult for many law enforcement jurisdictions, particularly those in rural areas. The lack of access to qualified forensic investigative support services by small rural police agencies causes them to rely on state or large police agencies for these services, which must be allocated to many geographic areas. Also, the medical examiner or coroner is frequently an elected official who is not a forensic pathologist. The problems of forensic support are further exacerbated in many agencies by a lack of standardized procedures for collecting and processing physical evidence.

Structural factors in the typical law enforcement agency's organizational arrangement further contribute to linkage blindness. The phenomenon of single-complaint policing rather than problem-based responses such as a problem-oriented approach (see Goldstein, 1977) results in police patrol units reacting to individual complaints without identifying multiple situations of a similar nature as part of a problem or pattern. The same is true for the criminal investigation function, where the case basis of investigative assignment also precludes rapid identification of a developing crime pattern.

As indicated earlier, law enforcement's response, or lack thereof, to reports of missing persons fails to create the necessary information from which a readily identified pattern may emerge. Although this has been changing in many agencies across the country, many agencies are still unwilling to respond actively to reports of missing persons or to treat them as serious and potentially violent criminal acts.

Linkage blindness also frequently results from the inability of policing organizations to deal with large amounts of information. Brooks et al. (1988) found that historically

the Achilles' heel of most prolonged serial murder investigations has not been that of the investigation function per se, but the viability of the law enforcement agencies involved to manage the massive amounts of information received and generated. (p. 2)

In most serial murder investigations, the vast amount of information and its rate of accumulation quickly exceed human capabilities for effective management. Although most governmental agencies in large metropolitan areas have installed computerized systems to increase the efficiency of their services, law enforcement agencies have for the most part been far behind the cutting edge of this development. Computer-assisted dispatching and automated records systems are commonplace today in many agencies. However, the use of computerized information systems to support investigation has lagged far behind. Even with the implementation of VICAP at the national level and HITS-like systems at the state level, acceptance and utilization of these important tools, particularly for cross-jurisdictional information sharing, remain far from normal in the operations of most law enforcement agencies.

Further, law enforcement agencies are generally accustomed to operating as self-contained units devoted to serving the public within their respective jurisdictional boundaries. The organizational structure hierarchically designed for vertical downward and upward communication is poorly suited to communication and coordination with agencies outside their jurisdiction.

Linkage blindness is the real and ever-present cause of law enforcement's inability to respond to serial murder in a timely and effective manner. As indicated earlier, linkage blindness has been defined as the lack of sharing or coordination of investigative information and the lack of adequate networking among law enforcement agencies and law enforcement officers in this country. Numerous direct or indirect references by others to the communication problem have been cited here. Further, this problem was noted earlier in describing the four well-known serial murder cases of Bundy, Gacy, the Hillside Strangler, and Lucas.

In the day-to-day operations of law enforcement agencies, little serious attention or resource allocation has been devoted to interagency communication, cooperation, or coordination of the criminal investigation function. Today the chances are high that linkage blindness will occur within the law enforcement community because of the decentralized and fragmented nature of policing that has resulted in thousands of law enforcement jurisdictions across the country. Regionalization of policing services or consolidation of police agencies has met with only limited success.

Jealousy, a sense of interagency competitiveness, and turf battles only add to the problem of linkage blindness, facilitating a systemic myopia. Limited forensic services, with coroners ill-prepared to support criminal investigations, are another contributor.

Structural factors, such as single-complaint policing and case-based investigative assignments within hierarchically designed levels of control, in most police agencies greatly inhibit interagency communication and increase the probability that linkage blindness will occur.

Also, law enforcement's response to reports of missing persons, though currently changing, has clouded the lenses of many agencies in their view of these cases and of evolving crime patterns. Fortunately, such reports are beginning to be viewed with increased awareness of their potential criminality.

Lack of timely and effective information management has also contributed to increased instances of linkage blindness. The inability to support criminal investigations with effective information management greatly inhibits multijurisdictional investigations of serial murder.

By the late 1990s most police departments had access to computer services. Access is, however, only the first step. Standardizing formats for the information that is processed must be the next step. Perhaps the most important next step must be training of police personnel. Otherwise, the benefits of automation will be negated by the unwillingness of personnel to take advantage of the computer, further exacerbating the problem of linkage blindness.

Serial killers are able to escape apprehension for long periods of time while they continue to kill. This has more to do with problems of law enforcement than with the special skills of these killers. Linkage blindness is the crux of the law enforcement problem. "Linkage blindness," a term I coined in 1984, refers to a serious communication problem among law enforcement agencies in this country. Briefly stated, law enforcement agencies do not willingly and as a matter of accepted procedure readily share information on unsolved murders with one another. This sharing of information, when it does occur, greatly assists law enforcement investigators in identifying a pattern of homicides committed in different jurisdictions. Sadly, this sharing of information does not occur often enough. Many mobile serial killers have killed in numerous jurisdictions across the country, and this mobility has protected them from being arrested. In effect, their mobility results in an immunity from quick and swift apprehension. This mobility does not have to occur across jurisdictions to be effective. Large urban police jurisdictions with numerous precincts or district stations have also had serial killers roaming their areas, killing with what might be considered an immunity from detection or apprehension.

"Linkage blindness" results from the lack of sharing of information on unsolved murders among interested officers and among different jurisdictions, homicide investigative information that is not coordinated among multiple jurisdictions or areas of a single jurisdiction, and the lack of adequate networking by law enforcement agencies and their officers. "Linkage blindness" is a systemic weakness of American policing resulting from the multitude of law enforcement agencies in every state and the different levels of policing (local, state, and national) that are present. The United States has the most decentralized policing system in the world, and since it also appears to be the leading hunting ground for serial killers, this decentralization, in the absence of a deliberate effort to share and communicate with one another on unsolved cases, increases the probability that the serial killer can continue to kill with a great deal of immunity from detection.

As Robert Keppel, who was involved in the serial murder investigations of Ted Bundy and the Green River Killer cases, has stated, in order for police departments to catch a serial killer, "[t]hey have to be more open to talk with other departments about what they have, because to identify the serial it may not be [all] within their jurisdiction . . . so just identifying the serial up front is one of the most important things" (CNN, 1993).

In my research, I found that in some of their responses to a serial murder, particularly those involving multiple jurisdictions, the police were actively attempting to increase common linkages or networks among the law enforcement officers or agencies involved in the investigation (Egger, 1990a). Further, these investigations focused on identifying, documenting, and verifying a serial murderer's trail of victims. In other words, these agencies have attempted to reduce the extent to which linkage blindness has allowed the serial killer to kill and kill again.

Information is necessary to establish that a single homicide event is part of a series of multiple homicide events. Second, information is necessary to establish modus operandi patterns. Information is also necessary to evaluate the physical evidence from the identified series. To obtain access to this kind of information, an investigator or his agency must expand and develop new sources of information beyond jurisdictional boundaries. The obvious sources for this information are other law enforcement agencies in other jurisdictions that encompass the series of common homicide events.

Unfortunately, the absence of law enforcement efforts to expand sources of information to other jurisdictions has been characteristic in most of the incidents of serial murder in this country, and to a great extent in other countries as well. Specifically, the United States law enforcement community only infrequently makes the necessary effort to seek sources of information outside an agency's jurisdictional boundaries because of a blindness, forced or intentional, to the informational linkages necessary to respond effectively to the serial murder. Criminal investigators have not seen, have been prevented from seeing, or have made little attempt to see beyond their jurisdictional responsibilities in homicide investigations that turned out to be of a serial nature.

I have documented this problem of "linkage blindness" in a number of serial murder cases (Egger, 1985). As has been noted, in analyzing four of the case studies presented earlier, in Part II, this problem is evident in all of them.

It is not my intent to focus on mistakes of law enforcement with such comments as "They should have" or "If they had only." It is nevertheless necessary when analyzing these cases and many others to highlight a major problem, that of "linkage blindness."

The next chapter discusses various police responses to serial murder. From this analysis, we will see how linkage blindness plays a part in each of these responses.

CHAPTER 15

Different Police Strategies for Investigating Serial Murder

Technically, the unsolved murder is never closed. But as other murders occur, "old" cases receive a lower priority. Scarce resources must be allocated on the basis of cost-effectiveness. Murders that are more recent are also more likely to be solved, and this higher solvability factor, as well as the currency of the event, means that investigative manpower is reallocated from older to newer cases. When an unsolved murder is part of an identified series, however, law enforcement agencies are under a great deal of pressure to continue the investigation regardless of the current likelihood of solving the crime or the cost-effectiveness of pursuing the case as compared to other criminal cases. When a killing is labeled a "serial murder," everything changes. As indicated in Chapter 14, pressure from politicians, the media, and the general public creates heightened expectations, and agencies involved in the investigation of a serial murder will use a variety of methods to catch the serial killer.

Regardless of the approaches selected, a serial murder case may remain unsolved. In the famous Green River investigation, after many years of trying to capture this elusive killer or killers, there have been no arrests. In the "Atlanta Child Murders" investigation, an arrest was made, and Wayne Williams was found guilty of two of the murders. However, few who have studied this case believe him to be responsible for killing all of the remaining twenty-seven missing and murdered children.

When police have been successful in solving serial murder cases, this success has not always been the direct result of a specific law enforcement strategy aimed at the serial killer. At times, in fact, this success may seem unrelated to such a strategy. As one example, Bobbie Joe Long was not caught as a result of the formation of a task force in Hillsborough County, Florida. He was arrested when one of his intended victims got away and reported her ordeal to the police. As will be noted later, the subsequent investigation is a textbook example of good investigative techniques and interagency cooperation. However, the actions of the task force alone did not identify Long. Rather, it was their response to a reported assault that led to his arrest and conviction for nine murders, as well as convictions for kidnapping and rape in Pasco and Hillsborough County, Florida.

Another case in which success in a serial murder investigation had little to do with the police strategies used is that of the "Michigan Murders." I was assigned to this investigation in 1969, when I worked for the Ann Arbor, Michigan, Police Department. The task force that was created, combining the resources of seven law enforcement agencies in Washtenaw County and those of the Michigan State Police, was indeed a frustrating exercise. Over a number of months, the task force had not been successful in identifying a viable suspect for the killings of seven young women in the area—that is, not until Michigan State Police Corporal David Leik returned to his home in Ypsilanti from a family vacation. While away, the Leiks had asked their nephew, John Norman Collins, to watch their house and care for their dog. Corporal Leik became suspicious of some red stains on washtubs in his basement after he learned that his cousin had been questioned in the deaths of seven young women killed in the area since 1967. Leik scraped off samples of these stains and collected hair clippings from the basement area where he had cut his children's hair before going on vacation. The stains revealed nothing connected to the murders, but the hair clippings were of great interest to the crime lab. By neutron activation analysis, crime lab technicians were able to match these clippings with the hair clippings taken from the body of the seventh female victim. Collins was arrested, and hair clippings taken from his car also matched the clippings from the basement and those from the victim. As a result, Collins was convicted of this seventh murder. Most investigators on the case remain convinced he was responsible for the deaths of at least four of the other six victims.

Luck, happenstance, being in the right place at the right time, routine police work, awareness of a serial murder investigation, or a fluke—all have played an important part in catching a number of serial killers, and they probably always will. This does not mean we should assume that the police are not doing much of a job at catching serial killers. With experience and the benefit and application of research, police do seem to be progressing in their efforts to catch serial killers. With the use of DNA fingerprinting, behavioral research, advanced crime link analysis, better computer utilization, and a greater awareness that sharing of information on unsolved cases should be a high priority, law enforcement agencies do appear to be moving forward in their effort to increase their effectiveness in serial murder investigations.

Notwithstanding these advances, police in this country (and in a number of other countries that have experienced serial murder) remain unsure of the correct response to a serial murder. A homicide investigation demands certain procedures and required skills. A multiple homicide that is the work of a serial killer is quite another matter, especially when it involves more than one jurisdiction. The police ask, "What strategy should we use? How should we respond?" Although law enforcement agencies are generally unwilling to admit to this frustration or lack of certainty about how to proceed, it takes only a quick review of the literature on serial murder to identify this problem. As indicated in the previous chapter, it can be very difficult to get police to admit to the problem of linkage blindness. However, to get police to admit that they lack information and knowledge about the best way to proceed in a serial murder investigation is, as a colleague once stated, "like pushing Jello up the side of a tree with a straw" (anonymous). Like those in any other profession, police don't like to acknowledge their uncertainty in responding to a difficult situation. Professionals are trained to respond to a variety of problems and situations. Unfortunately, this is not the case when police are confronted with a serial murder.

When police respond to what they believe is a serial murder, traditional approaches are the rule. Frequently, an agency may begin the investigation as it would any other homicide investigation, only with more resources and determination to solve the murders. In some cases, police managers may consult other agencies with experience of a serial murder investigation. At other times, the agency may call upon the expertise of the FBI Behavioral Science Unit in Quantico, Virginia. Very small agencies will sometimes call on the expertise of the state police. Requests for assistance from other agencies frequently depend on the interagency relationships involved, the willingness of the agency administrator to seek outside assistance, and the agency's commitment to searching beyond its jurisdictional boundaries for a solution to a crime. Of course, the agency must first be willing to consider that homicides committed within its jurisdiction are linked to other homicides in other jurisdictions.

When homicides are identified as part of a serial sequence, either by confessions of an apprehended serial murderer or through the occurrence of a number of similar murders in a relatively small or contiguous geographical area, the police must respond. A review of the various ways in which law enforcement has responded to serial murder reveals several categories of response: holding conferences with agencies that are involved or potentially involved; acting as a clearinghouse of information about the serial crimes; forming a task force for the coordination of multiple-jurisdiction investigations; using an outside investigative consultant team; or using psychological profiling. All of these responses, of course, come after the fact and are reactive in nature. A less reactive response, though certainly not preventive in a pure sense, is to develop a centralized point of analysis from which to identify patterns of serial murders as they emerge and to communicate such patterns to the appropriate agencies for necessary and combined action. Other responses to serial murder are used less frequently than those listed. These include using specially developed computer software programs; conducting geoforensic pattern analysis; using the services of a psychic, and paying an identified serial killer for criminal evidence necessary to locate all of his murder victims. Each of these categories of law enforcement response to serial murder is described in this chapter.

Before describing and analyzing various law enforcement responses to serial murder, we must restate the major conclusion of Chapter 1, which is, in effect, the premise of this book. A systematic search of the current literature and research on serial murder reveals that very little of scholarly substance or empirical knowledge is available on law enforcement's response to serial murder. Without such an empirically validated knowledge base, law enforcement's response to serial murder is frequently unsuccessful and, when successful, more a product of chance than of a sophisticated and carefully planned approach. Jenkins's (1989) description of research on serial murder, "The very rudimentary state of our knowledge of serial murder, even when our access to the facts of particular cases is extensive" (p. 2), should be warning to those who construe the following taxonomy as an indictment of law enforcement's investigative skills. In other words, those armed with the knowledge of this taxonomy and its apparent aggregate failures should resist the urge to be quick to criticize.

Figure 15.1 depicts the various strategies that police have used in responding to serial murder. These response strategies or combinations of these strategies were used by law enforcement agencies in serial murder investigations over the past twenty years in the United States and England.

FIGURE 15.1   Law Enforcement Strategies in Response to Serial Murder

Strategy	Examples	Networking Skills	Outside Assistance	Primary Expertise
1. Conference	• National Conference on Serial Murder, Unidentified Bodies, and Missing Persons (Oklahoma City, 1986) • Green River Killer (1986) • Henry Lee Lucas (LA, 1983–1984; WI & GA, 1984) • Bobby J. Long (FL, 1984) • Austin, TX, 1980	• Cooperation and sharing of information • Cross-case analysis	• Interagency emphasis	• Investigator skills • Ability to I.D. possible similarities between cases
2. Information clearinghouse	• Lucas Task Force (TX, 1983–1985) • Tennessee Bureau of Investigation (1985)	• Collection and sharing of information	• Interagency focus	• Interagency relationships

Strategy	Examples	Networking Skills	Outside Assistance	Primary Expertise
3. Task force	• Green River • Atlanta Child. Murders (1980) • San Diego, CA. • Hillside Strangler (1977) • Gainesville, FL (1990) • Zodiac, New York City (1990)	• Coordination • Organization of information	• Inter- and intra-agency concern	• Same as above • Willingness to ignore "turf battles" and share information
4. Central coordination without forming a task force	• Aileen Wuornos Case, Marion County, FL (1990)	• Communication • Coordination of information	• Interagency	• Same as above • Willing to trust agencies to share information and work together without a formal structure
5. Profiling	• FBI Behavioral Science Unit • State and local officers trained by FBI • Psychologists • Psychiatrists • Geographic profiling • Investigative psychology (University of Liverpool, U.K.)	• Cooperation • Liaison • Coordination	• Yes	• Investigative experience and exposure to a number of cases • Psychology • Psychiatry • Empirical research and statistical analysis
6. Investivgative consultants	• Investigative Team (Atlanta, 1980) • Gainesville, FL (1990)	• Cooperation • Liaison • Coordination	• Yes	• Special skills (investigation, criminology, research, analysis, and policing)

(continued)

FIGURE 15.1   Law Enforcement Strategies in Response to Serial Murder (*continued*)

Strategy	Examples	Networking Skills	Outside Assistance	Primary Expertise
7. Forensic consultants	• National, state, and local crime labs • Medical examiner	• Same as above	• Yes	• Forensic medicine • Criminalistics • DNA analysis • Hypnosis • Artist
8. Major incident room procedures	• Police forces in the United Kingdom	• Coordination	• Intra-agency focus possibly	• Investigative skills • Training and use of standard-ized procedures in serious crime investigations
9. Solicitation from public	• Clue tips or leads made to central tele-phone number (numerous cases) • Two-hour TV special request-ing information on Green River Killer	• Identifying and linking relevant information	• Yes	• Public relations • Communication • Electronic media
10. Computer analysis system	• HOLMES (UK, Toronto and St. Petersburg, FL) • Dr. Watson Case Management System (Ontario, Canada) • Expert Systems • Text management systems	• If multiple jurisdictions involved	• Possibly	• Systems analysis computer programs • Software development

Strategy	Examples	Networking Skills	Outside Assistance	Primary Expertise
11. Centralized investigative network	• INTERPOL • VICAP (FBI) • VICLAS (RCMP) • HALT (NY State Police) • HITS (Washington) • Other states	• All of above • Collecting information from police agencies • Communicating analysis results to appropriate agency	• Interagency emphasis	• Crime and pattern analysis • Software and hardware support communication • Interagency relations
12. Psychics	• Boston Strangler • Michigan Murders • J. W. Gacy • Atlanta Child Murders • Other cases where police do not acknowledge this assistance	• Liaison • Cooperation • Coordination	• Yes	• Parapsychology • Psychic phenomena
13. Offender rewards	• R. Hansen (Anchorage, AK): Confession and location of victims for out-of-state incarceration • Clifford Olsen (Vancouver, B.C.): Confession and location of victims for $110,000 (Canadian) to his family • Confession in return for no death penalty	• If multiple jurisdictions involved	• Yes	• Willingness to "deal" with killer • Interrogation

(continued)

FIGURE 15.1   Law Enforcement Strategies in Response to Serial Murder (*continued*)

Strategy	Examples	Networking Skills	Outside Assistance	Primary Expertise
14. Rapid Response Team	• St. Louis • FBI Rapid Start Team–San Francisco: 15-year investigation of 14 bombings aimed at educators • St. Louis kidnap murders of two girls • Florida Regional Coordination Teams	• Development of mutual aid pact • Liaison • Cooperation • Coordination	• Yes	• Crime and pattern analysis • Communication with national databases • Interagency relations • Investigative skills

Conferences

Law enforcement conferences are almost a tradition in police work, held on an annual basis by professional associations for socializing, sharing new techniques and technology, and generally getting brought up to date on the particular world of policing germane to the specialization of the attendees or members. Conferences are convened to address specific problems facing multiple law enforcement jurisdictions. Only very recently have such conferences attempted to deal with serial murder. Conferences dealing with serial murder have been of two types: those dealing with numerous unsolved murders and those responding to the ramifications of the identification and confessions of a serial murderer.

A conference dealing with numerous unsolved murders was held at the Texas Department of Public Safety Training Center in Austin, Texas, on October 28–30, 1980. The discovery of an unidentified homicide victim found along Interstate 35 near Waco, Texas, together with numerous other unsolved homicides occurring along this highway in a three-year period, was the catalyst for the conference. The conference coordinator, the late Jim Boutwell, Sheriff of Williamson County, Texas, stated: "We have a killer (or killers) still on the loose, traveling I-35. We know that the M.O. is not the same in all murders. Guns, knives, and strangulation have been utilized in killing these victims. Some may have been raped; some haven't" (J. Boutwell to F. Hacker, personal communication, August 29, 1980). Representatives from thirty-two cities, counties, and political jurisdictions in Texas attended this conference, and nineteen new leads to unsolved area crimes resulted from the information shared among law enforcement officers. Four years later, Boutwell stated, "If we'd only known about Henry [Henry Lee Lucas] back then!" (J. Boutwell, personal communication, July 18, 1984).

Other such conferences were held in response to the Green River Killings in the Seattle, Washington, area (1983); the Michigan Murders in the Ann Arbor–Ypsilanti, Michigan, area (1968); and the Hillside Strangler case in the Los Angeles, California, area (1979).

In Canada, the Royal Canadian Mounted Police (RCMP) in Vancouver, British Columbia, sponsored the first conference, entitled Project Eclipse, in October 1991. Experienced psychological profilers and crime analysts from New York, South Carolina, Seattle, the FBI, the Ontario Provincial Police, and the RCMP examined twenty-five unsolved homicides that had occurred in southwest British Columbia. The primary purpose of this conference was to seek the opinion of the attendees regarding linkages between cases and to develop psychological profiles. In April 1992 the Ontario Provincial Police sponsored a second conference with the same format analyzing eleven unsolved homicides within the province of Ontario. Attendees at this second conference came from New York, the FBI, the RCMP, Ontario, and Quebec. Building on the experience of these first two conferences, the RCMP sponsored a third conference, entitled Project Kayo, in Edmonton, Alberta, to analyze fourteen unsolved homicides occurring in that province. Profilers, crime analysts, and homicide investigators from New Jersey, Iowa, the FBI, the Ontario Provincial Police, the RCMP, and Montreal attended. They were provided with laptop computers. Thirteen investigative profiles of unknown offenders were developed. The RCMP plans to use the format and organization of Project Kayo as a model for future projects of this nature (MacKay, 1994).

An example of conferences convened in response to an identified person confessing serial murder were the two conferences organized by the Monroe, Louisiana, Police Department in October 1983 and January 1984. In a direct response to the arrest and subsequent confessions of the serial murderer Henry Lee Lucas in Texas, more than 150 investigators from twenty-four different states met during these two conferences, compared notes on unsolved murders in their area, and were briefed by the Texas Rangers regarding Lucas's known travels and modus operandi. Similar conferences in 1984 in Wisconsin and Georgia focused primarily on Henry Lee Lucas and on unsolved murders in those states (Gest, 1984; Lindsey, 1984).

Another example was the conference on December 10, 1984, organized by Florida agencies following the arrest of Robert Joe Long, charged with eight counts of sexual battery, nine counts of kidnapping, one count of aggravated assault, seven counts of murder, and one count of first-degree murder in the Tampa, Florida, area. The conference was attended by representatives of the Hillsborough County, Florida, Sheriff's Office, the Tampa Police Department, and the Florida Department of Law Enforcement from Florida, the Georgia Bureau of Investigation; and the Regional Organized Crime Information Center in Nashville, Tennessee. These agency representatives shared information on Long and on a series of unsolved murders and rapes in Florida and Georgia (*ROCIC Bulletin,* 1985, p. 13).

Information Clearinghouse

A response similar to the conference approach is the creation of an information clearinghouse. Again, such a response may occur because a serial murderer has been apprehended or because of a number of unsolved murders involving multiple law enforcement jurisdictions. An example of the former, on a national scale, was the Lucas Homicide Task Force in Texas. Established by the governor of Texas in November 1983, this task force, which operated until April 1985, was composed of Texas Rangers, the Texas Department of Public Safety, and the Williamson County Sheriff's Office. This organization, though called a task force, performed the function of an information clearinghouse by communicating with law enforcement agencies that requested information on Lucas, coordinating interviews with Lucas conducted by law enforcement investigators from numerous states, compiling and distributing information about Lucas to requesting agencies, conducting preliminary interviews with Lucas for agencies that sent investigative information by mail, and providing for Lucas's security. In addition, the Texas Rangers directly investigated sixteen homicides committed in Texas in which Lucas was a suspect and assisted in numerous other investigations within the state. Between November 11, 1983, and April 12, 1985, approximately six hundred different law enforcement agencies interviewed Lucas. Altogether, more than one thousand different people from forty states and Canada interviewed him. By the end of February 1985, the task force had cleared a total of 210 homicide cases, 189 of which were directly attributed to Lucas (B. Prince, personal communication, May 21, 1985). A more detailed description of this task force is documented in the Lucas case study in Chapter 7.

As another example, on April 24, 1985, the Tennessee Bureau of Investigation began serving as an information clearinghouse for law enforcement agencies from five states (Pennsylvania, Kentucky, Tennessee, Mississippi, and Arkansas) and the Federal Bureau of Investigation in response to eight unsolved homicides of unidentified females that had occurred since October 1983. The clearinghouse provided information to all jurisdictions and was the catalyst for the creation of a network among them (*Tennessean,* April 25, 1984, p. 1). These homicides remain unsolved.

Task Force

Gilbert (1983) contends that because of the increase of stranger criminal homicide, police administrators must pursue nontraditional methods of case reduction, such as aggressive patrol activity and the use of interdepartmental task forces (pp. 162–163). However, the formation of a task force is one of the most traditional methods of responding to a multijurisdiction criminal investigation.

In the early summer of 1969, a task force made up of the Michigan State Police, the Ann Arbor Police Department, the Ypsilanti Police Department, the Eastern Michigan University Police, and the Washtenaw County Sheriff's Office was established in Ann Arbor, Michigan, by the Washtenaw County Prosecutor's Office in response to six unsolved homicides of young females that had occurred in the county in the preceding two and one-half years. On July 28, 1969, a seventh young female homicide victim was found, and on July 30, 1969, the governor of Michigan ordered the Michigan State Police to take charge of the investigations, "to concentrate and coordinate the efforts of all state and local agencies" (*Detroit News*, July 30, 1969, p. 1). John Norman Collins was arrested on August 1, 1969, for the murder of the seventh homicide victim and was subsequently convicted. Homicide Captain Daniel C. Myre of the Michigan State Police, who participated in this task force and later directed it after the governor's order, refers to a task force as a crime center in his book *Death Investigation* (1974). Myre states:

> The investigation of a major crime sometimes requires various police departments to unite and form a single investigative unit with a central headquarters. Such major crime investigative centers are only as good as their organization and information retrieval systems. To eliminate duplication of effort and insure that evidence is handled properly by all investigators, a major crime center must have a definite command structure and well-defined rules of procedure. (p. 153)

Levin and Fox (1985) state that the usual law enforcement response to a difficult investigation is to form a task force, which, they argue, "has never proven to be overly successful" (pp. 168, 169). The task force in the Hillside Strangler case was, say Levin and Fox (1985), too large and decentralized. They contend that if Bianchi had not killed on his own in Washington, the killings never would have been solved. "Until his arrest in Washington, however, the Los Angeles Task Force had been stumped for a year and had been labeled a total failure" (Levin & Fox, 1985, p. 169).

In July 1980 Chief Lee Brown announced the formation of a task force to look into the problem of missing and murdered children in the Atlanta, Georgia, area. The original task force consisted of five police officers (Detlinger & Prugh, 1983, p. 68). This task force effort, which grew much larger, eventually resulted in the arrest and conviction of Wayne Williams for murdering two of the twenty-eight homicide victims. Williams was suspected as being responsible for the deaths of many of the other victims. Chet Dettlinger, formerly a police planner with the Kentucky Crime Commission and a former assistant to Atlanta's Chief of Police, is extremely critical of the Atlanta task force, particularly for its failure to place some homicide victims on a list of victims related to task force efforts and for its analysis of the geographic distribution of the homicides (Detlinger & Prugh, 1983). Levin and Fox (1985) are also critical of the Atlanta police for not forming a task force earlier and for their failure to consider the geographic evidence in a broader context.

Levin and Fox (1985) are also critical of the Boston Strangler task force, which they consider to have been poorly focused, with techniques ranging from traditional forensics to the use of psychics. They state: "The capture of Albert DeSalvo actually resulted from his arrest by the Cambridge Police for a breaking and entering and an assault, rather than for one of the stranglings" (Levin & Fox, 1985, p. 171).

Darrach and Norris (1984) contrast the Atlanta task force with the Green River task force, set up to investigate the killings of over thirty young women found in the general vicinity of the Green River in the Seattle, Washington, area. They state:

> Everything that went wrong in the Atlanta investigation has been going right in Seattle. The Green River Task Force, set up to investigate the killings, now includes 30 talented detectives and is clearly one of the best organized, least politicized and most effective units in the country. Protected by a strong sheriff, the group has shrewdly controlled the release of information to prevent hysteria and keep the killer guessing. (Darrach & Norris, 1984, p. 64)

Unfortunately, however, the Green River Task Force was not successful in solving these homicides, which would eventually claim more than forty victims.

Past experience of multijurisdictional task forces reveals the crucial need for a well-managed, coordinated response. To meet this need, specific guidelines in the form of a manual, the *Multi-Agency Investigative Team Manual* (MAIT) was developed through a National Institute of Justice grant of funds to Sam Houston State University in 1986. This manual resulted from the documentation and synthesis of a two-week conference of experienced serial murder investigators held in August 1986.

Although the MAIT manual was seen as a disappointment for some because of its traditional approach to organization and management and its "cookbook" approach to the problem, some particular points are worthy of highlighting.

> The serial murderer often selects his victim from an urban area but disposes of the body in the privacy of a rural area, crossing jurisdictions in the process. (p. 1)

> Law enforcement agencies are generally accustomed to operating as self-contained units and often do not have the organizational structure, personnel or inclination for coordinating with other agencies. (p. 7)

Historically, the Achilles' heel of most prolonged serial murder investigations has not been a failure of the investigative function itself but, rather, the capability of the law enforcement agencies involved to:

- Manage the massive amounts of information received and effectively generated.
- Communicate internally or externally with other involved agencies. (p. 23)
- With most serial murder investigations, the amount of information and the rate of accumulation far exceeds human capabilities for management. (p. 27)

- Case coordination, review and analysis provide an opportunity to examine all investigative activities so that leads are not overlooked or links between them missed. (p. 49)

A contemporary example of a task force formed to investigate a serial murder is the multistate task force formed to investigate the I-70 Murders, involving police agencies in the states of Kansas, Indiana, Missouri, and Texas and the Federal Bureau of Investigation in an investigation of possibly ten homicides. These homicides, tied to a single killer who preyed on retail clerks in stores located near interstate highways I-70 and I-35, occurred between April 8, 1992, and January 1994. Except for those in Texas, these killings were originally linked by their proximity to the interstate highway system and the fact that the victims were stalked before they were killed. This link was established more firmly when ballistics tests showed that the first six victims all had been shot with the same .22 caliber revolver. The links to Texas were confirmed as a result of the vocations of the victims and the fact that these killings also occurred near the interstate highway.

Law enforcement agencies from these states have been meeting periodically to share information. In 1994 it was determined that the St. Charles Police Department would set up a computerized database to collect information related to the killings. All of the victims were women with the exception of one man with long hair and a ponytail (believed to have been mistaken for a woman by the killer). Victims worked in shoe stores, bridal shops, a ceramics store, a video store, and a dance wear shop.

Central Coordination without Forming a Task Force

In September 1990, law enforcement agencies in north central Florida decided to take a less-than-traditional approach to a serial murder investigation. Investigators from five different county sheriff's departments began to see similarities among a series of unsolved homicides that had occurred since December of the previous year. These investigators began, informally, to share the results of their investigations. Shortly after the discovery of a seventh homicide victim who was believed to be part of this series, two female suspects were identified and linked to these murders. On July 4 of that year, these two suspects were seen leaving a car belonging to one of the victims after they had driven it off the road in the Ocala National Forest. Witnesses who saw these two women leaving the car and later hitchhiking away from the area helped a police artist develop a composite drawing of the two suspects.

In late November, the Marion County Sheriff's Department released information about these suspects and the composite drawing to a Reuters newspaper reporter and, the following day, held a news conference. For the first time, reporters learned that investigators from five Florida counties were seeking two young women for questioning in a string of unsolved killings of men driving through the state on business. The bodies of five middle-aged men had been found in secluded areas of north central Florida over a seven-month period. Victims ranged in age from their forties to their mid-sixties and were traveling by car on business. Each victim died of gunshot wounds from a small-caliber weapon.

This information was reported by a number of newspapers across the country along with the composite drawing of the suspects. Within three weeks over four hundred people had called the Marion County Sheriff's Office with leads to the case. On the basis of this information and fingerprints from a pawnshop where some of the victims' belongings had been pawned, the suspects were identified. By this time, the investigation, involving five county law enforcement agencies and the Florida Department of Law Enforcement, was being informally coordinated by the Marion County Sheriff's Office.

This informal coordination continued throughout the remainder of the investigation and the arrest of one of the suspects. The investigation culminated with the interrogation of Aileen Carol Wuornos and her confession to seven homicides. Throughout this serial murder investigation, once agencies had agreed that the pattern of homicides indicated that the same killer or killers were involved, these six law enforcement agencies cooperated without a formal agreement or the development of a formal multiagency investigative task force or team. The Marion County Sheriff's Office took the initiative to serve as information coordinator to these agencies by collecting information on the various ongoing investigations and keeping each agency informed about progress and developments. In the final stages of the investigation, the sheriff's office coordinated a multiagency surveillance of Wuornos and her arrest.

Psychological Profiling (Investigative Profiling)

It is seldom that any man, unless he is very full-blooded, breaks out in this way through emotion, so I hazarded the opinion that the criminal was probably a robust and ruddy-faced man. Events proved that I had judged correctly.

—SHERLOCK HOLMES, congratulating himself on the accuracy of his
   psychological profile in *A Study in Scarlet*

Psychological profiling is an attempt to provide investigators with more information on a serial murderer who is yet to be identified. A more current and perhaps more descriptive term for this strategy is "investigative profiling." The purpose of this profiling is to develop a behavioral composite combining sociological and psychological assessments of the offender. Profiling is generally based on the premise that an accurate analysis and interpretation of the crime scene and other locations related to the crime can provide clues to the type of individual who committed the crime. Because certain personality types exhibit similar behavioral patterns (in other words, behavior that becomes habitual or routine), an understanding of these patterns can lead investigators to potential suspects. Over the past twenty years, three types of investigative profiling have emerged. The first type was developed primarily by the Federal Bureau of Investigation, an agency that has consistently maintained a very visible role through the mass media as consisting of criminal profilers who help local police catch serial killers. Although the Bureau has changed the name of this service to investigative analysis, the media continue to use the term "psychological profiling." The FBI conducts most of the profiles in serial murder cases in the United States, but a number of psychologists, psychiatrists, and criminologists have also been involved in providing this service in serial murder cases. This type will be referred to as the "FBI model."

The second type of investigative profiling to emerge was developed in England at the University of Surrey in Guilford. In 1985 Dr. David Canter, a psychologist at the University of Surrey, was approached by Detective Vince McFadden, head of the Surrey Police Criminal Investigative Division, and asked for his assistance in a major inquiry into two murders and at least thirty rapes under investigation by Scotland Yard, the British Transport Police, and the constabularies of Surrey and Hertfordshire. Canter agreed to help, and investigators from the London Metropolitan Police and the Surrey Constabulary were assigned to assist him. Canter developed a profile of the unidentified murderer, who would be dubbed the "Railway Rapist" by the press. The profile was remarkably accurate and proved useful in the apprehension of the serial murderer and rapist, John Duffy. This second type will be referred to as the "Canter model."

The third type of investigative profiling was developed by the late Dr. Milton Newton, who referred to this strategy as "geoforensics." A number of agencies investigating a serial murder have attempted to conduct a geographical analysis for pattern identification. For the most part, these efforts have been merely an extension of placing pins in a map to show geographic relationships, an approach typically used in traffic accident and enforcement analysis. Dr. Newton carried this analysis to a more sophisticated level through the use of geographic topical analysis.

Dr. Newton presented a preliminary analysis of his research, entitled "Geoforensic Identification of Localized Serial Crime," to the Southwest Division of the Association of American Geographers in Denton, Texas, in October 1985. Newton's final research (unpublished) was entitled "Geoforensic Analysis of Localized Serial Murder: The Hillside Stranglers Located," co-authored with Elizabeth Swoope. In this work, which I received from Newton in January 1987, Newton used a geographic post hoc analysis of the points of fatal encounter and body dumps, resulting in a near geographic "hit" on Angelo Buono's home, where most of the murders had actually taken place.

Beyond my personal sense of loss of a friend and colleague, with Milton Newton's death the criminal investigation field in this country also unknowingly lost a valuable resource. Although Newton's analysis was conducted on a post hoc basis, his techniques could easily be used as an integral part of an ongoing serial murder investigation. Had he lived, his further research would have undoubtedly provided this capability to an ongoing serial murder investigation. Newton's research has been recognized by the small but evolving forensic geographic community, and his work is being continued.

D. Kim Rossmo (formerly an investigator with the Vancouver, British Columbia, Police Department and now with the Police Foundation) has continued the study of geoforensics, which he now refers to as "geographic profiling." Rossmo describes geographic profiling as the analysis of spatial behavioral patterns using a variety of techniques, including distance-to-crime research, demographic analysis, centrographic analysis, criminal geographic targeting, point-pattern analysis, point-spread analysis, crime site residual analysis, spatial-temporal ordering, and directional analysis (Rossmo, 1995). Each of the three types of investigative profiling is described next.

FBI Model

Hazelwood and Douglas (1980) define a "psychological profile" as:

[a]n educated attempt to provide investigative agencies with specific information as to the type of individual who committed a certain crime. A profile is based on characteristic patterns or factors of uniqueness that distinguishes certain individuals from the general population. (p. 5)

Reiser (1982) states:

The arcane art of psychological profiling of suspects in bizarre and multiple murder cases is actually a variant of psycho-diagnostic assessment and psychobiography. It involves an amalgam of case evidence, statistical probabilities based on similar cases, available suspect and victim psychodynamics, knowledge of unconscious processes, and interpretation of detectable symbolic communications. The factual materials and speculative possibilities are combined using an inferential-deductive process. (p. 53)

The origins of criminal profiling are obscure (Ault & Reese, 1980). It is known that during World War II, the Office of Strategic Services (OSS) employed the psychiatrist William Langer to profile Adolf Hitler (Ault & Reese, 1980, p. 23). The material assembled by Langer included a psychological description of Hitler's personality, a diagnosis of his condition, and a prediction of how Hitler would react to defeat (Pinizzotto, 1984, p. 32). Furthermore, such cases as the Boston Strangler and New York City's Mad Bomber in the 1960s were profiled in a similar manner by Dr. James A. Brussels (Geberth, 1983, p. 399).

The FBI became involved in psychological profiling in 1970, when Agent Howard Teten began developing profiles. Teten was teaching an applied criminology course at the FBI Academy, and students from various police departments would bring their criminal cases to him (Porter, 1983). The FBI began formally developing psychological profiles shortly thereafter, for, as noted by Ressler et al. (1984), "The FBI agents at the Behavioral Science Unit have been profiling murderers for approximately sixteen years" (p. 12). Roger L. Dupue, director of the FBI's Behavioral Science Unit, states: "We believe that in most crime scenes, the killer leaves his signature there. If you're sensitized to what these things are, you can construct a profile of the killer" (Kessler, 1984, p. A-16).

Ressler, Burgess, and Douglas (1985) describe psychological profiling as "the process of identifying the gross psychological characteristics of an individual based upon an analysis of the crimes he or she committed and providing a general description of the person, utilizing those traits" (p. 3). Ressler et al. (1982) state that the process normally involves five steps:

1. A comprehensive study of the nature of the criminal act and the types of persons who have committed this offense;
2. A thorough inspection of the specific crime scene involved in the case;
3. An in-depth examination of the background and activities of the victim(s) and any known suspects;
4. A formulation of the probable motivating factors of all parties involved; and
5. The development of a description of the perpetrator based upon the overt characteristics associated with his/her probable psychological makeup. (p. 3)

Swanson, Chamelin, and Terrieto (1984) state the purpose of the psychological profile as follows:

The purpose of the psychological assessment of a crime scene is to produce a profile; that is, to identify and interpret certain items of evidence at the crime scene which would be indicative of the personality type of the individual or individuals committing the crime. The goal of the profiler is to provide enough information to investigators to enable them to limit or better direct their investigations. (pp. 700, 701)

FBI Agent Robert K. Ressler, a former member of the profiling team in the Behavioral Science Unit, states:

All people have personality traits that can be more or less identified. But an abnormal person becomes ritualized even more so and there's a pattern in his behavior. Often times, the behavior and the personality are reflected in the crime scene of that individual. By studying the crime scene from the psychological standpoint, rather than from the technical, evidence-gathering standpoint, you could recreate the personality of the individual who committed the crime.
    If the crime scene is abnormal, it would indicate their personality is abnormal. (*Law Enforcement News*, December 22, 1980, p. 7)

Geberth (1983) discusses the utility of psychological profiling:

Psychological profiling is usually productive in crimes where an unknown subject has demonstrated some form of psychopathology in his crime. For example,

• Sadistic torture in sexual assaults
• Evisceration
• Postmortem slashing and cutting
• Motiveless fire setting
• Lust and mutilation murders

- Ritualistic crimes
- Rapes

Practically speaking, in any crime where available evidence indicates a mental, emotional, or personality aberration by an unknown perpetrator, the psychological profile can be instrumental in providing the investigator with information which narrows down the leads. It is the behavior of the perpetrator as evidenced in the crime scene and not the offense per se that determines the degree of suitability of the case profiling. (pp. 400, 401)

Roy Hazelwood, a former member of the FBI's profiling team, states: "We don't get hung up on why the killer does the things he does. What we're interested in is that he does it, and that he does it in a way that leads us to him" (Porter, 1983, p. 6).

In 1982 the FBI Behavioral Science Unit received a grant from the National Institute of Justice, U.S. Department of Justice, to expand its profiling capabilities by building a file of taped interviews with convicted murderers (Porter, 1983; Ressler et al., 1984). As of September 18, 1984, thirty-six convicted sexual murderers representing solo, serial, and mass murderers had been interviewed (Ressler et al., 1984, p. 5).

Evaluations of psychological profiling in the literature have been inconclusive. Godwin (1978) is critical of profiling, which he characterizes as dull, tedious, and of little use to the police. He states:

They play a blindman's bluff, groping in all directions in the hope of touching a sleeve. Occasionally they do, but not firmly enough to seize it, for the behaviorists producing them must necessarily deal in generalities and types. But policemen can't arrest a type. They require hard data: names, faces, fingerprints, locations, times, dates. None of which the psychiatrists can offer. (p. 276)

Dr. John Liebert, a Bellevue, Washington, psychiatrist and a consultant to Seattle's Green River Task Force, is distrustful of psychological profiles put together by police agencies and the FBI. He states: "I think the state of the art [profiling] leaves a lot to be desired" (McCarthy, 1984, p. 1).

Liebert further urges that law enforcement involved in a serial murder investigation utilize the services of a psychiatric consultant. He warns against phenomenological generalizations about the murderer and states: "Superficial behavioral scientific profiling that rigidly reduces serial murder to a few observable parameters can lead an investigation astray" (Liebert, 1985, p. 199).

Levin and Fox (1985) characterize psychological profiles as so vague and general as to be basically useless in identifying a killer. They state:

As with most things, however, the value and validity of a psychological profile depends mostly on the skills and experience of the profiler. Unlike a psychologist who might consult with police investigators on an occasional, ad hoc basis, a full-time team of FBI agents trained in behavioral sciences as well as law enforcement techniques prepares approximately three hundred criminal profiles a year. Because FBI profilers have extensive experience, they construct the most useful profiles. Unfortunately, this tool, no matter how expertly implemented, is inherently limited in its ability to help solve crimes. (p. 174)

The FBI's own recent evaluation of its profiling efforts, in our minds, underscores the limitations of this approach. A survey of 192 users of these profiles indicated, first, that less than half the crimes for which the profiles had been solicited were eventually solved. Further, in only 17% of these 88 solved cases did the profile help directly to identify the subject. While a "success" rate of 17% of those 88 cases may appear low (and even lower if one includes the unsolved cases), the profiles are not expected, at least in most instances, to solve a case, but simply to provide an additional set of clues in cases found by local police to be unsolvable. Indeed in over three-fourths of the solved cases, the profile did at least help focus the investigation. (p. 176)

Holmes and DeBurger (1988) warn against a trend in law enforcement toward contacting federal agencies for assistance in the development of profiles. They argue that because federal agencies have little experience in murder cases, rather than local agencies using a "specialist," it would be far better for them to train their homicide investigators in the recognition of psychological motives and other characteristics of the unknown killer that can be inferred from the crime scene.

Levin and Fox (1985) also indicate that the profile is intended to be a tool to allow investigators to focus on a range of suspects, rather than pointing precisely to a particular suspect. Campbell (1976) sees intensive investigative work to locate a suspect and find corroborating evidence following the development of a psychological profile, due to its general and nonspecific descriptors. Reiser (1982), however, notes that the profile may provide a starting point or focus from which an investigation can proceed.

Robert Keppel, investigator for the Washington Attorney General's Office, is also critical of profiling:

[F]or the most part, cases where you don't have a whole lot of information at the scene, profiling is nothing more than guess work. It's an art form, number one, to begin with, it's not real scientific, and there are some good profilers, and some very bad profilers, and the good ones are successful because they limit themselves to those cases where there is a lot of answers at the scene, and they're able to help the police in those matters. (CNN, 1993)

The FBI itself urges caution in perceiving profiling as an automatic solution to a difficult case. Hazelwood, Ressler, Depue, and Douglas (1987) state:

Profiles have led directly to the solution of a case, but this is the exception rather than the rule, and to expect this will lead to failure in most cases. Rather, a profile will provide assistance to the investigator by focusing the investigation towards suspects possessing the characteristics described. (p. 147)

Psychological profiling is a relatively new tool in criminal investigation and has had some success in assisting in a serial murder investigation. Pinizzotto (1984) states: "Currently, the Behavioral Science Unit of the Federal Bureau of Investigation is developing a variety of research methods to statistically test for reliability and validity" of profiling (p. 37). However, no evaluation has been forthcoming from the FBI.

West (1987), in his discussion of psychological profiling, states:

It can be seen that profiling owes more to experience and imagination than to scientific deduction. All the same, matches between the actual and predicted characteristics of an offender are sometimes very striking. (p. 183)

Geberth (1983) notes that the psychological profile "can be a valuable tool in identifying and pinpointing suspects; however, it must be noted that the profile has its limitations. It should be utilized in conjunction with the sound investigative techniques ordinarily employed at the scene of a homicide" (p. 399).

Most homicide investigators appear to be convinced of the potential value of the psychological profile. Geberth, an experienced homicide investigator of the New York City Police Department, argues that the serial murderer is a type of personality that can be profiled. Geberth (1983) states, "A description of the salient psychological and behavioral characteristics which identify personality and behavioral traits or patterns can be used to classify and distinguish such an individual from the general population" (p. 495).

The Behavioral Science Unit of the FBI had been working on an artificial intelligence software program to enhance the investigative tool's effectiveness. The status of this effort is currently uncertain. Recently, however, private vendors have developed software programs for personal computers with an application for psychological profiling, referred to as computer-aided profiling.

Psychological profiling by FBI agents of the Bureau's Behavioral Science Unit has received a great deal of criticism, as noted. These profiles, however, are not without substantial support. Park Elliott Dietz, a noted forensic psychiatrist and a professor of law and behavioral science and psychiatry at the University of Virginia, argues that the FBI profiles have no peer. Dietz has stated: "I think I know as much about criminal behavior as any mental-health professional and I don't know as much as the bureau's profilers do" (Michaud, 1986, p. 42).

An example of part of a profile prepared by the FBI on the Green River Killer is presented next:

PSYCHOLOGICAL PROFILE OF THE GREEN RIVER KILLER PREPARED BY THE FBI, SEPTEMBER 22, 1982

. . . Their [the victims'] ages and race showed a variance which indicated that the offender demonstrated no personal preference for race. It was determined through studies at the Behavioral Science Unit that even the best of the so-called street people can be tricked or fooled, and a frequent tactic repeatedly observed is where the offender impersonates a law enforcement official. During his contact with the victim, her safety will be the prime entree that he will use and he may even promise to take the victim home or to the police station. He may also admonish the victim for walking the streets in the evening hour and for soliciting sexual favors. The offender's biggest obstacle will be to gain control of the victims and while the victims will initially be willing to go with him for the solicited act of prostitution, at some point he will have to demonstrate power over the victim.

While in this particular case the victims are of different ages and races, including variances in modus operandi, the assumption is still made that all of the deaths are related and all are committed by the same individual. This is based on the location where the victims were initially confronted, that being the Pacific Highway South "stroll" area near the Seattle-Tacoma International Airport, and the location of the disposal of the bodies. Also due to the probable cause of death being strangulation asphyxia. All of the victims are categorized in this matter as high risk victims due to their involvement with drugs and prostitution, their life styles which makes them susceptible to be a victim of a violent crime. In other words, they are characterized as victim of opportunity, they are easy to approach on the street, and probably initiate the conversation with their prospective "John."

An analysis of the crime scene reflects a primary focal point being the disposal site for the offender. In the case of the Green River victims, namely [deleted], the offender dumped his victims in or near the Green River. Crime scene analysis further reflected the offender was comfortable at the crime scene where some of the victims were anchored down in the water with rocks. His efforts to secure victims to the bottom of the river by placing rocks on top of them demonstrates the fact that he spent a considerable period of time in or at this location. The other two bodies were dumped on the side of the Green River, evidence that the offender had to quickly dispose of his victims. The method of disposing of the victims indicates that offender does not, nor will not, demonstrate any remorse over the death of his victims and what the offender is telling the police is that the deaths of these victims are warranted and justified and he is even providing in his own mind a service to mankind.

The crime scene further reflects that the offender at this particular point in the investigation, is not seeking power or recognition or publicity as he is not

(continued)

displaying his victims after he kills them. He does not want his victims to be found and if they are eventually found, he has the mental faculties to understand that items of evidentiary value because of the bodies being place in the river, will not be found.

The offender is very familiar with the area where the victims are disposed, does not seek publicity, and demonstrates no remorse.

From the Medical Examiner reports and autopsy reports, it is learned the victims die from some sort of asphyxia. In some cases, the offender leaves the ligature around the victim's neck where in the other cases, none is evident. The primary element that surfaced with each victim is that the subject is not planning to kill his victim each night he sets out to the area where the victims solicit sexual favors. He does not bring a rape or murder kit with him, nor does he plan to put his victims through some sort of ritual sexual act of body positioning.

We learned that the offender commits post-mortem acts on two of the victims, that he placed pyramid rock in the vaginal canal, and by doing this act, the offender reveals further elements of his personality.

The offender is profiled basically as a psychopathic personality in that the offender is mobile, drives a vehicle quite a bit. The vehicle, according to the profile, will be conservative in make and model. Offenders of this type favor vans and four-door conservative automobiles. These vehicles would be a minimum of three years old, and will probably not be well maintained.

The offender, in all probability, has a prior criminal or psychological history, comes from a family background which includes marital discord between his mother and father, and in all probability was raised by a single parent. His mother attempted to fill the role of both parents by inflicting severe physical as well as mental pain on the victim. She consistently nagged her son, particularly when he rebelled against all authority figures. The subject had difficulty in school which caused him to probably drop-out during his junior or senior year and he probably had average intelligence. The offender has dated and in all likelihood, if he has been married, he is separated or divorced at this time. He does not, nor has he ever been or had an aversion towards women. He had felt that he has been "burned" or "lied to and fooled by women one too many times." In his way of thinking, women are no good and cannot be trusted and he feels women will prostitute themselves for whatever reason and when he sees women openly prostituting themselves, this makes his blood boil.

He is drawn to the vicinity where there is open prostitution because of recent failures with other significant women in his life, and in all probability, he has been dumped by a women for another man.

He seeks prostitutes because he is not the type of individual who can hustle women in a bar. He does not have any fancy line of speech as he is basically shy and has very strong personal feeling of inadequacy. Having sex with those victims may be the initial aim of the subject but when the conversation turns to "play for pay" this causes flashbacks in his memory to uncomfortable times he has had in the past with women. These memories, as stated previously, are not pleasant. The straightforwardness of prostitutes is very threatening to him. They demonstrate too much power and control over him, because of his personal feelings toward women and the action of prostitutes that will make it mentally comfortable to him to kill them.

The offender will be in relatively good shape and will not be extremely thin or fat. He is somewhat of an outdoors man, and would be expected to have an occupation that required more strength than skill, a "laborer, maintenance, etc." He does not have an aversion to getting wet or soiled. His employment or hobbies will get him this way all the time.

When it comes to determining the race of the subject, the probability factor is decreasing inasmuch as some of the victims are white, some are black, [some] are mulatto. Generally, crimes [of] this type are intra-racial, black on black, white on white. Using the hypothesis that the first victim was white and is related to the other four victims, this would lead to the fact that the offender, in all probability, is white.

The age of the offender can be determined by the amount of control and confidence he exhibits in initially confronting his victims as mobility. These factors place him in an age category between his mid-twenties to early thirties. If the age grouping is correct, a previous criminal and psychological history for the offender can be found. Criminally cases of assault and rape would be his typical criminal background. Schizophrenia or manic depressive psychosis is almost typically found. It is felt, however, the offender is not insane as evidenced by his ability to conceal his victim, have little or any tangible evidence, and drive a vehicle. Someone that is insane does not rationally think of concealing his crimes nor is he capable of driving a vehicle safely.

It should be noted any suspects developed cannot be eliminated by age alone. There is no burn-out with these types of offenders and they can kill easily at 40 years of age just as at 20 years. These homicides reflect rage and anger on the part of the subject and he will not stop killing until he is caught or moves.

Under post offensive behavior, it was noted that the offender does not stay idle. He is a nocturnal individual and is a cruiser in his automobile. He feels comfortable during the evening hours, and when there is stress at work or at home, he cruises to the area where prostitutes are available. He, in all probability, has returned on several occasions to the disposal dump sites, both prior and subsequent to the victims being found and he has in all probability had additional encounters with prostitutes since these homicides. His primarily typical areas of conversation with the prostitutes would be the homicides.

He has followed the newspaper accounts of these homicides and clipped them out for posterity, and for further fantasy and further embellishment.

(continued)

> If items belonging to the victim are missing, he will take them as souvenirs and will in all probability give them to a girlfriend, wife, or his mother.
>
> He has had difficulty sleeping and has been experiencing periods of anxiety. He fears being detected particularly if newspaper accounts report that investigators are conducting a thorough and exhaustive investigation.

Canter Model

A primary difference between the profiling developed by David Canter and that done by the FBI is that Canter is continually building an empirical base from which to operate, whereas the FBI model is based almost totally on intuition of the profiler and his or her experience in profiling previous crimes. Whereas the FBI model spends little effort on the victim of the crime, Canter's model considers victim information as crucial to the development of the investigative profile. Canter relies on statistical analysis and the use of probabilities derived from his continually updated empirical base. He also bases his finding on the accepted theoretical concepts of psychology, whereas FBI profilers rely almost solely on their own experience.

As a result of nine years of investigative profiling experience, Canter set up the first graduate degree in investigative psychology at the University of Surrey. He has moved this degree to the University of Liverpool, where it will continue to be offered. All of Canter's research focuses on the search for viable psychological principles that can be used to generate profiles to assist in crime investigations. Canter's profiling research is broken down into five basic aspects of the criminal transaction between the offender and the victim: interpersonal coherence, significance of time and place, criminal characteristics, criminal career, and forensic awareness.

Interpersonal coherence addresses whether variations in criminal activity relate to the variations in the ways in which the offender deals with other people in noncriminal situations. Focusing on this aspect of the transaction highlights the targeting of victims and the implied relationship of victim to offender. A coherence of behavior within subgroups provides a series of assumptions for the investigator to test.

The location and time of the criminal act may give investigators information regarding the way in which the offender conceptualizes temporal and spatial relationships. This may provide valuable information on the constraints of the offender's mobility.

Addressing the characteristics of the criminal allows researchers to determine whether the nature of the crime and the way it is committed can lead to classification of criminal characteristics. This may lead to common characteristics of a subgroup of offenders and may provide some guidance for the direction of a criminal investigation.

While the actual development of a person's criminal behavior may vary, the direction of this development, determined from empirical data, may give police a way to backtrack over the probable career of the unidentified offender and to narrow the possibilities. In other words, solid and probative evidence may well be available in the offender's earlier crimes, which may have led to his contact with the police.

"Forensic awareness," a term coined by Rupert Heritage during his research with Canter (see Canter, 1994), is any evidence that the offender has attempted to mask or hide physical evidence of the crime from the police. It implies that the offender probably has had earlier contact with the police and has learned some of the techniques and procedures of criminalistics. The presence of this awareness should lead investigators to suspect that the offender has a criminal record.

For Canter, research into the development of more accurate investigative profiles means interpreting the "criminal's shadow" (Canter, 1994). This shadow, or story, of the criminal, which Canter refers to as the "inner narrative," evolves from a series of cryptic signals provided by the actions of the offender. These cryptic signals, as adapted from Canter (1994), pp. 278–281, are as follows:

- The personal world the individual inhabits
- The degree of care the offender takes in avoiding capture
- The degree of experience the offender shows in his crime
- Unusual aspects of the criminal act that may reflect the type of individual involved
- Habits of the offender that may carry over into his daily life

In effect, Canter is saying that even though the serial murderer may be characterized as killing in a random manner, the killer will in fact act in a very coherent manner. Unless a person is totally out of control, random behavior does not occur.

Canter concludes his book *Criminal Shadows* by stating, "Although a shadow can be disguised, it can never be shaken off" (1994, p. 285). This self-challenge to his efforts in developing an applied investigative psychology with which to assist police in their investigation of crimes leads me to believe that the efforts of David Canter and the students of his investigative psychology curriculum will indeed make a great deal of progress toward the integration of applied psychology into the criminal investigative procedures in the near future and will thereby substantially reduce the number of unsolved serial murder cases in the United Kingdom.

Geographic Profiling

Geographic profiling provides an analysis of spatial behavioral patterns of the offender and is based to some extent on the military intelligence interrogation technique called "map tracking," developed by U.S. Army Intelligence. It also is based on the criminal geography research of Brantingham and Brantingham (1978). Map tracking was used to debrief a captured combat soldier from his point of capture backward in time and space to his origination point, or to the point at which he has no more information of intelligence value. Use of geographic targeting in crime analysis includes distance to crime research, demographic analysis, centrographic analysis, criminal geographic targeting, point-pattern analysis, point-spread analysis, crime site residual analysis, spatial-temporal ordering, and directional analysis (Rossmo, 1995). These various analytical techniques are particularly useful in responding to serial rape and serial murder. By an examination of the spatial data connected to a series of crime sites, a criminal geographic targeting model generates a three-dimensional probability map that indicates those areas most likely to be associated with the offender, such as home, work site, social venue, and travel routes.

Geographic profiling analyzes spatial information associated with a series of crimes that have been linked and directs investigators to the most likely areas in which to locate the offender. This analysis requires a special software mapping program. Using the relevant variables of offender types, activity spaces, hunting styles, and target backcloths, geographic profiling infers spatial characteristics of the offender behavior. At the very least, this profiling strategy can assist investigators in focusing their resources on specific geographic areas and can narrow the alternative scenarios to explore.

The geographic profiling technique generally requires information regarding the crime, geography, victimology, and suspect information, when available. In addition, this technique can be integrated with the psychological profile, which should increase the specificity of profile information provided to the criminal investigators.

Investigative Consultants

In October 1980 the late chief of police of Stamford, Connecticut, Victor Cizanckas, contacted Commissioner Lee Brown of the Department of Public Safety in Atlanta, Georgia, and offered his assistance regarding the missing and murdered children investigation in Atlanta. Specifically, Chief Cizanckas offered to loan Atlanta one of his skilled investigators with experience in a similar case. Further discussions ensued between Cizanckas, Brown, and the Police Executive Research Forum, to which both men belonged. As a result of these discussions, the Police Executive Research Forum agreed to underwrite a cooperative effort to provide a team of qualified, experienced investigators to assist in investigating the Atlanta child killings (Brooks, 1982). The Forum provided this investigative consultant team to Atlanta "in the hope that it would serve as a model and prompt others to undertake similar efforts in the future" (Brooks, 1982, pp. v, vi).

To select a group of investigators for the team, homicide detectives in police departments from all regions of the country were contacted and asked to name investigators in their area who had the expertise to deal with the Atlanta problem. Five investigators were selected from this nominated pool. Pierce Brooks, retired police chief of Eugene, Oregon, and formerly a homicide investigator with the Los Angeles, California, Police Department, was selected as the team leader. Other members were Detective Alex Smith of Oakland, California; Detective Gil Hill of Detroit, Michigan; Detective George Mayer of Stamford, Connecticut; and Detective Charles Nanton of New York City. On November 11, 1980, this team traveled to Atlanta and served in the capacity of investigative consultants for two weeks.

The Police Executive Research Forum paid the $7,000 cost for this team to travel to and live in Atlanta.

The responsibility of this investigative consultant team was:

> to come to Atlanta as consultants to the task force investigators and share with them any insights they might have by virtue of their experience in working complex cases in their respective jurisdictions. To that end, they were expected to review the case files and interact with the investigators responsible for the investigation involving the missing and murdered children. (Brooks, 1982, p. iii)

Commissioner Brown noted that the team's role, "was akin to lawyers asking for consultation from other lawyers or doctors receiving consultation from other doctors—in short, asking for a second opinion" (Brooks, 1982, p. iii).

Brooks (1982) notes that the team could be considered the experimental version of established methods of interagency assistance, the formal mutual aid agreement and the informal one-on-one exchange of information between detectives. Although the use of this team did not directly result in a successful resolution of the Atlanta homicides, Brooks states:

> The November 1980 venture of the Investigative Consultant Team (ICT) in Atlanta is believed to be the first time police investigators, all from separate departments, were invited to participate as consultants in a major criminal investigation in a city other than their own. (p. 6)

While psychiatrists, psychologists, forensic pathologists, and even psychics have been used by police as outside consultants in difficult criminal investigations, the participation of officers from other agencies not involved in the investigation was a bold and, to many, a creative step by the Atlanta police. The utilization of experienced homicide investigators from outside the involved jurisdictions in a serial murder investigation would undoubtedly bring fresh ideas and expertise to the case. This strategy used in Atlanta remains a unique experience that apparently has not been replicated in other serial murder investigations.

Forensic Consultants

"Forensics" means the use of scientific knowledge to answer legal questions. Because investigators are, in effect, attempting to answer legal questions so that the killer can be charged by the state with his crimes, it follows that forensic scientists will, from time to time, be asked to assist in serial murder investigations. Forensic scientists from a variety of disciplines have provided assistance in such cases. Scientists from national, state, and local crime laboratories provide a wide range of services in the analysis of physical evidence in order to make the identifications and comparisons that are necessary to prove the elements of the crime in a court of law. These services range from the actual identification of physical evidence at crime scenes, to its preservation and collection, to its examination (identification and comparison), to actually testifying in a criminal trial.

Experts on DNA, generally referred to as "genetic fingerprints," are frequently used in serial murder investigations when semen is found at the crime scene on the body of the victim. Hypnosis experts may be used to enhance the memories of crucial witnesses. Police forensic artists may be used in instances where witnesses are available. The forensic pathologist is a frequent contributor to a serial murder investigation regarding specific information surrounding the actions of the killer, the victim, cause of death, time of death, manner of death, and other physiological evidence found from the autopsy of the victim. Aside from the normal forensic assistance in a serial murder investigation, forensic anthropologists have been used to reconstruct the head of an unidentified victim from the skull; forensic entomologists have been useful in determining time of death from the examination of maggot larvae on the victim's body, and forensic odontologists have assisted in the examination of teeth of the victims for identification purposes. This group of investigative response strategies is always used in some fashion in a murder investigation, frequently as a complement to the other response strategies described.

Major Incident Room Procedures

Police services in the United Kingdom have, by tradition, used a somewhat standard procedure for organizing the investigation of a major crime. However, following the massive Yorkshire Ripper investigation, which culminated in 1981 with the conviction of Peter Sutcliffe, the need for a more uniform and systematic approach to a major inquiry was evident. Based on this serial murder investigation and research on other major inquiries, the Metropolitan Police Academy in London introduced a standardized method of operating a major investigation incident room. Subsequent to the development of this standardized method and its implementation in the London Metropolitan Police, the Home Office required that this method be implemented in all the police forces in the United Kingdom.

Much of this standardized method seeks to counter the problems identified in the Ripper case. During the Ripper investigation, several police forces possessed criminal information pertaining to the identity of suspects in the case. However, there was no systematic means for one of these agencies to cross-reference or retrieve information from the other. Thus the completion of investigative leads and the successful collation of criminal information was not well coordinated and "became a hit and miss proposition" (Hetzel, 1985, p. 15).

The primary purpose of the standardized incident room procedure is to improve the collation of criminal information and to enhance the flow of investigative documentation. In a criminal investigation in the United Kingdom, the major incident room is the nucleus of all investigative activity. This procedure is now standardized throughout all police forces in England, Scotland, Ireland, and Wales. Messages, reports, and calls, referred to as "actions," are received at a central point, documented, assigned a control number, and forwarded to an "action writer," who identifies leads to be documented and data to be recorded. The information is then researched in a series of files and indexes, reviewed by administrative personnel, and assigned for follow-up to investigative officers. This procedure ensures that the investigation makes full use of all information on file before conducting interviews or taking further action. Although this standardized procedure appears complex compared to typical American police procedure, it does accomplish two vital tasks: the efficient flow of investigative documentation and the efficient collation of criminal information in a manner that promotes rapid retrieval (see Hetzel, 1985).

Solicitation from the Public

When and if an agency or group of agencies chooses to make public the fact that they are investigating a series of homicides believed to have been committed by the same killer or killers, it logically follows that leaders of the agencies involved would ask the public for assistance in providing information to the investigation. Frequently, when the police announce that they are searching for a serial killer, they will set up a bank of telephones connected to a central number so that the public can call in information or leads to the police.

Making an investigation public is a strategic decision with a number of ramifications. A centralized telephone number made available to the public will require an additional allocation of investigative personnel to operate these telephones. Because of the large volume of information generated from these telephone banks, a number of potential suspects will be identified, necessitating investigative follow-ups. In addition, a great deal of information will be received from the public, necessitating the computerization of these data so that they can be managed effectively.

For example, in the Green River Murder investigation, still unsolved, 18,000 suspect names were collected, many from tips called in by the public to an advertised telephone hotline number. In this well-known serial murder investigation, additional avenues were utilized to seek the public's help in identifying the killer. On December 7, 1988, a two-hour television special seeking assistance from the public was aired; it was entitled "Manhunt Live: A Chance to End the Nightmare." A number of homicide investigators experienced in serial murder investigation were flown into Seattle by the local Crime Stoppers program to answer telephone calls from people viewing the program. During the program, a toll-free telephone number constantly flashed at the bottom of viewers' television screens. Prior to the broadcast, a press release from the Green River Task Force stated:

> The goal of this important special is straightforward and direct: to mobilize the country in an effort to track down the most prolific killer of all time, the Green River Killer. More vicious than Jack the Ripper, Ted Bundy, The Boston Strangler and Son of Sam combined, this killer has terrorized the West Coast for the last six years. (Smith & Guillen, 1991, p. 446)

As a result of this program, the telephone company in Washington reported that more than 100,000 people had attempted to call the toll-free number. (Fewer than 10,000 actually got through to the detectives operating the telephones for the broadcast.) This massive and unique effort to solicit information from a national television audience was to no avail: The Green River Killer has not yet been identified.

In Gainesville, Florida, in early September 1990, four young women and one twenty-three-year-old man were found murdered—the work, apparently, of a single serial killer. Within the first eleven days of this serial murder investigation involving three police agencies, three thousand telephone calls were made to a central murder hotline number.

There is currently no evaluation of this investigative response. Whether it has produced important information in a serial murder investigation has not been documented. Given the difficulty of a serial murder investigation, however, police agencies are generally unwilling to take the risk of not soliciting information from the public once the investigation has become public.

Computerized Analysis System

Those who watch the TV program *Mystery* on PBS, who consider themselves Anglophiles, who read mysteries by the British writers P. D. James or Anne Perry, will be familiar with the police sergeant who accompanies the inspector from Scotland Yard. This sergeant always has a "box" in which he maintains the records of the investigation. When the United Kingdom began to experience serial murder, the records of such an investigation necessarily outgrew this "box." Today, the box has been replaced in all police jurisdictions in the United Kingdom with a small portable computer running a software program appropriately labeled with the acronym HOLMES, for Home Office Large Major Inquiry System. This software is based on standardized criminal investigation procedure developed for the major criminal incidents referred to earlier. The location of such an investigation is referred to as the "major criminal investigation incident room" (see Doney in Egger, 1990a, for a more complete description).

The Major Crimes Files now in operation on the Canadian Police Information Centre (CPIC) system is a national system that operates in a somewhat similar manner to VICAP and HOLMES. In contrast to VICAP, where the analysis is conducted at a central site, the Major Crimes File allows the investigator to use the program for his own remotely located terminal (C. P. Clatney, personal communication, March 31, 1988). The utility of the system by a single investigator at a remote site is then similar to the function of HOLMES.

In addition to the computer software applications referred to earlier, other software is being developed to assist law enforcement agencies in responding to serial murder. One such program is the Dr. Watson Case Management System, which operates on a personal computer and was recently implemented by the Peel Regional Police Force in Brampton, Ontario. This system, very similar in some ways to the HOLMES System or the HALT System, was implemented in early 1988. Since that time the agency has utilized the system in several lengthy homicide investigations and has given it very positive evaluations (M. S. Trussler, personal communication; January 27, 1989; also see "Police track serial killer with commercial DBMS," *Government Computer News,* December 5, 1986, p. 78).

Centralized Investigative Network

Interpol

Interpol is primarily a criminal information exchange service that provides its members with studies and reports on individuals and groups involved in crime internationally. "The purpose of INTERPOL is to facilitate, coordinate, and encourage international police cooperation as a means for embattling crime" (Interpol General Secretariat, 1978, p. 94).

Interpol is becoming an increasingly important tool for criminal investigation in the United States to satisfy investigative leads that go beyond U.S. borders. To address the need for an international channel of communication for state and local law enforcement officials, each of the fifty states is setting up a point of contact within its own police system to serve as a focal point for all requests involving international matters. This effort was initiated and is being coordinated by the National Central Bureau of the U.S. Justice Department. Illinois was the first state to implement the program of state liaison, which it established within the Division of Criminal Investigation of the Illinois State Police.

Although Interpol was not specifically designed to respond to serial murder, the in-place system of this organization is uniquely qualified to provide assistance to investigators of a serial murder with potentially transnational characteristics. As each of the fifty states develops its liaison program, Interpol will become better known to the law enforcement community as a tool for international information and assistance.

Interpol has recently been instrumental in linking the location of eleven killings of a serial killer to Austria, Czechoslovakia, and the United States. As a result, on July 28, 1994, Jack Unterweger, an Austrian ex-convict, was found guilty of these murders in an Austrian court, where prosecution of crimes occurring in other countries is permissible.

FBI's Violent Criminal Apprehension Program (VICAP)

Control is currently law enforcement's only viable strategy for responding to the phenomenon of serial murder. "Control" means to identify, locate, and apprehend. Identifying is done to verify that similar patterns or modi operandi are present, suggesting a serial murder. This usually requires information from different jurisdictions. Once this information is collated and a strong probability of serial events is identified, the collator, at a central point, can then distribute the information from which a pattern has been determined to the original sources. These sources, a group of discrete investigative agencies, can then share this information in order to coordinate investigative action. The collator is necessary in order to ensure that a high-value piece of information is not missed (Willmer, 1970, p. 32). Creating a central point of analysis precludes this from happening. An investigative network is then in a position, through state-of-the-art investigative techniques, to attempt to locate and apprehend the serial murderer.

Such a centralized investigative network or system is currently operational at the national and state level in the United States, on a national level in Great Britain, and to some extent in Canada. The U.S. network, referred to as the Violent Criminal Apprehension Program (VICAP), is located at the FBI National Academy in Quantico, Virginia, as a component of the National Center for the Analysis of Violent Crime (FBI, 1983). The Behavioral Science Unit at the Academy is the central site for this system and that unit performs the aforementioned functions of collator. This unit of agents also currently provides a psychological profile of the perpetrator of an unsolved violent crime when requested by a local agency.

VICAP is reported to have been the brainchild of Pierce Brooks, a retired police chief of Eugene, Oregon, and a former homicide investigator with the Los Angeles, California, Police Department, and of other police officials in the Pacific Northwest. The VICAP concept was first put into operation during a multijurisdictional investigation of the killing of young children in Oakland County, Michigan, in 1976 and 1977 (Levin & Fox, 1985; see also McIntyre, 1988). This systematic approach coordinated the collection and distribution of case information to the team of investigators from different law enforcement jurisdictions in the county. The Oakland County Task Force, as the result of an LEAA grant, was to have served as a model in criminal investigation to other agencies facing a serial murder investigation. However, the task force's efforts have never been made available in document form to the law enforcement community.

Further developments concerning VICAP came in the form of a technical assistance task plan submitted to Integrated Criminal Apprehension Program (ICAP) Program Manager Robert O. Heck of the Law Enforcement Assistance Administration in September 1981. In this plan, written by Pierce Brooks, the following was stated:

VI-CAP, a product of ICAP, is a process designed to integrate and analyze, on a nationwide basis, all aspects of the investigation of a series of similar pattern deaths by violence, regardless of the location or number of police agencies involved. The overall goal of the VI-CAP is the expeditious identification and apprehension of criminal offender, or offenders, involved in multiple murders (also referred to as serial murders, sequential murders, or random and motiveless murders). (Brooks, 1981, p. 1)

Brooks (1981) also provided a statement of the problem, which the proposed VICAP system would address:

The lack of centralized automated computer information center and crime analysis system to collect, collate, analyze and disseminate information from and to all police agencies involved in the investigation of similar pattern multiple murders, regardless of date and location of occurrence, is the crux of the problem. Research of almost every multiple murder investigation indicates an absolute need for a centralized information center and crime analysis function as a nationwide all agency resource. There is no question that on a number of occasions multiple killers could have been apprehended much sooner if the several agencies involved in the investigation could have pooled and correlated their information.

Each agency alone had "bits and pieces" of suspect identity—together their information would have provided the murderers complete identity and early on apprehension. (p. 2)

Between November 1981 and May 1982, four VI-CAP planning sessions were held in Colorado, Texas, and Virginia. These sessions were funded from ICAP moneys and participants were investigators and crime analysts from law enforcement agencies involved in ICAP projects. However, the VI-CAP system was not implemented at this time.

Because of the demise of the Law Enforcement Assistance Administration, funds were suspended for any further VI-CAP planning efforts following the last planning session in May 1982. VI-CAP procedures, budget, and forms had been developed as a result of these planning sessions. A third revised VI-CAP crime report form with instructions and summary sheets was the product of the final session (Briggs, 1982).

On July 1, 1983, Sam Houston State University received a planning grant award from the Office of Juvenile Justice and Delinquency Prevention (OJJDP) and the National Institute of Justice, U.S. Department of Justice, entitled the National Missing/Abducted Children and Serial Murder Tracking and Prevention Program (MACSMTP) (OJJDP, 1983). This planning grant allowed for task force and workshop activities to plan, develop, and implement a National Center for the Analysis of Violent Crime, to include the VI-CAP system. A program workshop meeting in July 1983 included the following activities:

- Preliminary development of a conceptual model of a National Center for the Analysis of Violent Crime (NCAVC) consisting of four major program components:

  (1) training
  (2) research and development
  (3) profiling
  (4) the Violent Criminal Apprehension Program (VI-CAP)

The Behavioral Science Unit of the FBI Academy in Quantico, Virginia, was recommended as the site for the NVAVC.

- Preliminary development of the procedures and reporting mechanisms for collecting information on serial murders and incidents of missing/abducted children. Included here was the first draft of an offense report for the collection of VI-CAP murder-incident information. (OJJDP Memo, July 28, 1983)

An MACSMTP workshop meeting in August 1983 included the following activities:

- A preliminary VI-CAP standardized form was developed for collecting murder-incident information. Selected members of the planning group were designated to perform content analysis on this form and field-test the document.

- The conceptual model of the National Center for the Analysis of Violent Crime, to be located at the FBI Academy was further discussed and refined.
- Network linkages and collection, analysis and dissemination processes of NCAVC were discussed (OJJDP Memo, September 15, 1983).

The third workshop of the program, held in November 1983, included the revision of VI-CAP reporting forms (OJJDP Memo, November 20, 1983). As a result of program efforts and activities referred to here, specific planning was initiated within the U.S. Department of Justice to fund the National Center for the Analysis of Violent Crime. On March 31, 1984, the FBI received approximately $3.3 million to support the organizational development of NCAVC for twenty-four months. Funding for this development was provided by the Office of Juvenile Justice and Delinquency Prevention, the National Institute of Justice, and the Office of Justice Assistance and Research Statistics. Under this funding arrangement, the project stipulated that it would:

- Create, develop and test a criminal justice operations center for a national multi-jurisdictional investigative research information and assistance program addressing selective violent crimes. The center will be under the direction and control of the FBI training center at Quantico, Virginia.
- Include four major organizational components that will include a research, training, and investigative support and information assistance program.
- Provide a research and analysis center for the nation's law enforcement and criminal justice system that can coordinate, assist, and provide comparative investigative assistance between multijurisdictional criminal justice agencies having similar murder patterns showing violent sexual trauma; mysterious disappearances of adults and children who may have been abducted, sexually exploited, molested or raped. (OJJDP Interagency Agreement, December 19, 1983)

VICAP (the hyphen was deleted in 1984), a major component of the National Center for the Analysis of Violent Crime, currently operational, is a centralized data information center and crime analysis system that collects, collates, and analyzes all aspects of the investigation of similar-pattern, multiple murders, on a nationwide basis, regardless of the location or number of police agencies involved. VICAP is described by Brooks et al. (1988) as a "nationwide clearinghouse . . . to provide all law enforcement agencies reporting similar pattern violent crimes with the information necessary to initiate a coordinated multi-agency investigation" (p. 41). VICAP attempts to identify any similar characteristics that may exist in a series of unsolved murders, and to provide all police agencies reporting similar patterns with information necessary to initiate a coordinated multi-agency investigation.

Cases that currently meet the criteria for VICAP are:

1. Solved or unsolved homicides or attempts, especially those that involve an abduction; are apparently random, motiveless, or sexually oriented; or are known or suspected to be part of a series;
2. Missing persons, where the circumstances indicate a strong possibility of foul play and the victim is still missing;
3. Unidentified dead bodies where the manner of death is known or suspected to be homicide. (Howlett, Hanfland, & Ressler, 1986, pp. 15–16)

Levin and Fox (1985) argue that the value of VICAP is predicated in part on the presumption that serial murderers roam the country. They state: "Traveling serial killers like Bundy, Lucas, and Wilder are in the minority to those like Williams, Gacy, Corll, Buono, and Berkowitz who 'stay at home' and at their jobs, killing on a part-time basis" (p. 183). However, this statement is based on a data set of forty-two offenders involved in thirty-three acts of multiple murder, and only ten of these were committed serially (see Fox & Levin, 1983, p. 4).

The success of VICAP will not be known for some time. It is dependent on a number of factors, not the least of which is local law enforcement cooperation in completing a very detailed twenty-seven-page form and transmitting this form on unsolved cases to the FBI. The concept, however, appears to be moving in the right direction, since no database from which to identify serial murders currently exists in this country. Depue notes that his VICAP system will be expanded to include the crimes of rape, child sexual abuse, and arson (Ressler, Burgess, & Douglas, 1988). Darrach and Norris (1984) state that for over twenty years the United States has had a national system for reporting and tracing stolen cars, but that there is no national computerized clearinghouse for reporting unsolved homicides. When VICAP develops the appropriate database, the hope is that the identification of patterns will stimulate the necessary interagency communication and sharing of information that is currently, with a few laudable exceptions, almost nonexistent.

New York State's Homicide Assessment and Lead Tracking System

By the mid-1980s a number of states had initiated efforts to develop statewide analysis capabilities similar to the system evolving with VICAP. In 1986, fourteen states were involved in such an effort. I was the project director of one such system for the state of New York, the first statewide system to become fully operational, in 1987. The Homicide Assessment and Lead Tracking System (HALT) was developed with state funds by the New York Division of Criminal Justice Services and turned over to the New York State Police in 1987 to be fully implemented. To date, HALT is far from realizing its full potential because of the shortsightedness of the executive-level personnel of this agency, who have provided only one full-time investigator to the system. Nonetheless, HALT has become a model for other states to follow in terms of its design, computer software, functions, and established cooperative relationship with VICAP.

The development of HALT was a cooperative effort between the New York State Police and the Criminal Justice Institute, Division of Criminal Justice Services. From the onset of program development, plans were made for the operational control of the program by the New York State Police. This was a major planning assumption in program development.

The HALT program, initiated in January 1986, was designed to provide a systematic and timely criminal investigative tool to law enforcement agencies across the state. Through computer analysis of case incident information supplied by police agencies, HALT is able to determine when similar crime patterns exist in two or more jurisdictions. When patterns are identified, the appropriate local agencies are notified.

HALT was developed in cooperation with an FBI national effort addressing serial homicide so that it would be compatible with the FBI's Violent Criminal Apprehension Program (VICAP). However, HALT was not simply a conduit from New York to VICAP. The system is "value added" in order to provide communication linkages within the state, investigative support services, and a source center to refer law enforcement agencies to specific services or provide the appropriate applied research information.

HALT became fully operational by the New York State Police in 1987 and is considered to be a valuable resource in addressing the problem of serial violent crime in New York.

The program goals of HALT were developed to be as follows:

1. To provide an informational and investigative resource for law enforcement agencies in the state by facilitating effective responses by local police agencies to serial homicides.
2. To promote and facilitate communication, coordination and cooperation among law enforcement agencies in the state on unsolved serial homicides.
3. To be designed in a manner that will permit its extension to other serial crimes. (Egger, 1986a, pp. 1–2)

Examples of Other Computerized Analysis Systems

Another statewide computerized analysis system similar to HALT is the Homicide Investigation and Tracking System (HITS), which collects murder and sexual assault information and identifies similiar characteristics across cases (see Keppel & Weis, 1993).

The Royal Canadian Mounted Police has implemented the Violent Crime Linkage Analysis System (VICLAS), which uses a modified version of the FBI's VICAP form to conduct computer analysis.

Although little information is currently available on the extent to which serial murder is an international phenomenon (except for the research of Hickey, 1985, and Jenkins, 1988), one special international network should not be excluded from this discussion. Interpol, the International Criminal Police Organization, is an international networking and communication system that is in place to respond to the transnational character of serial crime. This organization is the one best suited to providing a centralized investigative network for the world.

To the extent that conflict continues to exist between law enforcement agencies, it will contribute to a continuing communication problem. Notwithstanding this conflict, a centralized investigative network can substantially contribute to the reduction of such conflict. Where conflict remains between two organizations, there will be less of it when one outside individual or group of individuals (VICAP or HALT) holds an acknowledged monopoly of relevant information. Thus, the ability of these agencies to access and retrieve information from a centralized investigative network may further reduce the conflict between involved agencies.

Psychics

The extent to which serial murder investigations have made use of parapsychology or the services of a psychic has not been well documented. Other than a survey by Sweat and Drum (1993), there are no empirical data on police use of psychics in any type of investigation. Although the use of a psychic in a criminal investigation always receives a great deal of publicity in the press, psychic involvement in a serial murder investigation has generally received notice and attention only in the most publicized and infamous cases. Also, in many instances, regardless of the nature of the criminal investigation, police agencies have been reluctant to admit to the use of psychics during or after the completion of an investigation given the risks of criticism from the public and from other members of the law enforcement community.

Invariably, psychics become involved in highly publicized serial murder investigations, either by making predictions about the killer to the media or, in other cases, by secretly providing advice to agencies or individual investigators.

During the early stages of searching for a missing teenage boy in December 1978, Des Plaines, Illinois, police began to suspect strongly that John Wayne Gacy was responsible for the boy's disappearance. A local psychic was used to uncover information about the missing youth. Information given to the police by this psychic was subsequently interpreted as very accurate in describing John Wayne Gacy, his method of killing his victims, and his disposal of their bodies. Gacy was later arrested and convicted of killing thirty-three young men and boys in Cook County, Illinois. The young boy missing in Des Plaines had been one of Gacy's victims; however, the boy's body was still missing. (According to Gacy's confession to the police, the boy's body had been thrown off a bridge into the Des Plaines River, about fifty-five miles south of Chicago.)

Search for the missing boy's body continued until April 1979, when his body was found floating in the Des Plaines River in Grundy County, Illinois. During the intensive search for the body, the local psychic and a well-known psychic from the East assisted the Des Plaines police.

The psychics used by the police did give investigators some "very pertinent information" (Kozenczak & Henrikson, 1989, p. 24) regarding the location of the missing boy's body. Had weather conditions not prohibited it, investigators argue, the boy's body might have been found earlier as a direct result of psychic assistance.

Peter Hurkos was well known to the law enforcement community in the early 1960s. This famous Dutch mystic had reportedly helped solve a number of murders in the United States and Europe and claimed to have helped Scotland Yard recover a famous painting that had been stolen.

In January 1964, at the urging of an anonymous citizen who offered to pay his fee, Hurkos was asked to assist the Massachusetts Attorney General's Office in its investigation of a series of homicides that had occurred in and around Boston since 1962. The homicides were already being referred to as the Boston Strangler case.

After spending a week in Boston, Hurkos identified a fifty-six-year-old shoe salesman with a history of mental illness as the killer. Hurkos assured the police they had to look no further. Boston police then coordinated an exhaustive investigation of this suspect, ruling him out as a suspect in the killings. Not long after this, Albert DeSalvo confessed to the killings (see Frank, 1967).

Over five years later in 1969, Hurkos, who by this time was working as a "psychic detective" in California theaters and night clubs, was contacted by private citizens from Ann Arbor, Michigan, and asked to assist police in Washtenaw County in solving the "Coed Murders," six deaths of young females in the Ann Arbor–Ypsilanti area between 1967 and 1969.

Although there was a great deal of controversy over whether the three major police agencies involved would cooperate with Hurkos, the Ann Arbor police finally agreed to provide some limited cooperation to the psychic. Hurkos agreed to come to Ann Arbor provided his travel expenses were paid. With a great deal of fanfare and media publicity, Hurkos arrived in Michigan in late July 1969. For almost a week, Hurkos was accompanied by two homicide detectives in his efforts to assist the investigation. Following the discovery of a seventh homicide victim during this time, Hurkos, claiming the police were too hostile to his presence in the investigation, left Ann Arbor (see Keyes, 1976).

In briefly discussing a psychic consultant brought in by the Atlanta Police Department to assist them in the Atlanta Child Murders, Detlinger and Prugh (1983) state that "the Atlanta Police did everything possible—including providing official police escort service—to facilitate her 'communion' with the killer(s) or the spirits "driving the killer(s)'"(p. 60). Detlinger and Prugh are no less strident in their criticism of this psychic consultant and others who attempted to assist the Atlanta police in investigating a serial murder that would officially list thirty victims. Media hype and self-promotion were apparently major problems in the use of psychics during this investigation.

Notwithstanding the tendency of law enforcement and, to a lesser extent, the public to respond negatively to the use of psychics in a serial murder investigation, psychic consultants are indeed a strategy used in these investigations. The extent to which these psychics are forced upon the police or the amount of cooperation police provide to them is not well understood or well documented. In some cases, when all leads have been exhausted, turning to a psychic may be necessary if only to show that the agency is willing to use all sources that may lead to the resolution of the murders.

There has been no credible evaluation of psychic effectiveness in assisting a criminal investigation. A review of a number of serial murder investigations conducted over the last twenty years reveals the presence of psychics (invited and uninvited) in a large number of these cases. A number of investigators claim that psychics are useful, but the majority remain skeptical. However, the involvement of a psychic in a serial murder investigation may provide an unintentional benefit to the investigation. Psychics approach the investigation from a very different perspective, and it is this perspective that may, through the questions asked by a psychic, cause investigators to begin to ask new questions. This in turn may result in new information that inadvertantly provides further progress in the investigation.

Offender Rewards

On January 14, 1982, Clifford Robert Olson pleaded guilty in a Vancouver, British Columbia, courtroom to the rape and murder of eleven young boys and girls. Olson's plea was entered in exchange for a promise by Canadian authorities to establish a $90,000 trust fund for his wife and son. In addition to the plea, Olson agreed to identify the locations of some of the buried victims. The story of this controversial plea bargain received a great deal of coverage in the Canadian press and was also reported extensively by U.S. media (*Criminal Justice Ethics*, Summer/Fall 1983, pp. 47–55). Although the intensely negative reaction of the public to this negotiated plea may preclude the probability of such an unusual event reoccurring, it is certainly noteworthy. One can only imagine the frustration of the criminal justice officials in Canada that led to such a negotiation. It is not unrealistic to contemplate that such a negotiation in the United States, in such well known cases as those of Ted Bundy and Henry Lee Lucas, might have resulted, at the very least, in a resolution of cases and an end to the "not-knowing" of the relatives of their victims.

In other cases, serial murderers have agreed to confess to their murders in return for prosecutors not seeking the death penalty against them or in return for incarceration at a specific location. Plea bargaining in serial murder criminal trials has not been well documented. However, the Robert Hansen case in Alaska does provide an example of a case where the serial murderer bargained with the legal system to ensure his incarceration away from the state in which he was convicted. Robert Hansen pled guilty to the murders of seventeen women and the rape of thirty additional women in Anchorage, Alaska, in early 1984. In return for this plea and confession, which enabled Alaska state troopers to locate and unearth his buried victims, Hansen was assured of incarceration at a federal prison outside of Alaska, and state officials agreed to assist in the relocation of his family to another state (see DuClos, 1993; Gilmour, 1991).

Specialized Response Team

The FBI has recently developed a strategy to assist local law enforcement agencies in conducting major criminal investigations. Upon the request of a local or state law enforcement agency, the FBI's Rapid Start Team has been developed to aid local task forces in their investigation. A team of FBI agents and computer special-ists, numbering from eight to twenty, can be on the site of the investigation within four hours. The team provides laptop and desktop computers, telephone modems, customized software, a portable generator, and a tent for the team to use. The team assists the task force in transferring data into a specialized database. Team mem-bers also recommend an organizational structure for the task force. The team is assigned to the task force on an indefinite basis; however, the overall goal of the team is to train the local departments involved and to provide the appropriate software for the investigation. The FBI's Rapid Start Team provides five basic ser-vices: (1) help in organizing and delegating jobs within the task force; (2) compil-ing and analyzing clues on the computer; (3) establishing an electronic message system for the task force; (4) providing links to national databases; and (5) estab-lishing communication links to national or international police forces. These teams have provided assistance in the Unabomber serial bombing case, which involved fourteen bombings of educators across the country, and in a serial kidnapping and murder case in the St. Louis area. Although this type of service is still available to local law enforcement, the Rapid Start Team is now called the Critical Incident Response Group.

At one time, the Florida Department of Law Enforcement planned a similar response at the state level. A series of six regional teams would be set up, each cov-ering a specific geographic area of the state. These teams would consist of mem-bers from the Florida Department of Law Enforcement, police departments, sheriff's offices, state's attorneys, medical examiners, and individuals with special training in polygraph and criminal profiling. The purposes of the Regional Coor-dination Team would be to provide a vehicle for local law enforcement to obtain assistance on major violent crime cases, to ensure that work group resources are appropriately committed, and to guarantee that the most advanced technologies are applied in each individual situation. A special agent of the Florida Department of Law Enforcement would be put in charge of each Regional Coordination Team and would have the primary duty of tracking the investigative case progress, ensuring that additional needs that surfaced during the course of the investigation were appropriately addressed, and making sure that additional agencies and/or expertise were involved in the case as needed.

All Investigative Response Strategies Share a Common Focus

All of the law enforcement investigative responses encompassed within this tax-onomy share a common focus: to reduce the extent to which linkage blind-ness occurs in a serial murder investigation. "Linkage blindness," a term I coined (see Egger, 1984a), was addressed in the previous chapter. In the future, criteria for the success of a serial murder investigation will necessarily include the ex-tent to which this shortsightedness or cross-jurisdictional myopia is reduced or eliminated.

PART IV

THE FUTURE

Part IV presents the reader with a perspective on the future serial murder. Chapter 16 looks at the future of the phenomenon by presenting an agenda for research on serial murder. Chapter 17 presents a brief discussion of the future of serial murder investigation by highlighting questions to answer and recommendations for training.

CHAPTER 16

Future of the Phenomenon

As the reader will have noticed by now, the previous chapters have left us with more questions about serial murder than definitive answers or complete descriptions of this phenomenon. That is appropriate, because we still have a lot to learn about serial murder.

Rather than summarizing previous chapters, highlighting what we know and what we don't know about serial murder, this brief chapter will provide a structure and context for the necessary future study and research agenda on serial murder.

Although all of these questions may never be answered, I hope that this agenda will stimulate sufficient research on the part of the academic and law enforcement communities to provide answers or partial answers to many of them. If sufficient resources are allocated to this end, it is quite possible that in the near future the problem of linkage blindness can be applied to the much larger and more complicated phenomenon of serial crime.

What follows is an agenda for research on serial murder. As the reader will note, a number of the questions posed in this agenda challenge the assertions and conclusions of this book. More research is needed to verify my own conclusions or to prove them false and in need of revision. This agenda should serve graduate students seeking a thesis or dissertation topic, funding agencies developing priorities, law enforcement agencies developing criminal investigative strategies for the implementation of community policing or problem-oriented policing, and the intense curiosity of faculty members in criminology and criminal justice academic programs. It is hoped that no one who chooses to address one of the research questions posed in this agenda will develop emotional calluses but, rather, that their research focus will continue to offend their sense of morality and value of life.

Ted Bundy told authors Michand and Aynesworth (1983), "It has always been my theory that for every person arrested and charged with multiple homicide, there are probably a good five more out there" (p. 322). It is hoped that the research agenda that follows will test Bundy's theory as well as provoke the research community to provide the study and research that such a serious phenomenon as serial murder deserves.

The following research agenda is presented in three categories, with questions regarding victimology, serial murderers, and policy.

A Research Agenda for Serial Murder

Victimology

- Are groups of people who lack prestige or power the most common victims of serial murderers, or is their vulnerability a precipitating factor, creating "attractive" targets of opportunity for the serial murderer?
- Do the characteristics of powerlessness or lack of prestige of most serial murder victims contribute to the initial priority given by law enforcement to singular acts of homicide, prior to any identification of a serial pattern?
- Does the sexual preference or chosen vocation of serial murder victims reduce the priority that law enforcement gives to their murder?
- How does the serial murderer select a victim, and how have selected victims escaped death?
- Can at-risk populations reduce the probability of their victimization by a serial murderer?

Serial Murderers

- What case study techniques or ideographic methodologies will better develop our understanding of the causes of serial murder?
- Is the definition of serial murder offered in this book useful in creating a systematic framework within which to study the phenomenon?
- Is the apparent fact that most serial murderers are males a significant characteristic of the phenomenon?
- Why are a large number of serial murders committed by a team of killers? Do causation theories of solo serial killers also apply to these teams of killers?
- Will the development of a typology of serial murder facilitate a clearer understanding of serial murderers and thus increase meaningful research and study of serial murder?

Policy

- How can the incidence and prevalence of serial murder be more accurately determined?
- Is the incidence of serial murder increasing in the United States? If so, why?
- What clarifications or explanations of the phenomenon of serial murder are necessary in order to develop strategies and policies for intervention, prevention, and deterrence?
- How can the significance or importance of serial murder be emphasized in order to warrant the necessary allocation of resources for its study?

- What are the preadolescent and adolescent characteristics of serial murderers that would distinguish them from their birth cohort? How can the identification of such characteristics be used to develop intervention techniques and strategies necessary to prevent the development of these individuals into serial murderers?
- What is the most effective methodology for estimating the number of serial murderers currently operating in a specific geographical area?
- Why does the United States appear to have so many serial murderers compared to other countries?

It is my fervent hope that this research agenda will stimulate the necessary study, beyond what has been provided in this book, to establish a basis for the development of tactics and strategies that can be readily shared with the law enforcement community to reduce the prevalence and increase control of the incidence of serial murder. The victims must not be forgotten, and their number must be reduced. For this to occur, the phenomenon of serial murder must indeed become less elusive.

Criminal Justice Failure: An Example

Larry G. Bell had a criminal history that should have alerted officials to his potential dangerousness. Unfortunately, criminal court judges and probation officials in South Carolina seem to have made a number of faulty decisions in attempting to change Bell's behavior.

Bell's juvenile record is reported to show involvement in a number of sexual offenses. When he was twenty-six, he attempted to force a woman into his car at knifepoint. As an alternative to prison, the courts ordered him to undergo psychiatric treatment. He saw a psychiatrist on only two occasions. A few months later, using a handgun, he tried to force another woman into his car. A psychiatrist recommended to the court that Bell be given a long sentence and intensive psychiatric treatment. Instead, the judge sentenced Bell to only five years in prison. When he was released on parole twenty-one months later, he began to harass a woman and her ten-year-old daughter with over seventy obscene telephone calls. He was arrested for these calls, pled guilty, and was given probation with the stipulation that he see a psychiatrist. He saw a psychiatrist only a few times and then, as before, abandoned treatment. Also as before, no one noticed that Bell had stopped seeing a psychiatrist.

Shortly thereafter, in 1985, Bell abducted a seventeen-year-old girl from her home and killed her. Two weeks later his victim was a nine-year-old girl. He was found guilty of both murders and is suspected of having committed at least three other homicides in South Carolina. He is currently on death row in South Carolina. For many, it is clear that the criminal justice system failed when it let Bell go free again and again, eventually to kill. One reporter stated: "Every time Bell got into trouble, he was ordered to get psychiatric treatment. Every time, he abandoned the treatment. And every time, the monitoring systems of the medical and criminal-justice systems failed" (Methvin, 1989, p. 138).

CHAPTER 17

Future Investigation of Serial Murder

A number of questions remain to be answered regarding the criminal investigation of a serial murder:

- Is there a correlation between the demographic or geographic patterns of serial murder? For instance, there appears to be a disproportionate number of serial murderers who have killed in the Pacific Northwest (R. Keppel, personal communication, July 1985).
- Is a national centralized investigative network such as VICAP in the United States or HOLMES in the United Kingdom the most effective system for assisting local law enforcement agencies with unsolved and potentially serial homicides, or should other alternatives, such as regional distributive networks, be considered?
- How effective is VICAP or HOLMES in assisting local law enforcement agencies in responding to serial murder?
- What is the best method for developing a national database on solved and unsolved serial murders?
- What investigative strategies or techniques are the most successful for law enforcement's response to an unsolved and potentially serial murder?
- Can the technique of developing solvability factors be used in assessing the investigation of a serial murder?
- Is collecting information on unsolved murders and communicating this information the most effective method of reducing the linkage blindness of law enforcement?
- What are the necessary components of a training program for criminal investigators that would increase their effectiveness and efficiency in the investigation of serial murder?

These questions must be addressed in order to increase the effectiveness of law enforcement's response to serial murder.

Serial murderers defy deterrence. Nettler's (1982) lesson following his discussion of serial lust-murder makes the point: "Lock your doors" (p. 138). More specific tactics are obviously necessary, but we do not know who the next intended victim will be. Until more research is conducted on serial murder, only the most general deterrence strategies can be suggested, and these are of little use to the citizen.

Control is currently law enforcement's only viable strategy for responding to the phenomenon of serial murder. To control means to identify, find, and apprehend. Identifying is to verify that similar patterns or modi operandi are present, suggesting a serial murder. This requires information, in most cases from different jurisdictional sources. Once this information from the various pertinent sources is collated and the strong suggestion or probability of the serial events is present, the collator, a central point functioning as a collector, processor, analyzer, and distributor of information, can then distribute to the original sources the information from which a pattern has been identified. These sources, a group of discrete investigative agencies, must then share this information in order to coordinate investigative action dictated by this distributed information. The collator is necessary in order to ensure that a high-value piece of information is not missed (Willmer, 1970, p. 32). A central point of analysis precludes this. An investigative network is then in a position though state-of-the-art investigative techniques to attempt to locate and apprehend the serial murderer.

For agencies or organizations that are developing training programs to increase effective serial murder investigations, the following topics are suggested:

- Review of appellate court decisions on serial murder cases to eliminate mistakes in the future
- Development of solvability factors (some clues may be more important than others) for a serial murder investigation
- Conducting psychological autopsies of serial murder victims to develop traits in identifying a serial killer
- Networking of information on unsolved murders
- Computer skills in analyzing large amounts of information in a serial murder investigation
- Basic skills in victimology of serial murder

Beyond the Dahmers of the 1990s

What kind of serial killers will haunt our world in the twenty-first century? Given the selectivity of our mass media, our newspapers and television news programs will find them somehow more horrific than Jeffrey Dahmer. Possibly they will be mass serial killers, using letter bombs, poison in our water supply, or poison gas in the subways of our urban centers.

In order for our society and the criminal justice system to respond and catch these serial killers of the new century, we must pay special attention to a number of critical issues:

1. Research into the phenomenon of serial murder must focus on the motivation of these killers and critically analyze how our society spawns these horrific and deadly craftsmen.

2. An extensive and detailed database on serial killers must be developed in order to facilitate the generation of correlations that can be used to build an accurate profile of these killers.

3. The "less-dead" victims of serial killers must be given more effective protection from these killers. This can only be realized by implementing the first two items in this list.

4. The mass media must be held accountable for the generation of myths and falsehoods regarding serial murder so that the public becomes accurately informed about the serial murder phenomenon.

5. More case studies of serial killers should be conducted by criminologists using a standarized protocol similiar to the cases presented in Chapters 6 through 12, so that cross-case analysis can be presented for a significant number of cases.

6. The seven major challenges confronting a serial murder investigation (as detailed in Chapter 14):

   a. Overcoming "linkage blindness"
   b. Public commitment
   c. Coordination of investigations
   d. Management of information
   e. Public pressure and the adversarial tone of the news media
   f. Recognition by law enforcement agencies of victim information so they can be adequately prepared to initiate an effective investigation
   g. Awareness by enforcement leaders of the various strategies that have been employed in serial murder investigations so that they can understand the ramifications of each and intellectually select appropriate methods to identify and apprehend the serial killer

Author's Final Comments

It is my fervent hope that this book will stimulate the necessary research and study to make a book like this obsolete in the near future. More realistically, perhaps, I hope that a number of law enforcement officials will read this book and understand the imperative of sharing information about unsolved murders with their counterparts on our rapidly shrinking globe.

The phenomenon of serial murder must become less elusive and better understood. **Serial killers remain among us.** We still count their victims. Serial killers must be found and apprehended! **Without the necessary research and study of these killers, they will remain free—to kill and kill again.**

References

Abrahamsen, D. (1973). *The murdering mind.* New York: Harper & Row.

———. (1985). *Confessions of Son of Sam.* New York: Columbia University Press.

American Psychiatric Association. (1968). *Diagnostic and statistical manual of mental disorders.* Washington, DC: American Psychiatric Association.

———. (1980). *Diagnostic and statistical manual of mental disorders,* 2nd ed. Washington, DC: American Psychiatric Association.

———. (1987). *Diagnostic and statistical manual of mental disorders,* 3rd ed., revised. Washington, DC: American Psychiatric Association.

———. (1994). *Electronic DSM-IV,* HDT Software. Jackson, WY: Teton Data Systems.

Apsche, J. A. (1993). *Probing the mind of a serial killer.* Morrisville, PA: International Information Associates.

Atkinson, R. (1984, February 20). Killing puzzle. *Washington Post,* pp. 1, 14–15.

Ault, R. L., & Reese, J. T. (1980, March). A psychological assessment of crime profiling. *FBI Law Enforcement Bulletin,* pp. 1–4.

Baden, M. M. (1989). *Unnatural death: Confessions of a medical examiner.* New York: Random House.

Banay, R. S. (1952). Study in murder. *Annals, 284,* 26–34.

———. (1956). Psychology of a mass murderer. *Journal of Forensic Science, 1*(1), 1–7.

Bardach, E. (1996). Turf barriers to interagency collaboration. In D. Kettl & H. B. Milward (Eds.), *The state of public management.* Baltimore, MD: Johns Hopkins University Press.

Barnes, M. (Producer and Director). (1984). *The mind of a murderer* [Videotape]. Washington, DC: Public Broadcasting Service.

Barrington, R. C., & Pease, D. M. S. (1985). HOLMES: The development of a computerised major crime investigation system. *The Police Journal, 63*(3), 207–223.

Bayley, D. H. (1977). The limits of police reform. In D. H. Bayley (Ed.), *Police and society* (pp. 219–236). Beverly Hills, CA: Sage.

BBC News Service. (2000, January 28). Rwanda: Child "serial killer" arrested in southwest. Radio Rwanda, Kigali, in English, 1145 GMT, 10 November 1999.

BBC World News Service. (1999, October 30). *World: America's Colombian child killer confesses.*

Berger, J. (1984, September 8). Mass killers baffle authorities. *New York Times,* p. 1.

Biondi, R., & Hecox, W. (1988). *All his father's sins: Inside the Gerald Gallego sex-slave murders.* Rocklin, CA: Prima Publishing and Communications.

———. (1992). *Dracula killer: True story of California's vampire killer.* New York: Pocket Books.

Bjerre, A. (1981). *The psychology of murder: A study in criminal psychology.* New York: Da Capo Press. (Originally published in 1927)

Blackburn, D. J. (1990). *Human harvest: The Sacramento murder story.* Los Angeles: Knightsbridge.

Bloch, H. (1999, December 27). The horror, the horror: As a slaughter of the innocents comes to light, a pained Pakistan searches its soul for explanations. *Time, 154*(25), Asia Week.

Bogdan, R., & Taylor, S. J. (1975). *Introduction to qualitative research methods.* New York: Wiley.

Brandl, S. G. (1987, October). *The managment of serial homicide investigations: Considerations for police managers.* Paper presented at the annual meeting of the Midwest Criminal Justice Association, Chicago.

Brantingham, P. J., & Brantingham, P. L. (1978). A theoretical model of crime site selection. In M. Krohn & R. Akers (Eds.), *Theoretical perspectives* (pp. 105–118). Beverly Hills, CA: Sage.

Brearley, H. C. (1969). *Homicide in the United States.* Montclair, NJ: Patterson Smith. (Originally published in 1932)

Briggs, T. (1982, March 4). *VI-CAP memo.* Colorado Springs Police Department, pp. 1–10.

Brittain, R. P. (1970). The sadistic murderer. *Medical Science and the Law, 10,* 198–207.

Britton, P. (1999, June 27). The killers who follow in Hannibal's footsteps. *Sunday Times* (London). Features, p. 1.

Broeske, P. (1998, October 7). Blood money serial killers continue to get their stab at Hollywood stardom. *Milwaukee Journal Sentinel,* p. 1.

Brophy, J. (1966). *The meaning of murder.* New York: Thomas Y. Crowell.

Brooks, P. R. (1981). *VI-CAP.* Unpublished report.

———. (1982). *The investigative consultant team: A new approach for law enforcement cooperation.* Washington, DC: Police Executive Research Forum.

Brooks, P. R., Devine, M. J., Green, T. J., Hart, B. J., & Moore, M. D. (1987, February). Serial murder: A criminal justice response. *The Police Chief,* pp. 37, 41–42, 44–45.

———. (1988). *Multi-agency investigation team manual.* Washington, DC: U.S. Department of Justice.

Brown, N., & Edwards, R. (1992). *Genene Jones: Deliver us from evil.* Unpublished case study, University of Illinois at Springfield.

Brussel, J. A. (1968). *Casebook of a crime psychiatrist.* New York: Bernard Geis.

Burgess, A. W., Hartman, C. R., Ressler, R. K., Douglas, J. E., & McCormack, R. (1986). Sexual homicide: A motivational model. *Journal of Interpersonal Violence,* pp. 251–271.

Burn, G. (1984). *"—Somebody's husband, somebody's son": The story of Peter Sutcliffe.* London: Heinemann.

Cahill, T. (1986). *Buried dreams: Inside the mind of a serial killer.* New York: Bantam.

Campbell, C. (1976, May). Portrait of a mass killer. *Psychology Today,* pp. 110–119.

Canter, D. (1989). Offender profiles. *The Psychologist.* 2(1), 12–16.

———. (1993). The environmental range of serial rapists. *Journal of Environmental Psychology. 13,* 63–69.

———. (1994). *Criminal shadows: Inside the mind of a serial killer.* London: Harper-Collins.

Canter, D., & Heritage, R. (1990). A multivariate model of sexual offence behavior: Developments in "offender profiling." *Journal of Forensic Psychiatry, 1*(22), 185–212.

Caputi, J. (1987). *The age of sex crime.* Bowling Green, OH: Bowling Green State University Press.

———. (1990, Fall). The new founding fathers: The lore and lure of the serial killer in contemporary culture. *Journal of American Culture,* pp. 1–12.

Centers for Disease Control. (1982). *Homicide—United States: Morbidity and mortality report, 31*(44), 594, 599–602.

Chambliss, W. (1972). *Box man: A professional thief's journey.* New York: Harper & Row.

Cheney, M. (1976). *The co-ed killer.* New York: Walker.

Clark, S., & Morley, M. (1993). *Murder in mind: Mindhunting the serial killers.* London: Boxtree Limited.

Clarke, R. V., & Cornish, D. B. (1985). Modeling offenders' decisions: A framework for research and policy. In M. Tonry & N. Morris (Eds.), *Crime and justice: An annual review of research* (Vol. 6, pp. 147–185). Chicago: University of Chicago Press.

Cleckley, H. (1964). *The mask of sanity,* 4th ed. St. Louis, MO: C. V. Mosby.

CNN. (2000, March 28). Islamic council rule Pakistan serial killer's sentence violates laws of Islam.

Colton, K. W. (1978). *Police computer technology.* Lexington, MA: Lexington Books.

Connor, S. (1994, March 6). Crimes of violence: Birth of a solution. *The Independent,* p. 19.

Conradi, P. (1992). *The red ripper.* New York: Walker.

Cornwell, P. D. (1994). *The body farm.* Boston: G. K. Hall.

Coston, J. (1992). *To kill and kill again.* New York: Penguin Books.

Cox, M. (1991). *Confessions of Henry Lee Lucas.* New York: Pocket Books.

Cressey, P. G. (1932). *The taxi-dance hall.* Chicago: University of Chicago Press.

Critchley, T. A., & James, P. D. (1987). *The maul and the pear tree: The Ratcliffe Highway murders, 1811.* Boston: G. K. Hall.

Cross, R. (1981). *The Yorkshire ripper.* London: Granada.

Cullen, R. (1993). *The killer department: Detective Viktor Burakov's eight-year hunt for the most savage serial killer in Russian history.* New York: Pantheon Books.

Dahmer, L. (1994). *A father's story.* New York: William Morrow.

Daley, R. (1983). *The dangerous edge.* New York: Dell.

Damore, L. (1981). *In his garden: The anatomy of a murderer.* New York: Arbor House.

Danto, B. L., Bruhns, J., & Kutcher, A. H. (Eds.). (1982). *The human side of homicide.* New York: Columbia University Press.

Darrach, B., & Norris, J. (1984, August). An American tragedy. *Life,* pp. 58–74.

Davies, N. (1981, May 23). Inside the mind. *The Guardian,* p. 6.

de River, J. P. (1958). *Crime and the sexual psychopath.* Springfield, IL: Charles C Thomas.

Denzin, N. K. (Ed.). (1970). *Sociological methods: A sourcebook.* Chicago: Aldine.

———. (1978). *The research act: A theoretical introduction to sociological methods.* New York: McGraw-Hill.

Detlinger, C., & Prugh, J. (1983). *List.* Atlanta, GA: Philmay Enterprises.

Deutsch, J., Hakim, S., & Weinblatt, J. (1984). Injurisdictional criminal mobility: A theoretical perspective. *Urban Studies, 21*, 451–458.

Dickson, A. G. (1975). *A descriptive study of male and female murderers.* Unpublished doctoral dissertation, U.S. International University.

Dietz, P. E. (1986). Mass, serial and sensational homicides. *Bulletin of the New York Academy of Medicine, 62*(5), 477–491.

———. (1987). Patterns in human violence. In R. E. Hales & A. J. Frances (Eds.), *American psychological association annual review, Vol. 6.* Washington, DC: American Psychological Association.

Dobson, J. (1992, Spring). Special report: Ted Bundy's last words. *Policy Council,* pp. 31–38.

Dominick, J. R. (1978). Crime and law enforcement in the mass media. In Charles Winick (Ed.), *Deviance and mass media* (pp. 105–128). Beverly Hills, CA: Sage.

Donohue, P. (1996, July 19). Zodiac told cops he envied Bundy. *New York Daily News,* p. 32.

Douglas, J. E., & Munn, C. (1992, February). Violent crime scene analysis: Modus operandi, signature, and staging. *FBI Law Enforcement Bulletin,* pp. 1–10.

Drapkin, I., & Viano, E. (1975). *Victimology: A new focus.* Lexington, MA: D. C. Heath.

DuClos, B. (1993). *Fair game.* New York: St. Martin's Press.

Eftimiades, M. (1993). *Garden of graves.* New York: St. Martin's Paperbacks.

Egger, K. (1999). [Preliminary database on serial killers from 1900 to 1999]. Unpublished data.

Egger, K., & Egger, S. (2001, forthcoming). Victims of serial killers: The less dead. In J. Sgarzi & McDevit, *Victims of Crime.* Upper Saddle River, NJ: Prentice Hall.

Egger, S. (1984a). A working definition of serial murder and the reduction of linkage blindness. *Journal of Police Science and Administration, 12*(3), 348–357.

———. (1984b, October). *Research in progress: Preliminary analysis of the victims of serial murderer Henry Lee Lucas.* Paper presented at the annual meeting of the American Society of Criminology, Cincinnati, Ohio.

———. (1984c, March). *Serial murder—the development of a preliminary research agenda: Order out of chaos.* Paper presented at the annual meeting of the Academy of Criminal Justice Sciences, Chicago.

———. (1985a, March). *Case study of serial murderer Henry Lee Lucas.* Paper presented at the annual meeting of the Academy of Criminal Justice Sciences, Las Vegas, Nevada.

———. (1985b). *Serial murder and the law enforcement response.* Unpublished dissertation, College of Criminal Justice, Sam Houston State University, Huntsville, Texas.

———. (1986a). *Homicide Assessment and Lead Tracking System (HALT) Briefing Document.* Albany: New York Division of Criminal Justice Services.

———. (1986b, October). *Utility of the case study approach to serial murder research.* Paper presented at the annual meeting of the American Society of Criminology.

———. (1986c). A challenge to academia: Preliminary research agenda for serial murder. *Quarterly Journal of Ideology, 10*(1), 75–77.

———. (1990a). *Serial murder: An elusive phenomenon.* Westport, CT: Praeger.

———. (1990b, March). *The future of criminal invesigation.* Paper presented at the annual meeting of Academy of Criminal Justice Sciences, Denver, Colorado.

———. (1992, March). *Serial killing of the lambs of our dreams.* Essay presented at the annual meeting of the Academy of Criminal Justice Sciences, Pittsburgh, Pennsylvania.

———. (1994). Psychics and law enforcement. *The REALL News, 1*(7), 1, 8.

———. (1999). The history, status, and future of psychogical profiling. *Journal of Contemporary Criminal Justice,* No. 4.

———. (1999, November). *Profile of the serial killer.* Paper presented at the International Workshop on Violence and Psychopathy at the Queen Sofia Center of the Study of Violence, Valencia, Spain.

———. (2000). Linked crimes, missing evidence. *The Forensic Panel letter, 4*(10). http://www.forensicpanel.com.

Egginton, J. (1989). *From cradle to grave: The short lives and strange death of Marybeth Tinning's nine children.* New York: William Morrow.

Elkind, P. (1990). *The death shift: Nurse Genene Jones and the Texas baby murders.* New York: Onyx.

Ellis, A., & Gullo, J. (1971). *Murder and assassination.* New York: Lyle Stuart Inc.

Fair, K. (1994, July). Kenneth McDuff: Death row. *Police,* pp. 56–58.

Federal Bureau of Investigation. (1983, July). *Violent criminal apprehension program: Conceptual model.* Unpublished working document, pp. 1–4.

Fero, K. (1990). *The zani murders: The true story of a 13-year killing spree in Texas.* New York: Dell.

Finkelhor, D., Hotaling, G., & Sedlak, A. (1990). *Missing, abducted, runaway, and throwaway children in America* (Cooperative Agreement #87-MC-CX-KO69). Washington, DC: U.S. Department of Justice, Office of Juvenile Justice and Delinquency Prevention.

Fisher, B. (1992). *Techniques of crime scene investigation,* 5th ed. New York: Elsevier Science.

Fisher, J. C. (1997). *Killer among us: Public reaction to serial murder.* Westport, CT: Praeger.

Fox, J. A., & Levin, J. (1983). *Killing in numbers: An exploratory study of multiple-victim murder* (draft). Unpublished manuscript.

———. (1999). Serial murder: Myths and reality. In M. D. Smith & M. A. Zahn (Eds.), *Studying and preventing homicide* (pp. 79–96). Thousand Oaks, CA: Sage.

Frank, G. (1967). *The Boston strangler.* New York: New American Library.

Franklin, C. (1965). *The world's worst murderers.* New York: Taplinger.

Freeman, L. (1955). *"Before I kill more . . ."* New York: Crown.

Ganey, T. (1989). *St. Joseph's children: A true story of terror and justice.* New York: Carol Publishing Group.

Garland, S. B. (1984, August 12). Serial killings demand new ways to analyze unsolved homicides. *Newhouse News Service.*

Gaskins, D. (as told to Wilton Earle). (1992). *The final truth: The autobiography of a mass murderer/serial killer.* Atlanta, GA: Adept.

Geberth, V. J. (1983). *Practical homicide investigation.* New York: Elsevier.

Gest, T. (1984, April 30). On the trail of America's "serial killers." *U.S. News & World Report,* p. 53.

Giannangelo, S. (1997). *The psychopathology of serial murder: A theory of violence.* Westport, CT: Praeger.

Gibbons, D. C. (1965). *Changing the lawbreaker.* Englewood Cliffs, NJ: Prentice Hall.

Gibney, B. (1984). *The beauty queen killer.* New York: Pinnacle.

Gilbert, J. (1983). A study of the increased rate of unsolved criminal homicide in San Diego, California, and its relationship to police investigative effectiveness. *American Journal of Police, 2,* 149–166.

Gilmour, W. (1991). *Butcher, baker: A true account of a serial murderer.* New York: Onyx.

Ginsburg, P. E. (1993). *The shadow of death: The hunt for a serial killer.* New York: Charles Scribner's Sons.

Godwin, J. (1978). *Murder USA: The ways we kill each other.* New York: Ballantine Books.

Goldstein, H. (1977). *Policing a free society.* Cambridge, MA: Ballinger.

Goodfellow, M. (1998, May 8). Italian serial killer case widens. Reuters News Service.

Goodwin, G. (1938). *Peter Kurten: A study in sadism.* London: Acorn.

Grant, C. (1999, January 9). Spend, spend, spend killer: Like many of us Dana loved to shop. But when the cash ran out she couldn't stop so she financed her sprees by murder. *The Mirror,* pp. 26, 27.

Gray, V., & Williams, G. (1980). *The organizational politics of criminal justice.* Lexington, MA: Lexington Books.

Graysmith, R. (1976). *Zodiac.* New York: Berkely Books, St. Martin's Press.

———. (1990). *The sleeping lady: The trailside murders above the Golden Gate.* New York: Dutton.

Green, T. J., & Whitmore, J. E. (1993, June). VICAP's role in multiagency serial murder investigations. *The Police Chief,* pp. 38–45.

Greombach, J. V. (1980). *The great liquidator.* New York: Doubleday.

Griffiths, R. (Producer and Director). (1993). *Murder by number* [Videotape]. Atlanta, GA: CNN.

Groth, A. H. (1979). *Men who rape: The psychology of the offender.* New York: Plenum.

Groth, A. H., Burgess, A. W., & Holmstrom, L. L. (1977). Rape, anger, and sexuality. *American Journal of Psychiatry, 134*(11), 1239–1243.

Gurwell, J. K. (1974). *Mass murder in Houston.* Houston: Cordovan Press.

Guttmacher, M. (1960). *The mind of the murderer.* New York: Grove Press.

Hare, R. D. (1993). *Without conscience.* New York: Pocket Books.

Hare, R. D., Forth, A. E., & Strachman, K. E. (1992). Psychopathy and crime across the life span. In R. D. Peters, R. J. McMahon, & V. L. Quinsey (Eds.), *Aggression and violence throughout the life span* (pp. 285–300). Newbury Park, CA: Sage.

Harrington, J., & Burger, R. (1993). *Eye of evil.* New York: St. Martin's Press.

Harris, T. (1981). *Red dragon.* New York: Putnam.

———. (1988). *The silence of the lambs.* New York: St. Martin's Press.

Harrison, F. (1986). *Brady and Hindley: Genesis of the Moors murders.* New York: Ashgrove Press.

Hazelwood, R. R., Dietz, P. E., & Warren, J. (1992, February). The criminal sexual sadist. *FBI Law Enforcement Bulletin,* pp. 12–20.

Hazelwood, R. R., & Douglas, J. E. (1980, April). The lust murderer. *FBI Law Enforcement Bulletin,* pp. 1–5.

Hazelwood, R. R., Ressler, R. K., Depue, R. L., & Douglas, J. E. (1987). Criminal personality profiling: An overview. In R. R. Hazelwood & A. W. Burgess (Eds.), *Practical aspects of rape investigation: A multidisciplinary approach* (pp. 137–149). New York: Elsevier.

Heilbroner, D. (1993, August). Serial murder and sexual repression. *Playboy,* pp. 78, 147–150.

Heimer, M. (1971). *The cannibal. The case of Albert Fish.* New York: Lyle Stuart.

Heritage, R. (1994, March). *A facet model of sexual offending.* Paper presented at annual conference of Academy of Criminal Justice Sciences, Chicago.

Hetzel, R. L. (1985). The organization of a major incident room. *The Detective: The Journal of Army Criminal Investigation, 12*(1), 15–17.

Hickey, E. W. (1985). *Serial murderers: Profiles in psychopathology.* Paper presented at the annual meeting of the Academy of Criminal Justice Sciences, Las Vegas, Nevada.

———. (1997). *Serial murderers and their victims,* 2nd ed. Belmont, CA: Wadsworth.

Hilberry, C. (1987). *Luke Karamazov.* Detroit, MI: Wayne State University Press.

Holmes, R. M., & DeBurger, J. (1985, March 18). *Profiles in terror: The serial murderers.* Paper presented at the annual meeting of the Academy of Criminal Justice Sciences, Las Vegas, Nevada.

———. (1988). *Serial murder.* Newbury Park, CA: Sage.

Holmes, S. T., Hickey, E., & Holmes, R. M. (1991). Female serial murderesses: Constructing differentiating typologies. *Journal of Contemporary Criminal Justice, 7*(4), 245–256.

Howlett, J. B., Hanfland, K. A., & Ressler, R. K. (1986, December). The violent criminal apprehension progam VICAP: A progress report. *FBI Law Enforcement Bulletin,* pp. 15–16.

Humes, E. (1991). *Buried secrets.* New York: Dutton.

Interpol General Secretariat. (1978). The I.C.P.O.—Interpol. *International Review of Criminal Policy, 34,* 93–96.

Isaacson, W. (1982, March 28). A web of fiber and fact. *Time,* p. 18.

Jackson, J., van Koppen, P. J., & Herbrink, J. C. M. (1993a). *Does the service meet the needs? An evaluation of customer satisfaction with specific profile analysis and investigative advice as offered by the Scientific Advisory Unit of the National Criminal Intelligence Division (CRI), The Netherlands.* Netherlands Institute for the Study of Criminality and Law Enforcement.

———. (1993b). *An expert/novice approach to offender profiling.* Netherlands Institute for the Study of Criminality and Law Enforcement.

Jaeger, R. W. (1991). *Massacre in Milwaukee: The macabre case of Jeffrey Dahmer.* Oregon, WI: Waubesa Press.

James, E. W. K. (1991). *Catching serial killers: Learning from past serial murder investigations.* Lansing, MI: International Forensic Services.

Jenkins, P. (1989). Serial murder in the United States 1900–1940: A historical perspective. *Journal of Criminal Justice, 17,* 377–392.

———. (1992). *Intimate enemies: Moral panics in contemporary Great Britain.* New York: Aldine De Gruyter.

———. (1995, January). The inner darkness: Serial murder and the nature of evil. *Chronicles: A Magazine of American Culture, 19,* 16–19.

Jenkins, P., & Donovan, E. (1987, July–August). Serial murder on campus. *Campus Law Enforcement Journal,* pp. 42–44.

Jesse, F. T. (1924). *Murder and its motive.* New York: Knopf.

Johnson, K. W. (1977). *Police interagency relations: Some research findings.* Beverly Hills, CA: Sage.

Jouve, N. W. (1986). *"The street cleaner": The Yorkshire ripper case on trial.* London: Marion Boyers.

Karmen, A. (1983). Deviants as victims. In D. E. MacNamara & A. Karmen (Eds.), *Deviants: Victims or victimized?* (pp. 237–254). Beverly Hills, CA: Sage.

Karpman, B. (1954). *The sexual offender and his offenses.* New York: Julian Press.

Kasindorf, J. R. (1993, August 9). The bad seed. *New York,* pp. 38–45.

Katz, J. (1982). A theory of qualitative methodology: The social system of analytic fieldwork. In R. M. Emerson (Ed.), *Contemporary field research* (pp. 127–148). Boston: Little, Brown.

Kennedy, D. (1992). *On a killing day: The bizarre story of convicted murderer Aileen "Lee" Wuornos.* Chicago: Bonus Books.

Kennedy, L. (1961). *10 Rillington Place.* London: Gollancz.

Keppel, R. D. (1989). *Serial murder: Future implications for police investigations.* Cincinnati, OH: Anderson.

Keppel, R., & Weis, J. (1993, August). *Improving the investigation of violent crime: The homicide investigation and tracking system.* Washington, DC: National Institute of Justice.

Keppel, R. D., Weis, J. G., & Lamoria, R. D. (1990). *Improving the investigation of murder: The homicide information and tracking system (HITS)* (Grant No. 87-IJ-CX-0026). Washington, DC: National Institute of Justice, U.S. Department of Justice.

Kershaw, A. (1999, March 27). Death on the rails. *The Guardian,* p. 38.

Kessler, R. (1984, February 20). Crime profiles. *Washington Post,* pp. 1, 16.

Keyes, D. (1986). *Unveiling Claudia: A true story of serial murder.* New York: Bantam.

Keyes, E. (1976). *The Michigan murders.* New York: Pocket Books.

Kidder, T. (1974). *The road to Yuba City.* Garden City, NY: Doubleday.

King, C. (1992). *Mama's boy.* New York: Pocket Books.

King, G. C. (1993). *Driven to kill.* New York: Pinnacle Books.

King, H., & Chambliss, W. J. (1984). *Harry King: A professional thief's journey.* New York: Wiley.

———. (1992). *A passing acquaintance.* New York: Carlton Press.

————. (n.d.). *The use of psychics in a serial murder investigation.* Unpublished paper.

Kraus, R. T. (1995). An enigmatic personality: Case report of a serial killer. *Journal of Orthomolecular Medicine, 10*(1).

Krivich, M. (1993). *Comrade Chikatilo: The psychopathology of Russia's notorious serial killer.* Fort Lee, NJ: Barricade Books.

Lane, B., & Gregg, W. (1992). *The encyclopedia of serial killers.* London: Headline House.

Laytner, R. (1998, December 6). Murderer of 350 children free to slaughter more. *Scotland on Sunday,* p. 19.

Lederman, D. (1993, July 17). Campuses search for proper response to letter bombing of 2 professors. *Chronicle of Higher Education,* pp. 18–19.

Leith, R. (1983). *The prostitute murders: The people v. Richard Cottingham.* New York: Lyle Stuart.

Leonard, V. A. (1980). *Fundamentals of law enforcement.* St. Paul, MN: West.

Levin, J., & Fox, J. A. (1985). *Mass murder.* New York: Plenum.

Leyton, E. (1986). *Hunting humans: The rise of the modern multiple murderer.* Toronto, Ont.: McClelland & Stewart.

Lichfield, J. (1999, June 18). French 'angel of mercy' is charged with murder. *The Independent (London),* p. 17.

Liebert, J. A. (1985, December). Contributions of psychiatric consultation in the investigation of serial murder. *International Journal of Offender Therapy and Comparative Criminology, 29,* 187–199.

Lindsey, R. (1984, January 21). Officials cite a rise in killers who roam U.S. for victims. *New York Times,* pp. 1, 7.

Linedecker, C. L. (1980). *The man who killed boys.* New York: St. Martin's Press.

————. (1990). *Serial thrill killers.* New York: Knightsbridge.

————. (1991). *Night stalker.* New York: St. Martin's Press.

Linedecker, C. L., & Burt, W. A. (1990). *Nurses who kill.* New York: Pinnacle.

Long trail to find Black. (1994, May 20). *The Independent,* p. 3.

Lourie, R. (1993). *Hunting the devil: The pursuit, capture and confession of the most savage killer in history.* New York: HarperCollins.

Lunde, D. T. (1976). *Murder and madness.* Stanford, CA: Stanford Alumni Association.

Lunde, D. T., & Morgan, J. (1980). *The die song: A journey into the mind of a mass murderer.* San Francisco: San Francisco Book Company.

Lundsgaarde, H. P. (1977). *Murder in space city.* New York: Oxford University Press.

MacDonald, J. M. (1961). *The murderer and his victim.* Springfield, IL: Charles C Thomas.

MacKay, R. (1994, May). Violent crime analysis. *The RCMP Gazette,* pp. 11–14.

MacNamara, M. (1990, November). Letters from San Quentin: Playing for time. *Vanity Fair,* pp. 80, 86, 88, 90, 92.

Maghan, J., & Sagarin, E. (1983). Homosexuals as victimizers and victims. In D. E. J. MacNamara & A Karmen (Eds.), *Deviants: Victims or victimized* (pp. 147–162). Beverly Hills, CA: Sage.

Magid, K., & McKelvey, C. A. (1987). *High risk: Children without a conscience.* New York: Bantam.

Marchbanks, D. (1966). *The moors murders.* London: Frewin.

Mariani, T., & Stover, M. (1999, March 18). Police tight-lipped on nature of evidence sent for analysis. *San Luis Obispo Telegram Tribune,* p. 1.

Markman, R., & Dominick, B. (1989). *Alone with the devil: Famous cases of a courtroom psychiatrist.* New York: Doubleday.

Marsh, H. L. (1989, September). Newspaper crime coverage in the U.S.: 1983–1988. *Criminal Justice Abstracts,* pp. 506–514.

Masters, B. (1985). *Killing for company: The case of Dennis Nilsen.* London: J. Cape.

———. (1991, May). Dahmer's Inferno. *Vanity Fair,* pp. 183–189, 264–269.

———. (1993). *The shrine of Jeffrey Dahmer.* London: Hodder & Stoughton.

McCarthy, K. (1984, June 28). Serial killers: Their deadly bent may be set in cradle. *Los Angeles Times,* p. 1.

McCauley, R. P. (1973). *A place for the implementation of a state-wide regional police system.* Unpublished doctoral dissertation, South Houston State University, Huntsville, Texas.

McDougal, D. (1991). *Angel of darkness.* New York: Warner Books.

McIntyre, T. (1988). *Wolf in sheep's clothing: The search for a child killer.* Detroit, MI: Wayne State University Press.

Megargee, E. I. (1982). Psychological determinants and correlates of criminal violence. In M. E. Wolfgang & N. A. Weiner (Eds.), *Criminal Violence* (pp. 14–23). Beverly Hills, CA: Sage.

Meloy, J. R. (1988). *The psychopathic mind: Origins, dynamics, and treatment.* Northvale, NJ: Jason Aronson.

———. (1989). Serial murder: A four-book review. *Journal of Psychiatry and Law,* pp. 85–108.

———. (1992). *Violent attachments.* Northvale, NJ: Jason Aronson.

Meredith, N. (1984, December). The murder epidemic. *Science, 84,* 4348.

Michaud, S. G. (1989, October 26). The F.B.I.'s new psyche squad. *New York Times Magazine,* pp. 40, 42, 50, 74, 76–77.

———. (1994). *Lethal shadow.* New York: Onyx.

Michaud, S. G., & Aynesworth, H. (1983). *The only living witness.* New York: Linden Press/Simon & Schuster.

———. (1989). *Ted Bundy: Conversations with a killer.* New York: New American Library.

Miller, R. (1999, June 20). The highway to hell that connects the rape and murder of 33 girls. *Mail on Sunday,* pp. 10–11.

Miller, T. (1993, September). Death row: Ray and Faye Copeland. *Police,* pp. 62–66.

Millikan, R. (1994, December 13). Backpacker murders. *The Independent,* p. 15.

Mitchell, E. W. (1993). *The Copeland killings.* New York: Pinnacle Books.

———. (1999). *The aetiology of serial murder: Towards an intergrated model.* Unpublished thesis, University of Cambridge, Cambridge, United Kingdom.

Moore, K., & Reed, D. (1988). *Deadly medicine.* New York: St. Martin's Press.

Morris, T., & Bloom-Cooper, L. (1964). *A calendar of murder.* London: Michael Joseph.

Moseley, R. (2000, February 1). Setting grisly record, British doctor convicted of killing 15. *Chicago Tribune*, p. 6.

Mott, N. L. (1999). Serial murder: Patterns in unsolved cases. *Homicide Studies, 3*(3), 241–255.

Mowday, B. E. (1984, July 26–29). Computer tracking violent criminals. *Police Product News*, p. 7.

Myre, D. C. (1974). *Death investigation.* Washington, DC: International Association of Chiefs of Police.

Naisbitt, J. (1982). *Megatrends.* New York: Warner Books.

Nelson, T. (1984, March 23). Serial killings on increase, study shows. *Houston Post*, p. 11.

Nettler, G. (1982). *Killing one another, Vol. 2: Criminal careers.* Cincinnati, OH: Anderson.

Neville, R., & Clark, J. (1979). *The life and crimes of Charles Sobhraj.* London: Jonathan Cape.

Newton, M. (1988). *Mass murder: An annotated bibliography.* New York: Garland.

———. (1990). *Hunting humans: An encyclopedia of serial murder.* Port Townsend, WA: Loompanics Unlimited.

———. (1992). *Serial slaughter.* Port Townsend, WA: Loompanics.

———. (2000). *The encyclopedia of serial killers.* New York: Checkmark.

Newton, M. B., & Newton, B. C. (1985, October 18). *Geoforensic identification of localized serial crime.* Paper presented at the Southwest Division of American Geographers Meeting, Denton, Texas.

Newton, M. B., & Swoope, E. A. (1987). *Geoforensic analysis of localized serial murder: The Hillside Stranglers located.* Unpublished manscript.

Nickel, S. (1989). *Torso: The story of Eliot Ness and the search for a psychopathic killer.* Winston-Salem, NC: J. F. Blair.

Norris, J. (1989). *Serial killers.* New York: Anchor Books.

Norton, C. (1994). *Disturbed ground: The true story of a diabolical female serial killer.* New York: William Morrow.

Office of Juvenile Justice and Delinquency Prevention. (1983a). *National missing/abducted children and serial murder tracking and prevention program.* Washington, DC: U.S. Department of Justice.

———. (1983b, November 20). *Memo.* Washington, DC: U.S. Department of Justice.

Olsen, J. (1974). *The man with the candy: the story of the Houston mass murders.* New York: Simon & Schuster.

———. (1993). *The misbegotten son: A serial killer and his victims. The true story of Arthur J. Shawcross.* New York: Delacorte Press.

Osterburg, J. W., & Ward, R. H. (1992). *Criminal investigation: A method for reconstructing the past.* Cincinnati, OH: Anderson.

Palmiotto, M. J. (1988). *Critical Issues in Criminal Investigation,* 2nd ed. Cincinnati: Anderson.

Paretsky, A. (1991, April 28). Soft spot for serial murder. *New York Times*, Section 6, p. 9.

Penn, G. (1987). *Times 17: The amazing story of the zodiac murder in California and Massachusetts.* San Francisco: Foxglove Press.

Pettit, M. (1990). *A need to kill.* New York: Ivy Books.

Philpin, J., & Donnelly, J. (1994). *Beyond murder: The inside account of the Gainesville student murders.* New York: Onyx.

Pinizzotto, A. J. (1984). Forensic psychology: Criminal personality profiling. *Journal of Police Science and Administration, 12*(1), 32–37.

Pinto, S., & Wilson, P. R. (1990). *Serial Murder.* Trends and Issues in Crime and Criminal Justice, No. 25. Canberra: Australian Institute of Criminology.

Porter, B. (1983, April). Mind hunters. *Psychology Today,* pp. 1–8.

Pretsky, R., Cohen, M., & Seghorn, T. (1985). Development of a rational taxonomy for the classification of rapists: The Massachusetts treatment center system. *Bulletin of the American Academy of Psychiatry Law, 13*(1), 39–70.

Pron, N., & Duncanson, J. (1994, May 1). Six sex slayings may be linked. *The Toronto Star,* p. 5.

Rae, G. W. (1967). *Confessions of the Boston strangler.* New York: Pyramid.

Regional Information Sharing Systems (RISS). (1984). *The RISS projects: A federal partnership with state and local law enforcement.* Washington, DC: Bureau of Justice Assistance.

Regional Organized Crime Information Center (ROCIC). (1985, January). *ROCIC Bulletin,* p. 13.

Reinhardt, J. M. (1960). *The murderous trail of Charles Starkweather.* Springfield, IL: Charles C Thomas.

————. (1962). *The psychology of a strange killer.* Springfield, IL: Charles C Thomas.

Reiser, M. (1982, March). Crime-specific psychological consultation. *The Police Chief,* pp. 53–56.

Ressler, R. K. (1992). *Whoever fights monsters.* New York: St. Martin's Press.

Ressler, R. K., et al. (1982). *Criminal profiling research on homicide.* Unpublished research report.

————. (1984). *Serial murder: A new phenomenon of homicide.* Paper presented at the annual meeting of the International Association of Forensic Sciences, Oxford, England, September 17.

Ressler, R. K., Burgess, A. W., & Douglas, J. E. (1988). *Sexual homicide.* Lexington, MA: Lexington Books.

Ressler, R. K., Burgess, A. W., Hartman, C. R., Douglas, J. E., & McCormack, A. (1986). Murderers who rape and mutilate. *Journal of Interpersonal Violence, 1*(3), 273–287.

Restak, R. M. (1992, July–August). See no evil. *The Sciences,* pp. 16–21.

Reuters News Service. (1995, August 10). Station strangler is charged.

Revitch, E., & Schlesinger, L. B. (1978). Murder, evaluation, classification, and prediction. In I. L. Kutash, S. B. Kutash, L. B. Schlesinger, & Associates (Eds.), *Violence: Perspectives on murder and aggression* (pp. 138–164). San Francisco: Jossey-Bass.

————. (1981). *Psychopathology of homicide.* Springfield, IL: Charles C Thomas.

Reynolds, M. (1992). *Dead ends.* New York: Warner Books.

Ritchie, J. (1988). *Myra Hindley: Inside the mind of a murderess.* London: Angus & Robertson.

Rogers, R., Craig, D., & Anderson, D. (1991, March). *Serial murder investigations and geographic information systems.* Paper presented at the annual conference of the Academy of Criminal Justice Sciences, Nashville, Tennessee.

Rose, H. M. (1979). *Lethal aspects of urban violence.* Lexington, MA: D. C. Heath.

Rosenbaum, R. (1993, April). The FBI's agent provocateur. *Vanity Fair,* pp. 122–136.

Rossmo, D. K. (1995). *Geographical profiling: Target patterns of serial murderers.* Unpublished dissertation, Simon Frasier University, Vancouver.

Royal Canadian Mounted Police. (1993, July) *VICLAS: Violent Crime Linkage Analysis System.* Crime Analysis Report Form 3364 Eng. (93-07), 1993.

Rule, A. (1980). *The stranger beside me.* New York: New American Library.

Rumbelow, D. (1988). *Jack the ripper: The complete casebook.* New York: Berkley.

Samenow, S. E. (1984). *Inside the criminal mind.* New York: Times Books.

Sam Houston State University Criminal Justice Center. (1983). *National Missing/ Abducted Children and Serial Murder Tracking and Prevention Program.* Grant application to Office of Juvenile Justice and Delinquency Prevention, U.S. Department of Justice, Huntsville, Texas.

Sare, J. (1986, March 7). Other slaying linked to Lancaster suspect. *Dallas Morning News,* pp. 1, 43.

Schaefer, G. J. (1990). *Killer fiction: Tales of an accused serial killer.* Atlanta, GA: Media Queen.

Schechter, H. (1990). *Deranged: The shocking true story of America's most fiendish killer.* New York: Pocket Books.

Schreiber, F. R. (1983). *The shoemaker: The anatomy of a psychotic.* New York: Simon & Schuster.

Schwartz, A. E. (1992). *The man who could not kill enough: The secret murders of Milwaukee's Jeffrey Dahmer.* Secaucus, NJ: Carol Publishing Group.

Schwartz, H., & Jacobs, J. (1979). *Qualitative sociology.* New York: The Free Press.

Schwarz, T. (1981). *The hillside strangler: A murderer's mind.* New York: Doubleday.

Scott, H. (1992). *The female serial killer: A well kept secret of the 'gentler sex.'* Unpublished thesis, University of Guelph, Guelph, Ontario.

Sears, D. J. (1991). *To kill again: The motivation and development of serial murder.* Wilmington, DE: SR Books.

Sereny, G. (1972). *The case of Mary Bell.* London: Methuen.

Serial killers and murderers. (1991). Lincolnwood, IL: Publications International.

Sewell, J. D. (1985). An application of Megargee's algebra of aggression to the case of Theodore Bundy. *Journal of Police and Criminal Psychology, 1,* 14–24.

———. (1991). Trauma stress of multiple murder investigations. *Journal of Traumatic Stress, 6*(1), 103–118.

Shaw, C. (1930). *The jack-roller.* Chicago: University of Chicago Press.

Sifakis, C. (1982). *The encyclopedia of American crime.* New York: Facts on File.

Skogan, W. G., & Antunes, G. E. (1979). Information, apprehension, and deterrence: Exploring the limits of police productivity. *Journal of Criminal Justice, 7,* 217–241.

Skrapec, C. (1984). *Psychological profiling and serial murderers*. Unpublished paper.

Smith, B. (1960). *Police systems in the United States*, 2nd ed., revised. New York: Harper & Row.

Smith, C., & Guillen, T. (1991). *The search for the Green River killer*. New York: Onyx.

Smith, H. (1987). Serial killers. *Criminal Justice International*, 3(1), 1, 4.

Smith, P. (1988, May 9). The literature of the American serial killer. *Cite AB*, pp. 1933–1988.

Snider, D., & Clausen, T. (1987). *A typology of serial murder*. Unpublished paper.

Sonnenschein, A. (1985, February). Serial killers. *Penthouse*. pp. 32, 34–35, 44, 128, 132–134.

Spiering, F. (1978). *Prince Jack*. New York: Jove.

Staff. (1969, July 30). State police to take charge of co-ed murder investigation. *Detroit News*, p. 1.

Staff. (1980, December 22). FBI develops profile to change face of sex probes. *Law Enforcement News*, p. 7.

Staff. (1982). Homicide—United States. *Morbidity and Mortality Weekly Report*, 31(44), 594, 599–602.

Staff. (1983). Paying a murderer for evidence. *Criminal Justice Ethics*, Summer–Fall, pp. 47–55.

Staff. (1984, April 25). Police search for killer of red-haired women. *Tennessean*, p. 1.

Staff. (1986, December 5). Police track serial killer with commercial DBMS. *Government News*, p. 78.

Staff. (1999, October 3). Trial told of butchery skills of alleged British serial killer. *The Herald (Glasgow)*, p. 8.

Staff. (2000, October 18). Yates to plead guilty. *The Seattle Times*, p. 1.

Starr, M., et al. (1984, November 26). The random killers. *Newsweek*, pp. 100–106.

State police to take charge of co-ed murder investigation. (1969, July 30). *Detroit News*, p. 1.

Stewart, J. R. (1992, January). A kiss for my killer. *Redbook*, pp. 76–83.

Storr, A. (1972). *Human destructiveness*. New York: Basic Books.

Strecher, V. G. (1957). *An administrative analysis of a multiple-agency criminal investigation within the suburban district of a large metropolitan area*. Unpublished master's thesis, Michigan State University, East Lansing.

Sullivan, T., & Maiken, P. (1983). *Killer clown*. New York: Grosset & Dunlap.

Sutherland, E. (1937). *The professional thief*. Chicago: University of Chicago Press.

Swanson, C. R., Chamelin, N. C., & Terrieto, L. (1984). *Criminal investigation*. New York: Random House.

Sweat, J. A., & Durm, M. W. (1993). Psychics: Do police departments really use them? *Skeptical Inquirer*, pp. 148–165.

Tanay, E. (n.d.). *The murderers*. Unpublished report.

Thibault, E. A., Lynch, L. M., & McBride, R. B. (1985). *Proactive police management*. Englewood Cliffs, NJ: Prentice Hall.

Thomas, J. (1993, September 29). Preble County strangler: The case of the clueless cops. *Gaybeat*, pp. 2, 6, 10, 13, 16.

Thompson, T. (1979). *Serpentine*. New York: Dell.

Travis, L. F. III. (1983). The case study in criminal justice research: Applications to policy analysis. *Criminal Justice Review, 8*(2), 46–51.

Treen, J. (1993, January 25). The killing field. *People,* pp. 74–80.

Tunnell, K. D., & Cox, T. C. (1991). Sexually aggressive murder: A case study. *Journal of Contemporary Criminal Justice, 7*(4), 232–244.

U.S. Congress. House. Committee on Government Operations. Government Information, Justice, and Agriculture Subcommittee. (1986). *The federal role in investigation of serial violent crime: Hearings before a subcommittee of the Committee on Government Operations, House of Representatives, Ninety-ninth Congress, second session, April 9 and May 21, 1986.* Washington, DC: U.S. Government Printing Office.

U.S. Congress. Senate. Committee on the Judiciary. (1984). *Serial murders: Hearing before the Subcommittee on Juvenile Justice of the Committee on the Judiciary, United States Senate, Ninety-eighth Congress, first session, on patterns of murders committed by one person, in large numbers with no apparent rhyme, reason, or motivation, July 12, 1983.* Washington, DC: U.S. Government Printing Office.

U.S. Department of Justice. *Uniform Crime Report, 1982.* Washington, DC: U.S. Government Printing Office.

———. (1994). *Crime Report, 1993.* Washington, DC: U.S. Government Printing Office.

———. (1999). *Crime Report, 1998.* Washington, DC: U.S. Government Printing Office.

VICAP Alert. (1992, February). *FBI Law Enforcement Bulletin,* pp. 20–21.

Villasenor, V. (1977). *Jury: The people vs. Juan Corona.* Boston: Little, Brown.

Vollmer, A. (1936). *The police and modern society.* Berkeley: Regents of University of California.

Wade, G., Davis, R. M., & Modafferi, P. A. (1993, September). Developing a model police for the multi-agency investigation of violent crime. *The Police Chief,* pp. 27–30.

Wagner, M. S. (1932). *The monster of Dusseldorf.* London: Faber.

Walstad, B. (1994). *Police use of psychics: Results of a 1993 questionnaire.* Unpublished manuscript.

Wambaugh, J. (1989). *The blooding.* New York: Perigord Press.

Wertham, F. (1966). *A sign for Cain.* New York: Paperback Library.

West, D. J. (1987). *Sexual crimes and confrontations: A study of victims and offenders.* Brookfield, VT: Gower.

Wilkinson, A. (1994, April 18). Conversation with a killer. *The New Yorker,* pp. 58–76.

Willie, W. S. (1975). *Citizens who commit murder: A psychiatric study.* St. Louis, MO: Warren H. Green.

Wilmer, M. A. P. (1970). *Crime and information theory.* Edinburgh: University Press.

Wilson, C., & Putnam, P. (1961). *The encyclopedia of murder.* New York: Putnam.

Wilson, C., & Seaman, D. (1983). *The encyclopedia of modern murder, 1962–1982.* New York: Putnam.

———. (1990). *The serial killers.* New York: Carol Publishing Group.

Wilson, J. Q. (1978). *The investigators.* New York: Basic Books.

Wilson, P. R. (1988). *Murder of the innocents: Child-killers and their victims.* Rigby, Australia: Adelaide.

Winn, S., & Merrill, D. (1980). *Ted Bundy: The killer next door.* New York: Bantam.

Wood, W. P. (1994). *The bone garden: The Sacramento boardinghouse murders.* New York: Pocket Books.

Wroe, G. (1999, April 18). Touching evil. *The Sunday Herald,* p. 6.

Yin, R. K. (1984). *Case study research: Design and methods.* Beverly Hills, CA: Sage.

Yallop, D. (1982). *Deliver us from evil.* New York: Coward, McCann.

Zahn, M. A. (1980). Homicide in the twentieth century. In J. A. Meicude & C. Farepel (Eds.), *History and crime: Implications for criminal justice policy.* Beverly Hills, CA: Sage.

———. (1981). Homicide in America: A research review. In I. L. Barak-Glantz & R. Huff (Eds.), *The mad, the bad and the different: Essays in honor of Simon Dinitz* (pp. 43–55). Lexington, MA: Lexington Books.

Appendix: Case Study Source Material

Theodore Robert Bundy

Books

Kendall, E. (1981). *The phantom prince: My life with Ted Bundy.* Seattle, WA: Madrona Publishers.

Larsen, R. W. (1980). *Bundy: The deliberate stranger.* Englewood Cliffs, NJ: Prentice Hall.

Michaud, S. G., & Aynesworth, H. (1983). *The only living witness.* New York: Linden Press.

Rule, A. (1980). *The stranger beside me.* New York: W. W. Norton.

Winn, S., & Merrill, D. (1980). *Ted Bundy: The killer next door.* New York: Bantam.

Magazine Articles

Bundy: Guilty. (1979, August 6). *Time,* p. 22.

Camera in the courtroom. (1979, July 23). *Time,* p. 22.

The case of the Chi Omega killer. (1979, July 16). *Time,* pp. 12, 13.

Marsh, H. L. (1989, September). Newspaper crime coverage in the U.S.: 1983–1988. *Criminal Justice Abstracts,* pp. 506–514.

Newspaper Articles

Jacksonville Journal, June 19, 1984.

Lake City Reporter (Florida), May 10 and 13, 1985.

Orlando Sentinel, February 10, 1980.

Sentinel Star (Orlando, Florida), June 30, July 15, August 1, 1979; March 16, May 20, 1982; May 10, 1985.

Other Sources

Interviews with Robert D. Keppel, Investigator, Attorney General's Office, State of Washington. (various dates 1983–1985).

King County Department of Public Safety. (1974). Summary of events July 14 and September 7. Seattle, WA: King County Department of Public Safety, Case No. 74-123376.

Letter from R. D. Keppel to R. H. Robertson, September 26, 1983, regarding Bundy's travels, known victims, and list of ninety similar victims.

Jeffrey Dahmer

Books and Reports

Davis, J. (1991). *Milwaukee murders: Nightmare in Apt. 213.* New York: St. Martin's Press.

Dietz, P. (1992, February 15). *Statement of Dr. Park Dietz, M.D., in reaction to Dahmer verdict.* Press release.

Dvorchak, R. J., & Holewa, L. (1991) *Milwaukee massacre.* New York: Dell.

Fisher, H. (1992). *Jeffrey Dahmer: An unauthorized biography of a serial killer.* Champaign, IL: Boneyard Press.

Jaeger, R. W., & Balousek, M. W. (1991). *Massacre in Milwaukee.* Madison, WI: Waubesa Press.

The Mayor's Citizen Commission on Police–Community Relations. (1991, October 15). *A Report to Mayor John O. Norquist and the Board of Fire and Police Commissioners.*

Norris, J. (1992). *Jeffrey Dahmer.* New York: Shadow Long Press.

Schwartz, A. E. (1992). *The man who could not kill enough: The secret murders of Milwaukee's Jeffrey Dahmer.* Secaucas, NJ: Carol Publishing.

Simon, R. I. (1996). *Bad men do what good men dream.* Washington, DC: American Psychiatric Press.

Journal and Magazine Articles

Black men tragic victims of white Milwaukee man's gruesome murder spree. (1991, August 12). *Jet,* pp. 16–17.

Caplan, L. (1992, March 2). Not so nutty. *New Republic,* pp. 18–20.

Chin, P. (1991, August 12). The door of evil. *People Weekly,* pp. 32–37.

Chin, P., & Tamarkin, C. (1991, August 12). The door of evil. *People,* p. 34.

Dahmer. (1984, November 26). *Newsweek,* p. 106.

Davids, D. (1992, February). The serial murderer as superstar. *McCalls,* p. 150.

DeBenedictis, D. J. (1992, April). Sane serial killer. *ABA Journal,* pp. 22, 78.

Dietz, Dr. Park. (1992, February 12). Court testimony. *Court TV.*

Gelman, D. (1991, August 5). The secrets of Apt. 213. *Newsweek,* pp. 40–42.

I carried it too far, that's for sure. (1992, May–June). *Psychology Today,* pp. 28–31.

Jeffrey Dahmer. (1991, January 6). *People Weekly,* p. 70.

Jeffrey Dahmer. (1992, December 30). *People Weekly,* p. 25.

The jury finds Dahmer sane. (1992, March 2). *Jet,* p. 15.

Kaufman, I. (1982, August). The insanity plea on trial. *New York Times Magazine,* p. 18.

Kaplan, D. A. (1992, February 3). Secrets of a serial killer. *Newsweek,* pp. 45–51.

Mackenzie, H. (1991, September 23). Infamous in Milwaukee. *MacLean's,* p. 28.

Masters, B. (1991, November). Dahmer's inferno. *Vanity Fair,* pp. 183–189, 264–269.

Mathews, T. (1992, February 3). Secrets of a serial killer. *Newsweek,* pp. 46–49.

Mathews, T. (1992, February 10). He wanted to listen to my heart. *Newsweek,* p. 31.

Miller, A. (1991, August 12). Serial murder aftershocks. *Newsweek,* pp. 28–29.

Post-mortem on the Dahmer trial coverage. (1992, February 29). *Editor & Publisher,* pp. 9, 125.

Prudhome, A. (1991, August 5). The little flat of horrors. *Time,* p. 26.

Prudhome, A. (1991, August 12). Did they all have to die? *Time,* p. 28.

Restak, R. M. (1992). See no evil: Blaming the brain for criminal violence. *The Sciences,* July–August, pp. 16–21.

Salholz, E. (1992, February 3). Insanity: A defense of last resort. *Newsweek,* p. 49.

Schneider, K. S. (1992, March 2). Day of reckoning. *People Weekly,* pp. 38–39.

Secrets of a killer. (1992, February 3). *Newsweek,* pp. 44–47.

Secrets of a serial killer. (1992, February 3). *Newsweek,* p. 49.

The Socrates option. (1992, May 24). *Reason,* p. 47.

So guilty they're innocent. (1992, March 2). *National Review,* pp. 17–18.

Tayman, J. C. (1991, August 12). The door of evil. *People,* pp. 32–35.

Toufexis, A. (1992, February 3). Do mad acts a madman make? *Time,* p. 17.

Treen, J., Toufexis, A., & Tamarkin, C. (1992, August 20). Probing the mind of the I-70 killer. *People Weekly,* pp. 37, 75–78.

Wroe, G. (1995, November 19). The real life Hannibal Lecter. *Mail on Sunday,* p. 49.

Newpaper Articles

Dahmer is given life in prison. (1992, February 18). *Boston Globe,* p. 3.

Dahmer shocks even expert on deviant psyches. (1992, February 18). *Los Angeles Times,* p. B4.

Defense gears for battle over Dahmer's sanity. (1992, January 26). *Springfield (Illinois) State Journal Register,* p. 3.

Expert: Dahmer sought control. (1992, February 9). *Boston Herald-American,* p. 4.

Expert says killer lived for morbid sex fantasies. (1992, February 6). *Boston Herald-American,* p. 3.

Expert tells of Dahmer's twisted acts. (1992, February 5). *Boston Herald-American,* p. 1.

He wanted "excitement, gratification." (1992, February 3). *USA Today,* p. 3A.

A horror warning for Dahmer trial. (1992, January 28). *Chicago Sun-Times,* p. 14.

Juror: Dahmer is a con artist. (1992, February 16). *Springfield (Illinois) State Journal Register,* p. 1.

Jury debates Dahmer's sanity after hearing final arguments. (1992, February 15). *Springfield (Illinois) State Journal Register,* p. 3.

Killer-cannibal Dahmer declared sane by jury. (1992, February 16). *Boston Herald-American,* p. 2.

Lawyer: Dahmer drawn to sex with the dead. (1992, January 31). *Springfield (Illinois) State Journal Register.*

Necrophilia drove Dahmer. (1992, February 9). *Decatur (Illinois) Herald & Review,* p. A4.

Officers dismissed in Dahmer case lose bid to get their job back. (1992, November 29). *New York Times,* p. 35.

Officers in Dahmer's case try to regain jobs. (1992, October 12). *New York Times,* p. 7.

Police in Dahmer case admit making error. (1992, October 17). *New York Times,* p. 14.

Psychiatrist: Dahmer gave up idea of freeze-drying victim. (1992, February 13). *Springfield* (Illinois) *State Journal Register.*

Psychiatrist says Dahmer fought his necrophilia. (1992, February 4). *Chicago Sun-Times,* p. 5.

Two serial killers' day in court. (1992, January 28). *USA Today,* p. 3A.

Victims' kin bring anger for Dahmer. (1992, January 29). *Chicago Tribune.*

Witness: Dahmer said he'd "eat my heart." (1992, February 1). *Springfield* (Illinois) *State Journal Register,* p. 3.

John Wayne Gacy

Books

Gacy, J. W. (1991). *A question of doubt: The John Wayne Gacy story.* (C. I. McClelland, Ed.).

Kozenczak, J., & Henrickson, K. (1992). *A passing acquaintance.* New York: Carlton Press.

Linedecker, C. L. (1980). *The man who killed boys.* New York: St. Martin's Press.

Sullivan, T., & Maiken, P. T. (1983). *Killer clown: The John Wayne Gacy murders.* New York: St. Martin's Press.

Magazine Articles

Darrach, B., & Norris, J. (1984, August). An American tragedy. *Life,* pp. 58–74.

Double life of a clown. (1979, January). *Newsweek,* pp. 24, 93.

Wilkinson, A. (1994, April 18). Conversation with a killer. *The New Yorker,* pp. 58–76.

Newspaper Articles

New York Times, December, 23, 24, 25, 28, 29, 30, 31, 1978; January 1, 2, 3, 8, 9, 10, 11, 12; March 1, 3, 11, 17; April 8, 10, 24, 1979; January 28, 29; February 2, 7, 16, 17, 22, 23, 24; March 8, 9, 11, 12, 13, 14, 16, 27; April 1; May 4, 1980; September 8, 1984.

Washington Post, March 3, 1980.

Other Source

Osanka, F. (1980, March 6). Sociological Evaluation of John Wayne Gacy for W. J. Kunkle, Jr.

"Hillside Strangler"

Books

Schwarz, T. (1981). *The hillside strangler: A murderer's mind.* New York: Doubleday.

Newspaper Articles

Bellingham (Washington) *Herald,* January 1, 1980.

Glendale (California) *News Press,* February 22, 1979.

Houston Chronicle, February 5, 1984.

Los Angeles Daily News, August 18; November 16, 19; December 2, 1982; January 7; March 20, 28; April 27, 29; May 4; June 22; August 3, 8; September 3, 29; November 1, 4, 7, 9, 11, 14, 15, 17, 18, 19, 20, 23, 25, 1983; January 5, 11, 14; March 19, 1984; January 14, 1985.

Los Angeles Herald Examiner, March 8, 1978; January 7; March 30; April 29; November 14, 15, 16; October 2, 16; November 2, 20, 21, 23, 25, 1983; January 8, 11; March 19, 31, 1984.

Los Angeles Times, November 22, 1977; August 22, 1978; January 1; March 5, 20, 27; May 6, 8, 12, 13; June 13, 17; September 11; October 3, 4, 6, 22, 25; November 14; December 4, 6, 1980; January 6; February 6; March 15; July 7, 8, 11, 13, 22, 23, 27, 29, 30, 31; August 6, 7, 9, 10, 11, 13, 14, 21, 28, 29; October 5, 23, 1981; February 8, 11, 27; March 2, 3, 4, 8, 9, 10, 11, 12, 15, 17, 19, 24, 25; April 6, 9, 14, 27, 29; May 31; June 5, 24; July 1, 8; October 4, 13, 26; November 1, 8, 10, 1982; January 7; February 24; September 2; October 21; November 1, 2, 4, 6, 8, 9, 10, 11, 12, 15, 16, 17, 19, 30, 1983; January 5; March 9, 19; August 19, 1984.

New York Times, February 24, 1979.

San Francisco Chronicle, May 7, 1994.

Other Sources

Barnes, M. (Producer and Director). (1984). *The mind of a murderer* [Videotape]. Washington, DC: Public Broadcasting Service.

Interviews with Frank Salerno, Sergeant, Los Angeles Sheriff's Office. (various dates, 1983–1985).

Henry Lee Lucas

Books

Call, M. (1985). *Hand of death: The Henry Lee Lucas story.* Lafayette, LA: Prescott Press.

Larson, B. (1984). *The story of mass-murderer Henry Lee Lucas.* Boulder, CO: Bob Larson.

Magazine Article

Cuba, N. (1985, July). The life and deaths of Henry Lee Lucas. *Third Coast,* 4(12), 44–59.

Newspaper Articles

Atlanta Constitution, April 10, 1985

Atlanta Journal, December 21, 1984; April 22, 1985.

Austin American Statesman, June 29; July 3; November 23, December 8, 1983; March 9, 12; April 4, 18, 24; May 11; July 26, 1984; April 21, 1985.

Avalanche Journal (Lubbock, Texas), June 3, 4, 5, 6, 28; September 2; October 31, 1984.

Baltimore Sun, February 20, 1984.

Beaumonth Enterprise, July 1, 29, 1984.

Dallas Morning News, June 30, July 7, August 3, 11, 25; December 8, 1983; June 8;
    August 1, 2, 9; October 28, 1984.

Dallas Times Herald, August 11, 1982; June 24, 26; August 13, 25, 26; November 26;
    April 5, 7, 11, 14, 23, 27; May 11, 17; October 6, 27; September 7, 1984; April 14, 15,
    16, 17, 18, 19, 20, 23, 24, 1985.

El Paso Herald Post, October 26, 27, 1984.

Fort Worth Star Telegraph, January 16, 29, 1984.

Herald Dispatch (Huntington, West Virginia), December 11, 17, 28; April 7, 13, 23;
    May 12; June 2, 17, 23; August 1; September 7; October 6, 1984; January 14; April
    15, 16, 18, 22, 23, 24, 25, 30; May 4; June 24, 1985.

Houston Post, June 30; August 11, 28; September 8, 9, 22, 23, 30; October 1, 4, 5, 8, 22,
    23, 25; April 5; July 1; August 18, 1984; April 15, 16, 18, 19, 20, 1985.

Law Enforcement News, September 24, 1984.

New York Times, April 18, 24, 29, 1985.

Rocky Mountain News (Denver, Colorado), September 13, 1984.

Tampa Tribune, June 9, 1985.

Toledo Blade, January 17, 19, 20, 1960.

Other Sources

Egger, S. A. (1985, March). *Case study of serial murder: Henry Lee Lucas.* Presented at
    the 1985 annual meeting of the Academy of Criminal Justice Sciences, Las Vegas,
    Nevada.

Henry Lee Lucas Homicide Task Force Investigative Reports:
- Index of Confirmed Homicides
- Court Action Involving Henry Lee Lucas
- Index to Supplements of Synopsis
- Synopsis of Confirmed Homicides
- Daily Log Activities of Lucas and Toole

Interviews with Henry Lee Lucas:
- June 5, 1984
- June 22, 1984
- July 18, 1984
- August 2, 1984
- August 14, 1984
- September 25, 1984
- February 8, 1985
- March 22, 1985

Mattox, J. (1986). *Lucas report.* Austin: Office of Texas Attorney General.

Regional Organized Crime Information Center. (1985). Travel Movements of
    Henry Lee Lucas and Ottis Elwood Toole, 1952–1985. Nashville, Tenn.: ROCIC.

Psychiatric Reports

Transfer to Ionia State Hospital, Michigan, July 14, 1961.

Ionia State Hospital Diagnosis, August 10, 1961.

Ionia State Hospital Record, January 28, 1965.

Psychological Evaluation, Center for Forensic Psychiatry, Ypsilanti, Michigan, November 17, 1971.

Jerry Marcus

Books

Douglas, J. E., & Olshaker, M. (1995). *Mindhunter: Inside the FBI's elite serial crime unit.* New York: Scribner.

Egger, S. (1998). *The killers among us. An examination of serial murder and its investigation.* Upper Saddle River, NJ: Prentice Hall.

Hickey, E. (1997). *Serial murderers and their victims,* 2nd ed. Belmont, CA: Wadsworth.

Matza, D. (1964). *Delinquence and drift.* New York: Wiley.

Ressler, R. K., Burgess, A., & Douglas, J. E. (1985). *Sexual homicide.* Lexington, MA: Lexington Books.

Interviews

Grant, Agent Jerome, Alabama State Police, telephone interview, 1998.

Jones, Ken, Public Information Officer, Mississippi Department of Corrections, Personal Interview, Jacksonville, Mississippi, 1998.

Lindley, Captain David, Starkville Police Department, Personal Interview, Starkville, Mississippi, 1998.

Lindley, Captain David, Starkville Police Department, Personal Interview, Starkville, Mississippi, November 1999.

Marcus, Jerry, Personal Interview, Parchman Penitentiary, Parchman, Mississippi, November 13, 1999.

Marcus, Ruth, Personal Interview, November 12, 1999.

Owens, Arthurlene, Personal Interview, November 12, 1999.

Patrick, Captain Lester, Tuskeegee Police Department, Personal Interview, Tuskeegee, Alabama, 1998.

Journals

Doener, W. G. (1975, May). A regional analysis of homicide rates in the United States. *Criminology, 13,* 90–101.

Hickey, E. (1986, October). The female serial murderer. *Journal of Police and Criminal Psychology, 2*(2), 2–81.

Newspaper Articles

Marcus may be linked to Knoxville death. (1987, April 22). *Starkville Daily News,* p. 1.

Town dumbfounded by murder charges against Marcus. (1987, April 23). *Birmingham Post-Herald,* p. 3C.

Police Records

Starkville Police Department; Marcus, Jerry case file, April 16, 1987.

Joseph Miller

Books

Canter, D. (1994). *Criminal shadows.* London: HarperCollins.
Egger, S. A. (1990). *Serial murder: An elusive phenomenon.* Westport, CT: Praeger.

Newspaper Articles

Car of missing woman found on East Bluff. (1993, September 24). *Peoria Journal Star,* p. A6.
Meidroth, T. (1993, October 27). Indictment returned in woman's vanishing. *Peoria Journal Star,* pp. A1, A2.
Moll, D. (1993, October 17). Search yields no clues. *Peoria Journal Star,* pp. A1, A12.
Moll, D. (1993, October 29). Sexual assaults preceded deaths. *Peoria Journal Star,* pp. A1, A2.
Okeson, S. (1993, September 28). Parents feared for daughter. *Peoria Journal Star,* p. A1.
Okeson, S. (1993, October 12). Volunteers will search for woman. *Peoria Journal Star,* pp. A1, A2.
Smothers, M. (1993, October 6). Miller's prosecutor hoped for execution. *Peoria Journal Star,* pp. A1, A2.
Williams, C. R. (1993, September 18). West Bluff woman, 88, missing nearly 3 weeks. *Peoria Journal Star,* p. A6.
Williams, C. R. (1993, September 19). Two bodies found nude in ditch. *Peoria Journal Star,* p. A1.
Williams, C. R. (1993, September 22). One murder victim stabbed, another asphyxiated: coroner. *Peoria Journal Star,* p. C1.
Williams, C. R. (1993, September 27). Body found in county. *Peoria Journal Star,* pp. A1, A2.

Other Sources

Federal Bureau of Investigation. *Criminal history record: Joseph Miller.*
Illinois Department of Corrections. (1978, September 27). *Intake assessment report: Joseph Miller.*
Illinois State Police. *Criminal history record: Joseph Miller.*
Interviews with Lieutenant David Briggs and Detective Steven Schmidt, Peoria County, Illinois, Sheriff's Police, February 9 and February 23, 1996.
Official autopsy photographs and records. (1993).
Perry, J. K. (1993, October 18). Leads report list.
Perry, J. K. (1993, November 10). Timeline for case M930004, Peoria County Sheriff Department.

Pyatt, T. (1993, October 5). Incident report.

Special Task Force Investigative Reports and Materials, Joseph Miller case: Peoria County, Illinois, Sheriff's Police; Peoria, Illinois, Police Department; Illinois State Police; et al. (Obtained via Freedom of Information request, February 23, 1996.) Including:

Taylor, C.D. (1994, February 1). Field report.

Index

Forensic profiler, 101
Fort, Dr. Joel, 27
Forth, A. E., 26, 312
47, XYY karyotype chromosome, as factor, 36
Fosdal, Dr. Frederick (testifying in Dahmer case), 222
Fox, J. A., 6, 14, 25, 26, 31, 60, 65, 66, 83, 153, 166, 244, 245, 269, 270, 276, 277, 290, 293, 311, 315
Frank, G., 42, 311
Franklin, C., 70, 311
Franklin, Joseph Paul, 92, 98
Freeman, L., 311
Freeway Killer. *See* Bonin, William.
Freight Train Riders of America (FTRA), 45
Fye, Heidi Villareal, 50

Gacy, John Wayne Jr., 8–9, 12, 15, 16, 25, 30, 31, 41, 47, 60, 61, 65, 81, 84, 96, 105, 112, 115–132, 230, 231, 232, 233, 234, 235, 236, 250, 256, 293, 295, 326
  attitudes of, 130–131
  case study of, 115–132
  case study source materials on, 326
  contact with defining agencies by, 120–126
  execution of, 126, 132
  family background of, 9, 117–119
  law enforcement response to, 249
  offense behavior by, 126–129
  peer group associations and personal relationships of, 119–120
  recall of events by, 131
  self-concept of, 129–130
  social environment of, 115–117
Gainesville Slayer. *See* Rolling, Danny.
Gallego, Gerald and Charlene, 43
Ganey, T., 311
Garavito, Luis Alfredo, 70
Garland, S. B., 312
Gary, Carlton, 98
Gaskins, Donald "Pee-Wee," 88, 312
Geberth, V. J., 274, 275, 278, 312
Gein, Ed, 61
Gelman, D., 324
Genetic factors in serial murder, 16, 22–23
Gerald, Hubert Jr., 45, 88
Gest, T., 312
Giannangelo, S., 28, 29, 312
Gibbons, D. C., 112, 312
Gibney, B., 312

Gilbert, J., 63. 268, 312
Gilmour, W., 297, 312
Godwin, J., 27, 42, 63, 276, 312
Goldstein, H., 245, 255, 312
Goodfellow, M., 76, 312
Goodwin, G., 312
Graham, Les, 78
Grant, C., 46, 312
Grant, J., 329
Gray, V., 252, 312
Gray, Dana, 46
Green River Killer, 13, 53–54, 65, 81, 86, 97, 100, 257, 259, 262, 263, 264, 270, 276, 287
  profile of, 278–282
Green River Killings, 60, 61, 65, 287
Green, T. J., 312
Greenwood, Vaughn, 98
Gregg, W., 20, 42, 71, 315
Greombach, J. V., 312
Griffiths, R., 312
Groth, A. H., 312
Guardado, Manuel, 78
Guillen, T., 54, 100, 287, 320
Gullo, J., 7, 30, 311
Gurwell, J. K., 312
Guttmacher, M., 25, 62, 312

Hakim, S., 244, 310
HALT System, 265, 288, 293–294, 295
Handguns, as weapons in serial murders, 99
Hanfland, K. A., 293, 313
"Hanley, James" (alias of John Wayne Gacy), 116
Hannibal (film), 4, 103
Hansen, R., 265
Hansen, Robert, 47, 60, 297
Hare, R. D., 26, 28, 312
Harlot killer, 73, 90. *See also* Yorkshire Ripper.
Harrington, J., 45, 312
Harris, Ralph, 46
Harris, T., 81, 313
Harrison, F., 313
Hartman, C. R., 31–32, 318
Harvey, Donald, 42, 84, 98, 102, 239–240
Hawn, Stacy, 47–48
Hazelwood, R. R., 4, 7, 29, 33, 62, 274, 276, 277, 313
Heck, Robert O., 65
Hecox, W., 43, 307